▲▲▲MOUND BUILDERS
OF ANCIENT AMERICA

MOUND BUILDERS OF ANCIENT AMERICA

The Archaeology of a Myth

ROBERT SILVERBERG

NEW YORK GRAPHIC SOCIETY LTD

GREENWICH, CONNECTICUT

Library of Congress Catalogue Card No. 68–12370

Text copyright © 1968 by Robert Silverberg
All rights reserved
No part of this book may be reproduced without permission
in writing from the publisher.

Composition & binding by The Book Press Incorporated
and printed by Halliday Lithograph Corporation
in the United States of America.
Design by Sophie Adler.
Maps by Jean Ivers

CONTENTS

▲▲▲

LIST OF ILLUSTRATIONS

▲▲▲

The diagrams of mound sites in this book are reproduced from *Ancient Monuments of the Mississippi Valley* by E. G. Squier and E. H. Davis, *Smithsonian Contributions to Knowledge,* No. 1, 1848. They do not therefore represent the present condition of the monuments.

I respect Assyria, China, Teutonia, and the Hebrews;

I adopt each theory, myth, god and demi-god;

I see that the old accounts, bibles, genealogies, are true,

> *without exception;*

I assert that all past days were what they should have been.

—WALT WHITMAN: *With Antecedents* (1860)

▲▲▲ *For Tom Allen*

▲▲▲MOUND BUILDERS
OF ANCIENT AMERICA

THE DISCOVERY OF THE MOUNDS

▲▲▲

The monuments of past civilizations lie scattered about the world in varying states of repair. Some are shattered by neglect; some are carefully tended, the object of pious cultural pilgrimages. Each land has its shrine of antiquity: Egypt her pyramids, England her Stonehenge, Greece her Acropolis. Out of the jungles of Cambodia rise the towers of Angkor. The isle of Crete offers the sprawling palace of Minoan Knossos. The stone cities of the Mayas adorn flat Yucatán.

In the continental United States the relics of the past are, for the time being, more meager. One day, hopefully not soon, tourists from other worlds will stare in wonder at the stump of the Empire State Building and the remains of Grand Coulee Dam; future archaeologists will plot our highways and will speculate on the possible ritual functions of the Pentagon. But in our own day we have little to show for our prehistory. In New Mexico and Arizona are the only ancient settlements of the American Indian that have survived: the cliff dwellings of Mesa Verde, the giant communal houses of Chaco Canyon, the many other village sites of the people we call the Pueblo Indians. Outside the Southwest, though, the architects of ancient America worked in wood and earth, and little of their work has endured. For signs of our past we must look, not to vast monuments of imperishable stone, but to subtler things: the arrowhead in the forest soil, the image carved on the face of a cliff, the potsherd and the bead.

When our forefathers came here in the seventeenth and eighteenth centuries, this was a great source of regret to them. They lamented the lack of a usable past. Many of them were educated men, aware of the archaeological treasures of Europe and the Near East. They expected to find in this green New World those traces of awesome antiquity on which romantic myths could be founded; they did not like to feel that they were coming into an empty land peopled only by naked wandering savages. Even as they transplanted the traditions of Western Europe to the new continent, they sought—and did not find —potent older traditions that would give their adopted land the cachet of great age.

Those early settlers in New England and Virginia knew nothing or next to nothing about the Pueblo cities of the Southwest, even though Spaniards had visited some of those cities in 1540 and had lived among them as conquerors since 1598. The cliff palaces and canyon cities of New Mexico might well have satisfied the American colonists' hunger for myth, but they were too far away, half a world away. Nor were they sufficiently romantic, since the descendants of the city-builders still lived nearby, and it would not have been difficult to discover the authors of these impressive ruins simply by questioning the inhabitants of the pueblos.

Thus the northern continent cheated its settlers, just as it had cheated the early explorers. In the sixteenth century, the Spanish *conquistadores* had reaped a rich harvest in Mexico and in South and Central America, finding not only an abundance of gold but also great kingdoms, awesome cities, high civilizations. Having raped the Aztecs and the Incas, the conquerors turned to the north expecting to find more wonders, and did not find them. The northern land held no cities to compare with Mexico's Tenochtitlán and Peru's Cuzco. There were no precious metals. Elaborately developed cultures were absent. It seemed a continent only of woods and plains, inhabited by simple huntsmen and equally simple sedentary farmers. The failure of the North to yield stone pyramids and golden treasure-vaults was painful to Europe in the years of the conquests, and it remained painful in the years of colonization that followed. True, the land was quite satisfyingly fertile, well suited for farms and plantations. But the men of the Thirteen Colonies lamented the absence of grand, imagination-stirring symbols of vanished greatness. In all this mighty continent, was there nothing to compare with the antiquities of the Old World?

Men in search of a myth will usually find one, if they work at it. In the fledgling Thirteen Colonies the mythmakers had little raw material with which to work; but as the colonists gradually spread westward and southward, they found the mounds, and the process of romantic embellishment began. At last, beyond the Alleghenies and in the valley of the Mississippi, ancient monuments came to light, monuments to rouse the poet and to create diversion for the amateur archaeologist.

The mounds were lacking, perhaps, in beauty and elegance. They were mere heaps of earth that mainly followed the lines of the Mississippi and Ohio rivers, though they were discovered in outlying regions as well. Some were of colossal size, like the Cahokia Mound in Illinois, 100 feet high and covering 16 acres of ground; others were mere blisters rising from the earth. Some stood in solitary grandeur above broad plains, while others sprouted in thick colonies. All were overgrown with trees and shrubbery, so that their outlines could barely be distinguished, although, once cleared, the mounds revealed their artificial nature through regularity and symmetry of shape. Within many of them there were evidences of past races: human bones, weapons, tools, jewelry.

Though few of these earthen heaps were impressive as individual sights, they had a cumulative effect. There were so many of them—ten thousand in the valley of the Ohio alone—that they seemed surely to be the work of a vanished race that had thrown itself into the task of construction with obsessive fervor. As the settlers fanned outward during the eighteenth and early nineteenth centuries they found scarcely an area that did not show traces of mound-building activity. The Atlantic coast, from North Carolina northward through New England, was devoid of mounds; but beyond the Alleghenies they were ubiquitous. In the North, the mound zone commenced in western New York, and extended along the southern shore of Lake Erie into what now are Michigan and Wisconsin, and on to Iowa and Nebraska. In the South, mounds lined the Gulf of Mexico from Florida to eastern Texas, and extended up through the Carolinas and across to Oklahoma. The greatest concentration of mounds lay in the heart of the continent: Ohio, Illinois, Indiana, Missouri. There were subsidiary mound areas in western Tennessee and Kentucky. Nearly every major waterway of the Midwest was rimmed by clusters of mounds.

To some of the settlers, the mounds were impediments to be ploughed flat as quickly as possible. To others, they were convenient places of refuge in times of high water. But to those of an antiquarian bent, the mounds were the handiwork of a vanished race, which with incredible persistence had erected them in the course of hundreds or thousands of years, and then had disappeared from the face of North America.

Why a vanished race?

Because the aborigines of the mound area were sparse in number and limited in ambition. The Indians of the Midwest, as the settlers found them, were seminomadic savages who seemed brutal and bestial—obviously incapable of the sustained effort needed to quarry tons of earth and shape it into a symmetrical mound. Nor did these savages have any traditions of their own about the construction of the mounds; when questioned, they shrugged the matter off, or spoke vaguely about ancient tribes.

The mounds, then, came under close scrutiny, for they filled a need of the colonial imagination. By the time Thomas Jefferson assumed the Presidency, hundreds if not thousands of mounds had been examined, measured, and partly excavated. (Jefferson himself was the most enlightened of these eighteenth-century archaeologists.) This early study of the mounds revealed, among much else, the extreme variety in the forms of the earthworks. In the region bordering the Great Lakes, the mounds tended to be low, no more than three or four feet in relief, and took the forms of gigantic effigies of birds, reptiles, beasts, and men. These huge and often fanciful image-mounds seemed quite clearly to be of sacred nature—idols, perhaps. Such effigies were common in Wisconsin, Michigan, and Iowa, more rarely seen in Ohio and Missouri, and scarcely ever found anywhere else. To the south, in the valley of the Ohio River, the customary shape of a mound was conical, the dimensions might be anything from a few yards in height to 80 or 90 feet. It appeared at first that the conical mounds had served as lookout posts or signal stations, but excavation showed that they invariably contained burials. In this region of conical burial mounds were also discovered isolated mounds of great size in the form of truncated pyramids. These immense, flat-topped mounds were usually square, but some were elliptical or pear-shaped. Some were terraced, or had graded roadways leading to their summits. To the discoverers it appeared probable that the flat-topped mounds had once been platforms for temples long since destroyed by the elements.

In the lower Mississippi area, conical mounds became scarce and truncated pyramids were the rule. These structures grew more imposing in bulk in the extreme South, increasing also in regularity of form. They reminded the discoverers of the *teocallis,* the stone pyramids of Mexico; and the presence of these earthen counterparts of the *teocallis* in the states bordering the Gulf of Mexico clearly indicated some link between the Aztec culture and that of the builders of the mounds.

In addition to the effigy mounds, the burial mounds, and the temple mounds, two types of embankments were observed, mainly in the central Ohio-Indiana-Illinois-Missouri zone. On hilltops overlooking the valleys, huge "forts" had been erected with formidable walls of earth, sometimes reinforced by stone. These obviously defensive works covered many acres and had been constructed at sites evidently chosen for their impregnability. In lowland sites were found striking geometric enclosures—octagons, circles, squares, ellipses—clearly nonmilitary in nature. The lines of embankment were 5 to 30 feet high, and the enclosures had areas of as much as 200 acres. Running out from the enclosures there often were parallel walls many miles long, forming great avenues.

The density and size of these structures astonished the early settlers. They delighted in calculating the cubic content of the great mounds: One near Miamisburg, Ohio, 68 feet high and 852 feet in circumference at the base, was found to contain 311,353 cubic feet of soil; another, in Ross County, Ohio, was shown to consist of 20,000 wagonloads of earth. Ross County alone proved to have 500 mounds and 100 enclosures.

The students of the mounds swiftly classified them: defensive enclosures, sacred and miscellaneous enclosures, mounds of burial, mounds of sacrifice, temple mounds, and so on. The spectrum of mound styles was quite clear at once: effigy mounds in the North, conical mounds and geometrical enclosures in the Midwest, Mexican-style truncated pyramids in the South. Surely, they argued, this indicated a migratory pattern for the builders of the mounds. Had they come from the north, building ever greater mounds as they moved south, and at last quitting Florida and Georgia and Louisiana to become the founders of the great Mexican civilization? By that theory, they had gained skills as they journeyed, so that when they reached Mexico they were able to abandon earthen constructions and create enduring monuments of stone. To this notion was offered an opposing one: that out of Mexico came colonists who moved northward across the continent, at first building earthen mounds in the style of the *teocallis,* then gradually transforming or forgetting their ancestral culture and producing the conical mounds of Ohio, and ultimately petering out as builders of effigy mounds near the Canadian border. The existence of the fortified enclosures gave scope for all sorts of speculations about prehistoric military encounters, while the mysterious and fascinating geometric earthworks provided a touch of the sacred and occult.

The discovery of the mounds was profoundly satisfying. At once these artificial hillocks and hummocks were invested with romance and myth. No longer did the continent seem a cheat to those who relished the thought of standing amid the relics of high antiquity. Scholars hurried to their books to find evidences of mound building in ancient times, and they were not disappointed.

From Herodotus, the Father of History, came the details of the burial of a Scythian king on the Russian plains: "The body of the dead king," says Herodotus, "is laid in the grave prepared for it, stretched upon a mattress; spears are fixed in the ground on either side of the corpse, and beams are stretched across above it to form a roof, which is covered with a thatching of osier twigs. In the open space around the body of the king, they burn one of his concubines, first strangling her, and also his cup-bearer, his cook, his groom, his lackey, his messenger, some of his horses, firstlings of all his other possessions, and some golden cups, for they use neither silver nor brass. After this they set to work and raise a vast mound above the grave, all of them vying with each other, and seeking to make it as tall as possible."[1]

The Old Testament was the authority for the statement that Canaanite tribes worshiped their deity in "high places"—and what were these "high places" if not temple mounds? The *Iliad* related how Achilles had heaped a great mound over the remains of his friend Patroclus, and how Hector, Patroclus' slayer, eventually was interred in such a mound as well. Alexander the Great, it was said, had spent a fortune to build a proper burial mound for his friend Hephaestion. The Roman Emperor Julian, who died near the Tigris in the year 363 while warring against the Persians, was buried beneath a "huge tumulus." Danish annals told of the mound burial of King Gorm and his queen, founders of the royal dynasty, in the middle of the tenth century. In the British Isles, antiquaries had long amused themselves by opening ancient mounds, which they termed "barrows."

The discovery of the mounds of North America provided a link to Herodotus and Homer, to Rome and the Vikings, to England's barrows, to all the mounds of Europe and Asia that had been known so long. In a stroke, North America was joined to the world's past, and no longer floated traditionfree and timeless. More than that: the presence of the mounds opened the floodgates of speculation. If the Israelites had built mounds in Canaan, why not in Ohio? Learned men came forth to suggest that our land had been visited in antiquity by Hebrews, Greeks, Persians, Romans, Vikings, Hindus, Phoenicians—anyone, in short, who had ever built a mound in the Old World. The silent structures along our rivers were credited to many nations; and then, of course, it became necessary to determine what had become of those ancient immigrants to America. The answer was obvious: they had been exterminated at some past date by the despicable, treacherous, ignorant red-skinned savages who even now were causing so much trouble for the Christian settlers of the New World.

In this way a legend was born, a governing myth that dominated the American imagination throughout the nineteenth century. The builders of the mounds were transformed into the Mound Builders, a lost race of diligent and gifted artisans, who had passed across the scene in shadowed antiquity. Perhaps they had come from the Old World, perhaps from Mexico; perhaps they had gone *to* Mexico once their work here was done. No one knew, but the scope for imaginative investigation was boundless. The myth took root, flourished, grew mightily, even spawned a new religion; then the scientists took over from the mythmakers and hacked away the luxurious growth of fantasy. Among the most vigorous of the demythologizers was one-armed Major J. W. Powell, conqueror of the Colorado River and later the founder of the Smithsonian Institution's Bureau of American Ethnology. When the Bureau put the myth of the Mound Builders to rest in the 1880's, it was with a certain regret. Powell himself sounded a rather wistful note in the 1890–91 *Annual Report of the Bureau of Ethnology:*

"It is difficult to exaggerate the prevalence of this romantic fallacy, or the force with which the hypothetic 'lost races' had taken possession of the imaginations of men. For more than a century the ghosts of a vanished nation have ambuscaded in the vast solitudes of the continent, and the forest-covered mounds have been usually regarded as the mysterious sepulchres of its kings and nobles. It was an alluring conjecture that a powerful people, superior to the Indians, once occupied the valley of the Ohio and the Appalachian ranges, their empire stretching from Hudson bay to the Gulf, with its flanks on the western prairies and the eastern ocean; a people with a confederated government, a chief ruler, a great central capital, a highly developed religion, with homes and husbandry and advanced textile, fictile, and ductile arts, with a language, perhaps with letters, all swept away before an invasion of copper-hued Huns from some unknown region of the earth, prior to the landing of Columbus. . . ."[2]

2

If more attention had been paid to the experiences of the first Europeans to visit the American mounds, the whole mythological concept of Mound Builders as a lost race might never have found support. In 1539, Hernando de Soto and an expedition of gold-seeking Spaniards landed in Florida and made their way through much of the Southeast, exploring a thickly populated territory where the mound-building tradition was still very much alive. Each town had one or more mounds, on which temples and the dwellings of chiefs and nobles were situated. It seemed quite logical to the Spaniards that these Indians would choose elevated sites for their important buildings, and the chroniclers of de Soto's* expedition touch quite briefly on the mounds, giving them no more space than any other ethnological feature. In the sixteenth century, the construction of mounds was a matter of custom to the Indians of the Southeast, and there was no reason whatever to attribute the structures then in use to some hypothetical ancient civilization. Yet the casual mentions of the mounds in the reports of de Soto's exploit failed to influence the course of future theories; within 250 years, some highly learned Americans were suggesting quite seriously that the mounds of the Southeast had been built by de Soto's own men!

In fact de Soto may not have been the first European visitor to the mound territory. Ponce de León, searching for the Fountain of Youth, visited Florida in 1513, landing near Palm Beach and following the coast northward to the

* Strictly speaking, we should refer to him simply as "Soto." But the Anglicized usage, "de Soto," has become too firmly entrenched to avoid.

St. John's River. He was greeted in unfriendly fashion by Indians whom we know to have been builders of mounds, but he left only sketchy accounts of what he saw on the verdant subtropical peninsula. In 1519, a fleet commanded by Alonso Alvarez de Piñeda carried out a survey of the northern perimeter of the Gulf of Mexico, hoping to find a sea route to Asia. Piñeda entered the mouth of a river which he said was "very large and very full," and spent six weeks on its waters, visiting large Indian villages that almost certainly contained mounds. Piñeda's river may well have been the Mississippi, although some geographers believe it was merely Mobile Bay. In 1520, another quester for the passage to the Indies, Lucas Vásquez de Ayllón, sent an exploratory mission up the Atlantic coast as far as South Carolina. Ayllón's men looked for gold and jewels, but found none, nor did they spy a sea passage. It did seem to them that the land held promise for colonization, and in 1526 Ayllón himself led a party of settlers perhaps as far as Chesapeake Bay, or possibly only to the Pedee River in South Carolina. There Ayllón perished during the grim winter, along with many of his men.

In 1528, came the sinister Pánfilo de Narváez, red-bearded, bass-voiced, unscrupulous. He had lost an eye trying to take Mexico away from Cortés; now, having managed to get himself named Governor of Florida, he arrived with 400 men and 80 horses, intending to plant a colony and grow wealthy at the expense of the natives. Narváez landed on the west side of Tampa Bay, and in the Indian village near the shore, quickly found a few objects of gold, enough to fire his greed. He moved north, through level, sandy country, invaded and plundered the large Indian town of Apalachee, then ran into tougher Indians near modern St. Marks. Their bows, "as thick as the arm, of eleven or twelve palms in length," took a terrible toll of the Spaniards; so did fevers, swamps, internal feuding, heat, and the strangeness of the land. They hastily built five boats, having misplaced their original fleet along the way, and the 250 survivors set sail for Mexico in September. Four of the boats went down with all hands off the mouth of the Mississippi; the other one, commanded by a junior officer named Alvar Nuñez Cabeza de Vaca, struggled on and was cast ashore near Galveston. Of the 80 men aboard, all but four met quick deaths. Those four, including Cabeza de Vaca, embarked on a bizarre odyssey through Texas and New Mexico which resulted in the eventual discovery of the pueblo country; after eight years of wandering Cabeza de Vaca and his companions stumbled into a Spanish camp in the Mexican province of Sinaloa, with a startling tale to tell.

All these, from Ponce de León to Cabeza de Vaca, almost certainly saw mound-building Indians, but left no hint of them in such accounts of their journeys as have reached us. Then it was the turn of de Soto to attempt the conquest of Florida.

"Hernando de Soto was the son of an esquire of Xeréz de Badajóz, and went to the Indias of the Ocean sea, belonging to Castile, at the time Pedrárias Dávila was the Governor. He had nothing more than blade and buckler: for his courage and good qualities Pedrárias appointed him to be captain of a troop of horse, and he went by his order with Hernando Pizarro to conquer Peru."[3] The words are those of a Portuguese knight known only as the Gentleman of Elvas, a witness to and survivor of the long and agonizing disaster that was de Soto's Florida enterprise.

The Gentleman of Elvas is one of several members of that expedition whose accounts have come down to us, and his was the first to be published, in 1557. An English translation by the geographer Richard Hakluyt appeared in 1609, and there were other English editions in 1611 and 1686, as well as Spanish and French versions in the seventeenth century; so there was never any question of the work's inaccessibility. Another account, by Luis Hernández de Biedma, remained unpublished until 1857, while that of de Soto's secretary, Rodrigo Ranjel, has never appeared except in severely abridged form. The most extensive work on the expedition, known as *The Florida of the Inca,* was written by a man born just a month before de Soto first set foot in Florida: Garcilaso de la Vega, known as "the Inca" because his mother, Chimpa Ocllo, had been a princess of Peru. (His father, Don Sebastián Garcilaso de la Vega Vargas, had seen action with the Pizarros during the Spanish conquest of Peru.) Garcilaso, an attractive and complex figure who spent most of his life in Spain but who was fiercely proud of his royal Inca ancestry, published his book on de Soto at Lisbon in 1605. His chief sources were the oral recollections of an anonymous Spaniard who had marched with de Soto, and the crude manuscripts of two other eyewitnesses, Juan Coles and Alonso de Carmona. From these Garcilaso wove a lengthy and vivid history, long thought to be largely fantastic, but now recognized as a trustworthy if somewhat romantic narrative. Its chief concern to us is the detailed descriptions it provides of Indian mounds of the Southeast.

De Soto had served with distinction in Peru. He fought bravely against the Incas, and acted as a moderating influence against some of the worst excesses of his fellow conquerors. The darkest action of that conquest—the murder of Atahuallpa, the Inca Emperor—took place without de Soto's knowledge and despite his advice to treat the Inca courteously. He shared in the fabulous booty of Peru and in 1537 came home to Spain as one of the wealthiest men in the realm. Seeking some tract of the New World that he could govern, he applied to the Spanish king, Charles V, for the region now known as Ecuador and Colombia. But Charles offered him instead the governorship of the vaguely defined territory of "Florida," which had lapsed upon the disappearance of Pánfilo de Narváez. By the terms of a charter drawn up on April 20, 1537, de Soto obligated himself to furnish at least 500 men and to equip and supply them for a minimum of eighteen months. In return, he would be made Governor of Cuba, and upon the conquest of Florida would have the rank of *Adelantado* of Florida, with a domain covering any two hundred leagues of the coast he chose. There he hoped to carve out a principality for himself as magnificent as that obtained by Cortés in Mexico and Pizarro in Peru.

In the midst of de Soto's preparations, Cabeza de Vaca turned up in Mexico, and at last revealed the fate of Narváez' expedition. De Soto invited Cabeza de Vaca to join his own party, but he had had enough of North America for a while, and went toward Brazil instead. De Soto collected men, sailed to Cuba, and recruited more men there. His reputation had preceded him from Peru; he was thought to have the Midas touch, and volunteers hastened to join him. He gathered 622 men in all, including a Greek engineer, an English longbowman, two Genoese, and four "dark men" from Africa. In April of 1539 they departed for Florida.

The expedition entered Tampa Bay a month later, and on May 30 de Soto's soldiers began going ashore. Their object was to find a new kingdom as rich as Atahuallpa's, and it seems strange that they would have begun the quest in the same country where Narváez had found only hardship and death. On the first of June they entered a town called Ucita in the narrative of the Gentleman of Elvas, and Hirrihigua in the version of Garcilaso de la Vega. "The town was of seven or eight houses, built of timber, and covered with palm-leaves," declares the Gentleman of Elvas. "The chief's house stood near the beach, upon a very high mount made by hand for defense; at the other end of the town was a temple, on the top of which perched a wooden fowl with gilded eyes, and within were found some pearls of small value, injured by fire, such as the Indians pierce for beads, much esteeming them, and string to wear about the neck and wrists."[4] Thus goes the first known description of a mound of the American Indians.

This town had been visited by Pánfilo de Narváez eleven years earlier, and its inhabitants did not remember their Spanish guests fondly. De Soto gave them no reason to revise their opinions. He took up lodging, with two of his lieutenants, in the chief's house. The rest of the dwellings were demolished, as was the temple atop the mound, and the Spanish soldiers flung together flimsy huts for themselves. De Soto sent scouts inland to survey the terrain, and soon smoke signals were rising as the Indians passed the word from village to village that intruders were again among them.

The scouts returned with dim tidings. The countryside was a maze of swamps and ponds and marshes; the horses had become enmeshed in thickets or had sunk into deep oozing mud; the only routes through the quagmires were Indian trails so narrow that the Spaniards had been able to travel only two abreast. Worse, the patrol had been ambushed by the Indians; two of the irreplaceable horses had been slain, and several of the men wounded.

If de Soto had been gifted with second sight, he would have sounded the order for withdrawal at that moment, put his men back on board the ships, and returned to Spain to fondle his gold for the rest of his days. Thus he would have avoided the torments of a relentless, profitless, terrible march over 350,000 square miles of unexplored territory, and would have spared himself the early grave he found by the banks of the Mississippi. This was no land for conquerors. But a stroke of bad luck, in the guise of seeming fortune, drew de Soto remorselessly onward to doom. His scouts, while fighting off the Indian ambush, had been about to strike one naked Indian dead when he began to cry in halting Spanish, "Do not kill me, cavalier! I am a Christian!" He was Juan Ortiz of Seville, a marooned member of the Narváez expedition, who, since 1528, had lived among the Indians, adopting their customs, their language, and their garb. He could barely speak Spanish now, and he found the close-fitting Spanish clothes so uncomfortable that he went about de Soto's camp in a long, loose linen wrap. He seemed precisely what de Soto needed: an interpreter, a guide to the undiscovered country that lay ahead.

Unhappily, Ortiz knew nothing of the country more than fifty miles from his own village, and each village seemed to speak a different language. Nevertheless, the Spaniards proceeded north along Narváez' route, looking for golden cities. Ortiz spoke to the Indians where he could and arranged peaceful passage through their territory. Where he could not communicate with them, the Spaniards employed cruelty to win their way—a cruelty that quickly became habitual and mechanical. The Indians were terrified of the Spaniards' horses, for they had never seen such beasts before. With the Spaniards there came also packs of huge dogs, wolfhounds of ferocious mien. The arquebuses of the invaders were clumsy weapons that could be fired only once every few minutes—time enough for the Indians to loose dozens of deadly arrows—but the flash and bang and smoke of the guns served to send the native warriors into flight. De Soto had hundreds of Indians enslaved and placed in irons to carry the baggage. Others he massacred for the sake of massacre, making slaughter an instrument of political policy, and as the march continued, the killing increased. In Peru, de Soto had been generous and noble with the conquered Incas; but here, vexed by the humid climate and the total absence of treasure, he grew stern, implacable, inflexible. At his command his men maimed, tortured, killed. The tale of the Gentleman of Elvas bristles with atrocities: "Many dashing into the flaming houses were smothered and, heaped upon one another, burned to death". . . . "Two the Governor commanded to be slain with arrows and the remaining one, his hands having first been cut off, was sent to the cacique [chief]" . . . . "The Governor sent six to the cacique, their right hands and their noses cut off. . . ."

When not slaughtering the Indians, de Soto's men took some trouble to observe their customs. Garcilaso de la Vega provides a description of their folkways covering several pages: "The Indians are a race of pagans and idolaters; they worship the sun and the moon as their principal deities, but, unlike the rest of heathendom, without any ceremony of images, sacrifices, prayers, or other superstitions. They do have temples but they use them as sepulchres and not as houses of prayer. . . ."[5] Garcilaso also sets down the plan of the Florida town of Osachile with the notation, "Having seen one town we shall have seen practically all of them." He offers this discussion of mound building:

"You may know therefore that the Indians of Florida always try to dwell on high places, and at least the houses of the lords and caciques are so situated even if the whole village cannot be. But since all of the land is very flat, and elevated sites which have the various other useful conveniences for settlements are seldom found, they build such sites with the strength of their arms, piling up very large quantities of earth and stamping on it with great force until they have formed a mound from twenty-eight to forty-two feet in height. Then on the top of these places they construct flat surfaces which are capable of holding the ten, twelve, fifteen or twenty dwellings of the lord and his family and the people of his service, who vary according to the power and grandeur of his state. In those areas at the foot of this hill, which may be either natural or artificial, they construct a plaza, around which first the noblest and most important personages and then the common people build their homes."[6]

To gain access to the houses atop the mounds, says Garcilaso, "the Indians build two, three or more streets, according to the number that are necessary, straight up the side of the hill. These streets are fifteen or twenty feet in width and are bordered with walls constructed of thick pieces of wood that are thrust side by side into the earth to a depth of more than the height of a man. Additional pieces of wood just as thick are laid across and joined one to the other to form steps, and they are worked on all four sides so as to provide a smoother ascent. The steps are four, six or eight feet apart and their height depends more or less on the disposition and steepness of the hill. Because of the width of these steps, the horses went up and down them with ease. All of the rest of the hill is cut like a wall, so that it cannot be ascended except by the stairs, for in this way they are better able to defend the houses of the lord."[7]

None of the villages possessed any gold. Each chief told the same story to get rid of the intruders: there was a golden land, yes, a village of incredible treasure, quite far away, in another part of the country entirely. Each chief supplied guides, either willingly or under duress, who took the Spaniards to the borders of their own territory and handed them on to the men of the next village, who told the same story. De Soto was aware of the deception, but there was little he could do save lead his men onward, north along the Florida coast. They came to the place near St. Marks where Narváez had built his boats, and there spent the winter of 1539–40. Then they moved on, engaging frequently in bloody battles with the Indians. Those Indians who did not attack practiced a scorched-earth policy, destroying their own crops and villages to make life harder for the advancing Spaniards. But in the spring came encouragement: stories of a land somewhere to the east and north, ruled by a corpulent queen who received tribute of furs and gold from surrounding tribes.

On March 3, 1540, de Soto's army crossed into Georgia, where the Indians lived in cane-roofed huts with mud walls. The land here, says the Gentleman of Elvas, was "abundant, picturesque, and luxuriant, well watered, and having good river margins." Shrewd chiefs sent gifts of rabbits, partridges, turkeys, and maize bread to the Spaniards to speed them on their way toward the land of gold. Then the country changed, and became a place of dense pine forests where the horses could not enter and hostile Indians lurked. Provisions dwindled. De Soto had brought thirteen sows to Florida, and by careful management had increased his herd of swine to three hundred head; now it became necessary to slaughter some of the animals and pass out half a pound of pork a day for each man. The horses grew thin; some died. There was no food to spare for the hapless Indian porters. By now the army was nearing the northern border of Georgia. At last came the word they were waiting to hear: they were approaching Cofachiqui, the realm

of the celebrated and wealthy queen. She ruled the area on the South
Carolina and Georgia sides of the Savannah River, with her capital near
present-day Augusta.

The queen herself—"brown but well proportioned," says Biedma—came
out to greet the Spaniards. She was the sole passenger in her canoe, which
was covered with a great canopy, adorned with ornaments, and towed by
another canoe carrying six Indian nobles and many oarsmen. Garcilaso
compares the scene to Cleopatra going forth to greet Marc Anthony, "although
less spectacular in grandeur and majesty."[8] The queen paid her respects to
de Soto, presenting him with shawls and skins, and throwing about his neck
a large string of pearls she had worn. Observing that de Soto was impressed
by the pearls, she invited him to search some sepulchers in a nearby town
that had been evacuated two years earlier because of a plague. He would find
pearls in the tombs, she said, and he might take all he desired.

1   Map of the de Soto explorations.

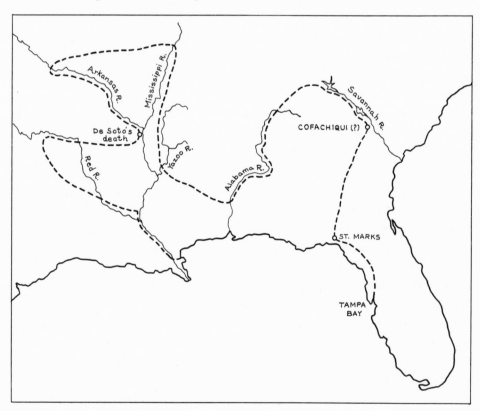

De Soto presented her with a gold ring set with a ruby—a fair exchange, Garcilaso thinks, for "a large strand of pearls as thick as hazelnuts which encircled her neck three times and fell to her thighs." The Spaniards crossed the river on rafts and canoes provided by the obliging Indians, and made their headquarters in the town of Cofachiqui, among "great and cool bowers of branches."[9] The natives sent the Spaniards turkeys and other provisions. Shortly de Soto brought up the subject of gold and silver. He produced two of his Indian slaves from Florida, who repeated their tales of Cofachiqui's horde of precious metals. The queen explained that no gold or silver was mined in her land, but that her people had obtained such metals by trade. "Immediately," says Garcilaso, "the lady issued an order for all the metals in her land of the colors the Spaniards were seeking to be brought before them, that is, all which were yellow and white; for they had shown her rings of gold and pieces of silver, and had asked for pearls and stones such as those that were set in the rings. The Indians having heard the command of their mistress brought with the utmost haste a great quantity of very golden and resplendent copper . . . for they were unable to distinguish between brass and gold. Instead of silver, these people fetched great slabs of iron pyrites* which were thick as boards. . . . As for the precious stones, the lady declared that there were none in her land except pearls, but that if the Spaniards wanted these they should go to the upper part of the town." She indicated a temple which, she said, was the burial place of the town's nobility, suggesting that the Spaniards loot it before they went on to the much larger temple in the abandoned town a league away.

Hiding their disappointment over the failure of Cofachiqui to yield gold and silver, the Spaniards hurried up the mound to the temple, within which they found wooden chests containing the decomposing bodies of Cofachiqui's late aristocrats. Next to these coffins were smaller chests containing great quantities of pearls. Oriental pearls are produced by ocean mollusks of the *Margaritifera* family, but the pearls of Cofachiqui came from fresh-water mussels of the *Unionidae*. Garcilaso says they were pearls of great beauty, but the Gentleman of Elvas, who was there, reports that they had been drilled by means of heat, "which causes them to lose their hue."[10] Discolored or not, the pearls were weighed out; de Soto's functionaries had parceled out five hundred pounds of them before the general observed that there was no need to carry such a "nonsensical and cumbersome load" through the rest of their travels. He would, he said, take only fifty pounds of pearls now, and pick up the rest from the subjects of the friendly queen after he had finished conquering Florida. But the officials insisted on taking the pearls, since they had already

* These were probably thick sheets of mica, rather than iron pyrites.

been weighed out, and de Soto relented. He took a double handful for himself, gave the same amount to each of his men, and instructed them "to make rosaries on which to pray. And indeed these pearls could have served adequately for such a purpose since they were as thick as fat chick-peas."[11]

Now the Spaniards moved on to Talomeco, the evacuated city, where as usual the chief's house and the temple stood on high artificial mounds. The temple was a hundred feet in length and forty in width, with a high roof of reeds and split canes covered with handsome sea shells, mother-of-pearl side out. Garcilaso supplies a detailed and perhaps fantastic description of the temple's interior, speaking of twelve giant wooden statues carrying clubs spiked with diamonds, strands of pearls strung along the ceiling, elegant images of the dead, and other wonders. On the floor of the temple were stacked chests of pearls, four, five, and six chests in a stack, with aisles between them. There were so many pearls, he says, that if the Spaniards had loaded themselves and all their horses with them, they still would not have been able to remove all that the temple contained. "Along with this splendor and wealth of pearls in the temple," Garcilaso declares, "there were likewise many enormous bundles of chamois. Some were white and some had been dyed various hues. . . . Furthermore there were great bundles of mantles of many colors that were made of chamois, and another great quantity made of skins dressed with their fur—skins of all the various animals both great and small which thrive in that land. Many were of different species and colors of cat, and others, of very fine marten, each of them being so well dressed that among the best of Germany and Muscovy one could not have found better."[12]

The dazzled Spaniards wandered through annexes containing weapons that seemed to be of gold, but which turned out to be merely of copper—pikes in one room, maces in another, battle-axes in a third. They eyed pearl-decorated broadswords and flawlessly worked bows and arrows, likewise set with pearls. Shields of wood, shields of cowhide, shields of woven cane, all of exquisite workmanship, delighted them. Even Spaniards who had beheld the golden riches of Mexico and Peru were awed by these humbler but no less beautiful objects. But again de Soto decided to leave the pearls behind rather than encumber his men. (Garcilaso finally admits that, according to one of his sources, the pearls were blackened and lusterless because the Indians had cooked the mussels before withdrawing the gems.)

At Cofachiqui de Soto had reached the high point of his expedition, but he did not know that. His mood seems to have been one of disappointment that the friendly town had yielded nothing but fresh-water pearls, when he sought gold and silver. The mood of his men was more cheerful; after enduring warfare and famine, they had found a peaceful place where food was plentiful and the maidens, apparently, were obliging. They wished to remain at Cofachiqui at least through the harvest season. But de Soto had heard of another supposedly wealthy province twelve days' march ahead. "Being an inflexible man, and dry of word," the Gentleman of Elvas says, he resolved to go there, and "there were none who would say a thing to him after it became known that he had made up his mind."[13]

On May 3, 1540, the Spaniards left Cofachiqui, unkindly taking with them the fat and friendly queen to serve as their guide. It was poor return for her hospitality, but she kept her own counsel, led the Spaniards to the borders of her territory, and gave them the slip in a thicket, taking with her a trunk of unmarred pearls that de Soto had coveted. According to legend, one of de Soto's "dark men" helped her escape and conducted her back to Cofachiqui, where he lived as her consort and co-ruler thereafter.

The Spaniards made their way onward, resuming their previous pattern of terrorizing the natives to win their co-operation. During the summer of 1540 they passed through what one day would be South Carolina, North Carolina, and Tennessee, into the Blue Ridge Mountains. They were disappointed in their hope of treasure, the Indians were more warlike, and their energies were waning. There were desertions, and de Soto had to post guards at night to prevent his men from slipping away to dwell with the natives. Now the land became too poor in agriculture to support them on their march, and the Spaniards swung south and then southwest, treating the Indians in an ever more callous manner. In October, they reached south-central Alabama, the country of the Choctaws, whose ruler was the great chief Tuscaloosa. De Soto had learned from Pizarro in Peru how to deal with Indian monarchs: seize them as hostages. He met Tuscaloosa face to face, won from the uneasy chief permission to cross his lands, then ordered him to be taken prisoner. But Tuscaloosa's people were not as meek as those of the Inca Atahuallpa; they prepared an ambush for de Soto as he entered the Choctaw capital, Mavila, with the captive chief at his side. Five Spaniards were slain protecting de Soto, and the general himself narrowly escaped death. De Soto's Indian porters escaped, taking with them into Mavila all the Spanish supplies, spare weapons, and gunpowder. De Soto had to invade the town to regain the equipment, but the Choctaws refused to surrender even after Mavila was ablaze, and by the time the Spaniards had finished the task of massacring the defenders the town was destroyed and with it the Spanish supplies. De Soto had lost 22 men besides, and 148 were wounded, including de Soto himself.

The expedition was crippled. Having doubled back nearly to the Gulf of

Mexico, the Spaniards' logical move was to board their waiting supply fleet and return to Cuba. But de Soto, who was in no need of further wealth, was hungry for power; he could not abandon his conquest now. He feared that his men would desert if they knew the ships were there. So the battered army limped inland without making rendezvous with the supply fleet, and set off, hungry and badly equipped, in search of new adventures. The fleet, laden with provisions, waited awhile and then, puzzled, sailed back to Cuba.

During the cold winter of 1540-41 the Spaniards camped near the Yazoo River in Mississippi. In March of 1541, traveling in the territory of the Chickasaw Indians, they provoked the natives into a surprise attack that became a greater debacle than Mavila. Striking by night, the Chickasaws set fire to the Spanish camp, transforming de Soto's herd of pigs into roast pork, killing nearly sixty horses, ruining the metal weapons, and taking the lives of a dozen Spaniards. Blankets and garments were destroyed, as were all wooden implements—lance shafts, ax handles, and more. The dazed, denuded Spaniards recovered, scavenging and salvaging what they could, rounding up runaway horses. They managed to defeat a second raiding party, but when they finally departed from Chickasaw country they were in sad straits.

Still, rumors of gold led them on, and they headed westward hunting for a tribe so rich that its warriors went into battle wearing golden helmets. On May 8, 1541, the straggling Spaniards came to the Mississippi River a few miles below the present site of Memphis. The river, nearly two miles wide there, was an amazing sight for these men from dry Spain. They spent a wearying month building barges to ferry themselves across. On the other side were more hostile tribes: Quapaws, Tulas, Tunicas, Caddos. The lust for gold enfevered the dreams of the wandering Spaniards and, now in the third year of their adventure, they drifted on, through the Ozarks, across Arkansas, into eastern Oklahoma. They were passing out of the country of the mound-building Indians; now they saw tepee-dwelling nomads on bison-cluttered plains. The winter of 1541-42 they passed at the junction of two rivers in Oklahoma, and there the interpreter, Juan Ortiz, died. His death brought home to the men their isolation in this strange land. Belatedly, the brooding de Soto admitted defeat, and commanded his men to turn southeast and make for the Gulf of Mexico. He hoped to reach the Mississippi near its mouth, build a small vessel, and send it to Cuba to bring a fleet to carry his men away. But when they came to the river, they were in northern Louisiana, far from the Gulf, hundreds of miles from the place they had been aiming for. De Soto withdrew into his tent, shivering with an illness that all knew would be fatal, and after ordering one last massacre of an Indian town, he gave up his life and was ceremoniously buried in the Mississippi.

His lieutenant, Lúis de Moscoso, took command of the despondent explorers and led them westward on what he hoped was the overland route to Mexico. Soon the Spaniards were in the deserts of eastern Texas, facing starvation. Moscoso backtracked, and early in December, 1542, the marchers came to the Mississippi for the third time. They spent a dismal winter there, building boats, and in July set out down the river, leaving behind all the slaves they had accumulated in their wanderings. Under a harsh sun they journeyed down the vast river, seven hundred miles in two weeks, and came at the end to the Gulf, where they set sail for Mexico. On September 10, 1543, fifty-two days after leaving the mouth of the Mississippi, the explorers made landfall at the Spanish settlement at Pánuco, on Mexico's Gulf Coast. The long nightmare was over. Strangely, of the 622 men who had set out with de Soto, 311 had survived all hardships and ambushes.

3

De Soto's Spaniards had had a lengthy exposure to the mound-building Indians of Florida, Georgia, the Carolinas, Tennessee, Arkansas, Alabama, Mississippi, and Louisiana, and the Indians had had a harrowing taste of the white man's ways. The effect of the collision on the Indians seems to have been a powerful one, causing a kind of culture-shock that may have given birth to a somber cult of death and terror, but the Europeans had found little of significance in the customs of the natives.

The next to arrive in the Southeast were French colonists under Jean Ribault, who, on April 30, 1562, landed near the present site of St. Augustine, Florida. Spain objected to this French intrusion, and sent a fleet to clear the French out; but by then the colony had already failed and its famine-stricken survivors had been taken away by an English ship. A second French expedition, equally ill-fated, arrived in 1564 and was driven out by Spaniards the following year. In this group was an artist, Jacques Le Moyne, who, after escaping to London, produced a series of watercolors depicting Indian life in "Florida" (by which he meant the entire Southeast up to the Carolinas). Le Moyne's paintings have been lost, with one exception, but engravings taken from them were published in 1591 by the Flemish house of De Bry. Among these engravings is one that shows the Indians mourning at a chief's burial mound. The mound is no more than a yard high and perhaps two yards across; arrows have been thrust into the ground around it to form a decorative palisade, and a large snail shell rests at the summit. Le Moyne's caption declares, "Sometimes the deceased king of this province is buried with great solemnity, and his great cup from which he was accustomed to drink is placed on a tumulus with many arrows set about it." As one archaeologist commented in 1881, the tumulus depicted by Le Moyne "scarcely rises to the dignity of a mound." But a burial mound in Naples, Illinois, excavated in April of that year turned out to contain, at its core, a single skeleton in an upright position, with "no objects . . . about it except a single sea-shell resting on the earth just over the head, and a number of . . . bone awls . . . sticking in the sand around the skeleton. The individual had been seated upon the sand, these awls stuck around him in a circle 4 or 5 inches in the sand, and the work of carrying dirt begun. When the mound had been elevated about 6 inches above the head the shell was laid on and the work continued."[14]

Cyrus Thomas, the Bureau of American Ethnology specialist in mounds, commented on this Naples mound in a report published in 1887, juxtaposing Le Moyne's picture and observing that the Naples mound, when completed, "formed an oval tumulus 132 feet long, 98 feet wide, and 10 feet high. It is therefore quite probable," Thomas went on, "that Le Moyne figures the mound at the time it reached the point where the shell cup was to be deposited, when, in all likelihood, certain ceremonies were to be observed and a pause in the work occurred." If this conjecture is true, as seems likely, then Le Moyne's painting as published by De Bry is the first depiction of an Indian burial mound —done while the mound was still under construction.

After the departure of the French from Florida, a long silence settled over the mound country. De Soto's men, the first Europeans to see anything of the Mississippi Valley, were the last to visit it for at least a century. The next thrust, when it came, was aimed down the valley from the north.

French explorers moving westward along the St. Lawrence River heard rumors about a much greater river inland. Jean Nicolet, an experienced French agent, may have reached the upper waters of the Mississippi in 1639; all we know for certain is that he went from Lake Michigan to Green Bay, then up the Fox River to the Wisconsin River, a tributary of the Mississippi. That may have taken him to the great river itself; in any event he was passing through effigy-mound country, but we do not know what he saw. Later in the seventeenth century, French Jesuit missionaries followed Nicolet's route; but the copiously detailed letters of these Jesuits lack any references to mounds.

About 1672, France commissioned a sturdy explorer named Louis Joliet "to discover the south sea" and to explore "the great river Mississippi, which is believed to empty in the California sea." Joliet, Jesuit-educated, had given up studying for the priesthood to make a career for himself in France's American empire. He took with him, as was customary, a missionary, the gentle, sweet-

2   A Florida mound burial. Engraving by De Bry from a painting by Jacques Le Moyne, sixteenth century.

souled Jesuit Jacques Marquette. Père Marquette was fluent in six Indian languages and had long experience among the wilderness tribes. They set out from Mackinac Island on May 17, 1673, to Green Bay, the Fox and Wisconsin rivers, and into the Mississippi. They journeyed south, seeing plenty of wild game but no sign of Indian life on the river until they were as far south as the present site of Quincy, Illinois. Until then, the valley had seemed virgin wilderness to them; but here they came upon Illinois Indians, friendly ones, whose language Marquette could speak. The explorers visited several villages and went on.

All about them lay the mounds of the past, but they saw none of them. From the river, mounds and embankments would have seemed mere natural formations; they would have had no reason to examine them more closely unless they had seen Indian settlements, and there were no settlements. A century and a half later, when this part of the continent was being carved into the farms of white settlers, the evidence of an immense prehistoric population would be found everywhere. But the builders of the valley's thousands of mounds had vanished by the time Joliet and Marquette came by in 1673, a fact that helped considerably to foster the legend of a lost ancient civilization.

This was burial-mound country, the land of conical tumuli and long parallel earthen walls. To Marquette and Joliet it was empty country, and they had no idea how long it had been that way—since the beginning of time, perhaps. The temple-mound people whose peace had been so catastrophically shattered by de Soto were nearly as numerous in 1673, probably, as they had been in 1539, but their territory lay far downriver in Mississippi and Alabama.

Marquette and Joliet did not get that far. Still in Illinois, they observed on the east bank several Indian rock paintings of frightening monsters; they went on, past the future site of St. Louis, without remarking on the huge mounds along the shore there; they entered into the fertile region later known as "the American Bottom," which seemed to them "an unbroken wild of timber . . . a continuous waste of forest, with its trees kissing the very wave." Presently they met Indians whose language was similar to that of the Iroquois encountered by Marquette in the North. These were Tuscaroras, kinsmen of the Five Nations of the Iroquois, who in the following century would move to New York and turn the Five Nations into Six Nations. They told Marquette of a "great village called Akamsea" to the south, possibly the village near which de Soto had died. By that time the explorers knew that the river they were on must empty into the Gulf of Mexico, and not, as they had hoped, into the Pacific; so in July, having come as far south as Arkansas, they turned back and, by September, after a voyage lasting three months, were again at Green Bay. Joliet set out for Quebec, losing all the notes he had taken when his canoe overturned in rapids on the St. Lawrence. Père Marquette, though weakened by his journey, embarked on a mission to the Illinois Indians, fell ill among them in November of 1674, and died near Lake Michigan.

The Mississippi had now been traversed for nearly its entire length, de Soto having covered the lower section, Marquette and Joliet the rest. Part of the mound region had proved to be depopulated, but in the South mound-building tribes still existed. The earthworks of the empty North continued to attract no attention as the eighteenth century dawned; a Jesuit named Jacques Gravier spent the winter of 1700 at an Illinois village he called "Kaowikia"—almost certainly Cahokia—but though he lived among an array of mounds that included one whose volume was greater than that of Egypt's largest pyramid, he made no mention of them when he published his journal. This is most curious, since Gravier did speak of mounds, though somewhat vaguely, in his narrative of a voyage farther down the Mississippi. He reached the village of "Akansea," the "Akamsea" of Marquette, which lay at the mouth of the Arkansas River. "We went out and cabined a league lower down," he says, "half a league from the old village of the Akansea, where they formerly received the late Father Marquette and which is discernible now only by the old outworks, there being no cabins left."[15] The "old outworks" quite likely were earthen fortifications. Speaking of the "Tounicas," a Southern tribe encountered by de Soto, Gravier says, "They have only one small temple, raised on a mound of earth."

So the process of depopulation was spreading now to the mound-building tribes of the lower Mississippi. An early eighteenth-century account by one Bénard de la Harpe, speaking of the Indians living along the Yazoo River, declares, "The cabins of the Yasous, Courois, Offagoula, and Ouspie are dispersed over the country upon mounds of earth made with their own hands, from which it is inferred that these nations are very ancient and were formerly very numerous, although at the present time they hardly number two hundred and fifty persons."[16]

One Southern tribe still pursued its ancient ways, and was the subject of detailed ethnological study by the Frenchmen who lived among them from 1698 to 1732. These were the Natchez, who at that time numbered about four thousand and lived in seven small villages grouped around an imposing mound 35 feet high, covering seven acres. An account by a certain Mathurin La Petit informs us that "the temple of the Natchez in shape resembles an earthen oven over 100 feet in circumference," and "to enable them better to converse together they raise a mount of artificial soil on which they build his [the chief's] cabin, which is of the same construction as the temple . . . and when the great chief dies they demolish his cabin and then raise a new mound, on which they build the cabin of him who is to replace him in this dignity, for he never lodges in that of his predecessor."[17] Le Page du Pratz, who visited the Natchez in 1720, writes, "As I was an intimate friend of the sovereign of the Natchez he showed me their temple, which is about thirty feet square, and stands on an artificial mount about eight feet high, by the side of a small river." The chief's own house, "not less than thirty feet on each face and about twenty feet high, is like that of the temple, upon a mound of earth about eight feet high and sixty feet across."[18] Nine years later, the Natchez launched a massacre against the French, the outcome of which was the destruction of the Natchez civilization. The tribe was all but exterminated, and the few survivors were dispersed among other tribes.

The fortunes of the Southern mound builders were ebbing, but even in the middle of the eighteenth century there was ample evidence that mounds were customary features of contemporary Indian cultures. The Northern mounds were not yet known, generally, but it would not have been difficult to assume that they were the work of now-departed tribes of the fifteenth or sixteenth centuries. One of the earliest notices of Northern mounds appeared in Cadwallader Colden's *History of the Five Nations,* published in 1747, in which he notes that "a round hill" was sometimes raised over the grave in which a corpse had been deposited. He saw nothing extraordinary in this custom.

By now the Thirteen Colonies were firmly established along the Atlantic seaboard, and these English settlements had begun to look toward the heartland of the continent, an unknown wilderness penetrated thus far only by French trappers and missionaries. The frontiers were converging. British settlers began to reach beyond the Appalachians, entering the valley of the Ohio in 1750. By 1756, France and Great Britain were at war over the control of the continent, and as the outcome of that war Canada became British, as did everything else east of the Mississippi except 2,800 square miles including the mouth of the river and the town of New Orleans. That much passed from France to Spain, along with the entire domain west of the Mississippi, the boundless Louisiana Territory.

The way was open for the Thirteen Colonies to sweep westward to the Mississippi, subject only to the objections of the Indian tribes that happened to be occupying the territory. Soon the wagons were rolling through the mountain passes. Soon the forests were falling and the ancient mounds were coming to light. And, shortly, the myth of the Mound Builders was born.

▲▲▲ 2

THE MAKING OF THE MYTH

▲▲▲

The first notices of the Northern mounds were sporadic and tentative. On May 3, 1772, a group of Christian Indians led by the Moravian missionary David Zeisberger came from western Pennsylvania to found a settlement called Schönbrunn, near the present site of New Philadelphia, Ohio. In the course of laying out the town, Zeisberger discovered Indian burial mounds, and mentioned them in his *History of the North American Indians.* This was possibly the earliest account of mounds in Ohio. Zeisberger (1721–1808) was a dedicated student of Indian lore; he had lived among the Onondagas for many years, publishing a dictionary of their language, and then had dwelt with the Delawares.

Three months after Zeisberger founded Schönbrunn, his fellow missionary, John Heckewelder (1743–1823), arrived with two hundred more Indian converts. Heckewelder, too, had studied the Delaware Indians at first hand; unlike most men of his day, he refused to regard Indians as beasts or worthless pagans, and thought it important to record their beliefs and mythologies. He compiled a work entitled *An Account of the History, Manners and Customs of the Indian Nations Who Once Inhabited Pennsylvania and the Neighboring States,* which did not, however, see print until 1819. At that time it served to magnify the rapidly growing Mound Builder myth, as we shall see.

The settlement of Christian Indians at Schönbrunn lasted only until 1777, when the hostility of the non-converted local tribesmen forced its abandonment. By then, several other accounts of the Ohio mounds had been published. The January 1775 number of the *Royal American Magazine,* a Boston enterprise, had included an anonymous contribution describing and illustrating the extensive earthworks at what would be the town of Circleville, Ohio. A missionary named David Jones, who had seen mounds in 1772, wrote briefly of them in his *Journal of Two Visits,* published in 1774. The Swedish traveler, Peter Kalm, after touring America in 1749, had mentioned mounds in his journal, published in German in 1764 and in an English translation in 1772.

James Adair, whose *History of the American Indians* appeared in 1775, noted that "great mounds of earth, either of a circular or oblong form, having a strong breastwork at a distance around them, are frequently met with." Adair also spoke of Indian tribes that built their important structures atop hills— presumably artificial ones. And in 1776 the mapmaker Jonathan Carver, a member of Rogers' Rangers, toured the north country under the spell of the dream of finding a Northwest Passage to the Pacific. Carver saw high embankments at Lake Pepin on the Mississippi, and wrote of them in his *Travels in the Interior Parts of North America,* published in 1778.

All these comments were cursory and unspeculative, but the first stirrings of the mythmakers were beginning. In 1785, a certain John Fitch published a map of the Northwest Territory, and in the region which is now Wisconsin he placed the inscription, "This country has once been settled by a people more expert in the art of war than the present inhabitants. Regular fortifications, and some of these incredibly large, are frequently to be found. Also many graves and towers like pyramids of earth."[19]

The "present inhabitants," though, were themselves still fairly "expert in the art of war." The new United States of America, hoping to open its Western territories to further settlement, found it necessary to send troops over the Appalachians to pacify the Indians. Some of the officers stationed in Ohio were attracted to the mounds and sent descriptions of them to men of science in the East. Treaties with the Indians in 1785 and 1786 failed to quiet them, and war was necessary in 1787. General Samuel H. Parsons, on active duty in Ohio, communicated an account of the mounds at Marietta, Ohio, to Ezra Stiles, the president of Yale College, causing a flurry of excitement in New Haven.

Stiles, Yale's seventh president, was a wise administrator under whose regime the college had prospered; a clergyman and lawyer as well, he served as professor of ecclesiastical history, kept silkworms, and at the age of 40 had commenced the study of Hebrew, becoming a notable Biblical scholar. His wideranging mind was of a speculative bent, and among his theories was the persuasion that the Indians of the Americas had a Biblical origin, being "Canaanites of the expulsion of Joshua." Addressing the General Assembly of Connecticut in 1783, Stiles had proposed this theory in some detail, though he admitted he did not know whether the fleeing Canaanites had trekked all the way across Asia to enter North America from Siberia, or had been transported by Phoenician seamen across the Atlantic to found the civilizations of Mexico and Peru.

Upon hearing of the Marietta mounds from General Parsons, he asked his good friend Benjamin Franklin for an opinion of them. Franklin shed no light on Stiles' Canaanite notions; he suggested that the Ohio earthworks might have been constructed by de Soto in his wanderings. This contention was echoed by the lexicographer Noah Webster in the December 1787 issue of *The American Magazine,* although Webster later abandoned the idea and credited the mounds to Indian aborigines.

Out in Ohio, General Parsons continued his researches heedless of these debates, and perhaps might have made a further valuable contribution to archaeology, had he not been drowned in the Ohio River in December, 1789. By then the local Indians had been thoroughly subdued and colonists from New England were settling in Ohio. Brigadier General Rufus Putnam, a veteran of the Revolutionary War, had been instrumental in the founding in 1786 of a joint-stock corporation, the Ohio Company, with the aim of buying cheap land in Ohio and founding settlements. Putnam had learned from a friend and fellow officer that the ideal spot for his project was the fertile Muskingum Valley, and, after he had raised $250,000, he sent an agent to New York, then the national capital, to buy land from the government.

Putnam's agent was the Reverend Manasseh Cutler, a cagey clergyman from Ipswich, Massachusetts. Cutler arrived in New York on July 5, 1787, and proposed to Congress that the Ohio Company be allowed to purchase a million acres of land at less than a dollar an acre, despite a 1785 government ordinance which set one dollar as the minimum price and prohibited such large purchases. Congress showed little enthusiasm, and Cutler was ready to retire in defeat when he was surreptitiously approached by Colonel William Duer, the government official in charge of land sales. Duer proposed to use his influence to get the sale through Congress, and to loan the Ohio Company $750,000 to complete the deal. He suggested that the company apply for 1,500,000 acres for itself, paying $1,000,000, and also take down 5,000,000 acres to be sold to Duer and his associates in a later transaction. Over a dinner of oysters in Brooklyn the two men came to an agreement whereby the Ohio Company would ultimately get 1,500,000 acres at a net cost of about eight cents an acre, Duer's Scioto Company would acquire without public knowledge a much larger tract, and Cutler would get an option on several million acres for his own account.

Duer steered the deal through Congress and, after a pretense of deliberating over Cutler's offer, had his own office approve it. Thus the heart of Ohio's mound country passed into the hands of private operators. In the winter of 1787–88, the Ohio Company's advance parties arrived from Massachusetts and Connecticut and commenced the construction of a Yankee village they called Marietta. Each settler got a 116-acre pasture along the Ohio; streets were laid out with care; free lands were awarded to "Warlike Christian Men" who agreed to occupy dangerous spots in the interior; and gristmills and sawmills were set up. In the course of these busy preparations the Marietta settlers paused to consider what to do with the ancient mounds at the center of their townsite.

They showed a surprisingly reverent attitude toward these monuments of a previous age. General Putnam himself prepared a detailed map of the Marietta earthworks, which is preserved in the library of Marietta College. The

3   The great mound at Marietta. Engraving from *Ancient Monuments of the Mississippi Valley,* by E. G. Squier and E. H. Davis, 1848, from an early painting.

general, who had been trained as a surveyor and military engineer, had earlier chosen the site for West Point and constructed the fortifications there. On his Marietta map he indicated the outlines of mounds, avenues, and enclosures, and in his own hand appended a sheet of "references" describing each feature. ("ABCD: Is the remains of an ancient wall or rampart of earth whose base is from 25 to 36 feet and its height from 4 to 10 feet, at a, it is 5, at b, 4, at c, 8 & at d, 6 feet high. . . . Fig. 13 is an artificial mound of earth whose base is about 4 perch diameter and forms a hillock about twelve feet high . . . .")

"This document may be regarded as the genesis of the science of archaeology in the United States," wrote the Ohio archaeologist Henry Clyde Shetrone in 1930. He was speaking perhaps too grandly, since he overlooked some excellent archaeological work carried out by Thomas Jefferson in the previous decade. But Rufus Putnam's map was the first comprehensive sketch of an important mound group.

The directors of the Ohio Company took action to preserve at least one of the earthworks Putnam had mapped. Three features in particular lay within the area intended for downtown Marietta, at the junction of the Muskingum and Ohio rivers. One was an irregular square enclosure covering about 40 acres and containing four truncated pyramids, of which the largest was 188 feet long, 132 feet wide, and 10 feet high, with a graded path along the sides. Near it was a similar square covering 27 acres. To the south of this lay a finely formed truncated mound, 30 feet high, surrounded by a nearly circular wall. At right angles to the larger enclosure an excavated pathway, promptly dubbed the *Sacra Via,* ran to the river; this was 680 feet long, 150 feet wide, and bordered by embankments 8 to 10 feet high. "This passage," wrote the archaeologist, E. G. Squier, in 1847, "may have been the grand avenue leading to the sacred plain above, through which assemblies and processions passed, in the solemn observances of a mysterious worship."[20]

One of the earliest official acts of the Ohio Company when it set up business in Marietta in 1788 was to pass a resolution reserving the two large enclosures and the great mound as public squares, the great mound to be included in a cemetery. The squares, the company directors decreed, should be embellished with shade trees once the wild forest growth was cleared away, and these trees, they added, should be of certain specified varieties native to Ohio. A separate resolution preserved the *Sacra Via,* "never to be disturbed or defaced, as common ground, not to be enclosed." But for these decisions, the Marietta earthworks would surely have been obliterated as thoroughly as those of Cincinnati, Circleville, Chillicothe, and many other Ohio cities. In practice, it proved impossible to preserve the walls of the enclosures, but the mounds sur-

vived. (Today Marietta's Warren Street follows the route of the *Sacred Via.*)
In the early nineteenth century, cattle grazing about the mounds stripped away
the grassy cover and laid them open to rain erosion, but in the 1830's the
citizens of Marietta raised a fund to restore and fence the earthworks, and they
remain on view today.

The wily Reverend Manasseh Cutler also distinguished himself in Marietta
archaeology. When he arrived at the settlement in 1788, he discovered the
dense forest about the mounds being cut down, and carried out a thoughtful
analytical study of the growth rings of these trees. It was already known that
each year, as a tree grows, it adds a new ring of wood around its heart, and
that these rings are visible when the tree is cut down. In the presence of Arthur
St. Clair, who represented the United States as the governor of the newly
created Northwest Territory, Cutler counted the rings on some of the trees that
had topped the mounds. One tree yielded a count of 463 rings, and round
about it Cutler noted decayed stumps in which new trees were growing. This
led him to conclude that the mound had been erected in the early fourteenth
century at the latest, and quite likely was over a thousand years old. Probably
never before had tree-ring dating been used on an archaeological site; and
Cutler's studies helped to establish the fact that the Ohio mounds were not
the work of the contemporary Ohio Indians. (What Cutler did not realize was
that some trees in some climates add more than one growth ring a year.)

Mounds were being discovered; mounds were being studied; some mounds
were being preserved. As the western movement across the Alleghenies accelerated, interest in the mounds and their builders became intense—and theories concerning their origin multiplied. One of the most fertile theorists of the
era was Benjamin Smith Barton of Philadelphia, a member of that city's remarkable eighteenth-century intelligentsia. Barton, born in 1766, was the
nephew of David Rittenhouse, an important political figure of the day and
even more important as an astronomer and mathematician. In 1875, Rittenhouse, commissioned to lay out the western boundary of Pennsylvania, took
his young nephew along as an assistant surveyor. Barton found opportunity on
the trip to investigate geography and geology, natural history, and most particularly the Indians of the area—and, of course, the mounds. That autumn he
went to Edinburgh to study medicine, and while still in Scotland wrote a little
book entitled *Observations on Some Parts of Natural History,* which was published in Edinburgh in 1787. Barton called it "Part I," and devoted nearly all
of its text to a discussion of the mounds and ancient fortifications along the
Ohio and Muskingum rivers; he never got around to writing the projected
later volumes of the work.

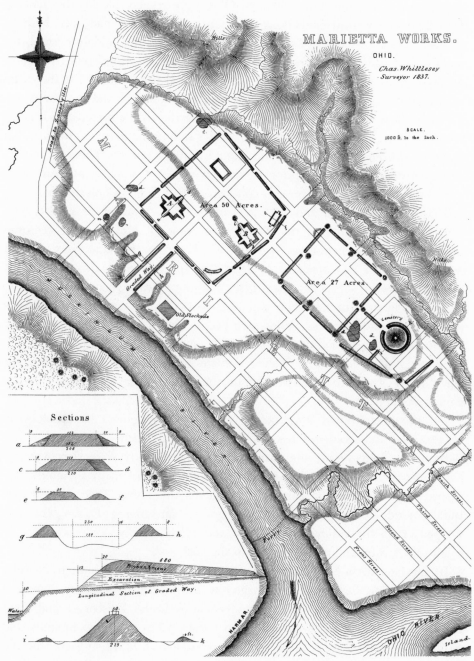

4   Diagram of the Marietta works. Squier and Davis, 1848.

Barton doubted that the Indians of Ohio were responsible for the mounds. In a kind of youthful exuberance he suggested that they had been built by Danish immigrants of pre-Columbian times—for, as was widely noticed, the Viking lords had been interred in burial mounds not much different from those of Ohio. Not content to stop there, Barton offered the opinion that the earthworks were religious in nature, rather than fortifications; and by way of explaining where his Danes had gone, he said that they had emigrated to Mexico, where they were known as "Toltecs." Barton's stab in the dark was the first, but by no means the last, linking of the Mound Builders and the Toltecs.

The history of Mexico prior to the arrival of Cortés' army was fairly well known, since some of the conquerors had been scholarly men who collected the chronicles and traditions of the Aztecs and their predecessors. The Toltecs, according to the Aztecs, had come to Mexico some centuries before the Aztecs themselves had arrived. Entering the land from the far west, the Toltecs had appeared at a time of anarchy in Mexico and quickly made themselves supreme. Their first great king was Quetzalcoatl, said to be a bearded man of fair skin, and later worshiped as a god in Mexico. In time Quetzalcoatl, expelled by his own people, fled with his supporters to the Mayan territories in Yucatán. Afterward, nomads called the Chichimecs, the "dog people," invaded the Toltec domain and destroyed it, clearing the way for the entrance and triumph of the Aztecs, last of Mexico's Indian empire builders.

All this was known long before the rise of systematic archaeology in Mexico, and archaeological research has confirmed much of it. To men like Barton, the Toltecs were tantalizing figures, particularly since they were reputed to have had fair skins. And Mexico was a land of many pyramids, flat-topped like some of the earthen mounds of the north. Ergo, the Mound Builders and Toltecs were the same group—far-ranging Danes who had stopped off in the valleys of the Ohio and Mississippi before proceeding on to Mexico, a thousand years or more in the past.

Barton later drew back from this youthful book, which he came to consider a premature publication, but his interest in American antiquity remained high. In 1797, he interviewed the missionaries David Zeisberger and John Heckewelder, taking down their data on Indian tribes and Ohio mounds, and in 1798 he published a book entitled *New Views of the Origins of the Tribes and Nations of America,* issued in Philadelphia and dedicated to Thomas Jefferson. This work was not primarily concerned with mounds or with Toltecs, but dealt with the vexed problem of American Indian origins. (Indians and Mound Builders were already beginning to fall into separate scientific compartments.) Barton believed that the Indians had come from Asia, and devoted most of this work to long tables of words from various Asian and American Indian languages, showing fancied resemblances. "The comparative vocabularies which are published in this memoir," Barton concluded, "seem to render it certain, that the nations of America and those of Asia had a common origin." In the same book he passed along a legend of a mysterious white race that had lived in the Tennessee Valley before the arrival there of the Cherokee Indians. "The Cheerake tell us," he wrote, "that when they first arrived in the country which they inhabit, they found it possessed by certain 'moon-eyed people,' who could not see in the day-time. These wretches they expelled."[21] He left the clear implication that these albino people were responsible for the Tennessee mounds. The myths of lost races were starting to come in clusters.

2

While the mounds of the Ohio Valley and surrounding regions were exciting these speculations, more sober investigations were being carried out upon the mounds of the Southeast, in territory visited long before by de Soto. William Bartram, another member of Philadelphia's eighteenth-century scientific pantheon, performed a tour of exploration there that won him worldwide fame and provided vivid descriptions of ancient monuments.

Bartram, who lived from 1739 to 1823, was the son of a Quaker botanist, John Bartram. The elder Bartram had founded a private botanical garden on the west bank of the Schuylkill River, near Philadelphia, and earned a substantial living supplying American plants and trees for the gardens of Europe. The big Bartram stone house was a gathering place for all Philadelphians interested in natural history; Benjamin Franklin was a frequent visitor, as was Hector Crèvecoeur, the famous traveler and author of *Letters of an American Farmer*. Among John Bartram's correspondents were Sir Hans Sloane, the British collector; Carolus Linnaeus, the great classifier; and botanists in Russia and France. Young William, one of seven sons, was apprenticed to a merchant, only to find the lure of natural history too strong. In 1761, he left Philadelphia to run a trading post on the Cape Fear River in North Carolina, but the store foundered while he studied the Carolina wildlife.

Four years later his father, newly appointed botanist to His Majesty George III, passed through North Carolina on his way to collect specimens in Florida. Father and son went to Florida together, William serving as an able assistant and causing a sensation by slaughtering a six-foot-long rattlesnake that the Bartrams presented to Governor James Grant of Florida. (Governor Grant promptly had the serpent served for dinner.)

The chief area of the Bartrams' Florida explorations was the St. Johns River. When John Bartram returned to Philadelphia in the spring of 1766, William remained by the St. Johns as a planter of indigo and rice. This business venture, too, was a disaster, and 1767 found him back in Philadelphia as an equally unsuccessful merchant. The following year he was elected a corresponding member of the American Society Held in Philadelphia for Promoting Useful Knowledge, which shortly was merged with the revered American Philosophical Society; but Bartram, in the 54 years remaining to him, managed to avoid attending every meeting of this celebrated group.

With bankruptcy threatening in 1770, he disappeared from Philadelphia and turned up, some months later, in North Carolina once more. There he remained, somewhat in disgrace, through 1772. He kept up a correspondence with his father, who urged him to return home; instead, William said, he planned to go back to Florida.

John Bartram wrote in surprise and annoyance to discourage this "wild notion." Nevertheless, William persevered. He found a London patron, Dr. John Fothergill, who commissioned him to collect plants and mollusks in Florida, offering a salary of £50 a year plus expenses. "It is a pity that such a genius should sink under distress," Fothergill wrote to John Bartram. Now that the Florida trip was a solid business proposition, the senior Bartram relented and gave his blessing.

William returned to Philadelphia late in 1772 to plan his journey, and set sail for the port of Charleston on March 20, 1773, beginning four years of peregrinations through wild and almost unknown territory. In 1774 and 1775, he dispatched specimens, drawings, and journals to Fothergill; these are preserved in the British Museum. The outbreak of the Revolution in 1776 cut off communication between Bartram and "the noble Fothergill," but William continued to travel and observe. When he returned from the South in 1777, he settled in Philadelphia and does not appear to have left it for the rest of his long life. Management of the famous botanical garden went to his brother John, for the elder John Bartram had good reasons to mistrust William's business abilities, but William, now a celebrity in his own right, was sought out and visited by all scientists and statesmen who passed through Philadelphia.

His literary masterpiece, *Travels through North & South Carolina, Georgia,*

East & West Florida. . . . etc., very nearly did not get published at all. Bartram had kept a colorful journal of his adventures, and in manuscript form this was examined by a number of Philadelphians. The details of Bartram's exploits thus circulated by word of mouth and greatly enhanced his fame: his meeting with the emperor of the Cherokees; his solitary wanderings up the Florida rivers; his idyll in the virgin forests; his dinners of venison and fresh trout; his encounters with roaring alligators, graceful cranes, wondrous fishes, otters and frogs, bears and wolves. There was magic and poetry in Bartram's work, and indeed when it finally appeared Samuel Taylor Coleridge would draw on its imagery for some of the most colorful passages of his "Kubla Khan." In 1786 a Philadelphia publisher, Enoch Story, Jr., issued a prospectus for a planned edition of the *Travels,* but the project somehow miscarried, and Bartram's nearly legendary manuscript remained unavailable.

The collapse of Story's plans may have been the work of young Benjamin Smith Barton, who, during his three-year stay in Edinburgh, exchanged five or six letters with Bartram. Under date of August 26, 1787, Barton wrote in harshly critical terms of Story as a publisher, and may have induced Bartram to break off negotiations with him. In several of these letters Barton asked to be allowed to publish Bartram's journal himself, with additions of his own; but the naturalist gently declined this offer. In 1789, Barton sent Bartram a lengthy list of questions about the customs of the Indians of the Southeast, to which Bartram replied in detail. Barton intended to use this material in a book of his own, but never did, and it remained unpublished until 1853.

Finally another Philadelphia firm, James and Johnson, arranged to bring out Bartram's *Travels* in 1791, by subscription, at a price of "two Spanish milled dollars." Among the subscribers were President Washington and Vice President Adams. The book was received enthusiastically, though some London reviewers were skeptical of the wonders described, and thought Bartram's style too imaginative. It was widely reprinted—in London in 1792 and 1794, in Dublin, in Berlin, in Paris, in Vienna, and perhaps in other European cities, and it rapidly established itself as a classic of American travel writing.

Bartram's chief concern was natural history; but, moving as he did through what had once been densely populated country, he could not avoid stumbling over mounds everywhere. On one of the early pages of his book he reports, "evident vestiges of an ancient Indian town may be seen, such as old extensive fields, and conical mounds, or artificial heaps of earth," and the refrain is a frequent one through the succeeding five hundred pages.

Sometimes he deceived himself in his mound-finding zeal. At a site along the north branch of Georgia's Little River Bartram reported "many very magnificent monuments of the power and industry of the ancient inhabitants of these lands. . . . I observed a stupendous conical pyramid, or artificial mount of earth, vast tetragon terraces, and a large sunken area, of a cubical form, encompassed with banks of earth; and certain traces of a large Indian town, the work of the powerful nation, whose period of grandeur perhaps long preceded the discovery of this continent."[22] But archaeologists have sought these "monuments" in vain. The only landmark that seems to fit Bartram's description is a large wooded hillock of natural origin; a nearby "sunken area" also appears to be a purely natural feature.

More authentic were the mounds Bartram discovered late in 1773 on the east side of the Ocmulgee River, opposite the present city of Macon, Georgia: "On the heights of these low grounds are yet visible monuments, or traces, of an ancient town, such as artificial mounts or terraces, squares and banks, encircling considerable areas. Their old fields and planting land extend up and down the river, fifteen or twenty miles from the site."[23] Two groups of these mounds now are included in Ocmulgee National Monument, and have been the subject of intensive modern study.

As he moved farther south, Bartram came to even more imposing mounds. The one that drew the most rapturous description from him was Mount Royal, on the east bank of the St. Johns River in Putnam County, Florida. He had first seen this mound in 1765, when he visited Florida with his father; it is possible that the elder Bartram gave Mount Royal its name. William returned alone in the summer of 1774 and, writing about 1780, declared, "About fifteen years ago I visited this place, at which time there were no settlements of white people, but all appeared wild and savage; yet in that uncultivated state, it possessed an almost inexpressible air of grandeur, which was now entirely changed. At that time there was a very considerable extent of old fields, round about the mount; there was also a large Orange grove, together with Palms and Live Oaks, extending from near the mount, along the banks, downward, all of which has since been cleared away to make room for planting ground. But what greatly contributed towards compleating the magnificence of the scene, was a noble Indian highway, which led from the great mount, on a strait line, three quarters of a mile, first through a point or wing of the Orange grove, and continuing thence through an awful forest, of Live Oaks, it was terminated by Palms and Laurel Magnolias, on the verge of an oblong artificial lake, which was on the edge of an extensive green level savanna. This grand highway was about fifty yards wide, sunk a little below the common level, and the earth thrown up on each side, making a bank of about two feet high. Neither nature nor art, could any where present a more striking contrast, as you approach this savanna. The glittering water pond, plays on the sight, through the dark grove, like a brilliant diamond, on the bosom of the illumined savanna, bordered with various flowery shrubs and plants; and as we advance into the plain, the sight is agreeably relieved by a distant view of the forests, which partly environ the green expanse, on the left hand, whilst the imagination is still flattered and entertained by the far distant misty points of the surrounding forests, which project into the plain, alternately appearing and disappearing, making a grand sweep round on the right, to the distant banks of the great lake. But that venerable grove is now no more. All has been cleared away and planted with Indigo, Corn and Cotton, but since deserted: there was now scarcely five acres of ground under fence. It appeared like a desert, to a great extent, and terminated, on the land side, by frightful thickets, and open Pine forests.

"It appears however, that the late proprietor had some taste, as he has preserved the mount, and this little adjoining grove inviolate. The prospect from this station is so happily situated by nature, as to comprise at one view, the whole of the sublime and pleasing."[24]

Other ancient structures were found nearby. On an island in adjoining Lake George Bartram found "a very pompous Indian mount, or conical pyramid of earth, from which runs in a straight line a grand avenue or Indian highway,"[25] and more lay not far away. "This island," he wrote, "appears to have been well inhabited, as is very evident, from the quantities of fragments of Indian earthenware, bones of animals and other remains, particularly in the shelly heights and ridges, all over the island."

Artifacts of many sorts came to light when Mount Royal received its first scientific excavation more than a century later. In 1893 there came to it Clarence B. Moore, whose mound work in Florida occupied him for a dozen years and did much to clarify the problems of this phase of Southern prehistory. Moore measured Mount Royal at 555 feet in circumference and 16 feet in height, and found within it numerous objects of stone, flint, copper, and clay, along with a great many human burials. Nothing found in the mound showed any sign of contact between its builders and Europeans, though other Florida mounds revealed traces of de Soto's visit.

Bartram managed to discover mounds even by accident. He camped one night a little farther along the St. Johns, and woke in the morning to find that "I had taken up my lodging on the border of an ancient burying ground. . . . These graves occupied the whole grove, consisting of two or three acres of ground; there were near thirty of these cemeteries of the dead, nearly of an equal size and form, they were oblong, twenty feet in length, ten or twelve feet in width and three or four feet high, now overgrown with Orange trees, Live Oaks, Laurel Magnolias, Red bays and other trees and shrubs, composing dark and solemn shades."[26] For the first time in his narrative Bartram ventured a theory of the origin of these mounds. He had picked up accounts of a battle between the Creek and Yamasee Indians at this site, and he declared that these were "sepulchres or tumuli of the Yamasees, who were slain by the Creeks in the last decisive battle, the Creeks having driven them into this point, between the doubling of the river, where few of them escaped the fury of the conquerors." Since this massacre had taken place in the early part of the eighteenth century, Bartram was attributing a relatively recent date to this group of mounds.

In September, 1774, Bartram visited an Indian town—at the site of the present town of Palatka, Florida—where mound building of a different sort was still being practiced. Here, as in de Soto's time, the Indians observed the custom of placing the important buildings of their village upon artificial elevations:

"We were received and entertained friendly by the Indians, the chief of the village conducting us to a grand, airy pavilion in the center of the village. It was four square; a range of pillars or posts on each side supporting a canopy of Palmetto leaves, woven or thatched together, which shaded a level platform in the center that was ascended to from each side, by two steps or flights, each about twelve inches high, and seven or eight feet in breadth, all covered with carpets or matts, curiously woven of split canes dyed of various colours; here being seated or reclining ourselves, after smoking tobacco, baskets of choicest fruits were brought and set before us."[27]

Despite such evidence, Bartram did not fall into the error of assuming that *all* the Southeastern mounds were of contemporary manufacture. Many were obviously ancient, though he did not know how ancient. When he questioned local Indians about them, he received vague replies that led him to suspect a considerable antiquity, but he was generally quite cautious in his guesses. Most of the Indians now inhabiting the Southeastern mound region were Creeks, and Bartram attempted to learn their traditions about the mounds; one day at the town of "Apalachucla" (Apalachicola, Florida) a trader took him to view the ruins of "the ancient Apalachucla," a mile and a half away. This, he saw, had been "a very famous capital," and he went among "the mounds or terraces, on which formerly stood their town house or rotunda and square or areopagus, and a little back of this, on a level height or natural step, above the low grounds is a vast artificial terrace or four square mound, now seven or eight feet higher than the common surface of the ground. . . . The Creeks or present inhabitants have a tradition that this was the work of the ancients, many ages prior to their arrival and possessing this country."[28]

Bartram carefully distinguished, then, between the mounds the Creeks themselves had built and those of their unknown predecessors. In his answers to the questions Benjamin Smith Barton had put to him in 1789, Bartram had gone into some detail about the Creek villages he had visited, describing the custom of placing important buildings on elevations. Publication of this manuscript might have helped to put down the impression, common in the early nineteenth century, that *all* mounds were the work of extremely ancient races. But Barton kept the manuscript in his possession, unpublished, until his death in 1815; then it vanished, not to reappear until 1852. The Mound Builder craze was at its peak then, and Bartram's work was edited by E. G. Squier and published in *Transactions of the American Ethnological Society* for 1853. However, fire destroyed all but twenty-five copies of this volume before they were distributed, and Bartram's discussion of Creek mounds remained virtually unknown until a second publication in 1909.

The Creeks were one of four Southeastern tribes of similar culture, the others being the Choctaws, Chickasaws, and Cherokees. The Creeks' own name for themselves was Muskhogee, "Creek Indians" being a designation given them by English traders, and all of these tribes but the Cherokees are are classed in the Muskhogean linguistic family. Though the Creeks were the dominant group at the time of Bartram's visit, he believed (incorrectly) that they were recent intruders who had dispossessed their northern neighbors, the Cherokees. Accordingly, when he doubled back through Cherokee country in the Carolinas, he investigated the possibility that they might have built the mounds he had see in Creek-held Georgia and Florida.

He found mounds in Cherokee villages, too. "The council or town-house," he wrote, " is a large rotunda, capable of accommodating several hundred people; it stands on the top of an ancient artificial mount of earth, of about twenty feet perpendicular, and the rotunda on the top of it being above thirty feet more, gives the whole fabric an elevation of about sixty feet from the common surface of the ground. But it may be proper to observe, that this mount on which the rotunda stands, is of a much ancienter date than the building, and perhaps was raised for another purpose. The Cherokees themselves are as ignorant as we are, by what people or for what purpose these artificial hills were raised; they have various stories concerning them, the best of which amounts to no more than mere conjecture, and leave us entirely in the dark; but they have a tradition common with the other nations of Indians, that they found them in much the same condition as they now appear, when their forefathers arrived from the West and possessed themselves of the country, after vanquishing the nations of red men who then inhabited it."[29] But these pre-Muskhogean "red men," Bartram learned, had not built the mounds either; they "themselves found these mounts when they took possession of the country, the former possessors delivering the same story concerning them: perhaps they were designed and appropriated by the people who constructed them, to some religious purpose, as great altars and temples similar to the high places and sacred groves anciently amongst the Canaanites and other nations of Palestine and Judea."

The Choctaws, too, he found to be builders of mounds, but they did not solve the mystery for him. Discussing Choctaw burial practices, Bartram told of "bone-houses" in which the flesh of corpses was allowed to decompose; when the house is full of skeletons, the tribe places each in "a curiously wrought chest or coffin, fabricated of bones and splints," and, with great lamentation, the mourners proceed "on to the place of the general interment, where they place the coffins in order, forming a pyramid, and lastly, cover all over with earth, which raises a conical hill or mount." But Bartram added in a footnote, "Some ingenious men, whom I have conversed with, have given it as their opinion, that all those pyramidal artificial hills, usually called Indian mounts were raised on this occasion, and are generally sepulchres. However I am of a different opinion."[30]

He expressed this opinion in considering a mound which, like Mount Royal, the Ocmulgee mounds, and other huge structures, did not seem to him to be the work of the Creeks, the Cherokees, or the Choctaws. This was the great mound in the group later called Rembert's Mounds on the Savannah River in Elbert County, Georgia. "These wonderful labours of the ancients, "he wrote, "stand in a level plain, very near the bank of the river, now twenty or thirty yards from it; they consist of conical mounts of earth and four square terraces, &c. The great mount is in the form of a cone, about forty or fifty feet high, and the circumference of its base two or three hundred yards, entirely composed of the loamy rich earth of the low grounds; the top or apex is flat; a spiral path or track leading from the ground up to the top is still visible, where now grows a large, beautiful spreading Red Cedar (Juniperus Americana;) there appear four niches, excavated out of the sides of this hill, at different heights from the base, fronting the four cardinal points; these niches or sentry boxes are entered into from the winding path, and seem to have been ment for resting places or look-outs."[31]

Nothing that Bartram had seen or heard among the various Muskhogean tribes led him to believe that this mound was their work, nor could he comprehend what functions it might have served for the ancients: "It is altogether unknown to us, what could have induced the Indians to raise such a heap of earth in this place, the ground for a great space around being subject to inundations, at least once a year, from which circumstance we may conclude they had no town or settled habitations here: some imagine these tumuli were constructed for look out towers. It is reasonable to suppose, however, that they were to serve some important purpose in those days, as they were public works, and would have required the united labour and attention of a whole nation, circumstanced as they were, to have constructed one of them almost in an age. There are several less ones round about the great one, with some very large tetragon terraces on each side, near one hundred yards in length, and their surface four, six, eight and ten feet above the ground on which they stand."

The best suggestion Bartram could offer, and he did not seem very convinced by it himself, was that these mounds had been erected as places of refuge in time of flood. Nevertheless, the passage is an important one. It provides a good description of a major temple mound no longer in existence (a flood in 1908 carried most of it away, and Smithsonian Institution archaeologists visiting the site forty years later found merely a stump four feet in height); it stresses the "united labour and attention of a whole nation" that must have been necessary to construct such mounds; and it refers to the builders of the mound as "Indians." Just which Indians, Bartram did not know, other than that they had vanished long before; but at no point did he speak of Toltecs, Danes, or other hypothetical non-Indian Mound Builders. At a time when mythmakers were beginning to exercise their fancies, Bartram took a position among the conservatives. In the closing pages of his *Travels* he put forth these conclusions about the Southeastern mounds and their creators:

"This region was last possessed by the Cherokees, since the arrival of the Europeans, but they were afterwards dispossessed by the Muscogulges [Creeks], and all that country was probably many ages preceding the Cherokee invasion, inhabited by one nation or confederacy, who were ruled by the same system of laws, customs and language; but so ancient, that the Cherokees, Creeks, or the nation they conquered, could render no account for what purpose these monuments were raised. The mounts and cubical yards adjoining them, seemed to have been raised in part for ornament and recreation, and likewise to serve some other public purpose, since they are always so situated as to command the most extensive prospect over the town and country adjacent. The tetragon terraces, seem to be the foundation of a fortress, and perhaps the great pyramidal mounts, served the purpose of look out towers, and high places for sacrifice.

The sunken area, called by white traders the chunk yard, very likely served the same conveniency, that it has been appropriated to by the more modern and even present nations of Indians, that is, the place where they burnt and otherwise tortured the unhappy captives, that were condemned to die, as the area is surrounded by a bank, and sometimes two of them, one behind and above the other, as seats, to accommodate the spectators, at such tragical scenes, as well as the exhibition of games, shews and dances."[32]

3

Another cautious observer of the Southern mounds was Thomas Jefferson. In 1787, writing of mounds in a letter to his friend Charles Thomson of Philadelphia, Jefferson declared, "It is too early to form theories on those antiquities, we must wait with patience till more facts are collected. I wish our philosophical societies would collect exact descriptions of the several monuments as yet known and insert them, naked, in their *Transactions*."[33]

To another correspondent, E. I. du Pont de Nemours, Jefferson said in 1809, "Nature intended me for the tranquil pursuits of science." He was writing at the end of his second term as President of the United States, a few days before he was to put aside the burdens of office and return to more congenial pastimes. Not only a statesman but an astronomer, a physicist, an architect, a naturalist, a mathematician, and a draftsman, Jefferson was the outstanding example of the American eighteenth-century version of the renaissance man. His unusual achievements in many fields of learning need no further rehearsing here; it is Jefferson the archaeologist that concerns us.

He had studied Indian lore since his Virginia boyhood. Indian languages in particular interested him, and he collected linguistic data on some forty tribes, hoping eventually to publish a definitive work on the subject. His manuscript, though, was lost en route from Washington to Monticello in 1809, and the book never appeared. He remained preoccupied with Indian languages as a clue to Indian origins; like Benjamin Smith Barton he believed the ancient homeland of the American Indians to have been Asia, though his own discussion of the subject was ambiguous, and left him puzzling over the possibility that "the red men of America" were of greater antiquity than the inhabitants of eastern Asia.

Jefferson dealt with these topics and many more in the only book he ever published, *Notes on the State of Virginia*. The genesis of this work was almost accidental; in 1780, the 37-year-old Jefferson was serving as Governor of

Virginia when he received a questionnaire from the French government, asking for information of all sorts on his state. The French, who had backed the American colonists in their revolution, were trying to find out more about these people with whom they had become involved, and sent similar queries to leading figures of other states.

The questionnaire arrived at a grim time for Jefferson and for Virginia. The outcome of the Revolutionary War seemed in doubt; the Virginia militia was demoralized; on the eve of 1781 the traitor Benedict Arnold led a British army into the state and burned the capital city of Richmond, while Jefferson and his fellow officials fled. A few months earlier he had begun to draw up answers to the French document, but now, he told the French legate in Philadelphia, "present occupations disable me from completing" the work. When his infant daughter died, his wife fell ill, and the Virginia legislature moved to investigate his official conduct, Jefferson retired as governor and in June, 1781, depressed and exhausted, headed for the seclusion of his Monticello. He even refused appointment to the peace commission sent by Congress to Paris to end the war, saying, "I have taken my final leave of everything of that nature, I have retired to my farm, my family, and my books, from which I think nothing will evermore separate me."

In this period of self-imposed inner exile from his nation, Jefferson worked energetically on the questionnaire, producing not the expected brief series of answers, but an extended treatise of considerable scientific and philosophical importance. The manuscript was completed by the autumn of 1781, and that December he forwarded it to the French legation. But he retained a copy of his text and circulated it among his friends, seeking suggestions for revision. Over a period of several years he corrected and enlarged it, at the same time gradually returning to public life. By 1784, when Jefferson was sent to France as a representative of the newly independent United States, the manuscript had swelled to triple its original length, and he was under heavy pressure to publish it.

He hesitated, partly because of the expense, partly out of the perfectionist feeling that the work was worthy neither of its subject nor of its author. But while in Paris he found a printer who agreed to do the job cheaply, and in May, 1785, he had an edition of two hundred copies struck off, for private circulation only, of what he now called *Notes on the State of Virginia*. These went to select friends; but soon came the threat of publication of an unauthorized French translation, and Jefferson was compelled first to license a French edition of his own, then to produce a second English-language edition for general distribution. In the summer of 1787 the English printer John Stockdale issued this edition, and Jefferson's book at last reached the wider public it deserved.

In form it was still a series of replies to queries; the chapters were headed, "Query I," "Query II," and so forth, and dealt with such topics as, "Boundaries of Virginia," "Productions Mineral, Vegetable and Animal," "Religion," "Manners," "Weights, Measures, and Money," and "Laws." The subject of Query XI was "Aborigines." In this section Jefferson listed and described the tribes of Virginia and their histories since the settlement of Jamestown in 1607; offered speculations on the origin of the Indians of North America; provided a census of Virginia's current Indian population; and, perhaps of greatest scientific interest, set down an account of his own archaeological work.

Sometime prior to 1781, Jefferson had excavated an Indian mound. He refers to such mounds as "barrows," following the English usage; England, like many Western European lands, contains thousands of low rounded burial mounds of prehistoric times, and it had long been a pleasing Sunday occupation for English gentlemen to open these "barrows" and collect the pottery, weapons, and other artifacts they contained. Jefferson's large private library undoubtedly included some accounts of English barrow-digging, and it must have been a great delight to him to find domestic barrows close at hand.

His account of a mound excavation merits quoting in full for several reasons: it shows that Jefferson regarded the burial mounds of Virginia, at least, as the work of Indians, and it reveals that he anticipated the techniques of modern field archaeology by at least a century. Until recent times the aim of most archaeologists was to uncover attractive ancient treasures, and they dug quickly and carelessly until they reached the buried hoards of antiquity. Gradually professional archaeologists came to realize the importance of recording such seemingly minor features as the stratification of the earth and the sequence of discovery at a site. Jefferson, seemingly intuitively, hit upon such methods as the cutting of a trial trench to get a preliminary understanding of his site's structure, the meticulous recording of the juxtaposition of features, and the necessity to dig through a site until the level of virgin soil is reached.

He begins by indicating that Virginia lacks the lengthy earthen embankments of the Western territories and the large flat-topped pyramids of the South, although it has an abundance of burial mounds: "I know of no such thing existing [in Virginia] as an Indian monument: for I would not honour with that name arrow points, stone hatchets, stone piles, and half-shapen images. Of labour on the large scale, I think there is no remain as respectable as would be a common ditch for the draining of lands: unless indeed it be the Barrows, of which many are to be found all over this country. These are of different sizes, some of them constructed of earth, and some of loose stones. That they were repositories of the dead, has been obvious to all: but on what particular occasion constructed, was matter of doubt. Some have thought they covered the bones of those who have fallen in battles fought on the spot of interment. Some ascribed them to the custom, said to prevail among the Indians, of collecting, at certain periods, the bones of all their dead, wheresoever deposited at the time of death. Others again supposed them the general sepulchres for towns, conjectured to have been on or near these grounds; and this opinion was supported by the quality of the lands in which they are found, (those constructed of earth being generally in the softest and most fertile meadow-grounds on river sides) and by a tradition, said to be handed down from the Aboriginal Indians, that, when they settled in a town, the first person who died was placed erect, and earth put about him, so as to cover and support him; that, when another died, a narrow passage was dug to the first, the second reclined against him, and the cover of earth replaced, and so on. There being one of these in my neighbourhood, I wished to satisfy myself whether any, and which of these opinions were just.

"For this purpose I determined to open and examine it thoroughly. It was situated on the low grounds of the Rivanna, about two miles above its principal fork, and opposite to some hills, on which had been an Indian town. It was of a spheroidical form, of about 40 feet diameter at the base, and had been of about twelve feet altitude, though now reduced by the plough to seven and a half, having been under cultivation about a dozen years. Before this it was covered with trees of twelve inches diameter, and round the base was an excavation of five feet depth and width, from whence the earth had been taken of which the hillock was formed. I first dug superficially in several parts of it, and came to collections of human bones, at different depths, from six inches to three feet below the surface. These were lying in the utmost confusion, some vertical, some oblique, some horizontal, and directed to every point of the compass, entangled, and held together in clusters by the earth. Bones of the most distant parts were found together, as, for instance, the small bones of the foot in the hollow of a scull, many sculls would sometimes be in contact, lying on the face, on the side, on the back, top or bottom, so as, on the whole, to give the idea of bones emptied promiscuously from a bag or basket, and covered over with earth, without any attention to their order.

"The bones of which the greatest numbers remained, were sculls, jaw-bones, teeth, the bones of the arm, thighs, legs, feet, and hands. A few ribs remained, some vertebrae of the neck and spine, without their processes, and one instance only of the bone which serves as a base to the vertebral column. The sculls were so tender, that they generally fell to pieces on being touched. The other bones were stronger. There were some teeth which were judged to be smaller than those of an adult; a scull, which, on a slight view, appeared to be that of an infant, but it fell to pieces on being taken out, so as to prevent satisfactory examination; a rib, and a fragment of the under-jaw of a person about half grown; another rib of an infant; and part of the jaw of a child, which had not yet cut its teeth. This last furnishing the most decisive proof of the burial of children here, I was particular in my attention to it. It was part of the right-half of the under-jaw. The processes, by which it was articulated to the temporal bones, were entire; and the bone itself firm to where it had been broken off, which, as nearly as I could judge, was about the place of the eye-tooth. Its upper edge, wherein would have been the sockets of the teeth, was perfectly smooth. Measuring it with that of an adult, by placing their hinder processes together, its broken end extended to the penultimate grinder of the adult. This bone was white, all the others of a sand colour. The bones of infants being soft, they probably decay sooner, which might be the cause so few were found here.

"I proceeded then to make a perpendicular cut through the body of the barrow, that I might examine its internal structure. This passed about three feet from its center, was opened to the former surface of the earth, and was wide enough for a man to walk through and examine its sides. At the bottom, that is, on the level of the circumjacent plain, I found bones; above these a few stones, brought from a cliff a quarter of a mile off, and from the river one-eighth of a mile off; then a large interval of earth, then a stratum of bones, and so on. At one end of the section were four strata of bones plainly distinguishable; at the other, three; the strata in one part not ranging with those in another. The bones nearest the surface were least decayed. No holes were discovered in any of them, as if made with bullets, arrows, or other weapons. I conjectured that in this barrow might have been a thousand skeletons. Every one will readily seize the circumstances above related, which militate against the opinion, that it covered the bones only of persons fallen in battle; and against the tradition also, which would make it the common sepulchre of a town, in which the bodies were placed upright, and touching each other. Appearances certainly indicate that it has derived both origin and growth from the accustomary collection of bones, and deposition of them together; that the first collection had been deposited on the common surface of the earth, a few stones put over it, and then a covering of earth, that the second had been laid on this, had covered more or less of it in proportion to the number of bones, and was then also covered with earth; and so on. The following are the particular circumstances which give it this aspect. 1. The number of bones. 2. Their confused position. 3. Their being in different strata. 4. The strata in one part having no correspondence with those in another. 5. The different states of decay in these strata, which seem to indicate a difference in the time of inhumation. 6. The existence of infant bones among them. [Here Jefferson appends a footnote in Greek, quoting examples of mound burials from Homer and Herodotus.]

"But on whatever occasion they may have been made, they are of considerable notoriety among the Indians: for a party passing, about thirty years ago, through the part of the country where this barrow is, went through the woods directly to it, without any instructions or enquiry, and having staid about it some time, with expressions which were construed to be those of sorrow, they returned to the high road, which they had left about half a dozen miles to pay this visit, and pursued their journey. There is another barrow, much resembling this in the low grounds of the South branch of Shenandoah, where it is crossed by the road leading from the Rock-fish gap to Staunton. Both of these have, within these dozen years, been cleared of their trees and put under cultivation, are much reduced in their height, and spread in width, by the plough, and will probably disappear in time. There is another on a hill in the Blue ridge of mountains, a few miles North of Wood's gap, which is made up of small stones thrown together. This has been opened and found to contain human bones, as the others do. There are also many others in other parts of the country."[34]

4

Papers on mounds and their contents now began to appear frequently in the learned journals of the young republic. Towns were being founded with great regularity in the Ohio Valley and along the Ohio's tributaries, the Miami, Scioto, and Muskingum Rivers; each townsite had its complement of mounds, and generally each town had its antiquarian who studied them before they were swept away by progress. Cincinnati was settled in 1788 by a contingent of land speculators from Kentucky; soon came Athens, Manchester, Chillicothe, Portsmouth, and a dozen more. In nearly every case, the site that the settlers found best suited for a town was the same that the ancient inhabitants of the land had found a desirable location for earthworks.

The mounds of Cincinnati were explored in 1794 by Colonel Winthrop Sargent, whose findings were published in the fourth volume of the *Transactions of the American Philosophical Society*, 1799. Colonel Sargent took a number of artifacts from a mound at the intersection of Third and Main streets in Cincinnati, all of stone or bone; he failed to discover the copper objects that the mound also contained. These were unearthed in 1815, and caused quite a stir, since the North American Indians had not been thought to be users of metal.

That same number of the *Transactions* contained a further article by Benjamin Smith Barton on mounds: "Observations and conjectures concerning articles which were taken out of an ancient tumulus, or grave, at Cincinnati, in the County of Hamilton, and Territory of the United States, northwest of the River Ohio." Barton's secondhand observations were typical of the growing tendency to comment in a theoretical way on other men's discoveries in the West. But he had nothing of importance to offer.

The English astronomer Francis Baily, accompanying a party of settlers down the Ohio River in 1796, stopped to examine a group of mounds on what is today the West Virginia side of the river, and made the first recorded notice of the striking Grave Creek tumulus, which had already been discovered and partly excavated by unknown pioneers. The mounds, Baily wrote, must have been "built by a race of people more enlightened than the present Indians, and at some period of time very far distant; for the present Indians know nothing about their use, nor have they any tradition concerning them."[35] Others who published comments on the Ohio Valley mounds at the close of the century included Major Jonathan Heart (*Observations on the Ancient Mounds*), the French traveler Constantin Volney (*Ruins: or a Survey of the Revolution of Empires*), and the Moravian missionary G. H. Loskiel (*Mission of the United Brethren among the Indians*). But shortly after the turn of the century there appeared two papers that were far more influential, since they served to polarize the controversy that raged over the mounds for the next hundred years.

The first was the work of the Right Reverend James Madison, first Protestant Episcopal Bishop of Virginia, and at one time president of William and Mary College. In 1803, Bishop Madison published in the sixth volume of the *Transactions of the American Philosophical Society* a closely reasoned essay entitled, "The Supposed Fortifications of the Western Country." In this he dismissed the various lost-race theories of Mound Builders, and asserted that the mounds and other earthworks had been built by the ancestors of the contemporary Indians of the mound regions.

Two years later, a New England minister, the Reverend Thaddeus M. Harris, published his book, *Journal of a Tour into the Territory Northwest of the Alleghany Mountains*. He had visited Ohio in 1803, spending much of his time examining the Marietta mounds, and it was his conclusion that the earthworks were too elaborate an engineering feat to have been the work of mere savage Indians. They must have been created, he argued, by some higher race, and he revived Barton's notion that the Mound Builders were identical to the Toltecs of Mexican tradition. (He did not, like the young Barton, claim that the two groups were descended from Vikings; he suggested only that this noble mound-building civilization lived in the Ohio Valley at some early date, ultimately migrating to Mexico while Indians replaced it in the North.)

Neither the opinions of Madison nor those of Harris were new, but the two men came to symbolize the opposite schools of thought. As the archaeologist Samuel Haven noted in 1856, "These two gentlemen are among the first who, uniting opportunities of personal observation to the advantages of scientific culture, imparted to the public their impressions of western antiquities. They represent the two classes of observers whose opposite views still divide the sentiment of the country; one class seeing no evidence of art beyond what might be expected of existing tribes, with the simple difference of a more numerous population, and consequently better defined and more permanent habitations; the other finding proofs of skill and refinement, to be explained, as they believe, only on the supposition that a superior race, or more probably a people of foreign and higher civilization, once occupied the soil."[36] In Haven's day, and for a generation thereafter, the supporters of the Reverend Mr. Harris had very much the best of the argument.

The reintroduction of the Toltecs into the controversy caused renewed interest in the debate over pre-Columbian voyages to the Americas. It was a debate that had been running for several centuries, ever since the Spaniards had discovered the high civilizations of Mexico and Peru. The cities of the Aztecs and Incas were in some ways grander and more advanced than those of sixteenth-century Europe, a fact that persuaded early theorists that their builders could not possibly have been indigenous to the American continents. No, they must have come from the Old World, settling among the red-skinned savages and erecting their great metropolitan centers. But where had they come from, and how long ago? Were they of Phoenician descent? Did they come from the lost continent of Atlantis? Were they Greeks? Persians? Hindus? Vikings? For that matter, how had the red-skinned savages themselves come to the Americas? That was an entirely separate problem, whose source was theological, not ethnological.

The civilized natives of the Americas must have come from the Old World, it was argued, merely because they were civilized. But the savages could not have been indigenous to the Americas either, since the Bible spoke of just one act of creation, that having taken place in the Garden of Eden. Eden was considered to be in Asia, and Asia thus must have been the homeland of America's red men, as it was of all other human beings.

Long before anything was known about the geography of western North America, clergymen were worrying over the route by which the Indians had traveled. In 1590, the Spanish priest José de Acosta wrote, "It is not likely that there was another Noah's Ark, by the which men might be transported into the Indies, and much less any angel to carry the first man to this world, holding him by the hair of the head, like to the Prophet Habakkuk. . . . I conclude, then, that it is likely that the first that came to the Indies was by shipwreck and tempest of weather." Since shipwreck would not account for the presence of animals in the New World, Acosta went on to guess that somewhere in the North there was a part of America joined to eastern Asia, or at least "not altogether severed and disjoined."

The idea was taken up by others. The English philologist Edward Brerewood, in his work of 1614, *Enquiries Touching the Diversity of Languages, and Religions, Through the Chief Parts of the World,* reasoned that the North American Indians must be akin to the "Tartars," by which he meant the inhabitants of Siberia and Mongolia. This was so, he argued, because of their skin color, neither an African black nor a European white, but rather a coppery hue. Also, he observed, "the West side of America respecting Asia, is exceeding much better peopled then the opposite or East side, that respecteth toward Europe. And, as for these reasons it is very likely, that America received her first inhabitants, from the East border of Asia." Brerewood noted that the Indians, "in their gross ignorance of letters, and of arts, in their Idolatry, and the specialties of it, in their incivility, and many barbarous properties, they resemble the old and rude Tartars, above all the nations of the Earth." As for their migration route, Brerewood was not sure that "that Northeast part of Asia possessed by the Tartars is . . . continent with the West side of America," but that, "without all doubt, it is the least disjoined by sea, of all that coast of Asia, for that those parts of Asia and America, are continent one with the other, or at most, disjoined by some narrow channell of the Ocean."[37] Thus "the ravenous and harmful beasts, wherewith America is stored, as Bears, Lions, Tigers, Wolves, Foxes, &c. (which men as is likely, would never to their own harm transport out of the one continent to the other)" had come over from Asia.

In the first half of the eighteenth century, the arduous explorations of Vitus Bering proved at last the correctness of the speculations of Acosta and Brerewood: there was indeed a place where the New World and the Old were "not altogether severed and disjoined," a 56-mile strait separating Alaska from Siberia. The discovery of what now is known as Bering Strait settled the controversy over the origin of the Indians; it was generally agreed, by the time of Thomas Jefferson and Benjamin Smith Barton, that they had come out of Asia via the Bering Strait, either by boat or over a bridge of winter ice, and then had spread through the two continents of the Americas. There has been no serious challenge to this theory since it was first proposed.

Yet some inhabitants of the Americas were clearly superior to others, and the origin of such higher peoples as the Aztecs, the Mayas, and the Incas aroused much fanciful thought long before the Mound Builders entered the story. The most persistent theory was that the Indians, or at least the cleverest of them, were descendants of the Ten Lost Tribes of Israel. Edward Brerewood regarded this as "a vain and capricious phantasy" in his book of 1614, but it endured despite all scorn and ultimately entangled itself thoroughly in the history of the Mound Builders.

The Biblical account describes how after the death of King Solomon, the twelve Hebrew tribes divided into two kingdoms, Israel in the north, Judah southward from a point a few miles north of Jerusalem. Both kingdoms had their troubles, but Israel in particular developed a tendency to backslide into idolatry; despite the threats and admonitions of their prophets, the Israelites "built them high places [mounds?] in all their cities," as we learn in II Kings, 17. "And they set them up images and groves in every high hill, and under every green tree: And there they burnt incense in all the high places, as did the heathen. . . ." These altars on the "high places" were frequently thrown down by reformist priests and kings, but were just as frequently rebuilt, and eventually God brought upon Israel a sign of His displeasure in the form of the bloodthirsty Assyrian legions. The Assyrians fell upon the idolatrous Israelites and carried them off into captivity, the climax coming in 722 B.C. when Sargon of Assyria captured Israel's capital and removed 27,290 of its inhabitants, settling them "in Halah and in Habor by the river of Gozan, and in the cities of the Medes." Eventually the surviving kingdom of Judah fell too, and its population was led into exile in Babylonia, but these Hebrews were later allowed to return to Palestine. Of the vanished ten northern tribes of Israel nothing more was heard.

The fate of those ten tribes remained moot until the 1560's, when Diego de Landa, the Bishop of Yucatán, wrote his treatise on Mayan civilization, *Relación de las Cosas de Yucatán*. Landa is at once the hero and the villain of students of Mayan history, for after the conquest of Yucatán, he carried out a relentless and unfortunately highly successful effort to eradicate what he deemed to be the idolatrous and devil-worshiping culture of the Mayas, and then, as if repenting, became interested in it and set down a detailed account of everything that had escaped his own bonfires. In his *Relación* he wrote, "Some of the old people of Yucatán say that they have heard from their ancestors that this land was occupied by a race of people, who came from the East and whom God had delivered by opening twelve paths through the sea. If this were true, it necessarily follows that all the inhabitants of the Indies are the descendants of the Jews. . . ."

This was not the only farfetched theory, as we see from a passage in Fray Gregorio García's book of 1607, *The Origin of the Indians of the New World:* "The Indians proceed neither from one nation or people, nor have they come from one part alone of the Old World, or by the same road, or at the same time, in the same way, or for the same reason; some have probably descended from the Carthaginians, others from the Ten Lost Tribes and other Israelites, others from the lost Atlantis, from the Greeks, and Phoenicians, and still others from the Chinese, Tartars, and other groups."[38] But the Israelite theory retained special favor. A seventeenth-century adventurer named Aaron Levi told Rabbi Manasseh ben Israel of Amsterdam about his visit to a colony of Jewish Indians in Peru, descended from the lost tribe of Reuben; the rabbi published this tale in a book, *The Hope of Israel,* which aroused the sympathetic interest of Oliver Cromwell and other English Puritans. The Quaker William Penn also subscribed to the Lost Tribe theory; he remarked that when among the Indians he could easily imagine himself in the Jewish quarter of London, so great were the resemblances of features and gestures between Indians and Jews. The most dedicated of the Lost Tribesmen was the eccentric nineteenth-century Irish peer, Lord Kingsborough, who in the 1820's contracted the obsession that the Mayas and Aztecs were of Hebraic extraction, and who in 1830 released the first of nine ponderous folio volumes to prove it. He consumed his entire inheritance to produce these elegant books, and died in a Dublin debtor's prison.

Lord Kingsborough did not attempt to include the Mound Builders in his survey of American antiquity. But many scholars did; the temptation to link the "high places" of Israel with the mounds of North America was simply too great. And so, while the legend of a great and lost race of Mound Builders was taking form in the first two decades of the nineteenth century, they were often given an Israelite ancestry.

A typical expression of this belief was stated in 1820 by Caleb Atwater of Ohio, one of the important early figures in American archaeology. He discusses the Biblical "high places" and observes that upon these mounds "great national affairs were transacted. Here they crowned and deposed their kings; here they concluded peace and declared war. Here the nation assembled at stated seasons, to perform the solemn worship of their deities. Here they celebrated anniversaries of great national events, and buried the illustrious dead."

Then he points out: "The Jews, on many great occasions, assembled at Gilgal. The name of the place, signifies 'a heap.' Here was a pile of stones, which were brought from the bed of the river Jordan, and piled up on the spot where they encamped for the first night after they crossed that river, on their entrance into 'the promised land.' Let the reader examine similar piles of stones on the water of the Licking, near Newark, in the counties of Perry, Pickaway, and Ross [all in Ohio], and then ask himself, Whether those who raised our monuments, were not originally from Asia? Shiloh, where the Jews frequently assembled to transact great national affairs, and perform acts of devotion, was situated upon a high hill. When this place was deserted, the loftier hill of Zion was selected in its stead. Upon Sinai's awful summit the law of God was promulgated. Moses was commanded to ascend a mountain to die. . . . How many hundreds of mounds in this country are situated on the highest hills, surrounded by the most fertile soils? Traverse the counties of Licking, Franklin, Pickaway and Ross; examine the loftiest mounds, and compare them with those described as being in Palestine, Through the wide world, such places seem to have been preferred by the men of ancient times who erected them."[39]

To be fair to Atwater, he should not strictly be placed in the group who advocated the Ten Lost Tribes theory. As we shall see when we return to his work shortly, he believed that the Mound Builders were a non-Indian race out of Asia, and that they were culturally akin in many ways to the Hebrews of Palestine, but he does not make the specific claim that they were the up-rooted victims of the Assyrians; at another point in his book he suggests that the Mound Builders reached North America "as early as the days of Abraham and Lot."

Others were less cautious. They wrote vociferously about the Hebrew migration to the Americas, giving the dates of arrival, the routes taken by specific tribes, and the mounds erected by each. The fantasies grew more detailed with each retelling, and their authors, generally rural clergymen, won transient but dazzling fame.

Even the conservatives now followed the Reverend Mr. Harris' school of thought rather than that of Bishop Madison; few voices were raised to claim that the mounds were the work of Indians. In 1811, the highly respected De Witt Clinton, who had examined the mounds of western New

York State, came before the New-York Historical Society to speak on behalf
of the theory that their builders were Scandinavian in origin. Clinton amplified
his ideas in a paper read to the Literary and Philosophical Society of New
York in 1817, and the following year published at Albany his *Memoir on the
Antiquities of the western part of New York,* again affirming his belief that
the mounds had been erected by errant Vikings.

Since Barton had said the same thing in 1787, this hardly was a novel
approach. But in 1819 the venerable missionary John Heckewelder released
his long-overdue work on the history, manners, and customs of the Indians
of Pennsylvania and neighboring states, and introduced a fresh aspect.

Heckewelder had lived among the Delaware Indians, also known as the
Lenni-Lenape, in the latter part of the eighteenth century. From them he
gathered a tradition of war between the Delawares and the Ohio Mound Builders, but it remained unpublished for decades, finally appearing in the first volume of the *Transactions of the Historical & Literary Committee of the American Philosophical Society.* He wrote:

"The Lenni Lenape (according to the traditions handed down to them
by their ancestors) resided many hundred years ago in a very distant
country in the western part of the American continent. For some reason which
I do not find accounted for, they determined on migrating to the eastward, and
accordingly set out together in a body. After a very long journey and many
nights' encampments by the way, they at length arrived on the *Namaesi-Sipu*
[*Namaes*=fish, *sipu*=river; River of Fish, or Mississippi], where they fell in
with the Mengwe [perhaps the Iroquois], who had likewise emigrated from a
distant country, and had struck upon this river somewhat higher up. Their object
was the same with that of the Delawares; they were proceeding on to the
eastward, until they should find a country that pleased them. The spies which
the Lenape had sent forward for the purpose of reconnoitring, had long
before their arrival discovered that the country east of the Mississippi was inhabited by a very powerful nation who had many large towns built on the
great rivers flowing through their land. Those people (as I was told) called
themselves *Talligew* or *Tallegewi.* . . . Many wonderful things are told of this
famous people. They are said to have been remarkably tall and stout, and there
is a tradition that there were giants among them, people of a much larger
size than the tallest of the Lenape. It is related that they had built to themselves regular fortifications or intrenchments, from whence they would sally
out, but were generally repulsed. I have seen many of the fortifications said to
have been built by them, two of which, in particular, were remarkable. One
of them was near the mouth of the river Huron, which empties itself into

the Lake St. Clair, on the north side of that lake, at the distance of about 20 miles northeast of Detroit. This spot of ground was, in the year 1776, owned and occupied by a Mr. Tucker. The other works, properly intrenchments, being walls or banks of earth regularly thrown up, with a deep ditch on the outside, were on the Huron River, east of the Sandusky, about six or eight miles from Lake Erie. Outside of the gateway of each of these two intrenchments, which lay within a mile of each other, were a number of large flat mounds in which, the Indian pilot said, were buried hundreds of these slain Tallegewi, whom I shall hereafter, with Colonel Gibson, call Alligewi. . . .

"When the Lenape arrived on the banks of the Mississippi they sent a message to the Alligewi to request permission to settle themselves in their neighborhood. This was refused them, but they obtained leave to pass through the country and seek a settlement farther to the eastward. They accordingly began to cross the Namaesi-Sipu, when the Alligewi, seeing that their numbers were so very great, and in fact they consisted of many thousands, made a furious attack upon those who had crossed, threatening them all with destruction, if they dared to persist in coming over to their side of the river. Fired at the treachery of these people, and the great loss of men they had sustained, and besides, not being prepared for a conflict, the Lenape consulted on what was to be done; whether to retreat in the best manner they could, or to try their strength, and let the enemy see that they were not cowards, but men, and too high-minded to suffer themselves to be driven off before they had made a trial of their strength and were convinced that the enemy was too powerful for them. The Mengwe, who had hitherto been satisfied with being spectators from a distance, offered to join them, on condition that, after conquering the country, they should be entitled to share it with them; their proposal was accepted, and the resolution was taken by the two nations, to conquer or die.

"Having thus united their forces the Lenape and Mengwe declared war against the Alligewi, and great battles were fought in which many warriors fell on both sides. The enemy fortified their large towns and erected fortifications, especially on large rivers and near lakes, where they were successfully attacked and sometimes stormed by the allies. An engagement took place in which hundreds fell, who were afterwards buried in holes or laid together in heaps and covered over with earth. No quarter was given, so that the Alligewi at last, finding that their destruction was inevitable if they persisted in their obstinacy, abandoned the country to the conquerors and fled down the Mississippi River, from whence they never returned.

"The war which was carried on with this nation lasted many years, during

which the Lenape lost a great number of their warriors, while the Mengwe
would always hang back in the rear leaving them to face the enemy. In the
end the conquerors divided the country between themselves. The Mengwe
made choice of the lands in the vicinity of the great lakes and on their
tributary streams, and the Lenape took possession of the country to the south.
For a long period of time, some say many hundred years, the two nations
resided peacefully in this country and increased very fast. Some of their most
enterprising huntsmen and warriors crossed the great swamps, and falling on
streams running to the eastward followed them down to the great bay river
(meaning the Susquehanna, which they call the great bay river from where
the west branch falls into the main stream), thence into the bay itself, which
we call Chesapeake. As they pursued their travels, partly by land and partly
by water, sometimes near and at other times on the great salt-water lake, as
they call the sea, they discovered the great river which we call the Delaware."[40]

Heckewelder's retelling of this Delaware tradition served as fuel for both
factions. No one doubted the accuracy of the old missionary's quotations from
Delaware lore, and, since Heckewelder had collected these stories in the 1770's,
before most of the Ohio mounds and fortifications had been discovered, it could
not be said that he was concocting a tradition to fit any preconceived theories.
Those who believed, with Bishop Madison, that the builders of the mounds
were the ancestors of contemporary Indians used the Heckewelder story as
proof that the Tallegewi or Alligewi were really the Cherokees. They based
this partly on the supposed similarity between the names "Tallegewi" and
"Cherokee," an alternate form of which was "Chellakee." They drew on Cherokee migration myths, which told of a trek from the northwest to their ultimate
Carolina domain. And they pointed to the evidence that the Cherokees were
builders of burial mounds, sidestepping the Cherokees' own admission that they
habitually built their important lodges atop the mounds left by unknown
predecessors. By carefully selecting their facts, the partisans of this faction were
able to "prove" that the Cherokees had built the mounds of the Ohio Valley,
then had been invaded by an alliance of Delawares and Iroquois, and had
thrown up most of the Ohio embankments as defensive measures in this war;
at length the Cherokees were vanquished and fled eastward, their lands being
divided between the two conquering tribes, and in time the Delawares migrated
to their historic homeland along the coast, leaving the Iroquois in possession
of the mound country.

This identification of the Cherokees as the Ohio Mound Builders was first
set forth in 1823 by one John Haywood, in an odd work called *Natural and
Aboriginal History of Tennessee,* published at Nashville. Haywood collected

traditions among the Cherokees of Tennessee—who seven years later would be forcibly removed to Oklahoma by order of the United States Government—and correlated them with Heckewelder's Delaware traditions. Naturally, the Cherokees did not admit to having been expelled from the Ohio Valley by the Delaware-Iroquois combination, but merely said that they had dwelt along the Ohio for many years in the course of their gradual migration out of the vicinity of Iowa. They claimed to have built the Grave Creek Mound and others along the upper Ohio.

Haywood did not pretend to have settled the question of the Southeastern mounds as easily. While crediting the Cherokees with the Ohio earthworks, he said they expressly disclaimed responsibility for the numerous mounds in their later territory in the Carolinas and Tennessee. Those mounds, according to Haywood's Cherokee informants, had been there when the Cherokees arrived. This tallied with what Bartram had learned from the Cherokees fifty years earlier. "They came from the west and exterminated the former inhabitants," Haywood explains. To provide the proper mythological touch, Haywood adds that the invading Cherokees found "white people" near the head of the Little Tennessee River, with forts extending down the Tennessee as far as Chickamauga Creek, and drove them from the country. So the same book provided a prosaic Cherokee origin for the Ohio mounds—via Heckewelder—and a romantic and mysterious origin for the mounds of Tennessee, Kentucky, and the Carolinas.

The wholehearted romantics also made use of Heckewelder. They rejected the Cherokee theory altogether and fastened on the description of the Tallegewi as "remarkably tall and stout . . . a tradition that there were giants among them, people of a much larger size than the tallest of the Lenape." Clearly these were not Cherokees or any other known Indian tribe; and so began the vain search for a race of giant Mound Builders in the Ohio Valley.

In such an intellectual environment it was difficult for the conservatives to make themselves heard and almost impossible for them to find a following. Some deep national need was fulfilled by the myth of the Mound Builders, and debunkers were unpopular. The dream of a lost prehistoric race in the American heartland was profoundly satisfying; and if the vanished ones had been giants, or white men, or Israelites, or Danes, or Toltecs, or giant white Jewish Toltec Vikings, so much the better. The people of the United States were then engaged in undeclared war against the Indians who blocked their path to expansion, transporting, imprisoning, or simply massacring them; and as this century-long campaign of genocide proceeded, it may have been expedient to conjure up a previous race whom the Indians had displaced in the same way.

Conscience might ache a bit over the uprooting of the Indians, but not if it could be shown that the Indians, far from being long-established settlers in the land, were themselves mere intruders who had wantonly shattered the glorious Mound Builder civilization of old. What had been a simple war of conquest against the Indians now could be construed as a war of vengeance on behalf of that great and martyred ancient culture.

Some staid scholars heeded Jefferson's advice, and went about the job of digging up mounds and examining their contents without seeking to venture into mythmaking. Among them was Dr. J. H. McCulloh, Jr., of Baltimore, who saw military service in Ohio during the War of 1812 and took the occasion then to study the ancient earthworks. He published his first essay on the mounds in 1813, followed it with *Researches on America* in 1817, and with a lengthier statement, *Researches, Philosophical and Antiquarian, concerning the Aboriginal History of America,* in 1829. McCulloh was a muddy, unpersuasive writer, but even if he had organized his material in masterly fashion he probably would not have found many disciples, for his ideas ran counter to many popular delusions. McCulloh concluded that the Indians of the Americas all belonged to the same race, albeit with sharp local variations in physical appearance and cultural attainment; and this race, he said, comprised the first human inhabitants of the New World. He found no need to invent a prior race of Mound Builders to account for the antiquities of North America.

Cyrus Thomas, the archaeologist who did most to deflate the myth of the Mound Builders, wrote of McCulloh at the close of the nineteenth century, "His conclusions, based, as they were, on the comparatively slender data then obtainable, are remarkable, not only for the clearness with which they are stated [!] and the distinctness with which they are defined, but as being more in accordance with all the facts ascertained than perhaps those of any contemporary."[41] But in his own time McCulloh was a prophet without honor. In the two major syntheses of mound research published in the first half of the nineteenth century—Atwater (1820) and Squier and Davis (1848)—McCulloh's labors and theories do not earn him so much as a single footnote.

▲▲▲ 3

THE TRIUMPH OF THE MYTH

▲▲▲

During the early years of the republic, the learned organization most concerned with mound research was the Philadelphia-based American Philosophical Society. The large quarto pages of its *Transactions* had harbored the writings of Benjamin Smith Barton, John Heckewelder, Winthrop Sargent, and others preoccupied with the mounds; Thomas Jefferson had been an active member and a president of the Society; and in later years there would be other important archaeologist-contributors. But the American Philosophical Society was not primarily an archaeological group, as was, for example, the Society of Antiquaries of London, which traced its founding to 1572. In open imitation of this and other European antiquarian societies, a group of New England scholars petitioned the Massachusetts legislature in October, 1812, for a charter to incorporate an American Antiquarian Society.

"Its immediate and peculiar design," the founders declared, "is, to discover the antiquities of our own continent; and, by providing a fixed and permanent place of deposit, to preserve such relicks of American antiquities as are portable." The legislators responded enthusiastically, and the organization came into being, holding its first meeting at the Exchange Coffee House in Boston on November 19, 1812. It began at once to collect specimens for its museum cabinet, to assemble a library, to encourage archaeological research, and to prepare to publish a journal. One of its specific goals was to introduce a more rational approach to the study of the Ohio mounds. In 1856, assessing the condition of American archaeology at the time of the founding of the American Antiquarian Society, Samuel F. Haven, its librarian, wrote:

"Objects of archeological interest were known to exist in great numbers; but in the crude and defective state of information respecting them, no inferences worthy the name of scientific deductions could be derived from the features they presented. Not only accurate delineations and trustworthy descriptions, but aggregation and classification, were wanting to a development of their real nature and probable origin. . . . Vestiges of human forms of unnatural dimensions, were supposed to have been discovered. The valley of the Mississippi was like a wonder-book, full of marvels and mysteries, and productive of vague and dreamy lucubrations. While men of education were reviving one or another of the many theories of colonization from the Old World, at some dim and distant period, faintly indicated by history or tradition, another class convinced themselves that giants and pigmies had, in turn or together, inhabited that region."[42]

The first volume of the *Transactions and Collections of the American Antiquarian Society,* bearing the additional title, *Archaeologia Americana,* was published at Worcester, Massachusetts, in 1820. Its 436 octavo pages covered a variety of topics ("Specimens of the Poetry and Singing of the Osages"; "Description of the Mummy found in Kentucky"; "Account of the Discovery of the River Mississippi, and the adjacent Country by the Lakes"). But some 150 pages are devoted to an essay on the Ohio mounds by Caleb Atwater of Circleville, Ohio, and there were supplementary notices by other hands.

Atwater, who lived from 1778 to 1867, was the postmaster of Circleville at the time he wrote his "Description of the Antiquities Discovered in the State of Ohio and other Western States." In the preface to *Archaeologia Americana,* the editor apologizes on Atwater's behalf, calling his writings "the hurried productions of a professional man, constantly engaged in various branches of business," and notes that "the distance of the Author from the place of publication, rendered it impracticable to forward to him either the written copy, or the printed proof sheets, for his revisal and correction." Despite certain "errours which have unavoidably occurred from reading letters not written in a manner the most legible," the Atwater work, we are told, is "interesting and valuable," and is confidently "presented to the perusal of the intelligent and candid reader."

The evaluation is a just one. Atwater's conclusions—"that the works described in this publication were erected by a race of men widely different from any tribe of North American Indians, known in modern times"—were not substantiated by later research; but his work is nevertheless a landmark in the history of American archaeology, being the first serious and comprehensive survey of the antiquities of a single region.

Atwater grew up among the Ohio mounds, and lived among them nearly all his long life, studying them even as they disappeared with the spread of civilization. His own town of Circleville, founded in 1806, was laid out following the outlines of two concentric circular earthworks, the outer one a thousand feet in diameter. These became Circle Street and Circle Alley, and an octagonal courthouse was placed at the center; but the courthouse burned in 1841, and no trace remains either of the earthworks or of the original town plan. They still existed when Atwater completed his manuscript in 1820, although he noted that the circular walls, five or six feet in height, "are disappearing before us daily, and will soon be gone." With great diligence he toured the rest of Ohio, describing and surveying other prehistoric earthworks that were then succumbing to progress, and his essay provides unique data on the state of these monuments just before they vanished forever. He had the assistance of a few antiquarian-minded friends, such as Dr. Samuel P. Hildreth of Marietta and Samuel Williams of Chillicothe, but mainly he worked alone, a scholar among rough pioneers, painstakingly compiling information for the enlightenment of his correspondents of the American Antiquarian Society in remote New England. In his dedicatory letter to the Society's president, Atwater touches a poignant note as he describes his isolation from the world of the intellect: "Seated upon the summit of a lofty tumulus, which overlooked all the works belonging to some once celebrated spot, gilded by the rays of the setting sun—how anxiously have I wished for the company of some one like the person to whom these observations are addressed, so that he might participate with me in the emotions which filled my breast!"

Atwater strikes a tone of sobriety in his opening pages. He scoffs at the "crude and indigested statements" of those travelers who dashed off theories "after having visited a few ancient works," and mocks those who conclude from a single example that all the earthworks were devoted to sun worship or were raised for military purposes. Mentioning the supposed Roman coins found in various parts of the country, he warns against assuming that Romans had built the mounds, insisting that such ancient coins had been brought here after the discovery of America by Columbus.

Atwater divides the antiquities of the New World into three classes: "Those belonging to Indians," "To people of European origin," and "Those of that people who raised our ancient forts and tumuli." He dismisses the antiquities of the North American Indians as "neither numerous nor very interesting. They consist of rude stone axes and knives, of pestles used in preparing maize for food, of arrowheads," and other humble products of "men in a savage state, little versed in the arts of civilized life, who look upon all pursuits as degrading to their dignity as men, except such as belong either to war or the chase."[43] The device of classifying the Indians a priori as rude savages, necessitating the invention of an earlier race of Mound Builders to explain any artifact or monument deemed beyond the capabilities of such savages, was a common one at this time.

In the class of antiquities belonging to people of European origin Atwater places the coins, medals, knives, guns, and other objects scattered through the Ohio Valley by the French explorers and soldiers of the seventeenth and eighteenth centuries. He brushes aside as unlikely the probability of pre-Columbian visits to the Americas by European seafarers.

Turning next to "the third, last, and most highly interesting class of Antiquities, which comprehends those belonging to that people who erected our ancient forts and tumuli," Atwater declares that the Ohio earthworks "owe their origin to a people far more civilized than our Indians, but far less so than Europeans"—a cautious view for its day, since it leaves out of consideration the possibility of an ancient high civilization in North America. Atwater's main interest is in the mounds he knows best, those of Ohio, but he observes that "these works are thickly scattered over the vast plain from the southern shore of lake Erie, to the Mexican Gulph, increasing in number, size and grandeur as we proceed towards the south. . . . They abound most in the vicinity of good streams, and are never, or rarely found, except in a fertile soil. They are not found in the prairies of Ohio, and rarely in the barrens, and there they are small, and situated on the edge of them, and on dry ground."[44]

He proceeds to a systematic description, accompanied by charts, of the most prominent Ohio earthworks, most of which exist today in fragmentary form, if at all. The ones he begins with, those of Newark, Ohio, have survived better than most, though doubtless Atwater would be surprised to find that Newark's large octagonal "fort" and its adjoining circular enclosure today are included in a municipal golf course. The octagon, as he saw it, covered some 40 acres, with walls about ten feet in height. Eight openings, 15 feet wide, pierced these walls, and in front of each was a small mound of earth. Two parallel embankments ten feet high linked this structure to the nearby round "fort," which Atwater estimated at an area of 22 acres; at a greater distance was another large circular enclosure, with a square "fort" beside it. "If I might be allowed to conjecture the use to which these works were originally put," Atwater wrote, "I should say, that the larger works were really military ones of defence; that their authors lived within the walls; that the parallel walls were intended for the double purposes of protecting persons in times of danger, from being assaulted from one work to another; and they might also serve as fences, with a very few gates, to fence in and enclose their fields. . . ."[45]

Dealing next with the Marietta earthworks, Atwater expresses his pleasure that "no despoiling hand has been laid upon them," and cites the work of his predecessors, Manasseh Cutler, Rufus Putnam, and the Reverend Thaddeus M. Harris. He quotes Harris' description of Marietta's square forts, the pyramids

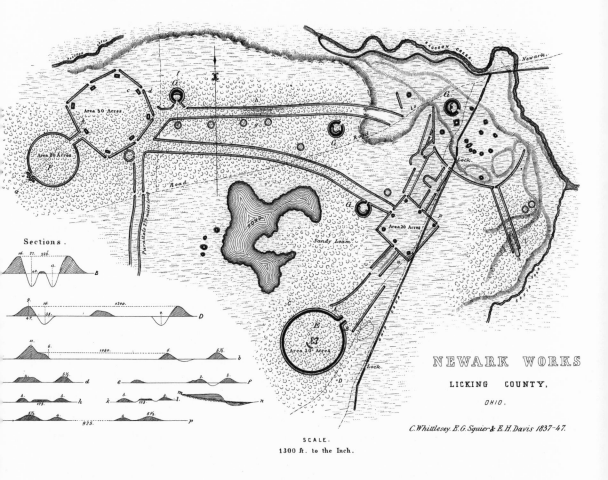

Sections.

NEWARK WORKS

LICKING COUNTY,

OHIO.

C.Whittlesey. E.G.Squier & E.H.Davis 1837-47.

SCALE.
1300 ft. to the Inch.

5 Diagram of the Newark works. Squier and Davis, 1848.

within them, and the *Sacra Via* leading toward the river. This is supplemented by quotations from a letter written by the Marietta physician, Samuel Hildreth, who had carried out excavations in these fortifications in the spring of 1819. Atwater's own contribution to this section is a discussion of the Mound Builders' tools: "It has excited some surprize here that the tools have not been discovered here, with which these works were constructed. Those who have examined these ruins, seem not to have been aware, that with shovels made of wood, earth enough to have constructed these works might have been taken from the surface, with as much ease, almost, as if they were made of iron. . . . Besides, had the people who raised these works, been in possession of, and used ever so many tools, manufactured from iron, by lying either on or under the earth, during all that long period which has intervened between their authors and us, they would have long since oxydized by 'rusting,' and left but faint traces of their existence behind them."[46]

Atwater's belief that the Mound Builders used wooden spades and shovels was clearly enough stated here. Yet this passage was conveniently overlooked or misinterpreted in later years by those who used other sections of Atwater's text to "prove" that he and Dr. Hildreth had found cast-iron implements and even steel swords in the Ohio mounds.

Not surprisingly, Atwater devotes a good deal of space to the earthworks of his own town of Circleville. He describes the double circular enclosure that gave the town its name, the square one that adjoined it, and "a once very remarkable ancient mound of earth, with a semicircular pavement on its eastern side," entirely removed before 1820. "These fortifications, where the town stands, will entirely disappear in a few years," he says, "and I have used the only means within my power, to perpetuate their memory, by the annexed drawing and this brief description."

He expresses his awe at the geometrical regularity of the two Circleville enclosures: the circle is a perfect circle, the square a perfect square. The walls of the latter work "vary a few degrees from north and south, east and west; but not more than the needle varies, and not a few surveyors have, from this circumstance, been impressed with the belief that the authors of these works were acquainted with astronomy. What surprized me, on measuring these forts, is the exact manner in which they had laid down their circle and square; so that after every effort, by the most careful survey, to detect some errour in the measurement, we found that it was impossible, and that the measurement was much more correct, than it would have been, in all probability, had the present inhabitants undertaken to construct such a work. Let those consider this circumstance, who affect to believe these antiquities were raised by the ancestors of the present race of Indians."[47]

Atwater speaks indignantly of the "hasty travellers, who have spent an hour or two here," and who have "concluded that the 'forts' at Circleville were not raised for military, but for religious purposes." With some passion he sets forth his reasons for believing that the enclosures were indeed defensive forts, adding, "These works have been examined by the first military men now living in the United States, and they have uniformly declared their opinion to be, that they were military works of defence." Here Atwater's judgment sadly failed him. About a decade later no less a military figure than General William Henry Harrison examined the Ohio earthworks, and, while agreeing that some were undoubtedly defensive forts, Harrison pointed out that at some, such as those of Newark and Circleville, the Mound Builders had placed deep ditches just *within* the ramparts and not where they would be much more useful defensively, outside them. "Great as some of these works are, and laborious as was their construction, particularly those of Circleville and Newark," he wrote, "I am persuaded they were never intended for military defences."[48]

After discussing several other groups of Ohio embankments and fortifications, Atwater turns to a consideration of Ohio's burial mounds. Quoting Virgil and other classical authorities, he makes the obligatory demonstration that mound burial has been a custom of mankind since earliest days, and then takes up those of his vicinity. "They are," he writes, "of various altitudes and dimensions, some being only four or five feet in height, and ten or twelve feet in diameter at their base, whilst others, as we travel to the south [of Ohio], rise to the height of eighty and ninety feet, and cover many acres of ground. They are generally, where completed, in the form of a cone."[49]

The first mounds he discusses are those of Cincinnati, for which his source is a book called *Pictures of Cincinnati,* published in 1815 by Daniel Drake, an officer of the American Antiquarian Society. "The mounds or pyramids found on this plain," Drake wrote, "were four in number. The largest stands directly west of the central enclosure, at the distance of five hundred yards. Its present height is twenty-seven feet." About eight feet were cut from the top of this mound in 1794 by order of General Anthony Wayne, to prepare it for the erection of a lookout tower. Today it is gone, along with the mound at Third and Main streets that was excavated in 1794 by Colonel Winthrop Sargent.

Sargent had found artifacts of stone and bone in that mound, some of them carved with "hieroglyphics" and the sculptured representation of a rapacious bird. He had also discovered some lumps of lead ore and a sheet of copper. In 1815, Drake re-excavated the mound before its final obliteration and uncovered twenty or thirty human skeletons, a number of beads, some large sea shells cut to serve as domestic utensils, and "several copper articles, each consisting of two sets of circular concavo-convex plates; the interior one of each set connected with the other by a hollow axis, around which had been wound some lint; the whole encompassed by the bones of a man's hand. Several other articles resembling these have been found in other parts of the town. They all appear to consist of pure copper, covered with the green carbonate of that metal."[50]

This was exciting news, for it gave evidence of Mound Builder metallurgy and, so it seemed, reinforced the belief in the Mound Builders' superiority to ordinary savage Indians. But Atwater was able to cite an even more spectacular find communicated to him by his friend Samuel Hildreth, the Marietta physician, under date of July 19, 1819:

"In removing the earth which composed an ancient mound in one of the streets of Marietta, on the margin of the plain, near the fortifications, several curious articles were discovered the latter part of June last. They appear to have been buried with the body of the person to whose memory this mound was erected.

"Lying immediately over, or on the forehead of the body, were found three large circular bosses, or ornaments for a sword belt, or a buckler; they are composed of copper, overlaid with a thick plate of silver. The fronts of them are slightly convex, with a depression, like a cup, in the centre, and measure two inches and a quarter across the face of each. On the back side, opposite the depressed portion, is a copper rivet or nail, around which are two separate plates, by which they were fastened to the leather. . . . Near the side of the body was found a plate of silver which appears to have been the upper part of a sword scabbard; it is six inches in length and two inches in breadth, and weighs one ounce; it has no ornaments or figures, but has three longitudinal ridges, which probably correspond with edges, or ridges, of the sword; it seems to have been fastened to the scabbard by three or four rivets, the holes of which yet remain in the silver.

"Two or three broken pieces of a copper tube, were also found, filled with iron rust. These pieces, from their appearance, composed the lower end of the scabbard, near the point of the sword. No sign of the sword itself was discovered, except the appearance of rust above mentioned. . . .

"This mound must originally have been about ten feet high, and thirty feet in diameter at it base. At the time of opening it, the height was six feet, and diameter between thirty and forty. It has every appearance of being as old as any in the neighbourhood, and was, at the first settlement of Marietta, covered with large trees, the remains of whose roots were yet apparent in digging away the earth. . . ." Dr. Hildreth estimated the age of these trees as "between four and five hundred years each," by "counting the concentrick circles in the stumps after the trees were cut down." He declared, "Of what language, or of what nation were this mighty race, that once inhabited the territory watered by the Ohio, remains yet a mystery, too great for the most learned to unravel. But from what we see of their *works*, they must have had *some* acquaintance with the arts and sciences. They have left us *perfect* specimens of circles, squares, octagons, and parallel lines, on a grand and noble scale. And unless it can be proved that they had intercourse with Asia or Europe, we now see that they possessed the art of working in metals."[51]

The Cincinnati and Marietta discoveries took their places in the furniture of the Mound Builders mythos. Again and again they were cited as instances of the technological superiority of this vanished race. True, E. G. Squier, in his then-definitive 1848 summary of the prehistory of the Mississippi Valley, took a wary posture, saying, "It is clear that, so far as the specimens here obtained are concerned, they did not understand the art of *plating,* in the proper meaning of the term. They had taken but the first step towards it. That art is certainly one which follows, instead of preceding, the knowledge of welding and of working metals through the assistance of fire, which knowledge does not seem to have been possessed by them. Their acquaintance with metallurgy appears to have been confined to working the native metals in a cold state; in which, it must be admitted, they evinced considerable skill. Further than this, little can be claimed for them."[52] But after taking a closer look at the Hildreth artifacts, Squier reversed himself, observing in his second book on the mounds (1849), "These articles have been critically examined, and it is beyond doubt that the copper 'bosses' are absolutely plated, not simply overlaid, with silver. Between the copper and the silver exists a connection such as, it seems to me, could only be produced by heat; and if it is admitted that these are genuine remains of the Mound-builders, it must at the same time be admitted that they possessed the difficult art of plating one metal upon another. There is but one alternative, viz: that they had occasional or constant intercourse with a people advanced in the arts, from whom these articles were obtained."[53] The idea that the Mound Builders were expert metallurgists was not laid to rest until 1883.

Atwater himself reports some metallic artifacts that came to have an exaggerated importance in archaeological mythology. He speaks of several mounds at Circleville, "which the ruthless hand of man is destroying," and describes the finds he made in one mound of 30-foot diameter while it was being leveled:

"1. Two human skeletons, lying on what had been the original surface of the earth.

"2. A great quantity of arrow heads, some of which were so large, as to induce a belief that they were used for spear heads.

"3. The handle either of a small sword or a large knife, made of an elk's horn; around the end where the blade had been inserted, was a ferule of silver, which, though black, was not much injured by time. Though the handle showed the hole where the blade had been inserted, yet no iron was found, but an oxyde remained of similar shape and size. . . .

"6. A plate of iron, which had become an oxyde; but before it was disturbed by the spade, resembled a plate of cast iron. . . ."[54]

Atwater was often referred to, but rarely actually consulted, by those who wrote on mounds in the middle of the nineteenth century. So the legend emerged, and took on the semblance of fact after a while, that he had found a steel sword and a piece of cast iron in the Circleville mound. His own report said nothing of the kind, but the story, once in circulation, was difficult to squelch. Thus the presence of traces of what perhaps was unworked meteoric iron in the mound metamorphosed into proof of Mound Builder greatness—and then was used, just as improperly, by those who tried to show that the mounds had all been constructed in recent times, after the contact of the Indians with white men.

After giving some space to a burial mound at Circleville which, like Jefferson's, contained "a great quantity of human bones . . . . here in the utmost confusion," and which Atwater assumes "were the remains of those who had been slain in some great and destructive battle," he touches on some mounds at Chillicothe that had been demolished a few years earlier, to his great distress, and then turns briefly to mounds outside the boundaries of the State of Ohio. These he had not surveyed himself, so he quotes the descriptions of H. H. Brackenridge, whose paper, "On the population and tumuli of the aborigines of North America," had appeared in the *Transactions of the American Philosophical Society* in 1818. Brackenridge had pointed out that the mounds along the lower Mississippi were different both in shape and in size from most of those of Ohio, being much larger and flat on top. Among the mounds he mentions are those at St. Louis, the Cahokia mounds in western Illinois, and others in Mississippi, Louisiana, and Arkansas. "I have been sometimes induced to think," he wrote, "that, at the period when these were constructed, there was a population as numerous as that which once animated the borders of the Nile, or of the Euphrates, or of Mexico. . . . I am perfectly satisfied that cities, similar to those of ancient Mexico, of several hundred thousand souls, have existed in this country."[55]

2

Atwater the surveyor of mounds is methodical, careful, and reasonably accurate. Atwater the speculative philosopher is more in the manner of his day. He opens the final section of his essay with the words, "The reader, after having become acquainted with many of our ancient works, naturally inquires, Who were their authors? Whence did they emigrate? At what time did they arrive? How long did they continue to inhabit the country? To what place did they emigrate? and, Where shall we look for their descendants?"

Though he admits that "the nature of the subject does not admit of [mathematically precise] proof," he begs leave to offer some considered conjectures.

He cites the Biblical references to "high places" and the Palestinian worship of hills and mountains. Then, just as one thinks he is about to bring forth the Ten Lost Tribes theory, he changes ground and discusses the mounds and earthworks built by the ancient Pictish inhabitants of the British Isles. "The strong resemblance between the works in Scotland and ours," he says, "I think no man will deny."[56]

Are the Mound Builders, then, a band of fugitive Picts? Or Hebrews? Or Egyptians, whom Atwater mentions next, or Mexicans, or Russians? He speaks of Egypt's pyramids and of the pyramids of Mexico. He notes mounds in Russia, where they "are numerous, and were every where seen by the learned Adam Clarke, LL.D. in his tour from St. Petersburg to the Crimea, in the year 1800." The learned Dr. Clarke had reported "conical mounds of earth or tumuli" occurring frequently between Moscow and St. Petersburg. The same author, quoted by Atwater, had observed mounds in other parts of the world: "They seem to mark the progress of population in the first ages, after the dispersion, rising wherever the posterity of Noah came. Whether under the form of a mound in Scandinavia and Russia, a barrow in England, a *cairn* in Ireland, Scotland, and Wales, or those heaps, which the modern Greeks and Turks call *Tepe;* lastly, in the more artificial shape of a pyramid in Egypt; they had universally the same origin. They present the simplest and sublimest monuments, which any generation could raise over the bodies of their progenitors; calculated for almost endless duration, and speaking a language more impressive than the most studied epitaph upon Parian marble."[57]

Out of that passage from the travel book of Adam Clarke, Atwater develops his own theory of the mounds, based on the concept of the unity of mankind. All human cultures, he concludes, radiated from a single point: the point at which Noah's Ark came to rest, in the mountains of Armenia, when the waters of the Deluge began to recede. The descendants of Noah spread out through Russia, some going westward to Europe's termination at the British Isles, some going eastward into Asia. "Let those who are constantly seeking for some argument, with which to overthrow the history of man by Moses, consider this fact," he says. "Such persons have more than once asserted, that there were different stocks or races of men; but this similarity of works almost all over the world, indicates that all men sprung from one common origin. I have always considered this fact, as strengthening the

Mosaic account of men, and that the scriptures throw a strong and steady light on the path of the Antiquarian."[58]

One of the running battles of antiquarians over the last century or so has been diffusionism versus independent invention—that is, the question of whether cultural similarities in remote parts of the world are the result of vast migrations of people or ideas, or simply the outcome of separate acts of thought. Atwater was a diffusionist among diffusionists. The "similarity of works" of which he speaks is linguistic (he finds that rivers in Britain and "Tartary" have the same names) and artistic (vases found by Cossacks in Russia resemble pottery found in barrows in Scotland and in mounds in Ohio) and technological (architects of ancient times throughout the world constructed mounds). The mounds are the key to Atwater's diffusionism. He lumps together structures as different in form as the pointed pyramids of Egypt, the flat-topped pyramids of Mexico, the stone burial mounds of ancient Europe, the conical tumuli of Ohio, and the truncated earthen mounds of the lower Mississippi, and finds a common denominator in the mere fact that all are mounds of one sort or another. "Unless we knew to the contrary, who of us in Ohio, would ever suspect, that Dr. Clarke was not describing with fidelity, our western mounds?" asks Atwater after discussing the shapes of the mounds of Russia.

In passing, he pauses to demolish the theory that America's Mound Builders could have been the ancestors of the American Indians. He finds it implausible that the Indians of Ohio—a sad and demoralized culture in his time—could have reverted to such a state of barbarism after building the mounds. Nor could such savages ever have possessed the skills of the Mound Builders. "Have our present race of Indians ever buried their dead in mounds?" he asks. "Have they constructed such works as are described in the preceding pages? Were they acquainted with the use of silver, or iron, or copper? All these, curiously wrought, were found in one mound at Marietta. Did the ancestors of our Indians burn the bodies of distinguished chiefs on funeral piles, and then raise a lofty tumulus over the urn which contained their ashes? . . . If any person can answer any one of these questions in the affirmative, let him state facts minutely; and let this be done, not by a mere traveller, whose credulity has been practiced upon by either red or white men."[59]

What, then, was the route of the Mound Builders on their journey from Mount Ararat to southern Ohio?

Despite the presence of barrows in Wales, Atwater does not think that voyagers brought the mound-building concept across the Atlantic from Western Europe. He traces the route the other way around the world, from

Asia into Alaska via the Bering Strait. He sees a double migration into the western part of North America. Out of Siberia came the Tartars of the north, hunters and savages, to become the ancestors of the American Indians. Also out of Asia over the same route came shepherds and husbandmen from India, China, and the Crimea, a more civilized lot who built the mounds. India seems to be his chief source for the Mound Builders. "The temples, altars, and sacred places of the Hindoos," he notes, "were always situated on the bank of some stream of water. The same observation applies to the temples, altars, and sacred places of those who erected our tumuli. To the consecrated streams of Hindostan, devotees assembled from all parts of the empire, to worship their gods, and purify themselves by bathing in the sacred water. In this country, their sacred places were uniformly on the bank of some river; and who knows but that the Muskingum, the Scioto, the Miami, the Ohio, the Cumberland, and the Mississippi, were once deemed as sacred, and their banks as thickly settled, and as well cultivated, as are now the Indus, the Ganges, and the Burrampooter?"[60]

Not by cultural resemblances alone does Atwater derive the Mound Builders from India. He offers the evidence of a "triune idol" found in Tennessee, a vessel consisting of three heads, joined together at the back, from which rises a hollow container. The features on the three heads are forceful ones, and "all the strong marks of the Tartar countenance are distinctly preserved, and expressed with so much skill, that even a modern artist might be proud of the performance."[61] But whose heads does this remarkable triune vessel display? "Does it not represent the three chief gods of India, Brahma, Vishnoo, and Siva?" asks Atwater. Surely it shows these three deities. And what of the "nine murex shells, the same as described by Sir William Jones in 'Asiatic Researches' . . . found within twenty miles of Lexington, Kentucky, in an ancient work. . . . These shells, so rare in India, are highly esteemed and consecrated to their god Mahadeva." There are other reasons, too, for thinking that the Mound Builders began their long trek near the banks of the Ganges. "All I pretend to do," Atwater declares, "is to lay an unvarnished statement of facts before the reader, who can form what opinion he chooses on the subject."

When did they come to Ohio, then?

"It was in an early age of the world," replies Atwater, drawing the inference "from the rude state of many of the arts among them." He compares the antiquities of Italy—paved roads, stone aqueducts, marble statues, stately palaces, fragments of amphitheaters—with the humble earthen heaps of Ohio. He points out the stone axes, the mica mirrors, the simple pottery, of

America's ancient inhabitants. So clearly the migration occurred long ago, perhaps quite soon after the Ark itself came to rest—"as early as the days of Abraham and Lot," perhaps. Rome had not yet been founded when the earthworks were going up in Ohio, for otherwise, if all cultures had the same source, why would that of Rome have been so superior to that of Ohio? Nor could the Lost Tribes have come to America after 722 B.C.; by then the world had attained a higher civilization than was found in the mounds.

In the middle of the seventeenth century, James Ussher, Archbishop of Armagh in Ireland, had calculated the age of the world by adding up every bit of chronological information in the Old Testament, totaling all the begats right back to Adam. He had set the time of Creation in the year 4004 B.C. A few years later his colleague, Dr. John Lightfoot, vice-chancellor of the University of Cambridge, refined the Ussher estimate by determining that "man was created by the Trinity on the twenty-third of October, 4004 B.C., at nine o'clock in the morning." Although certain godless men in France and other wicked lands had begun to challenge the Ussher-Lightfoot chronology in the late eighteenth century, we may be sure that Caleb Atwater accepted it fully, and thus believed that he was writing in the year 5824 since the Creation. The same chronology placed the Deluge in the year 2349 B.C., and from other sources Atwater was aware that the city of Rome had been founded in 753 B.C. Sometime between those two dates, therefore, the Mound Builders had crossed out of Asia into the New World. To Atwater's credit, he does not try to pinpoint the date. There is actually a vestige of science in his method as he offers various geological observations to support the theory of the antiquity of the mounds and calls up the evidence of the Marietta tree-ring counts. "Trees of the largest size, whose concentrick annular rings have been counted, have, in many instances, as many as four hundred, and they appear to be at least the third growth since the works were occupied," he says.

Curiously, unlike virtually everyone else who believed that the Mound Builders and the American Indians were of separate cultures, Atwater felt that the Mound Builders reached the Americas *after* the Indians. He was led to this odd inversion by his single-point-of-origin theory of cultural spread. Although the Mound Builders were not as advanced as the Romans, say, they were culturally superior to the Indians; and that, to Atwater, meant that the Indians had broken away from the ancestral Asian homeland first, coming here to lead their simple lives, while the Mound Builders, moving in later, brought with them the cultural advances that some human groups had recorded in the intervening years.

He sees the movement of the Mound Builders through North America as slow and marked by steady progress. The proof of this, he says, is in the mounds themselves. Those in the North, along the Great Lakes, "are comparatively few in number and small in size, but increase in both respects, greatly, as their authors proceeded towards the south. Their numbers must have wonderfully increased as they slowly descended the water courses, and their improvement in the useful arts is every where visible."[62]

He adds, "That they lived here for a long time, appears evident from the very numerous cemeteries, and the vast numbers of persons of all ages who were here buried. It is highly probable that more persons were buried in these mounds than now live in this state." He wrote at a time when Ohio's population was about 700,000. Correctly, Atwater saw that such elaborate earthworks must have been the products of a dense population well supplied with food; for a sparse tribe of huntsmen, preoccupied with the need simply to keep alive, could never have thrown up the mounds and embankments he knew. And their complex culture—here he brings up the plated silver of the Circleville and Marietta mounds, among other things—must have evolved only in favorable conditions among a large populace.

Atwater rejects the idea that the Mound Builders, so powerful and prolific, were driven out of Ohio by savages. "That they contended against some people to the northeast of them is evident," he says, "but that they leisurely moved down the streams, is also evident, from their increased numbers, and their improvement in the knowledge of the arts. These required time and a settled state of society."[63] The migration out of Ohio took place at least a thousand years ago, he suggests, taking into account the tree-ring tallies.

Where did the Mound Builders go?

Clearly to Mexico. "Our ancient works," he remarks, "continue all the way into Mexico, increasing indeed in size, number, and grandeur, but preserving the same forms, and appear to have been put to the same uses. The form of our works is round, square, semicircular, octagonal, &c. agreeing in all these respects with the works in Mexico." Postulating that "the first works built by the Mexicans were mostly of earth, and not much superiour to the common ones of the Mississippi," he argues that the later stone temples were simply improvements on the familiar styles of antiquity. He quotes various Aztec traditions of a migration across North America into Mexico, claims that the idols worshiped in Mexico resemble those found in Ohio and Lower Mississippi Valley mounds, and to clinch his case appends Alexander von Humboldt's description of Mexican "pyramids."

"We see a line of ancient works," Atwater says in summary, "reaching from the south side of lake Ontario across this state, on to the banks of the

Mississippi; along the banks of that river; through the upper part of the province of Texas, around the Mexican Gulph, quite into Mexico. And the evidence is as strong, when thoroughly examined, that they were erected by the same people as there would be, that a house found standing alone, on some wild and uninhabited heath, was erected by the hand of man."[64]

It is a neat, clear, and—given the incomplete knowledge of the day— reasonably convincing theory. Against some of the wilder and woollier notions of his era, Atwater seems like a monument of sweet reason as he traces his Hindu shepherds across the face of North America and down the valley of the Mississippi into Mexico. Since most of the continent west of the Mississippi was unexplored, he had no way of knowing that the trail of mounds from Alaska down to the Great Lakes was nonexistent, or that there was another large gap in the evidence of migration between the Gulf Coast and the centers of Mexican civilization. The continuous distribution of mounds that Atwater saw from the landing place of the Ark to the capital of the Aztecs was a myth; but Atwater deserves the respect due a pioneer.

The contrast between his controlled, judicious speculations and those of his contemporaries can be seen a hundred pages further along in the same volume of *Archaeologia Americana,* where the views of Samuel L. Mitchill, M.D., are related. Dr. Mitchill, Professor of Natural History in the University of New York, believed that the natives of the Americas belonged to the same racial stock as those of Asia, but picked up from Jefferson the notion that the American population was of greater antiquity. Sarcastically describing his interchange with a skeptical English scholar, Dr. Mitchill declared, in a letter written in 1816 to De Witt Clinton and reprinted here, "I avoided the opportunity . . . of stating, that America was the cradle of the human race; of tracing its colonies westward over the Pacifick ocean, and beyond the sea of Kamschatka, to new settlements; of following the emigrants by land and by water, until they reached Europe and Africa; and lastly, of following adventurers from the former of these sections of the globe, to the plantations and abodes which they found occupied in America. . . . I thought it was scarcely worth the while to inform an European, that on coming to America, he had left the *new* world behind him for the purpose of visiting the OLD."[65]

Though the human race, said Dr. Mitchill, had originated in America, undergoing various physical adaptations as it spread out to other continents, he did agree that at a later date the Americas had been visited and settled by emigrants from abroad, among them Norsemen, Welsh, Malays, and Tartars. The Tartars came across Bering Strait, the Malays journeyed by boat from the Pacific isles to the California coast, and the Norsemen and Welsh crossed the Atlantic. Thus Mitchill envisioned a grand collision of intruders in pre-Columbian North America: "In their course, these Asian colonists [the Tartars] probably exterminated the Malays, who had penetrated along the Ohio and its streams. . . . Having achieved this conquest, the Tartars and their descendants had probably a much harder task to perform. This was to subdue the more ferocious and warlike European colonists, who had already been intrenched and fortified in the country, before them. There is evidence enough that long and bloody wars were waged among the tribes. In these, the Scandinavians or Esquimaux seem to have been overpowered and destroyed in Newyork. The survivors of the defeat and ruin retreated to Labrador, where they have continued secure and protected by barrenness and cold. . . . Think, what a memorable spot is our Onondaga, where men of the Malay race from the southwest, and of the Tartar blood from the northwest, and of the Gothick stock from the northeast, have successively contended for supremacy and rule; and which may be considered as having been possessed by each before the French, the Dutch, and the English visited the tract, or indeed knew anything whatever about it."[66] And so on, identifying the Iroquois as of Tartar stock and the exterminated Mound Builders of Ohio and western Pennsylvania as "the Eries, an indigenous nation of the Malay race."

3

Caleb Atwater's thorough study of the Ohio mounds had two immediate successors, both the work of men who, like himself, were eminent public figures and generally temperate in their speculations. Each made an important contribution to American archaeology, although both succumbed at least in part to the prevailing atmosphere of fantasy that shrouded the mounds.

The first was William Henry Harrison, best known to us for the brevity of his term as President of the United States. Harrison, the ninth President, had had a long and distinguished career before he commenced his one-month occupancy of the White House in 1841. Born in Virginia in 1773, he abandoned a Philadelphia medical education to enter the army at the age of 18, upon the death of his father. The Indians of Ohio, attempting to destroy the new white settlements there, had gone on the warpath in the autumn of 1789, and two years later Ensign Harrison found himself at Fort Washington, Cincinnati, taking part in a full-scale Indian campaign. He soon became a lieutenant, and then aide-de-camp to General Anthony Wayne, who crushed

the Indians at the Battle of Fallen Timbers in 1794. (It was Wayne who had
had the top cut off the great Cincinnati mound so that his sentries could
mount a tower there and watch for parties of Indian raiders.) In the course
of this warfare Harrison saw a good deal of the mound country. In 1800,
he became President John Adams' appointee as governor of the newly
created Indiana Territory, and three years later President Jefferson gave him
the additional task of representing the government in various treaty negotiations with the Indians. For a while in 1804 he served also as governor of the
Louisiana Territory, which in effect made him the administrator of much of
North America.

Under the famed Chief Tecumseh, the Indians of the Midwest rose again in
1810, receiving British encouragement to rebel against the authority of the United
States. Harrison defeated the Indians in November, 1811, at the Tippecanoe
River near the present Lafayette, Indiana, and, as "Old Tippecanoe," took
his place among the nation's military heroes. He also saw important action
in the War of 1812. From 1816 to 1819 he was a member of the House of
Representatives and then of the Ohio Senate. Encountering political reverses, he
lived in retirement for a few years, then served in the United States Senate
from 1825 to 1828 and in the latter year was named the United States'
first minister to Colombia. When Andrew Jackson replaced John Quincy
Adams as President, Harrison was recalled and again retired to Ohio, where
for the next decade he figured prominently in American political life, becoming a presidential candidate in 1836, then the successful nominee in 1840.

Although he posed in his campaigns as a simple backwoodsman of log-
cabin birth, Harrison had his roots in the Virginia aristocracy, and he was a
man of culture and attainment. Archaeological matters were of high interest
to him; after his return from Colombia in 1829 he undertook an examination
of the earthworks in the vicinity of his Ohio home. Three years later he delivered before the Historical Society of Ohio an address on the mounds, which
was published in 1838 as *Discourse on the Aborigines of the Valley of the
Ohio.*

Harrison's approach was basically romantic. He saw the mounds as relics of
a lost race of undoubted greatness; he imagined stirring battles, sweeping
migrations of tribes under attack, mighty hosts of enlightened beings stream-
ing through the heartland of what one day would be the United States of
America. Describing what a traveler descending the Ohio River in the days
before white settlement might have seen, Harrison wrote, "His eye might have
rested on some stupendous mound, or lengthened line of ramparts . . . which
proved that the country had once been possessed by a numerous and laborious

people. But he would have seen, also, indubitable evidences that centuries had passed away since these remains had been occupied by those for whose use they had been reared. . . . He would not fail to arrive at the conclusion that their departure . . . must have been a matter of necessity. For no people in any stage of civilization, would willingly have abandoned such a country; endeared to them, as it must have been, by long residence and the labor they had bestowed upon it."[67]

If the Mound Builders had been driven from Ohio, though, where did the fugitives go? And what became of the conquerors? For the answers, says Harrison, "we must search amidst the remains which are still before us. . . . We learn first, from the extensive country covered by their remains, that they were a numerous people. Secondly, that they were congregated in considerable cities. . . . Thirdly, that they were essentially an agricultural people; because, collected as they were in great numbers, they could have depended on the chase but for a small portion of their subsistence." He invokes the existence of "a national religion, in the celebration of which, all that was pompous, gorgeous, and imposing, that a semi-barbarous nation could devise, was brought into occasional display." He sees "altars often smoking with hetacombs of victims." Then he expresses his belief "that they were compelled to fly from a more numerous or a more gallant people. No doubt the contest was long and bloody, and that the country, so long their residence, was not abandoned to their rivals until their numbers were too much reduced to continue the contest. Taking into consideration all the circumstances . . . I have come to the conclusion that these people were assailed both from their northern and their southern frontier; made to recede from both directions, and that their last effort at resistance was made on the banks of the Ohio."

To support this view General Harrison notes the hilltop fortifications found in the area. "The engineers . . . who directed the execution of the Miami works, appear to have known the importance of flank defenses. And if their bastions are not as perfect, as to form, as those which are in use in modern engineering, their position, as well as that of the long line of curtains, are precisely as they should be." But this veteran warrior, as we have seen, paused in his evaluation to challenge Atwater's view that the geometrical enclosures at such lowland sites as Newark and Circleville were also built for military purposes; they seemed to Harrison, as they do to modern archaeologists, purely ceremonial in nature.

Harrison provides a vivid picture of the last stand of the Mound Builders. He invites his readers to stand, as he did, atop the fortified hill overlooking the Great Miami River in Hamilton County, Ohio, where they could view "this elevated ridge, from which are now to be seen flourishing villages, and

plains of unrivaled fertility," and consider that "it was here that a feeble band
was collected . . . to make a last effort for the country of their birth, the ashes
of their ancestors, and the altars of their gods. That the crisis was met with
fortitude, and sustained with valor, need not be doubted. . . . But their efforts
were in vain, and flight or death were the sad alternatives. . . ."

He says little about the conquerors of the Mound Builders, other than to
state that in the valley of the Ohio "there are indubitable marks of its being
thickly inhabited by a race of men, inferior to the authors of the great works we
have been considering, after the departure of the latter. Upon many places,
remains of pottery, pipes, stone hatchets and other articles, are found in great
abundance, which are evidently of inferior workmanship to those of the
former people. But I have one other fact to offer, which furnishes still
better evidence of my opinion. I have before mentioned Cincinnati as one
of the positions occupied by the more civilized people. When I first saw
the upper plain on which that city stands, it was literally covered with
low lines of embankments. I had the honor to attend General Wayne, two years
afterward [in 1793], in an excursion to examine them. . . . The number and
variety of figures in which these lines were drawn, was almost endless, and as
I have said, almost covered the plain. . . . Now, if these lines were ever of the
height of the others made by the same people . . . or unless their erection was
ages anterior to the others [elsewhere in Ohio], there must have been some
other cause than the attrition of the rain (for it is a dead level) to bring them
down to their then state. That cause I take to have been continued cultivation . . . of another people, and the probability is, that people were the conquerors of the original possessors."

This was a useful contribution to archaeological thought. The Ohio Valley
had been inhabited only by sparse nomadic hunting tribes when the American settlers arrived in the 1780's; Harrison was apparently the first to point out
that between the end of the mound-building period and the appearance of the
Indian hunters there had probably been a lesser agricultural occupation of the
valley by Indians who represented a transitional state between the glories of
the Mound Builders and the savagery of the eighteenth-century tribesmen.

His attempt to determine the antiquity of the mounds also shows a thoughtful approach:

"The process by which nature restores the forest to its original state, after
being once cleared, is extremely slow. The rich lands of the West [today's Mid-
west] are, indeed, soon covered again, but the character of the growth is entirely
different, and continues so for a long period. In several places upon the Ohio,
and upon the farm which I occupy, clearings were made in the first settlement

of the country and subsequently abandoned and suffered to grow up. Some of these new forests are now sure of fifty years' growth, but they have made so little progress towards attaining the appearance of the immediately contiguous forest, as to induce any man of reflection to determine that at least ten times fifty years must elapse before their complete assimilation can be effected. We find in the ancient works all that variety of trees which give such unrivalled beauty to our forests, in natural proportions. The first growth on the same kind of land, once cleared and then abandoned to nature, on the contrary, is nearly homogeneous, often stinted to one or two, at most three kinds of timber. If the ground has been cultivated, the yellow locust will thickly spring up; if not cultivated, the black and white walnut will be the prevailing growth. . . . Of what immense age then must be the works so often referred to, covered as they are by at least the second growth, after the primitive forest state was regained?"[68]

When it came to suggesting the ultimate destination of the fugitive Mound Builders, Harrison followed what was becoming the conventional theory: that they had gone on to Mexico. "The pictural records of that nation," he wrote, "ascribe their origin to the Astecks, a people who are said to have arrived first in Mexico about the middle of the Seventh century.* An American author, the Rt. Rev. Bishop Madison, of Virginia, having with much labor investigated this subject, declares his conviction that these Astecks are one and the same people with those who once inhabited the valley of the Ohio. . . . There is every reason to believe, that they were the founders of a great empire, and that ages before they assumed the more modern and distinguished name of Mexicans, the Astecks had lost in the more mild and uniform climate of Anhuac, all remembrance of the banks of the Ohio. . . ."

Another cogent, though occasionally inconsistent, analysis of the mounds was produced about the same time as Harrison's by Albert Gallatin (1761–1849), the brilliant Swiss-born economist who was Thomas Jefferson's Secretary of the Treasury. Gallatin, one of the ablest public servants the nation ever had, was an important figure in the government from 1789, when he helped write the Constitution of the State of Pennsylvania, through his twelve years at the Treasury, to his service as American minister to France and England. In 1827, he left public life and became a New York banker, exerting considerable influence over national fiscal policy; but in his later years he concerned himself largely with the study of American Indians. In particular his research centered on Indian languages; in 1836, he published an important work, *A Synopsis of*

* Modern archaeologists place the arrival of the Aztecs in Mexico in the thirteenth century.

the Indians within the United States east of the Rocky Mountains and in the British and Russian Possessions in North America, as Volume Two of the *Transactions and Collections of the American Antiquarian Society.* It included a map of the distribution of the Indian population according to tribes and linguistic groups. In 1842, Gallatin founded and was the first president of the American Ethnological Society, and his final contribution to his chosen science appeared in 1848, when he was 87 years of age—a 188-page introduction to Horatio Hale's *Indians of North-West America.* This essay distinguished thirty-two American Indian linguistic families, a pioneering classification.

In his public career Gallatin was cool and prudent, somewhat conservative of thought, and immune to popular delusions and fantasies. Much the same attitude can be seen in the discussion of mounds that he included in his *Synopsis* of 1836. "How," he asked, "shall we account for those ancient tumuli, fortifications, and the remnants, both east and west of the Mississippi, the origin of which is entirely unknown to the Indians, who in the seventeenth century were the sole inhabitants, and still continue to occupy a part of that country? On this, as on many other subjects relative to our Indians, we are still in want of facts. We are not yet sufficiently acquainted with the extent of the country over which the monuments are spread, or how far they differ in character, extent, or number in the different sections of the country. They only appear to have been more numerous and of greater importance in the vicinity of the Mississippi and the valley of the Ohio. There is nothing in their construction or the remnants which they contain indicative of a much more advanced state of civilization than that of the present inhabitants. But it may be inferred from their number and size that they were the work of a more populous nation than any now existing; and if the inference is correct it would necessarily imply a state of society in which greater progress had been made in agriculture. For wherever satisfactory evidence of a greater population is found this could not have existed without adequate means of subsistence, greater than can be supplied by the chase alone."[69]

The large flat-topped mounds, of which the Cahokia Mound near East St. Louis, Illinois, was then the best-known example, struck Gallatin and many others as having "a strong family likeness to the Mexican pyramids," and he thought such mounds "were probably connected with the worship of the nation." The earthen ramparts and embankments of Ohio puzzled him, though. They appeared to be fortifications, yet he did not see how they could easily have been defended. Furthermore, they were different in form from any Indian fortifications encountered by the first European explorers, which "all consisted of wooden palisades strongly secured, with an internal gallery, from which the besieged party might under cover repel the assailants with missile weapons. And they were also of a moderate size, and such as could be defended by the population of an Indian village. Wood affords the natural means of fortification against a savage enemy, where the material is abundant."

Therefore, though Gallatin had already stated that the Ohio earthworks show nothing "indicative of a much more advanced state of civilization than that of the present inhabitants," he found it necessary to postulate that they were the work of a different race. These predecessors of the contemporary Indians were agriculturalists, built temple pyramids similar to those of Mexico, and also constructed "ramparts" inefficient for military purposes. Like Atwater, Gallatin saw a link between the Mound Builders and the high civilizations of Mexico, but he did not suggest that the sequence of events had involved an Aztec sojourn in Ohio followed by a migration to the south. Rather he approached more nearly the modern theory: "We may easily understand that the civilization of Mexico gradually extended its influence, as from a common center, northwardly as well as southwardly; that the northerly tribes, as far north as the thirtieth degree of latitude, and perhaps the Rio Gila, without having made the same progress in arts or attained the same degree of wealth as the ancient inhabitants of Mexico, may have been gradually converted into an agricultural people."

Gallatin's picture of the gradual diffusion of agriculturalist ideas out of Mexico into the United States is in keeping with modern archaeological thinking; and it follows, too, that such Mexican traits as the construction of flat-topped temple mounds may have traveled the same route. The agricultural pueblo villages of Arizona and New Mexico, which lie directly north of Mexico, were surely subjected to powerful influences from the south. Gallatin was uncomfortably aware, though, of a huge tract of desert land that lies between the civilized provinces of ancient Mexico and the agricultural settlements of the pre-Columbian United States. The best he can do is suppose that the Mexican influence passed through this barren tract, leaving no influence, until the fertile Mississippi Valley region was reached. This gives him a possible explanation for the earthworks of Ohio and their militarily ineffective pattern. "The only conjecture I can form, and it is but a conjecture, is that the people who erected those works came from the west, and that it was during their residence on the prairie country that they were compelled to resort to that species of defensive works. They may, as is often the case, have persisted in the habit when there was no longer occasion for it." That is, the ramparts of Ohio were symbolic representations of the fortifications thrown up in harder times as the Mound Builders made their way across northern Mexico and Texas to the

Mississippi. The trouble with this conjecture is that it presupposes formidable defensive works in the prairie and desert country of the West, and those works do not exist.

Gallatin did not attempt to explain what had become of the Mound Builders, or how it had come to pass that the natives of the Ohio Valley had lost the skills of agriculture while those of the Southeast had retained them. But by suggesting that the mounds were the work of prehistoric farming folk under influence from Mexico, he provided one of the foundations for later understanding of the mound-building phenomenon.

4

When we turn from Atwater, Harrison, and Gallatin to some of their contemporaries, we plunge into a very different universe of discourse. We find ourselves among authors like John Ranking, whose book, published in London in 1827, was entitled, *Historical Researches on the Conquest of Peru, Mexico, Bogota, Natchez, and Talomeco, in the Thirteenth Century, by the Mongols, Accompanied by Elephants*. The myth of the Mound Builders had caught the public fancy, and what delighted the public most keenly was the stirring depiction of a great empire dragged down to destruction by hordes of barbarians.

The images of this myth had been taking form at least since 1795, when a piece on the mounds by Jacob Bailey was published in *Collections of the Massachusetts Historical Society, IV*. Bailey described the gory struggle between the Mound Builders and fierce savages, driven on by famine, who "burst, like an impetuous torrent, upon their polished and more effeminate neighbors, involving in destruction, all their monuments of industry, art, and refinement. If a spirited resistance is made, extirpation often becomes the consequence of a victory; and in case of a timid submission, the most humiliating and servile dependence ensues."[70] Those who survive "terror, havock, and desolation" become "slaves to savages" and are swallowed up by barbaric tribes, or in "rugged climates and unsubdued wilds" they find refuge but labor so hard for mere subsistence that they forget "every elegant and even useful improvement," and lapse into barbarism themselves. The destruction of the Mound Builders, Bailey thought, had occurred between A.D. 795 and A.D. 995.

Steadily the images accumulated. De Witt Clinton wrote of the "vast population" of the Mound Builders' towns and of their "numerous nations." Benjamin Smith Barton said they must have been "extremely numerous;" Caleb Atwater spoke of a population of millions, and cited the "immense number" of skeletons in the mounds. In their *History of the State of New-York* (1824–1826), John V. N. Yates and Joseph W. Moulton termed the mounds "monuments of buried nations . . . unsurpassed in magnitude and grandeur," and called Ohio "nothing but one vast cemetery of the beings of past ages."

The identity of the Mound Builders was always kept separate from that of the "savage" Indians. Even Gallatin, who was willing to believe that the Mound Builders were racially kin to the Indians, insisted that they were distinct in culture. Others, like Harrison and Atwater, saw them as the ancestors of the Aztecs, while Samuel Mitchill suggested they were Malays. John Delafield, in his 1839 book, *An Inquiry into the Origin of the Antiquities of America,* said they were Egyptians. Yates and Moulton used Indian legends to show that the mounds were fortifications built by prehistoric white men who had been exterminated by barbarous red men. (Heckewelder's giant Tallegewi were frequently mentioned in this respect.)

These wild notions crystallized in a single work, a best seller of the day, Josiah Priest's *American Antiquities and Discoveries in the West.* Published at Albany, New York, in 1833, Priest's book was drummed from household to household by subscription agents, who rolled up a sale of 22,000 copies in thirty months. Samuel Haven, assessing the Mound Builder myth in 1856, called Priest's book "a sort of curiosity-shop of archaeological fragments, whose materials are gathered without the exercise of much discrimination, and disposed without much system or classification, and apparently without inquiry into their authenticity,"[71] but by then the damage had long since been done; the book had established itself among laymen as a kind of archaeological classic.

Priest knew which chords to touch. "Ancient millions of mankind had their seats of empire in America," he announced. "Many of the mounds are completely occupied with human skeletons, and millions of them must have been interred in these vast cemeteries, that can be traced from the Rocky Mountains, on the west, to the Alleghenies on the east, and into the province of the Texas and New Mexico on the south: revolutions like those known in the old world, may have taken place here, and armies, equal to those of Cyrus, of Alexander the Great, or of Tamerlane the powerful, might have flourished their trumpets, and marched to battle, over these extensive plains." In his patriotic and well-received attempt to extend the horizons of American prehistory, Priest argued that America was the land where Noah's Ark came to rest, and attributes at least some of the mounds to antediluvian inhabitants of the continent. He surveyed the prevailing theories of Mound Builder origin, reviewing the evidence for their having been antediluvians, Polynesians, Egyptians, Greeks,

Romans, Israelites, Scandinavians, Welsh, Scots, and Chinese, and decided that at the very least they must have been white men. Of course, he did not neglect the obligatory scene of their destruction, imagining "the remnant of a tribe or nation, acquainted with the arts of excavation and defense, making a last struggle against the invasion of an overwhelming foe; where, it is likely, they were reduced by famine, and perished amid the yells of their enemies."

The speculative ferment over the mounds naturally had its impact on the imaginations of poets and novelists. One of the first to respond was England's Robert Southey, whose long poem of 1805, *Madoc,* made use of an earlier fantasy and combined it with that of the Mound Builders. The story of Madoc ap Owen Gwynnedd, the twelfth-century Welsh prince who sailed to America, had apparently first been told in a pamphlet published in 1583, and the following year was elaborated upon in Caradoc of Llancarfan's *Historie of Cambria, now called Wales,* translated by Humphrey Lhoyd and "corrected and continued" by David Powell. The Caradoc-Lhoyd-Powell version was reprinted in 1589 in Richard Hakluyt's widely circulated collection of voyages, giving the Madoc legend a permanent audience, and providing the British with a claim to having discovered America before the caravels of Ferdinand and Isabella arrived.

According to the story Hakluyt used, Prince Madoc had left Wales in distress over a war between his father and his brothers and, with several hundred followers, had sailed westward into the Atlantic. (Evidently Madoc was a genuine historical figure of twelfth-century Wales, an expert sailor and fisherman.) As the tale goes, Madoc "came to a land unknown, where he saw many strange things." In time he returned to Wales, "and declared the pleasant and fruitful countries that he had seen without inhabitants; and . . . he prepared a number of ships and got with him such Men and Women as were desirous to live in quietness, and taking leave of his friends, took his journey thitherwards again." There was no further word from the Welsh colonists of the New World.

Caradoc, or rather David Powell, who seems to have inserted this fable in Caradoc's history, was of the belief that Madoc had landed in the West Indies. Hakluyt added a note of his own to the effect that the Prince probably had landed in Mexico, deducing this from the fancied resemblance of certain Aztec words to words in Welsh. Subsequent geographers placed Madoc's destination in Florida, Nova Scotia, South America, and even the Azores. But in the early eighteenth century there appeared the narrative of one Morgan Jones, supposedly a Welsh chaplain who was captured by Tuscarora Indians while traveling between Virginia and South Carolina in 1660. The Tuscaroras held a tribal council and decided to put their captive to death, upon which Jones became "very much dejected" and cried out in Welsh, bemoaning his fate. An Indian of the Doeg tribe, otherwise unknown to history, overheard him, understood him, for the Doegs were speakers of the Welsh tongue, and had him spared. To Jones' delight he found a village of Welsh-speaking Indians, evidently descendants of Madoc's band, and preached to them in Welsh three times a week until he returned to civilization.

There were other supposed discoveries of Welsh Indians—in 1764, it was reported that one Maurice Griffiths, also Welsh, was taken by Shawnee Indians to visit a white-skinned Welsh-speaking tribe far up the Missouri River—and the excitement grew until, in the 1790's, patriotic Welshmen sent a missionary named John Evans to find these long-lost cousins and reconvert them to Christianity. He did not succeed. Later, the American artist George Catlin identified the Mandan Indians of the Great Plains as the stock of Madoc and after their near destruction by a smallpox epidemic in 1837 the search for the Welsh tribesmen continued in such places as Utah and British Columbia.

Southey's poem *Madoc* employs this imaginative material in connection with the Mound Builder legend and the Aztec traditions collected by Cortés' men. It relates the adventures of Madoc and his followers as they settle in North America, convert many of the natives to Christianity, and do battle with the Aztecs, who then purportedly lived much farther north than they did at the time of the Spanish invasion of Mexico. The work abounds in warfare, human sacrifice, fierce duels, and romantic deeds. Eventually the Aztecs are defeated and move to Mexico, leaving behind the mounds that mark the sites of their ruined cities. (Some of the mounds, Southey says, are the remains of Welsh cities.)

But the literary artists of the American republic were more likely to be moved by the theme of the Mound Builders than were sophisticated Europeans. Perhaps the first domestic treatment of the subject in verse was "The Genius of Oblivion," published in 1823 by the New Hampshire poet Sarah J. Hale. Her thesis, at least for imaginative purposes, was that the Mound Builders were fugitives from the Phoenician city of Tyre. One evening at twilight a sensitive young man named Ormond, sitting upon one of the great mounds of the West, expresses a longing to know who built it. The Genius of Oblivion appears and sings to him about the countless millions of men of vanished empires now gone to eternity. Before him glows a vision of majestic Tyre; a handsome couple in glittering robes is being wed; but the ceremony of marriage is interrupted by the tyrant king of Tyre, who desires the bride for himself and suspects the loyalty of the bridegroom. The lovers take ship, fleeing across the Atlantic to found a city in America, and from their loins springs the race of Mound Builders. Mrs. Hale planned to continue her poem to tell of the destruction of the Mound Builders, but the reception accorded the first section discouraged her from doing so.

A far more richly endowed New England poet, William Cullen Bryant, also fell under the spell of the mounds. While still a boy in Massachusetts he wrote "Thanatopsis," a reflective, somewhat Wordsworthian lyric that attracted wide attention when it appeared in the *North American Review* in 1817, some years after its composition. The 18-year-old Bryant had brooded over the thought of death, and his somber dreams led him to a contemplation of the millions of ancient warriors lying interred in the soil of the American wilderness, in "one mighty sepulchre" among "the hills rock-ribbed and ancient as the sun." He did not need to allude directly to the Mound Builders; his readers knew of whom he spoke in such passages as:

> The golden sun,
> The planets, all the infinite host of heaven,
> Are shining on the sad abodes of death,
> Through the still lapse of ages. All that tread
> The globe are but a handful to the tribes
> That slumber in its bosom.—Take the wings
> Of morning, traverse Barca's desert sands,
> Or lose thyself in the continuous woods
> Where rolls the Oregon, and hears no sound,
> Save his own dashings—yet—the dead are there:
> And millions in those solitudes, since first
> The flight of years began, have laid them down
> In their last sleep—the dead reign there alone.

In 1832, Bryant, by that time an established voice in American letters and the editor and owner of an important New York newspaper, traveled to Illinois to visit his two brothers. Riding on horseback over the prairies, he paused to meditate on the ancient tumuli and embankments, and the result was "The Prairies," which he included in his *Poems* of 1832. Here, in these "gardens of the Desert," this vast and swelling ocean whose "surface rolls and fluctuates to the eye," Bryant was stirred by the popular fantasies of the mounds, by the tales of bygone races and forgotten battles, and the poem breaks forth in its thirty-fifth line with an undisguised evocation of the vanished Mound Builders:

As o'er the verdant waste I guide my steed,
Among the high rank grass that sweeps his sides
The hollow beating of his footsteps seems
A sacrilegious sound. I think of those
Upon whose rest he tramples. Are they here—
The dead of other days?—and did the dust
Of these fair solitudes once stir with life
And burn with passion? Let the mighty mounds
That overlook the river, or that rise
In the dim forest crowded with old oaks,
Answer. A race, that long has passed away,
Built them;—a disciplined and populous race
Heaped, with long toil, the earth, while yet the Greek
Was hewing the Pentelicus to forms
Of symmetry, and rearing on its rock
The glittering Parthenon. These ample fields
Nourished their harvests, here their herds were fed,
When haply by their stalls the bison lowed,
And bowed his maned shoulder to the yoke.
All day this desert murmured with their toils,
Till twilight blushed, and lovers walked, and wooed
In a forgotten language, and old tunes,
From instruments of unremembered form,
Gave the soft winds a voice. The red man came—
The roaming hunter tribes, warlike and fierce,
And the mound-builders vanished from the earth.
The solitude of centuries untold
Has settled where they dwelt. The prairie-wolf
Hunts in their meadows, and his fresh-dug den
Yawns by my path. The gopher mines the ground
Where stood the swarming cities. All is gone;
All—save the piles of earth that hold their bones,
The platforms where they worshipped unknown gods,
The barriers which they builded from the soil
To keep the foe at bay—till o'er the walls
The wild beleaguerers broke, and, one by one,
The strongholds of the plain were forced, and heaped
With corpses. The brown vultures of the wood
Flocked to those vast uncovered sepulchres,
And sat unscared and silent at their feast. . . .

To Bryant the mounds uttered a silent sermon on the transience of man and his works: "Thus change the forms of being. Thus arise races of living things, glorious in strength, and perish." He tells how a "solitary fugitive," escaping the holocaust that shattered the civilization of the Mound Builders, is captured by the destroying red men; the "rude conquerors" offer him a bride, and he seems to forget the past; yet there still lingers the memory of "the wife of his first love, and her sweet little ones, butchered, amid their shrieks, with all his race." But then "the red man, too, has left the blooming wilds he ranged so long." Driven westward, he seeks a wilder hunting ground near the Rocky Mountains, leaving the mound-haunted prairies desolate. Still they are "quick with life—myriads of insects, gaudy as the flowers they flutter over, gentle quadrupeds, and birds." The poet, among "sliding reptiles" and "the graceful deer," listens to the hum of bees and thinks he hears

The sound of that advancing multitude
Which soon shall fill these deserts. From the ground
Comes up the laugh of children, the soft voice
Of maidens, and the sweet and solemn hymn
Of Sabbath worshippers. The low of herds
Blends with the rustling of the heavy grain
Over the dark brown furrows. All at once
A fresher wind sweeps by, and breaks my dream,
And I am in the wilderness alone.

5

Nor did the novelists neglect the subject with which Caleb Atwater, Josiah Priest, and other students of the past had provided them. For a while the genre of Mound Builder fiction was an active sub-branch of American popular literature. A typical example of the species is Cornelius Mathews' *Behemoth: A Legend of the Mound-Builders* (1839). Mathews, a strongly nationalistic novelist eager to supply America with a tradition worthy of Greece's *Iliad* and Rome's *Aeneid,* pictures the continent thick with the great cities of civilized Mound Builders. He does not linger on details of their civilization, nor does he tell what by then had become the hackneyed tale of their probable destruction. Taking such aspects of the genre for granted, Mathews spins a fable which at least one recent contemporary literary critic has suggested was ancestral to *Moby Dick.* A generation before Mathews wrote, paleontologists had determined that the giant bones frequently unearthed in America belonged to certain extinct species of elephants known as mammoths and mastodons. Mathews invents a mammoth of supernal size and strength, named Behemoth, which terrorizes the Mound Builders and threatens them with destruction. The great beast rampages through their cities; several armies go out against him and fail to slay him; not even the fortifications of earth thrown up by the Mound Builders can deflect the charging Behemoth. As catastrophe threatens, a Mound Builder hero named Bokulla devises a way of penning the monster in, and kills him.

Behemoth had dozens of contemporaries. As late as 1864 the theme still found an audience; in that year Daniel Pierce Thompson's melodramatic story, "Centeola; or, The Maid of the Mounds," appeared in a collection called *Centeola; and Other Tales.* The plot concerned the sufferings of a lovely maid of the Mound Builders and her lover, who are persecuted by lustful and lawless tyrants. They are about to endure a terrible death when a great earthquake providentially saves them, though it wreaks havoc on the Mound Builders' cities. Thompson assumed that the Mound Builders were ancestral to the Aztecs.

Probably the most influential of these romances remained unpublished for generations after it was written, but circulated in manuscript form with remarkable effect. This was the Reverend Solomon Spaulding's unfinished story *Manuscript Found,* composed about 1809. This work is ostensibly a translation of twenty-eight rolls of parchment found in an artificial cave covered by large flat stones atop a mound near Conneaut, Ohio. The rolls, inscribed in elegant Roman writing, relate the adventures of a party of Christian Romans who, while sailing from Italy to Britain in the fourth century A.D., are blown off course and carried across the Atlantic to America. There they found a colony, despite the onslaughts of "innumerable hordes" of savages, and attempt to carry on civilized life as they had known it in Rome. But, troubled by the fear that in this barbarous land they will degenerate into savages themselves, they press on westward in the hope that they will find their way back to Europe.

As they move inland they find the mighty cities of the Mound Builders, who are taller than the Indians and have fairer skins; they are workers in iron and lead, keep herds of horses, have domesticated the mammoth, and possess a noble written literature. The parchment rolls describe in great detail their cities, culture, political system, and daily lives, and provide the history of two great nations of the Mound Builders over a period of five hundred years. (The Roman wanderers are forgotten.) The Mound Builders' expansion across the continent is shown; then the long era of harmony ends, and for a trivial reason the two nations commence a war of extermination. The "translation" from the parchment rolls does not continue to describe this war, but its outcome is made clear: the Mound Builders will destroy one another, leaving only the remains of their fortified cities and the huge mounds that cover the bodies of their millions of slain warriors. Once more images of the American wilderness as a vast graveyard are summoned up:

"Gentle reader, tread lightly on the ashes of the venerable dead. Thou must know that this Country was once inhabited by great and powerful nations considerably civilized & skilled in the arts of war, & that on ground where thou now treadest many a bloody Battle hath been fought, & heroes by thousands have been made to bite the dust."[72]

As this brief sample should indicate, Spaulding's *Manuscript Found* was an indifferent literary performance, and it would long ago have joined the Mound Builders in oblivion but for its supposed role in the founding of the Church of Jesus Christ of Latter-day Saints, popularly known as the Mormon Church. Here we are on delicate ground, for the Mormons are a large and active religious group in modern America, and their beliefs, which have inspired such derision among what they term "Gentile" scholars, are matters of serious value to them. The Mormons hold that the tenets of their creed are divinely inspired and deserve the same respect accorded the teachings of such prophets as Moses, Jesus, and Mohammed. Critics of the Mormons claim that their scriptures are nothing more than a tedious, long-winded, inflated plagiarism of Solomon Spaulding's clumsy fantasy about the Mound Builders.

The first of the Saints, as the Mormons prefer to call themselves, was Joseph Smith, born on a Vermont farm in 1805. When young Joseph was ten, his family moved to Palmyra, New York, where the farmers were much given to theological disputation. Most of the Smith family joined the Presbyterian Church, but Joseph was dissatisfied with any of the organized creeds. Reading his Bible, he came upon the passage, "If any of you lack wisdom, let him ask of God," whereupon he retired to the woods, fell on his knees, and sought counsel. There appeared to him a vision: thick darkness fell, and a pillar of light descended; two bright personages came into view in the sky, one pointing to the other and saying, "This is my beloved son; hear him." Joseph Smith asked which sect he should choose, and was told to join none, that all were abominations in the eyes of the Lord. This occurred in 1820, when Joseph was fifteen.

The farmers to whom he related his vision scoffed at him and called him a madman. He continued to pray for enlightenment, and on the night of September 21, 1823, a supernatural visitor robed in white entered his bedroom. This is Smith's own account of what occurred, as published by the Latter-day Saints:

"He called me by name, and said unto me that he was a messenger sent from the presence of God to me, and that his name was Moroni; that God had a work for me to do; and that my name should be had for good and evil among all nations, kindreds and tongues, or that it should be both good and evil spoken of among all people.

"He said there was a book deposited, written upon gold plates, giving an account of the former inhabitants of this continent, and the source from whence they sprang. He also said that the fulness of the everlasting Gospel was contained in it; as delivered by the Savior to the ancient inhabitants.

"Also, that there were two stones in silver bows—and these stones, fastened to a breastplate, constituted what is called the Urim and Thummim—deposited with the plates; and the possession and use of these stones were what constituted 'seers' in ancient or former times; and that God had prepared them for the purpose of translating the book."[73]

Joseph watched the light grow dim and the angel go "right up into heaven." But Moroni returned twice more that night to describe the location of the golden plates. The next day, after another visit from the angel, Joseph went to the hill now called Cumorah, near Palmyra, and found the plates stored in a stone vault under a flat rock on the west side of the hill. With them were the Urim and Thummim, the translating devices. When he tried to take the plates out, though, Moroni appeared and told him the time had not yet come. He was to return to Cumorah each year for four more years.

Joseph obeyed; and on September 22, 1827, Moroni at last delivered up the plates to him, with the Urim and Thummim, and charged him to guard them well while preparing his translation. At once persecutions descended on him; his claim to divine inspiration was met with scorn, and several times he was shot at, or beset by mobs. Realizing that he was in danger of his life, Joseph hid the plates in a barrel of beans and set out for his wife's family's farm in Pennsylvania. There he began the work aided by a certain Martin Harris, who had received a revelation commanding him to serve as Joseph Smith's scribe. By the summer of 1828, Smith and Harris had compiled a 116-page manuscript, which Harris managed to lose. In the spring of 1829, after resting awhile by divine order, Smith began to translate the plates from the beginning again, this time with the assistance of a schoolteacher named Oliver Cowdery. They completed their task with great swiftness, and in 1830 a printer in Palmyra, New York, produced a 5000-copy edition of the 588-page *Book of Mormon.* Afterward Moroni took back the golden plates, though not before Joseph had shown them to Cowdery, Harris, and nine other disciples.

Now began the perilous growth of the Church of Latter-day Saints—an epic of faith which must move even those who regard the Mormon creed as preposterous. Slowly Smith gathered followers, opposed at all times by bloody-minded mobs eager to stamp out the heresy. The Mormons were forced westward; Joseph Smith met martyrdom at the hands of a lynching party in an Illinois jail in 1844; an infuriated nation, maddened chiefly by the Mormon practice of polygamy, continued to persecute the adherents of the new faith until, after an attempt to found a colony in Missouri, the Mormons undertook their great desert trek into unknown Utah. There they remain, no longer beset by mobs, but still the center of controversy.

The *Book of Mormon,* which the Saints consider as sacred a volume as the Old and New Testaments, is a narrative that owes much in style to the King James Bible, and that derives much of its thematic matter from the tempestuous historical sections of the Old Testament, running from *Joshua* through *Chronicles.* The tone is set at once, on the opening pages of *The First Book of Nephi:*

"1. I, Nephi, having been born of goodly parents, therefore I was taught somewhat in all the learning of my father; and having seen many afflictions in the course of my days, nevertheless, having been highly favored of the Lord in all my days; yea, having had a great knowledge of the goodness and the mysteries of God, therefore I make a record of my proceedings in my days.

"2. Yea, I make a record in the language of my father, which consists of the learning of the Jews and the language of the Egyptians.

"3. And I know that the record which I make is true; and I make it with mine own hand; and I make it according to my knowledge.

"4. For it came to pass in the commencement of the first year of the reign of Zedekiah, king of Judah, (my father, Lehi, having dwelt at Jerusalem in all his days); and in that same year there came many prophets, prophesying unto the people that they must repent, or the great city Jerusalem must be destroyed."

Nephi describes how, at the time of the Confusion of Tongues following the building of the Tower of Babel, a group of settlers from the Near East was led by the Lord across the ocean to America. These were the Jaredites, named for their leader, Jared. In the New World the Jaredites established great cities and increased to a population of several millions; but then fraternal warfare divided them, and they fought to total extinction, the last survivors being destroyed in a fierce seven-day battle near the hill Cumorah, in New York State. As their prophets had predicted, their homes become mere "heaps of earth upon the face of the land." But a Jaredite historian, Ether, descended from Jared himself, survived long enough to set down the account of his people's downfall on golden plates. Ether predicts that in days to come new settlers will come to America and found a New Jerusalem.

Many centuries pass. About 600 B.C., in the time of Jeremiah, a party of Israelites of the tribe of Joseph escapes from the original Jerusalem just prior to its destruction at the hands of Nebuchadnezzar. They are led by Lehi, the father of Nephi. Through God's guidance they survive their wanderings in the desert, learn how to build ships, cross the ocean, and settle in America, "choice among all other lands." As the Jaredites had done before them, they prosper and multiply, build mighty cities, and surround them with huge fortifications. They find the golden plates inscribed by Ether, and learn of the history of the vanished Jaredites.

But the cycle repeats itself. This second group of colonists splits into two factions, the Nephites and the Lamanites. The Nephites enjoy the benefits of civilization; they till the land and become rich. But the Lamanites are ungodly, and sink into savagery. To punish them, God turns their skins a dark reddish hue. They are, in fact, the ancestors of the American Indians, although it is made clear that those Lamanites who return to the ways of virtue can recover the light skin of their Hebrew forefathers.

There are few repentant Lamanites. Rather, the Nephites grow corrupt themselves, backsliding into idolatry. About A.D. 300, angered by the repeated sins of the Nephites, who are the Mound Builders, God resolves to destroy their civilization. Their cities are invaded and laid waste by the Lamanites. Those few Nephites who have kept the ways of the Lord fight on, but they, too, are engulfed by the tide of red-skinned barbarians. Once more there is a climactic battle at the hill Cumorah, in A.D. 401, and nearly all of the Nephites are exterminated. Again, a solitary priest and scholar survives to compose the history of his kind. This last Nephite prophet is Mormon, who inscribes the records of his nation on golden plates (including an abridgement of Ether's earlier narrative) and gives them to his son, Moroni, who in A.D. 421 deposits them in the stone vault atop the hill Cumorah. There they rest until discovered and translated by Joseph Smith.

By some two million Americans today the *Book of Mormon* is regarded as at least as reliable a work of history as the Gospels or the Five Books of Moses. They accept as literal truth the assertions that America was twice populated by emigrants from the Near East, that the mounds and embankments discovered by later European explorers are the cemeteries and fortifications of these vanished peoples, and that the Indians trace their descent from the Israelite tribe of Joseph. To those who are hostile to Mormonism, though, these beliefs are merely amusing fantasies, and the sacred *Book of Mormon* itself is just another literary expression of the Mound Builder mythology.

The anti-Mormon literature is vast in scope. In the nineteenth century, books with titles like *Mormonism Unveiled* and *Mormonism Exposed* found immense audiences; they seem to have been particularly relished by pious Christians who enjoyed the opportunity to deplore the wild heresies of the Saints while simultaneously vicariously tasting the forbidden pleasures of polygamy. (No anti-Mormon book was complete without a lingering, graphic account of the Saints' marital practices, slanted to appeal to the prurient.) Today, when religious tolerance is more firmly established and the Mormons have officially abandoned polygamy, the task of denouncing the followers of Joseph Smith has fallen almost entirely to renegade members of his faith. A good example is Fawn Brodie, the niece of David O. McKay, the president of the church. In 1945 she published a not entirely complimentary biography of Joseph Smith, *No Man Knows My History,* and shortly was excommunicated for heresy by her fellow Mormons. Other attempts to debunk the divine nature of the prophet's inspiration have followed.

The essential charge against Joseph Smith is that, far from having consorted with angels and deciphered golden plates, he was simply a dreamy farm boy who became carried away by the fiction of the Mound Builders, and eventually found himself enmeshed in the synthetic religion that cost him his life. One possible source for Smith's *Book of Mormon* is said to have been *Views of the Hebrews* by the Reverend Ethan Smith of Poultney, Vermont. The Reverend Mr. Smith, no relation of the prophet, published this work in 1823, the same year Joseph Smith claimed to have been visited by Moroni. It was subtitled *The Tribes of Israel in America,* and told of the migration of the Lost Tribes to the banks of the Ohio, where they divided into two races and annihilated each other. *Views of the Hebrews* made much of the prediction that the records of these ancient Israelites would eventually be found in one of the mounds.

However, the most frequently repeated accusation is that Smith pirated the unpublished manuscript of Solomon Spaulding, eliminating Spaulding's Christian Romans and transforming the Mound Builders into sons of Israel. This charge was originally made in 1834 in E. D. Howe's *Mormonism Unveiled,* the first of many works of that title. It was picked up and expanded upon by others, and this summary of the case appeared in the introduction to a nineteenth-century edition of the *Book of Mormon* published in New York by anti-Mormon individuals:

"About the year 1809, the Rev. Solomon Spaulding, a clergyman who had graduated from Dartmouth college, and settled in the town of Cherry Valley, in the State of New York, removed from that place to New Salem (Conneaut), Ashtabula county, Ohio. Mr. Spaulding was an enthusiastic archaeologist. The region to which he removed was rich in American antiquities. The mounds and fortifications which have puzzled the brains of many patient explorers attracted his attention, and he accepted the theory that the American continent was peopled by a colony of the ancient Israelites. The ample material by which he was surrounded, full of mythical interest and legendary suggestiveness, led him to the conception of a curious literary project. He set himself the task of writing a fictitious history of the race which had built the mounds. The work was commenced and progressed slowly for some time. Portions of it were read by Mr. Spaulding's friends, as its different sections were completed, and after three years' labor, the volume was sent to the press, bearing the title of *The Manuscript Found.*

"Mr. Spaulding had removed to Pittsburgh, Pa., before his book received the final revision, and it was in the hands of a printer named Patterson, in that city, that the manuscript was placed with a view to publication. This was in the year 1812. The printing, however, was delayed in consequence of a difficulty about the contract, until Mr. Spaulding left Pittsburgh, and went to Amity, Washington county, New York, where in 1816 he died. The manuscript seems to have lain unused during this interval.

"But in the employ of the printer Patterson was a versatile genius, one Sidney Rigdon, to whom no trade came amiss, and who happened at the time to be a journeyman at work with Patterson. Disputations on questions of theology were the peculiar delight of Rigdon, and the probable solution of the mystery of the book of Mormon is found in the fact that, by this man's agency, information of the existence of the fictitious record was first communicated to Joseph Smith. Smith's family settled in Palmyra, New York, about the year 1815, and removed subsequently to Ontario county, where Joseph became noted for supreme cunning and general shiftlessness. Chance threw him in the company of Rigdon soon after Spaulding's manuscript fell under the eye of the erratic journeyman, and it is probable that the plan of founding a new system of religious imposture was concocted by these two shrewd and unscrupulous parties. The fact that the style of the book of Mormon so closely imitates that of the received version of the bible—a point which seems to have been constantly kept in view by Mr. Spaulding, probably in order to invest the fiction with a stronger character of reality—answered admirably for the purposes of Rigdon and Smith."[74]

Howe, in his *Mormonism Unveiled,* remarks that "an opinion has prevailed to a considerable extent that Rigdon has been the Iago, the prime mover of the whole conspiracy." The debate over how Joseph Smith might have come by the text of Spaulding's manuscript continued through much of the century. Rigdon himself denied that he had ever been in Pittsburgh prior to 1822, or

that he had had access to Spaulding's work at any time; various relatives of
Spaulding, of the printer Patterson, and of other interested parties made their
depositions, pro and con, and from their headquarters in Salt Lake City the
Mormons released pamphlets disclaiming any connection between the *Book
of Mormon* and *The Manuscript Found*. Spaulding's book was finally published
at Lamoni, Iowa, in 1885. It contains just enough parallels to the *Book of
Mormon* to arouse suspicion, and yet is just different enough to deflect
the charge of plagiarism from Joseph Smith. The official Mormon position
remains, of course, that any resemblances between the two works are coincidental; those hostile to the Mormons continue to bring up Spaulding's text
as the source for the work of Joseph Smith; neutral observers generally suggest the possibility that both works drew their inspiration from the fund of
Mound Builder legends then in circulation, leaving aside the question of
possible borrowing by Smith from Spaulding.

In any event, the legend of the Mound Builders achieved its apotheosis
when a major religious creed was founded upon it by Joseph Smith and made
lasting by his successor, Brigham Young. The essence of the continuing Mormon
beliefs concerning the mounds is that proposed by Orson Pratt, an early apostle
of the Saints, in a pamphlet of 1851, describing the warfare between the
Nephites and the Lamanites:

"The bold, bad Lamanites, originally white, became dark and dirty, though
still retaining a national existence. They became wild, savage, and ferocious,
seeking by every means the destruction of the prosperous Nephites, against
whom they many times arrayed their hosts in battle; but were repulsed and
driven back to their own territories, generally with great loss to both sides.
The slain, frequently amounting to tens of thousands, were piled together in
great heaps and overspread with a thin covering of earth, which will
satisfactorily account for those ancient mounds filled with human bones, so
numerous at the present day, both in North and South America."[75]

▲▲▲ 4

THE GREAT DEBATE

▲▲▲

By the fourth decade of the nineteenth century, the country between the Alleghenies and the Mississippi was ceasing to be a sparsely populated wilderness. The pioneering villages were becoming towns and even cities; territories were achieving statehood; the once troublesome Indian marauders had largely been shoved westward, beyond the rim of civilization. The great outward push of American expansion had halted for the moment, although soon, under the banner of Manifest Destiny, we would seize the Southwest from Mexico, and the lure of gold would draw men to California. But now came a time of taking stock, of theorizing, of examining, of classifying, of coming to terms not only with the present but with the prehistoric past.

Earlier, such intellectual activities had been the province of an elite centered in Boston, Philadelphia, and Jefferson's Virginia. The American Philosophical Society, a profoundly Philadelphian organization, spread its aegis over all speculative thought; its companion, the Boston-based American Antiquarian Society, also seemed rooted in the eighteenth-century elitist foundation. But once the task of breaking the soil and slaughtering the Indians was concluded, there was a westward shift in American archaeology. Thus we have Caleb Atwater, the Ohio postmaster, producing the first substantial work on his region's mounds. Thus we have Virginia-born William Henry Harrison, transplanted to Ohio, offering his ideas on the earthworks. And there were others, amateur and professional, farmers and academics, who sought answers to the riddles of the past not in Beacon Hill studies but out in the field, digging for the evidence. In 1800, an Ohioan with a mound on his property was likely to level it so he could plant his crops; by 1840 it was more probable that he would conduct a careful excavation and fill his house with an array of ancient artifacts. This sudden surge of archaeological activity continued alongside the feverish and romantic public interest in the Mound

Builders, each serving to fuel the other. Out of the new work came a renewed debate on the origin of the Mound Builders.

One extreme was represented by the Massachusetts historian George Bancroft, who, in the third volume of his *History of the United States* (1840), dismissed the mounds and earthworks as nothing but natural knolls and water-worn passages. (He abandoned this view in later editions.) At the opposite pole were those who championed unprovable hypotheses that the Mound Builders had been Israelites, Phoenicians, Malays, or members of some other immigrant group. Ideas that had been proposed first by De Witt Clinton, Caleb Atwater, or Samuel Mitchill were brought forth, embellished, and given to the world as new theories. There was never any shortage of imaginative philosophers. In 1851, the *Proceedings of the American Ethnological Society* published a paper by Dr. C. A. A. Zestermann of Leipzig entitled, "A Memoir on the European Colonization of America in ante-historic times," which sought to connect the Mound Builders of Ohio with the early peoples of northwestern Europe. Zestermann was particularly eager to prove that the mounds had been built by bearded men from Ireland, at least twelve hundred years before Christ. (They were, he said, the same bearded white-skinned strangers who turned up in the mythology of the Aztecs as Quetzalcoatl and in Mayan lore as Kulkulcan.)

But these were parlor theorists. In the open country, soiling their hands in the earth of the mounds, were men who split the tumuli apart and, at least, based their ideas on some sort of solid evidence. One of these was Dr. Montroville Wilson Dickeson, who excavated in the mounds and then capitalized on his labors by staging a kind of road show. From 1837 to 1844, Dickeson toured the United States with a painted panorama, which was constantly enlarged to include new discoveries. As it unrolled, it graphically displayed such scenes as the burial of de Soto, the great tornado of 1844, and views of the mounds and earthworks of the Mississippi Valley in both their unexcavated and excavated conditions. Among the mound groups shown were those at Marietta, Circleville, and Portsmouth in Ohio, and others in Louisiana and Arkansas. One of the handbills for this traveling show proclaimed:

"MONUMENTAL GRANDEUR OF THE MISSISSIPPI VALLEY, with scientific lectures on AMERICAN AERCHIOLOGY. . . . THIS GORGEOUS PANORAMA with all the ABORIGINAL MONUMENTS of a large extent of country once roamed by the RED MAN, was painted by the EMINENT ARTIST I. J. EGAN, ESQ., and covers 15,000 feet of Canvass. . . ."[76]

The admission charge was twenty-five cents, no small sum for Americans in the era of President Van Buren, but the panorama was a popular attraction even though, handbills to the contrary, it turned out to cover only 2,500 square feet. When Dickeson wearied of his show, he presented his collection of artifacts to the Academy of Natural Sciences in Philadelphia; the famous panorama itself was acquired about 1899 by the University Museum, Philadelphia, but is now owned by the St. Louis Art Museum.

6   *Dr. Dickeson excavating a mound, from the Panorama of the Monumental Grandeur of the Mississippi Valley.* Painting on muslin by John J. Egan, 1850. Courtesy of the City Art Museum of Saint Louis.

2

One of the important mound excavations of the day was carried out in 1838 at the Grave Creek Mound on the banks of the Ohio in what was then Virginia, but since 1863 has been West Virginia. This mound was one of the first major earthworks to be discovered by white men. The astronomer Francis Baily gave it his attention in 1796. A quarter of a century later, Caleb Atwater's paper on the mounds included a letter from "the Rev. Dr. Doddridge, of Brooke county, Virginia," describing Grave Creek in these terms:

"Wellsburgh, Va. May 27, 1819

"Dear Sir,
    "As to your inquiry concerning the ancient works at Grave Creek, below Wheeling, I will give you the best account which I can. Grave Creek flat is about eleven miles below Wheeling. It is about two miles square, consisting, for the most part, of second bottom, the most ancient alluvion; about the middle of it, little Grave Creek puts into the Ohio, and Great Grave creek, at the lower end of this flat. Between these creeks stand the ancient works, at the distance of about a quarter of a mile from the Ohio.
    "The 'fortifications,' as they are called, are not remarkable ones, though a number of small mounds stand among them. In one of the tumuli, which was opened about twenty years since, sixty copper beads were found. Of these, I procured ten, and sent them to the Museum in Philadelphia. They were made of a coarse wire, which appeared to have been hammered out and not drawn, and were cut off at unequal lengths. They were soldered together in an awkward manner, the centre of some of them uniting with the edges of others. They were incrusted with verdigrise, but the inside of them was pure copper. This fact shows that the ancient inhabitants were not wholly unacquainted with the use of metals.
    "The 'Big Grave,' as it is called, stands about half way between the two creeks, and about one fourth of a mile from the river. It is certainly one of the most august monuments of remote Antiquity any where to be found. Its circumference at the base, is three hundred yards; its diameter, of course, one hundred. Its altitude, from measurement, is ninety feet; and its diameter, at the summit, is forty-five feet. The centre, at the summit, appears to have sunk several feet, so as to form a small kind of amphitheatre. The rim enclosing this amphitheatre, is seven or eight feet in thickness. On the south side, in its edge, stands a large beach tree, whose bark is marked with the initials of a great number of visitants.
    "This lofty and venerable tumulus has been so far opened, as to ascertain that it contains many thousands of human skeletons, but no farther.

The proprietor of the ground, Mr. Joseph Tomlinson, will not suffer its demolition in the smallest degree. I, for one, do him honour for his sacred regard for these works of Antiquity. . . ."[77]

7   The Great Mound at Grave Creek. Engraving from *Ancient Monuments of the Mississippi Valley,* by E. G. Squier and E. H. Davis, 1848.

On March 19, 1838, Abelard B. Tomlinson, a member of the family that owned the Grave Creek property, began an extensive excavation of the big mound. At a cost of $2,500, he sank a shaft from the "amphitheatre" at the summit of the mound to its base. When he had gone down 77 feet, he found a stone-covered log-walled chamber which enclosed a skeleton decorated with a profusion of copper rings, shell beads, and mica plates. There were 2,350 disks cut from the shell of the large marine mollusk known as the conch, and 500 smaller beads. Tomlinson extended the shaft, and, he wrote, "At the distance of one hundred and eleven feet we came to a vault, which had been excavated before the mound was commenced, eight by twelve feet and seven in depth. Along each side and across the ends, upright timbers had been placed, which supported timbers thrown across the vault as a ceiling. These timbers were covered with loose unhewn stone, common to the neighborhood. The timbers had rotted and had tumbled into the vault. . . . In this vault were two human skeletons, one of which had no ornaments; the other was surrounded by six hundred fifty ivory [shell] beads, and an ivory [bone] ornament, six inches long."[78] Another observer, a Dr. Clemens, told of a horizontal trench cut through the mound which revealed "numerous masses composed of charcoal and burnt bones. . . . On reaching the lower vault from the top, it was determined to enlarge it for the accommodation of visitors, when ten more skeletons were discovered."[79]

To modern archaeologists, Abelard Tomlinson's notes on the Grave Creek work are important because they comprise the first clear description of the log tombs of what now is called the Adena Culture. Tomlinson's contemporaries, though, simply described the vaults as the tombs of Mound Builder kings, and turned their attention to a much more exciting discovery: the Grave Creek Tablet.

About 1840, Tomlinson made known the existence of this tablet, claiming to have discovered it on June 16, 1838. It was an oval white sandstone disk, ¾ of an inch thick and 1½ inches in diameter, on which were inscribed three lines in an unknown alphabet. The agitation over the Mormons had then reached one of its many peaks; the whole nation knew of Joseph Smith and the golden plates he had claimed to have found in the hill Cumorah. The uproar over the discovery of the Grave Creek Tablet is easy to imagine.

Among the authorities who descended on Grave Creek to examine the tablet was Henry Rowe Schoolcraft (1793–1864), who is considered one of the great early figures in American anthropology. The son of a New York State glass manufacturer, Schoolcraft studied mineralogy in college, and after the War of 1812 went west by way of Pittsburgh to make a mineralogical survey of the country beyond the Alleghenies. He came back with a trunkload of specimens that revealed the wealth of the Mississippi Valley, but he had also become infected with an interest in American Indians.

In 1820 and 1821, he served as geologist and mineralogist to government expeditions into the Indian territory. Then, in 1822, President Monroe appointed him the agent for Indian affairs at the remote outpost of Sault Ste. Marie, on what then was the northwest frontier of American civilization. Here Schoolcraft mastered the language of the Ojibwa Indians, and married a half-Ojibwa girl; he compiled a grammar of the Ojibwa tongue and listened in fascination to the tales the Indians told in their camps. Schoolcraft was one of the first to recognize the worth of Indian poetry and folklore, and he worked to assemble a collection of their myths and legends while their cultures still were intact. *Algic Researches,* his anthology of Indian tales, was the fruit of seventeen years' field work, and permanently established Schoolcraft's fame as an anthropologist. (To geographers he became famous for a different reason: he discovered Lake Itasca, the source of the Mississippi River.)

By 1836, he was acting Superintendent of Indian Affairs for the state of Michigan, and his importance was growing, both as a scholar and as a government official. He received a variety of public appointments, founded scholarly societies, and engaged in international correspondence with archaeologists and ethnologists. In 1842, he joined Albert Gallatin as a founder of the American Ethnological Society. That same year he traveled to Europe to read a paper before the British Association for the Advancement of Science, and when he returned, carrying the prestige of a member-in-full of the scientific establishment, he headed for Grave Creek to see the tablet.

Schoolcraft pondered the twenty-five characters on the tablet and pronounced twenty-two of them alphabetic and one a hieroglyph. But *which* alphabet? It seemed to him that at least four of the letters bore strong resemblances to letters of the ancient Celtic alphabet. But this was beyond his competence as a scholar, and he sent copies of the inscription off to Professors Jomard of Paris and Page of Copenhagen, as well as to several other European authorities. Professor Page reported that the characters, whatever they might be, were not ancient Norse runes. Professor Jomard, after a laborious analysis, claimed to see the ancestry of the inscription in the Lybian writing of North Africa. One of his colleagues disagreed, and ascribed the tablet to the Numidians, also of North Africa.

As the controversy over the Grave Creek Tablet drew in more experts, the opinions multiplied astonishingly. One man found four characters which he claimed were ancient Greek; another saw four Etruscan figures; five were said to be Runic; six, ancient Gaelic; seven, old Erse; ten, Phoenician; fourteen, old British; and sixteen, Celtiberic. Soon not merely identifications but translations were forthcoming, not from cranks but from leading philologists. In 1857, Maurice Schwab of France published his version: "The Chief of Emigration who reached these places (or this island) has fixed these statutes forever." A decade later, Jules Oppert, who was instrumental in deciphering the cuneiform writing of the Sumerians, provided a different interpretation of the Grave Creek message: "The grave of one who was assassinated here. May God to avenge him strike his murderer, cutting off the hand of his existence." And in 1875, when Schoolcraft and Abelard Tomlinson had gone to their rewards, M. Levy Bing told the Congress of Americanists meeting at Nancy, France, that he had found twenty-three Canaanite letters on the tablet, which read, "What thou sayest, thou dost impose it, thou shinest in thy impetuous clan and rapid chamois."[80]

Schoolcraft, who despite certain romantic tendencies was a generally sober-minded scholar, probably would have found M. Levy Bing's "rapid chamois" too much to swallow. Certainly that was the reaction of Dr. Daniel Wilson, who, in 1876, commented in the third edition of his cautious *Prehistoric Man,* "It thus appears that this ingenious little stone is even more accommodating than the Dighton rock [a supposed Phoenician or Viking inscription in New England] in adapting itself to all conceivable theories of ante-Columbian colonization, and, in fact, constitutes an epitome of the prehistoric literature of the new world. Had Sir Henry Rawlinson dug up such a medley of languages at one of the corners of the tower of Babel it might have less surprised us. This curious analysis, so contrary to all previous philological experience, does not seem to have staggered the faith of the elucidator."[81] Thereafter there were few scholarly efforts to "translate" the Grave Creek Tablet.

Schoolcraft's account of his researches at Grave Creek and his general thoughts on the Mound Builders appeared in the *Transactions of the American Ethnological Society* in 1845 under the heading, "Observations respecting the Grave creek mound, in Western Virginia; the antique inscription discovered in its excavation; and the connected evidence of the occupancy of the Mississippi valley during the mound period, and prior to the discovery of America by Columbus."

The Grave Creek Mound provoked a host of questions in his mind: "What are the facts connected with the position of this giant structure? Its dimensions, its contents, and the era and purpose of its construction? Who erected it? What is the language and purport of the recently found inscription? Who were the mound-builders? Was the continent known to Europeans before the era of Columbus? What race of Red Men first entered the Mississippi valleys? Whence came they? Whither went they? Do their descendants remain? What are the leading facts of the mound period of our history?"[82] He could not, of course, answer these questions, but he offered some reasonable preliminary thoughts.

His essay provided more ammunition for those who argued that the Mound Builders had been an advanced civilized race. Under the subtitle, "*Antique tube: telescopic device,*" he presented this description while discussing certain West Virginia tumuli:

"In the course of excavations made in 1842 in the easternmost of the three mounds of the Elizabethtown group, several tubes of stone were disclosed, the precise object of which has been the subject of various opinions. The longest measured twelve inches, the shortest eight. Three of them were carved out of steatite, being skillfully cut and polished. The diameter of the tube externally was one inch and four tenths; the bore, eight tenths of an inch. This calibre was continued till within three eighths of an inch of the sight end, when it diminishes to two tenths of an inch. By placing the eye at the diminished end, the extraneous light is shut from the pupil, and distant objects are more clearly discerned."[83]

Schoolcraft pointed out that the carving and workmanship were generally quite superior to that of Indian pipe carvings, and added that if this article were indeed a work of the Mound Builders, "intended for a telescopic tube, it is a most interesting relic." But soon Schoolcraft was retreating from the suggestion that the Mound Builders had been practicing astronomers. His final views on Grave Creek and the related earthworks appeared in the huge, muddled six-volume encyclopedia that was his masterpiece, *Historical and Statistical Information Respecting the History, Condition, and Prospects of the Indian Tribes of the United States* (1851–1857).

In the first volume of the *Indian Tribes,* Schoolcraft lined himself up among the not very numerous disciples of Bishop Madison and Dr. McCulloh, expressing his opinion that the mounds were the work of the ancestors of the North American Indians, and not of a fancied nation of Mound Builders. He commented, "There is little to sustain a belief that these ancient works are due to tribes of more fixed and exalted traits of civilization, far less to a people of an expatriated type of civilization, of either an ASIATIC or EUROPEAN origin, as several popular writers very vaguely, and with little severity of investigation, imagined. . . . There is nothing, indeed, in the magnitude and structure of our western mounds which a semi-hunter and semi-agricultural population, like that which may be ascribed to the ancestors of Indian predecessors of the existing race, could not have executed." Therefore, Schoolcraft went on, "aboriginal archaeology has fallen under a spirit of misapprehension and predisposition to exaggeration. The antiquities of the United States are the antiquities of barbarism, not of civilization."

This was a forthright and uncompromising statement, and, in the context of its era, a well-nigh astonishing one. It was the first time in nearly thirty years that anyone of note had taken the conservative position in the great debate; and Schoolcraft's book, compiled under government auspices and published in Washington, carried a quasi-official authority. Nevertheless, he was ahead of his time by at least a generation, and his assessment was ignored by those convinced of the Mound Builder fantasy.

In taking his stand, Schoolcraft not only had to step back from his "tele-

scope" passage and admit that the polished tubes were probably mere ornaments, but he also had to account for the Grave Creek Tablet. That tablet had
not yet been discredited; Maurice Schwab was at that very moment producing
his decipherment of the commandment of "the Chief of Emigration." No
forms of alphabetic writing were known among the North American Indians,
not even in the high civilizations of Mexico. Schoolcraft's explanation came in
the fourth volume of his *Indian Tribes,* where he termed the tablet an "intrusive antiquity." He did not pretend to know whether Phoenicians or
Numidians or Celts had visited the Ohio Valley, but he insisted, at any rate,
that whoever had inscribed the tablet had no cultural connection with the red
men who had heaped up the Grave Creek Mound.

3

While Abelard Tomlinson was sinking his shaft at Grave Creek, a distinguished American physician was seeking the answer to the Mound Builders
riddle in another fashion. He was Dr. Samuel G. Morton of Philadelphia, who
has been termed the father of American physical anthropology.

Morton was born in 1799 and took his medical degree at the Medical
College of the University of Pennsylvania in 1820; he received a second degree
from the medical school of the University of Edinburgh three years later. In
1826 he began to practice medicine in Philadelphia, also giving private instruction in medicine and anatomy. He became a member of the Academy of
Natural Sciences of Philadelphia, helped to classify and arrange its collections,
and developed an active interest in paleontology and archaeology. He made
use of his professional training to carry out studies in what today is called
anthropometry or physical anthropology—the analysis of anatomical evidence
in determining variations in human types.

Like a number of other sciences, physical anthropology has its roots in
pseudo-science—in this case, the pseudo-science of phrenology, which purported
to divine human psychological attributes through the study of bumps and
hollows on the cranium. Morton was a phrenologist of sorts himself, though he
bore no tinge of the charlatanism of other practitioners; he investigated phrenology in a sympathetic way out of the hope that it would produce meaningful
results, but his conclusions were moderate ones. In the course of his "cranio-
graphic" researches, Morton found himself led more or less accidentally into
anthropology. As he related it in 1848 in the *Transactions of the American
Ethnological Society,* "Having had occasion, in the summer of 1830, to deliver

an introductory lecture to a course in Anatomy, I chose for my subject: The different forms of the skull, as exhibited in the Five Races of Men. Strange to say, I could neither buy nor borrow a cranium of each of these races; and I finished my discourse without showing either the Mongolian or the Malay. Forcibly impressed with this great deficiency in a most important branch of science, I at once resolved to make a collection for myself."[84] Between 1830 and the year of his death, 1851, Morton gathered 968 crania, the largest collection of its kind then in existence. Included in his gallery of skulls were a number that came from mounds and aboriginal Indian sites, and Morton set about using purely physical methods to determine if the Mound Builders and the Indians were indeed separate races.

He was not the first to have made such studies. In 1819 Caleb Atwater had examined the skeletons in Ohio burial mounds, concluding that they "never belonged to a people like our Indians. The latter are a tall, rather slender, straight limbed people; the former [the Mound Builders] were short and thick. They were rarely over five feet high, and few indeed were six. Their foreheads were low, cheek bones rather high; their faces were very short and broad; their eyes were very large; and, they had broad chins. I have examined more than fifty skulls found in tumuli, several of which I have before me. . . . The limbs of our fossils are short and very thick, and resemble the Germans, more than any Europeans with whom I am acquainted."[85] A decade later, in 1829, Dr. McCulloh of Baltimore examined some burials from the mounds and came to just the opposite conclusion: that the Mound Builders and the Indians were physiologically of the same race.

Morton, aided by John S. Phillips of the Academy of Natural Sciences in Philadelphia, virtually invented physical anthropology from scratch. He devised measuring instruments, selected the most significant areas of the skull to compare, and spent "some years of toil and anxiety" preparing a work whose intention was "to give accurate delineations of the skulls" representing as many Indian nations, from all parts of the American continent, as he could bring together in his collection, to show the relation of American crania to those found on other continents, and to determine, "by the evidence of osteological facts, whether the American aborigines of all epochs have belonged to one race or to a plurality of races."[86]

In 1839, Morton was named Professor of Anatomy at Pennsylvania Medical College, and in that same year his anthropological landmark, *Crania Americana* was published. In this impressive volume, handsomely illustrated with lithographs of his specimens, Morton presented the results of his investigations. He had systematically measured hundreds of skulls, taking ten measurements on each—longitudinal diameter, facial angle, internal capacity, horizontal periphery, and so on. He took note of such practices as the artificial deformation of the skull through binding the heads of infants, common among the Mayas of Mexico and other groups. To explain the variations in the skulls he had examined, he made use of all that was known of the theory of the races at that time, which was not very much.

Of the hundreds of crania Morton measured, eight had been taken from mounds. Three came from sepulchral tumuli in Peru; one had been found in the Grave Creek Mound, one in a mound near Circleville, Ohio, and the other three came from Tennessee, Alabama, and Wisconsin. As his controls in the study of Mound Builders skulls, Morton used the crania of four recent Indians intrusively buried in a mound in Ohio's Scioto Valley, a skull found in Mammoth Cave, Kentucky, and the skull of a desiccated body found in the same cave. His table of measurements showed that there was no significant difference between the eight Mound Builder skulls, the four modern Indian skulls, and the two crania from Mammoth Cave, although American aborigines as a whole appeared to belong to a race distinct from those of other parts of the world.

He drew two conclusions: "That the American nations, excepting the Polar tribes [the Eskimos] were of one Race and one Species, but of two great families (Toltecan and Barbarous), which resemble each other in physical, but differ in intellectual character," and "That the cranial remains discovered in the Mounds, from Peru to Wisconsin belong to the same race (the Indian), and probably to the Toltecan family."[87]

These findings, buttressed by formidable statistical evidence, undercut the position of those who claimed that the Mound Builders had been a race apart from the lowly Indians. Morton grouped both in the same racial category: the American Indian race, which he distinguished from the Caucasian, Malay, Mongolian, and Ethiopian races. In this he differs from modern physical anthropologists, who class American Indians and Eskimos in the Mongoloid race, which also includes most Asiatic peoples. Morton's error can be explained, perhaps, by the fact that his "Mongolian" race was determined on the basis of the examination of only ten Chinese and Eskimo skulls, and he failed to see that the resemblances between his "Mongolians" and the American aborigines were far greater than the differences.

Having lumped Mound Builders and Indians into a single race, Morton nevertheless felt constrained to account for the cultural gap separating the high civilizations of Mexico from the nomadic Indians of the United States, whose supposed savagery and vicious stupidity was then a matter of current political policy as well as prejudice. Thus he divided his American Indian race into two families, the "Toltecan" and the "Barbarous." The various

Mexican civilizations he assigned to the Toltecan group, which was marked by the fact that it "bears evidence of centuries of demi-civilization." The Mound Builders, too, he felt were probably Toltecan. All the other American aborigines were classed with the Barbarous family. Here Morton revealed his adherence to the tenets of phrenology, for he claimed to be able to detect cultural factors through physical measurements. The intellectual faculties of his Barbarous people "appear to be of a decidedly inferior cast when compared with those of the Caucasian or Mongolian races,"[88] he wrote. The "structure" of the Indian mind, as represented by the Barbarous family, "appears to be different from that of the white man,"[89] and these Indians "turn with avulsion from the restraints of civilized life."

Despite these dubious conclusions, Morton had made a valuable contribution by demonstrating the racial unity of the American Indians and their mound-building predecessors. Those who still insisted on the existence of a non-Indian race of Mound Builders could not assail the accuracy of Morton's measurements nor could they hope to deny his high standing in the scientific community. But they could complain, with some justice, that conclusions based on the examination of a mere five skulls from the North American mounds need not be accepted as final. Some went further and tried to throw out Morton's evidence on the ground that he had mistaken intrusive modern skulls for the authentic relics of Mound Builders. A representative of this viewpoint is E. G. Squier, who wrote in 1847, "The first two [the Grave Creek and Tennessee skulls] may be regarded as genuine remains of the mound-builders; but it is more than probable . . . that the rest are skulls of the recent Indians, who, as we have seen, often buried in the mounds."[90] So, despite the care and labor that went into Morton's researches, the case against the Mound Builders remained unproven. It is just as well, possibly, for later anthropologists were able to show that Morton had reached the right answer on the basis of faulty, incomplete, and erroneous data. Mound Builders and American Indians did indeed both belong to the same racial stock; but that did not mean at all that they were identical in physical appearance. Those subleties, though, were decades away from discovery when Samuel Morton, his work unfinished, died twelve years after the publication of *Crania Americana.*

4

It was time once more for a synthesis of mound research. A quarter of a century had passed since the publication of Caleb Atwater's pioneering essay. Atwater had shirked almost entirely any description of mounds outside Ohio, while his hasty surveys of the Ohio mounds had not been of professional quality. Moreover, his speculations on the mounds, sound enough for 1820, had by 1845 come to seem naïve and thin. Gallatin and Schoolcraft's American Ethnological Society began to search for a man who would compile all that was known about the mounds, conduct extensive new research, and produce a definitive study.

They found their man in Ephraim George Squier (1821–1888), an Ohio newspaper editor. Squier, born in Bethlehem, New York, had entered journalism in early manhood. He agitated for prison reform as a young newspaperman in Albany, New York, and in 1844 moved to Connecticut to found a newspaper of his own in Hartford. He campaigned vigorously for the Whig party, whose presidential candidate, Henry Clay, was defeated in the 1844 election. Squier's paper failed at about the same time, and he went on to Chillicothe, Ohio, to edit the Scioto *Gazette*.

Chillicothe lies at the very heart of the Ohio mound country, and since his editorial duties were not burdensome, Squier had ample time to examine the prehistoric earthworks in the vicinity. Even after he was elected clerk of the Ohio House of Representatives in 1846 he continued his mound research. In company with Dr. E. H. Davis, a Chillicothe physician, Squier opened over two hundred mounds, explored about a hundred earthwork enclosures, and gathered a sizable collection of artifacts, all between 1845 and 1847. In addition they surveyed in a quite expert manner many of the earthworks, preparing detailed contour maps of acceptable accuracy and, incidentally, of great beauty.

During this time they received the encouragement and the financial support of the American Ethnological Society. In 1846, Squier appeared before that group to read a paper on "Aboriginal Monuments of the Mississippi Valley," which was published two years later in its *Transactions,* Volume II. Describing his work, Squier said, "At the outset all preconceived notions were abandoned, and the work of research commenced, as if no speculations had been indulged in, nor anything before been known, respecting the singular remains of antiquity scattered so profusely around us. It was concluded that, either the field should be entirely abandoned to the poet and the romancer, or, if these monuments were capable of reflecting any certain light upon the grand archeological questions connected with the primitive history of the American continent, the origin, migration, and early state of the American race, that then they should be carefully and minutely, and above all, systematically investigated." There have been "too few well-authenticated facts," he declared, and "their absence has been poorly supplied by speculations. . . . It seems strange that hitherto, while every other branch of research has enlisted active and enlightened minds in its elucidation, the archeological field has been left comparatively unoccupied."[91]

Squier's talk was in the nature of a preliminary, as was the book he published at New Haven in 1847, *Observations on the Uses of the Mounds of the West, with an attempt at their Classification*. He informed the officers of the American Ethnological Society that he was nearing completion of the manuscript of his intended definitive work, which would have to be published as a lavishly illustrated folio volume of more than three hundred pages. The American Ethnological Society, only five years old, did not have the resources to underwrite the publication of such a tome; so aid was sought from an even more youthful but far better endowed body, the Smithsonian Institution.

James Smithson, a wealthy Englishman of illegitimate birth and eccentric tastes, had died in 1829. His chief heir was his nephew, Henry James Hungerford, but Smithson specified that upon Hungerford's death without issue, the whole estate should go "to the United States of America to found at Washington, under the name of the Smithsonian Institution, an establishment for the increase and diffusion of knowledge among men." Since Smithson had never visited or shown any particular interest in the United States, it was hard to see why he should make such a bequest, and the speculation on his motives has continued to this day. Nevertheless, Hungerford did die without issue in 1835, and three years later some 105,000 gold sovereigns, the principal of Smithson's estate, were delivered by clipper to the Philadelphia mint, where they were recoined into $508,318.46 of United States money.

The government was leery of the gift. Such men as John C. Calhoun argued that Congress had no power under the Constitution to accept the money, but President John Quincy Adams prevailed, and after years of controversy the Smithsonian Institution began its official existence on August 10, 1846. The physicist Joseph Henry became its first secretary.

Henry was chiefly interested in matters such as electromagnetism and meteorology, and cared very little about the Mound Builders or the American Indians. But one of the ways he planned to increase and diffuse knowledge among men was to use the Smithsonian's bank account to finance the publication of a series of folio monographs on science. Hardly had he settled into his office than the officers of the American Ethnological Society were upon him, offering Squier's massive manuscript on the mounds. The subject was uncongenial to Henry, but he needed something to publish in his proposed series, *Smithsonian Contributions to Knowledge*. So it befell that the first volume of the series was the majestic *Ancient Monuments of the Mississippi Valley*, bearing the bylines of E. G. Squier, A.M., and E. H. Davis, M.D.

Thus began the involvement of the Smithsonian Institution with the Mound

Builders. Somewhat against Secretary Henry's intentions, the second, third, seventh, and eighth volumes of *Smithsonian Contributions to Knowledge* also contained essays on the mounds; then he managed to divert the series more successfully toward discussion of barometers, weather maps, and electricity. But after Henry's death in 1878 the Smithsonian would grow so concerned with the mounds that some archaeologists would accuse it of trying to impose a dictatorship of ideas on them.

Squier and Davis submitted their manuscript to Henry from Chillicothe on May 15, 1847. Henry referred the work to the venerable Albert Gallatin, President of the American Ethnological Society, the following month, asking for a report of its suitability for publication. Gallatin duly appointed a committee of five, including Dr. Samuel Morton, and within ten days the committee produced a favorable report. Three of its members said they had "examined the work in question, and regard it not only as a new and interesting, but an eminently valuable addition to our stock of knowledge on a subject little understood, but in which is felt a deep and constantly increasing interest, both in our country and abroad." A fourth committeeman added a comment that "my previous impressions concerning the value of the researches of that gentleman [Squier] and his associate [Davis] are fully confirmed," while Morton wrote from Philadelphia to call the work "by far the most important contribution to the Archaeology of the United States, that has ever been offered to the public."

It is not surprising that the American Ethnological Society, which had been following the progress of Squier and Davis since the beginning of 1846, would provide the formal seal of approval that the Smithsonian's Joseph Henry felt he needed. But the committee report was not merely a self-serving operation. *Ancient Monuments of the Mississippi Valley,* when it came from the press in 1848, instantly established itself as a work of commanding importance in American archaeology. As a summary of the knowledge of its particular field at that time, it was remarkable; as a model for later workers, it was invaluable; as a detailed record of the Ohio mounds as they appeared in 1847, it was and remains unique. Its value to archaeologists was underscored in 1965 when a New York firm published a complete photographic reprint of the original text.

In his opening pages, Squier—for he did most of the writing, despite the shared byline—reviews the work of his predecessors, mentioning de Soto's chroniclers, William Bartram, the Reverend Mr. Harris, Bishop Madison, De Witt Clinton, and many others. He gives Atwater credit for "the first attempt towards a general account of the ancient monuments of the West," though noting that his paper "contains many errors, for which however we can find a ready apology in the unsettled state of the country, and the attendant difficulties of investigation at the time it was written,—errors which, under present advantages of research, would be inexcusable."[92] He states his own intention of abandoning preconceived notions and speculations, and this he observed fairly faithfully throughout his report.

After some preliminary words on the geographic distribution of the ancient earthworks, Squier attempts an analysis by types: "The Earth and Stone Works resolve themselves into two classes, viz: ENCLOSURES, bounded by embankments, circumvallations, or walls; and simple tumuli, or MOUNDS. They constitute, together, a single system of works; but, for reasons which will satisfactorily appear, it is preferred to classify them as above. These grand classes resolve themselves into other subordinate divisions: ENCLOSURES FOR DEFENCE, SACRED AND MISCELLANEOUS ENCLOSURES: MOUNDS OF SACRIFICE, TEMPLE MOUNDS, MOUNDS OF SEPULTURE, etc."[93]

There follows a discussion by types, beginning with the enclosures:

"The square and the circle, separate or in combination, were favorite figures with the mound-builders; and a large proportion of their works in the Scioto valley, and in Ohio generally, are these forms. Most of the circular works

8 A group of sepulchral mounds. Engraving from *Ancient Monuments of the Mississippi Valley,* by E. G. Squier and E. H. Davis, 1848.

are small, varying from two hundred and fifty to three hundred feet in diameter, while others are a mile or more in circuit. Some stand isolated, but most in connection with one or more mounds, of greater or less dimensions, or in connection with other more complicated works. Wherever the circles occur, if there be a fosse, or ditch, it is almost invariably *interior* to the parapet. . . . Another fact, bearing directly upon the degree of knowledge possessed by the builders, is, that many, if not most, of the circular works are *perfect circles,* and that many of the rectangular works are accurate squares."[94]

Having established that most of the lowland earthworks were probably religious centers, since they could not have served any effective defensive purpose, Squier examines the hilltop embankments. "The natural strength of such positions, and their susceptibility of defence, would certainly suggest them as the citadels of a people having hostile neighbors, or pressed by invaders. . . . While rugged and steep on most sides, they have one or more points of comparatively easy approach, in the protection of which the utmost skill of the builders seems to have been exhausted. They are guarded by double, overlapping walls, or a series of them, having sometimes an accompanying mound, designed perhaps for a look-out. . . . The usual defence is a simple embankment, thrown up along and a little below the brow of the hill, varying in height and solidity, as the declivity is more or less steep and difficult of access."[95]

Squier presents a series of descriptions of individual forts, based on his and Davis' personal examinations and supplemented, where appropriate, by the observations of others. Each is accompanied by a detailed plan, drawn by Squier from survey work done in some cases by himself and Davis, in some by others. Squier's draftsmanship is surprisingly elegant, and the plans are delightful to behold. Visitors to the surviving Ohio earthworks today may often see blowups of the charts from Squier and Davis posted to provide an over-all view of the monuments.

In his descriptions of the various earthworks, Squier offers careful and extensive accounts of all features, natural and man-made, keying them to his charts. This part of the text is handled well, and is still useful, although Squier transgresses against modern archaeological custom by sliding swiftly from objective reportage to speculative conclusions. For example, he spends several pages on Fort Hill, in Highland County, Ohio: "Unlike the hills around it, this one stands detached and isolated, and forms a conspicuous object from every approach. Its sides are steep and precipitous; and, except at one or two points, if not absolutely inaccessible, extremely difficult of ascent. The points most easy of access are at the southern and northern angles, and may be reached on horseback. [Today picnickers from the state park at the foot of the hill go

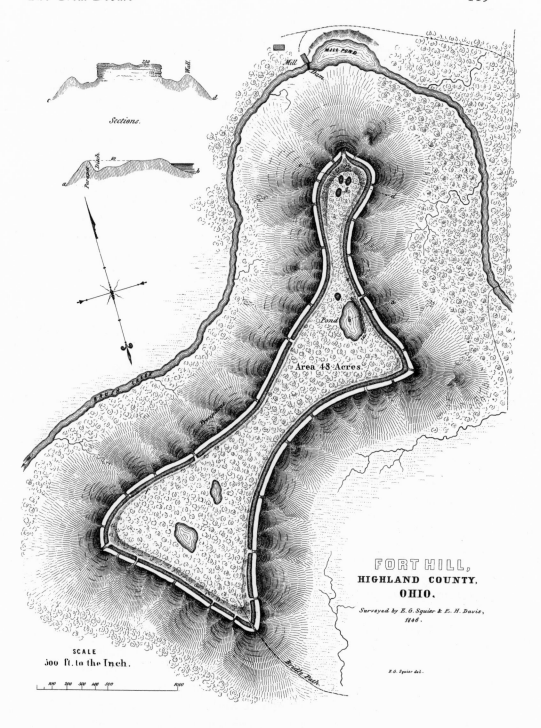

FORT HILL,
HIGHLAND COUNTY,
OHIO.

Surveyed by E. G. Squier & E. H. Davis,
1846.

9   Diagram of the Fort Hill works. Squier and Davis, 1848.

huffing and puffing up the difficult path in search of the virtually indetectible "fort" at its summit.] The top of the hill is level, and has an area of not far from fifty acres, which is covered with a heavy primitive forest of gigantic trees. One of these, a chestnut, standing on the embankment near the point indicated by the letter *e* [on his plan], measures *twenty-one feet* in circumference; another, an oak, which also stood on the wall, at the point *f,* though now fallen and much decayed, still measures *twenty-three feet* in circumference. All around are scattered the trunks of immense trees, in every stage of decay; the entire forest presenting an appearance of the highest antiquity."[96]

After a discussion of the embankment of earth and stone, "interrupted at intervals by gateways," which is so difficult for casual visitors to locate today, Squier returns to the trees of Fort Hill and reports two hundred annual rings per foot in the trunk of the large chestnut. "This would give nearly *six hundred years* as the age of the tree," he says. "If to this we add the probable period intervening from the time of the building of the work to its abandonment, and the subsequent period up to its invasion by the forest, we are led irresistibly to the conclusion, that it has an antiquity of at least *one thousand years.* But when we notice, all around us, the crumbling trunks of trees half hidden in the accumulating soil, we are induced to fix upon an antiquity still more remote."[97]

He continues his survey of ancient fortifications through some, like Fort Ancient in Warren County, Ohio, that have been preserved to our day, and many that have long since disappeared. Most of these were in Ohio, although he includes a few from adjoining states. He makes use of the work of Colonel Charles Whittlesey of Cleveland in describing the earthworks of northern Ohio, which differed in major respects from those of the region about Chillicothe. "The most natural inference in respect to the northern cordon of works," Squier quotes Whittlesey as writing, "is, that they formed a well-occupied line, constructed either to protect the advance of a nation landing from the lake [Lake Erie] and moving southward for conquest; or, a line of resistance for a people inhabiting these shores and pressed upon by their southern neighbors. The scarcity of mounds, the absence of pyramids of earth, which are so common on the Ohio, the want of rectangular and other regular works, at the north,—all these differences tend to the conclusion that the northern part of Ohio was occupied by a distinct people."[98] Whittlesey suggests "that the northern were warlike, and the southern peaceful and agricultural in their habits," and asks, "May we not suppose that the latter were overcome by their northern neighbors, who built the military works to be observed upon the Ohio and its tributaries, while the more regular structures are the remains of the conquered people?"

Whittlesey is groping here toward something not established by archaeology until the twentieth century: that there were at least two mound-building cultures in Ohio. But in the primitive state of archaeology at the time, he could do no more than conjecture, while today, when much more is known, the vanished mounds bordering Lake Erie are beyond the reach of scholarship.

Squier did not accept Whittlesey's two-culture idea. "The differences between the northern and southern earthworks," he says, "are not greater than would naturally be exhibited between the structures of a sparse frontier population, and those erected by more central and dense communities." On the same page he proposes for the first time in the work his theory of the origin of the mounds, which was implicit in many of his earlier comments: "The examples of defensive works here presented will serve to give a very accurate conception of this class of structures. By a minute attention to their various details, we are prepared to estimate the judgment, skill, and industry of their builders. No one can rise from such an examination, except with the conviction that the race, by whom these works were erected, possessed no inconsiderable knowledge of the science of defence,—a degree of knowledge much superior to that known to have been possessed by the hunter tribes of North America previous to the discovery by Columbus, or indeed subsequent to that event. Their number and magnitude must also impress the inquirer with enlarged notions of the power of the people commanding the means for their construction, and whose numbers required such extensive works for their protection."[99] Thus Squier joins the ranks of believers in the fabled Mound Builders.

Following Caleb Atwater, Squier seems to think that the Mound Builders' civilization "spread southward, constantly developing itself in its progress, until it attained its height in Mexico." On the evidence of the fortifications, he suggests that this migration was not a voluntary one. He traces a line of fortifications diagonally across the continent from western New York State through central and northern Ohio into southern Illinois, and from this he infers that out of the northeast "came the hostile savage hordes, before whose incessant attacks the less warlike mound-builders gradually receded, or beneath whose exterminating cruelty those who occupied this frontier entirely disappeared, leaving these monuments alone to attest their existence, and the extraordinary skill with which they defended their altars and their homes. . . . It is clear that the contest was a protracted one, and that the race of the mounds were for a long period constantly exposed to attack."[100] He is not altogether wedded to the theory of invasion by savages from the northeast, though; he offers the alternate possibility that "the tide of migration flowed from the south" and "received its final check upon this line [of forts]."

He sounds a note of nineteenth-century racial prejudice in his hypotheses of a Mound Builder civilization. In a nation where Indians still were looked upon as vermin, as troublesome obstructions to the expansion of the United States, there were sociological as well as archaeological implications in the creation of the myth of superior, vanished Mound Builders. Hence Squier writes, "It may be suggested that there existed among the mound-builders a state of society something like that which prevailed among the Indians; that each tribe had its separate seat, maintaining, with its own independence, an almost constant warfare against its neighbors, and, as a consequence, possessing its own 'castle,' as a place of final resort when invaded by a powerful foe. *Apart from the fact, however, that the Indians were hunters averse to labor, and not known to have constructed any works approaching in skilfulness of design or in magnitude those under notice,** there is almost positive evidence that the mound-builders were an agricultural people, considerably advanced in the arts, possessing a great uniformity throughout the whole territory which they occupied, in manners, habits, and religion,—a uniformity sufficiently well marked to identify them as a single people, having a common origin, common modes of life, and, as an almost necessary consequence, common sympathies, if not a common and consolidated government."[101]

5

The second part of Squier's book is devoted to what he called "sacred enclosures." It seemed to him, as indeed it has seemed to most modern observers, that the function of the geometrical earthworks of the Ohio Valley must have been ritualistic—that this once was consecrated ground. He suggests that the Mound Builder society may have been a theocracy, "in which the priestly and civil functions were jointly exercised, and one sufficiently powerful to have secured in the Mississippi valley, as it did in Mexico, the erection of many of those vast monuments, which for ages will continue to challenge the wonder of men."[102] He speaks of the "devotional fervor or superstitious zeal which induced their erection," and expresses his awe for their magnitude: "It is difficult to comprehend the existence of religious works, extending, with their attendant avenues, like those near Newark [Ohio], over an area of little less than *four square miles!*" He compares the Newark works to "the great temples of Abury and Stonehenge in England, and Carnac in Brittany," associating them all "with sun worship and its kindred superstitions."

* Emphasis added—R.S.

With many attractive diagrams he proceeds to describe the enclosures and avenues of southern Ohio: Ross County's High Bank, Hopeton, and Cedar Bank works; the Mound City group north of Chillicothe; the ancient works at Liberty Township and on Paint Creek; the earthworks of Seal Township, Pike County; and in particular the imposing octagon and circle of Newark. Most of these are gone today. Not merely the size but the precision of the enclosures awes Squier. "*The builders,*" he says, and the emphasis is his own, "*possessed a standard of measurement, and had some means of determining angles.* The most skilful engineer of the day would find it difficult, without the aid of instruments, to lay down an accurate square of the great dimensions of those above represented, measuring as they do more than *four fifths* of a mile in circumference. It would not, it is true, be impossible to construct circles of considerable size, without instruments; the difficulty of doing so, when we come to the construction of works five thousand four hundred feet, or *over a mile* in circumference, is nevertheless apparent. But we not only find accurate squares and perfect circles, but also, as we have seen, *octagons* of great dimensions."[103] Although it was the mere bulk of burial mounds such as that at Grave Creek, and temple mounds such as Cahokia, that had fascinated earlier observers, the intricacy of the Ohio enclosures now was becoming the most mystifying aspect of the story, and the one most likely to keep alive the concept of a superior race.

Having dealt with dozens of "sacred enclosures" and miscellaneous small earthworks, including one in the form of a serpent, one in the form of a cross, and one thought (without much justice) to resemble an alligator, Squier turns to the Southern mounds and finds himself confessing, as Atwater before him had done, "We are in possession of very little authentic information respecting the monuments of the Southern United States." It was not that the region bounded by Florida, North Carolina, Arkansas, and Texas was unsettled— much of it had been populous while Ohio was still a wilderness—but that the Southerners had displayed remarkably little curiosity about the mounds in their midst. No one since William Bartram's day had attempted a comprehensive exploration of the Southern mounds, with the exception of Dr. Montroville Wilson Dickeson, who had done a good deal of work in Louisiana and surrounding areas. But Dickeson had not published his findings, choosing instead to tour the country with his gaudy panorama, and Squier can only express his hope that "the public will soon be put in possession of the results of his labors."

He is forced instead to rely chiefly on Bartram and on those few archaeologists who had done work in the South. For certain Carolina mounds Squier's informant is William Blanding, M.D., of Camden, South Carolina, who had

written a letter on his research to Dr. Samuel Morton. An account of the great
Etowah earthworks in Alabama, sketchy and haphazard, is taken from a manuscript by the flamboyant naturalist Constantine Rafinesque. There are similar
sketchy descriptions of mounds in Mississippi and Louisiana, including the vast
Seltzertown Mound near Washington, Mississippi, which, Squier says, "is one
of very singular construction. It consists of a truncated pyramid six hundred
feet long by about four hundred broad at its base, covering nearly six acres
of ground. Its sides correspond very nearly with the four cardinal points, its
greatest length being from east to west. It is forty feet in perpendicular height;
and is surrounded by a ditch at its base, of variable dimensions, but averaging
perhaps ten feet in depth. It is ascended by graded avenues. The area on the
top embraces about four acres. Near each of the ends, and as nearly as may
be in the longitudinal centre of the elevation, is placed a large conical mound.
The one towards the west is represented to be not far from forty feet in
height, and truncated, with a level area at its summit of thirty feet diameter.
The opposite mound is somewhat less in size, and is also truncated. Eight other
mounds are regularly placed at various points; they are of comparatively small
size, measuring from eight to ten feet in height."[104]

It had been clear since the eighteenth century that the most important Southern mounds were fundamentally different in type from the conical, rounded
burial mounds of the Ohio Valley. Though some conical mounds were found
in the Southern states, Squier notes, they are "overshadowed by the more remarkable structures which surrounded them. . . . There are no perfect pyramids. . . . *All* appear to be truncated, and to have, in most instances, graded
ascents to their tops." He doubts that they could have been connected with
any military system, "their form and structure, so far as developed, pointing to
a religious origin."

Here the lack of any report of a mound excavation in the South made itself
felt. "We must seek therefore in the contents, as well as in the form and position of these works, for the secret of their origin and purposes," Squier writes.
"And it is at this stage of our inquiry, that the lack of a systematic and extended investigation, conducted on philosophical principles, is most sensibly
felt. Some of these structures, it is stated, where their formation is disclosed
by slides or the wasting action of the rivers, exhibit alternate layers or *platforms* of earth and burned clay, from base to summit. Others are represented
as having alternate layers of earth and human bones in various stages of decomposition. And others still, we are assured, have various horizontal strata of
earth and sand, upon which are deposited at various points human remains,
implements, pottery, and ornaments. Many of the remains of art exhibit great

skill in their construction, more especially the pottery and articles of similar composition. The conical mounds, so far as we are informed, have many features in common with those of a higher latitude. How far the coincidences between them may be traced can only be settled by future inquiries.

"From what has been presented above, it will readily be seen that it is impossible, with our present limited knowledge concerning them, to form anything like a determinate or satisfactory conclusion respecting the numerous and remarkable remains of the South. The immense mounds that abound there may be vast sepulchres in which the remains of generations were deposited; they may have been the temples and 'high places' of a superstitious people, where rites were celebrated and sacrifices performed; or, they may have answered as the places of last resort, where, when pursued by foes, the ancient people fled to receive the support of their gods and to defend the altars of their religion."[105]

Squier offers a variety of possibilities. Perhaps the Southern mounds are the work of a people contemporary with but distinct from those of Ohio. Or possibly they were built by the Ohio people during the course of a migration southward. Unless, that is, the Ohio mounds represent the efforts of colonists expanding northward from Mississippi and Florida, or even from Mexico or Peru.

While this portion of the book was going through the press, Samuel Morton discovered and sent to Squier a portion of William Bartram's long-lost manuscript on the customs of the Creek Indians. Squier incorporated it in his text as an insert. He quotes Bartram on the mounds found in inhabited Creek towns, including "a circular eminence, at one end of the yard, commonly nine or ten feet higher than the ground round about. Upon this mound stands the great *Rotunda, Hot House,* or *Winter Council House* of the present Creeks. . . ." and "a square terrace or eminence, about the same height with the circular one just described, occupying a position at the other end of the yard. Upon this stands the *Public Square.*"[106]

Bartram had questioned the Creeks and come away with the belief that these mounds had already existed when the Creeks entered the region, which was probably true. "From the above quotations," writes Squier, "it appears that, less than one century ago, a portion of the monuments of the South were in actual use by the Indians. It will be observed, however, that our authority [Bartram] ascribes their construction to an anterior race and assigns to them a high antiquity." So Squier persists in the common impression that there was a cultural gap, and not merely a gap in time, between the builders of the mounds and the Muskhogean Indians who came to make use of them. The idea of a continuous spectrum of occupancy linking Mound Builders and Creeks was still an alien one.

Leaving the puzzles of the South, Squier turns to the mysteries of the Northwest, which then consisted of Wisconsin, Michigan, and Minnesota. This was the land of the effigy mounds. Those low-relief elevations of earth or clay, modeled in the forms of animals, men, or abstract figures, had first been brought to the public attention by Richard C. Taylor in an article published in the *American Journal of Science and Art* for April, 1838. Several subsequent brief notices had appeared, but Squier's was the first comprehensive account of the effigies. He depends entirely on the surveys made by Taylor and by John Locke in 1840, and reproduces many of their outline plans of the effigies, with suggestions that they represent otters, lizards, buffalos, turtles, bears, and many other creatures. Squier is unable to offer conclusions about the effigy mounds. He is not sure if they can be credited to outlying settlements of Ohio Mound Builders, or if "they occupy an exclusive field, and possess characteristics sufficiently striking to warrant us in ascribing them to a different race or era. Their purposes, in our present state of information concerning them, do not seem to be satisfactorily settled: it is still a matter of doubt whether they are sepulchral in their origin, connected with the superstitions of their builders, or erected as the monuments and memorials of migrations and events unrecorded by the pen of history. Certain it is that they are now invaded by a busy population, careless alike of their origin and of their future fate, before whose encroachments they are rapidly disappearing."[107]

At the halfway point in his book, Squier reaches the monuments he knows best: the burial mounds of Ohio. "While the enclosures impress us with the number and power of the nations which built them . . . the mounds and their contents, as disclosed by the mattock and the spade, serve to reflect light more particularly upon their customs and the condition of the arts among them," he tells us. "Within these mounds we must look for the only authentic remains of their builders. They are the principal depositories of ancient art; they cover the bones of the distinguished dead of remote ages; and hide from the profane gaze of invading races the altars of the ancient people."[108]

He indulges in some preliminary reflections on the universal human impulse to build mounds, catalogues the distribution of mounds around the world, and establishes categories for the American tumuli: "Altar Mounds," "Mounds of Sepulture," "Temple Mounds," and "Anomalous Mounds." Then he tackles each category in turn.

His class of Altar Mounds, he says, occurs only in the vicinity of "enclosures or sacred places." They are stratified, and they contain "symmetrical altars of

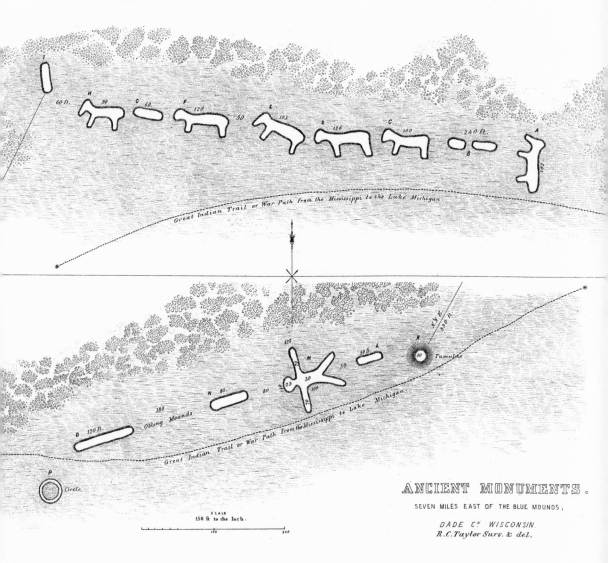

10 Diagram of Wisconsin effigy mounds. Squier and Davis, 1848.

burned clay or stone; on which are deposited various remains, which in all cases have been more or less subjected to the action of fire."[109] He illustrates this class of mounds with reference to the Mound City group, which, in 1847, was a group of twenty-six mounds within one enclosure, on the banks of the Scioto River three miles north of Chillicothe, Ohio. Squier and Davis had excavated many of these mounds by driving shafts through them from their summits, and the report Squier provides indicates that he and his colleague were the most painstaking observers of stratification since Thomas Jefferson. While modern archaeologists would find fault with many aspects of the Squier-Davis technique, they must certainly recognize the superiority of their reports to those of any of their contemporaries. This, for instance, is Squier's summary of the structure of one Mound City tumulus:

"It is seven feet high by fifty-five feet base. A shaft, five feet square, was sunk from its apex, with the following results:

"1st. Occurred a layer of coarse gravel and pebbles, which appeared to have been taken from deep pits surrounding the enclosure, or from the bank of the river. This layer was one foot in thickness.

"2d. Beneath this layer of gravel and pebbles, to the depth of two feet, the earth was homogeneous, though slightly mottled, as if taken up and deposited in small loads, from different localities. In one place appeared a deposit of dark-colored surface loam, and by its side, or covering it, there was a mass of the clayey soil from a greater depth. The outlines of these various deposits could be distinctly traced, as shown in Fig. 30.

"3d. Below this deposit of earth, occurred a thin and even layer of fine sand, a little over an inch in thickness.

"4th. A deposit of earth, as above, eighteen inches in depth.

"5th. Another stratum of sand, somewhat thinner than the one above mentioned.

"6th. Another deposit of earth, one foot thick; then—

"7th. A third stratum of sand; below which was—

"8th. Still another layer of earth, a few inches in thickness; which rested on—

"9th. An altar, or basin, of burned clay."[110]

Squier was careful to distinguish between the burials found at the bases of these mounds and the intrusive recent burials in their upper levels. Here he obeyed the precept of the English antiquary Sir Richard Colt Hoare (1758–1838), who, writing on the barrows and tumuli of Great Britain, had observed, "In the investigation of barrows, marks of interment are frequently found near the surface; but investigation must not terminate upon such a discovery. Experience has convinced me that these were subsequent interments, and that the primary deposit was always laid on the floor of the barrow, or within a cist in the native soil."[111] This was as reasonable a proposition in Ohio as it was in Wiltshire, and Squier emphasized it by way of avoiding the errors of some of his predecessors. Pointing out that it was an "almost invariable custom" of Indians to select "elevated points and the brows of hills as their cemeteries," Squier says, "that their remains should be found in the mounds, is therefore a matter of no surprise. They are never discovered at any great depth, not often more than eighteen inches or three feet below the surface. Their position varies in almost every case: most of them are extended at length, others have a sitting posture, while others again seem to have been rudely thrust into their shallow graves without care or arrangement."[112] He notes that "modern implements and ornaments, in some cases of European origin, are found with the recent burials. The necessity, therefore, of a careful and rigid discrimination, between these deposits and those of the mound-builders, will be apparent. From the lack of such discrimination, much misapprehension and confusion have resulted. Silver crosses, gun-barrels, and French dial-plates, have been found with skeletons in the mounds; yet it is not to be concluded that the mound-builders were Catholics, or used fire-arms, or understood French. . . . It may be safely assumed, that whatever deposits occur near the surface of the mounds, are of a date subsequent to their erection."[113]

This was good archaeological thinking as far as it went; but, carried to extremes, it could and did itself foster "misapprehension and confusion." Squier was correct in arguing that European artifacts found in the Ohio mounds were of necessity intrusive. In other regions, though, mound building had continued on into historic times—as indicated by the chroniclers of de Soto's expedition— yet the argument of intrusiveness could be used to controvert this, and make it seem as though even the Southern mounds were of great antiquity. And not even in Ohio were all burials in the upper strata of the mounds necessarily those of recent Indians.

After his lengthy and valuable exposition of his Mound City excavations, Squier passes to an account of his class of Mounds of Sepulture. "Mounds of this class are very numerous," he declares. "They are generally of considerable size, varying from six to eighty feet in height, but having an average altitude of from fifteen to twenty or twenty-five feet. They stand without the walls of enclosures, at a distance more or less remote from them. Many are isolated, with no other monuments near them; but they frequently occur in groups, sometimes in close connection with each other, and exhibiting a dependence which was probably not without its meaning. They are destitute of altars, nor do they possess that regularity which characterizes the temple mounds. Their usual form is that of a simple cone; sometimes they are elliptical or pear-shaped."[114]

He describes the contents of several large burial mounds on the Scioto south of Chillicothe, once more detailing the stratification and reporting the discovery, at a depth of 22 feet and on a level with the original surface of the ground, of "a rude sarcophagus or framework of timber, now reduced to an almost impalpable powder, but the *cast* of which was still retained in the hard earth. This enclosure of timber, measuring from outside to outside, was nine feet long by seven wide, and twenty inches high. It had been constructed of unhewn logs laid one upon the other, and had evidently been covered with other timbers, which had sunk under the superincumbent earth, as they decayed. The bottom had also been covered with bark, matting, or thin slabs of wood,—at any rate, a whitish stratum of decomposed material remained, covering the bottom of the parallelogram. Within this rude coffin, with its head to the west, was found a human skeleton, or rather the remains of one; for scarcely a fragment as long as one's finger could be recovered. It was so much decayed that it crumbled to powder under the lightest touch."[115] This was, apparently, a log tomb of what today is called the Adena Culture; its extreme state of decay served as one of the chief arguments for the cosmic antiquity of the Mound Builders, since archaeologists working in the Near East at the same time, excavating the remains of Assyrian palaces known to be at least twenty-five hundred years old, did not report a comparable situation.

Squier's survey of the class of Temple Mounds is brief because such flat-topped terraced mounds were rare in Ohio, and he did not have firsthand familiarity with those of the South. After a perfunctory analysis of his class of Anomalous Mounds—irregular ovals and possible lookout posts—Squier proceeds to his most original contribution, a lengthy stylistic consideration of the artifacts found in the mounds. No one had attempted such a survey before; and Squier's, misguided as it was, provided a point of departure for his successors.

He begins with pottery—"the first domestic art practised by man." Squier was familiar with many types of Indian pottery, from the crude ware of the North to the more sophisticated product of the Gulf Coast and the masterpieces of Mexico and Peru. Very little in the way of pottery had then come from the Ohio mounds, and almost none from those of the South, where artistic standards had been higher in prehistoric times. Yet Squier asserts, "Among the mound-builders the art of pottery attained to a considerable degree of perfection. Various though not abundant specimens of their skill have been recovered, which, in elegance of model, delicacy, and finish, as also in fineness of material, come fully up to the best Peruvian specimens, to which they bear, in many respects, a close resemblance."[116] In terms of the artifacts known in 1847, this was a notably overgenerous appraisal, and even the more extraordinary Arkansas and Tennessee pots unearthed a generation later fall well short of the Peruvian standard, though they have a certain raw power of their own. But the high rating Squier gives to Mound Builder pottery is part of his implied thesis; he insists that their pots "far exceed anything of which the existing tribes of Indians are known to have been capable," and the theme recurs as he takes up other classes of artifacts.

His views on metal implements from the mounds were more straight-forward. "The mound-builders were acquainted with several of the metals, although they do not seem to have possessed the art of reducing them from the ores," he states. "Implements and ornaments of copper are found in considerable abundance among their remains; silver is occasionally found in the form of ornaments, but only to a trifling amount; the ore of lead, galena, has been discovered in considerable quantities, but none of the metal has been found under such circumstances as to establish conclusively that they were acquainted with the art of smelting it. No iron or traces of iron, except with the recent deposits, have been discovered; nor is it believed that the race of the mounds had any knowledge of that metal. The copper and silver found in the mounds were doubtless obtained in their native state, and afterwards worked without the intervention of fire."[117] As we have seen, he rejected the possibility that the metal artifacts found by Hildreth at Marietta in 1819 indicated that the Mound fore; and Squier's, misguided as it was, provided a point of departure for his mind and supported that view.

With many fine woodcuts Squier depicts the copper axes, bracelets, and spear points from the mounds; he shows the finely wrought weapon points of chipped stone, some of them so delicate that they must have been purely ornamental pieces; he illustrates grooved axes of stone, and celts, or polished grooveless hand axes. He shows the odd, attractive stone implements called bannerstones, which he believed might have been the heads of ceremonial hatchets. (Their function still is a matter of doubt, though the most widely accepted theory is that they served as weights for *atlatls,* or spear throwers.) He portrays awls and needles of bone, and the curious stone objects known as discoidals, which were probably counters in a prehistoric game. He shows the stone pipes from the mounds, with their bowls rising from the centers of flat or convex platforms, and he presents details of Mound Builder beads of shell and the fresh-water pearls that bedazzled de Soto's followers. He describes a variety of "gorgets," flat pendant ornaments worn on necklaces, and shows the enigmatic, highly abstract "birdstones" found in many sites.

The stone implements, he says, "display no inconsiderable degree of taste and skill. There is, however, a large class of remains, comprising sculptural tablets, and heads and figures of animals, which belongs to a higher grade of art. Many of these exhibit a close observance of nature and a minute attention to details, such as we could only expect to find among a people considerably advanced in the minor arts, and to which the elaborate and laborious, but usually clumsy and ungraceful, not to say unmeaning, productions of the savage can claim but a slight approach."[118] Though Squier was quick to add "that nothing of the imposing character of many of the sculptured relics of Central America is found in the mounds," his strong advocacy of the esthetic superiority of Mound Builder art to that of the Indians was an important feature of the continuing controversy over the relation of those two "races." Squier claimed to see in the portrait sculptures from the mounds a beauty and strength that need not be denied; but he extrapolated from that an argument for the advanced nature of Mound Builder civilization that later archaeologists found a *non sequitur.*

Another controversial Squier conclusion stemmed from his attempt to trace migration routes or international communication channels from Mound Builder animal-effigy pipes. He identified certain animals of doubtful species as manatees, toucans, and other tropical exotics; but here he was severely challenged a generation later.

Squier sums up his view of Mound Builder relics by saying, "as works of art, they are immeasurably beyond anything which the North American Indians are known to produce, even at this day, with all the suggestions of European art and the advantages afforded by steel instruments."[119] But in this judgment he betrays his era's esthetic prejudices. What he dislikes about Indian art is that it makes much of "distorted caricatures," while Mound Builder works strike him as a higher rank because they are extremely realistic: "They display not only the figures and the characteristic attitudes, but in some cases . . . the very habits of the objects represented. So far as fidelity is concerned, many of them deserve to rank by the side of the best efforts of the artist-naturalists of our own day." It is difficult to see how he would have supported this line of argument if he knew of the grotesque, fantastic works of art that one day would be discovered in the giant mounds of the centers of the so-called Southern Cult.

He spends little time on the inscribed tablets from the mounds, with their alleged alphabetic and hieroglyphic messages. Noting that not even the Mexican civilizations had arrived at the use of writing, he comments, "It would be unwarrantable therefore to assign to the race of the mounds a superiority in this respect over nations palpably so much in advance of them in all others." Thus he casts into limbo the Grave Creek Tablet that so fascinated his correspondent Schoolcraft. Likewise he gives short shrift to six inscribed brass plates that had turned up in 1843 in a mound near Kinderhook, Illinois. These plates, bell-shaped and four inches in length, were fastened together by two corroded iron wires, and allegedly lay twelve feet below the surface of the mound. They bore "ancient characters" said to resemble Chinese. With the nation in the throes of the Mormon crisis, the discovery of the plates gained enormous notoriety, but, as Squier relates, "subsequent inquiry has shown that the plates were a harmless imposition, got up for local effect." The village blacksmith, taking his inspiration for the hieroglyphics from the lettering on the lid of a Chinese tea chest, had produced them.

11   The Cincinnati tablet. Engraving from *Ancient Monuments of the Mississippi Valley,* by E. G. Squier and E. H. Davis, 1848.

A tablet that Squier does not dismiss, and which archaeologists still consider authentic, is the Cincinnati Tablet, found in a mound in December, 1841. "The material is a fine-grained, compact sandstone, of a light brown color," Squier writes. "It measures five inches in length, three in breadth at the ends, two and six tenths at the middle, and is about an inch in thickness." Pondering the strange, seductive pattern of curves inscribed on the face of this tablet, Squier sidesteps a suggestion of Egyptian influence and the possibility that it represents some sort of calendar stone, and proposes tentatively that the tablet was a stamp used for imprinting ornaments on the clothing or skins of its makers.

Squier's section on crania from the mounds is based almost entirely upon the research of Dr. Samuel Morton. It is a little puzzling, in view of Morton's enthusiastic support for and praise of Squier and Davis, to find that their book employs his statistics while largely rejecting his conclusions. Despite Morton's belief in a single Indian race embracing both Mound Builders and modern aborigines, Squier speaks of "the race of the mounds" and depicts "the only skull incontestibly belonging to an individual of that race." Most of the skulls recovered from mounds Squier insists were intrusively buried; true "Mound Builder" skeletal evidence is rare because "the skeletons are almost invariably found at the base of the mounds, and in such a state of decay as to render all attempts to restore the skull, or indeed any part of the skeleton, entirely hopeless. The crania, when not so much decomposed as to crumble to powder beneath the touch, are crushed and flattened by the falling in of the sepulchral chambers, and by the weight of the superincumbent earth."[120] Squier did well to distinguish between ancient burials and modern ones; where he faltered was in his insistence on referring to a separate Mound Builder race, rather than seeing the Mound Builders as physical variants of the basic American Indian stock.

His "Concluding Observations" are brief and clearly stated. He expresses his belief in a populous, widespread civilization of Mound Builders, "essentially homogeneous, in customs, habits, religion, and government." He does not venture to decide whether "the ancient race was at one time diffused over the entire valley, or . . . migrated slowly from one portion of it to the other, under the pressure of hostile neighbors or the attractions of a more genial climate. The differences which have already been pointed out between the monuments of the several portions of the valley, of the northern, central, and southern divisions, are not sufficiently marked to authorize the belief that they were the works of separate nations."[121]

Skirting the subject of the origin and disappearance of the Mound Builders, Squier notes "a connection more or less intimate between the race of the mounds and the semi-civilized nations which formerly had their seats among the sierras of Mexico, upon the plains of Central America and Peru. . . ." The Mound Builders, though not as advanced as these people, "were also stationary and agricultural," he asserts. "It may safely be claimed, and will be admitted without dispute, that a large local population can only exist under an agricultural system. Dense commercial and manufacturing communities, the apparent exceptions to the remark, are themselves the offspring of a large agricultural population, with which nearly or remotely they are connected, and upon which they are dependent." The size and scope of such earthworks as the Newark embankments and the Cahokia Mound prove, for Squier, that the ancient population must have been exceedingly dense and thus agricultural, for, working with simple stone and wooden tools, thousands of men must have been employed in these projects. In this he follows the thinking of Albert Gallatin, who, correctly ascribing the origin of American aboriginal agriculture to the tropics, called agriculture "that first, difficult, and indispensable preliminary step before any advance whatever can be made towards civilization."

Gallatin had also observed of the great mound at Grave Creek that "it indicates not only a dense agricultural population, but also a state of society essentially different from that of the modern race of Indians north of the tropic." Squier regards both these propositions as truisms. So did most of his successors, until quite recent times; not until the 1950's did any archaeologists mount a challenge against the seemingly self-evident idea that the existence of vast mounds presupposes a well-developed agricultural system.

After some final thoughts on the possible functions of the enclosures and hilltop embankments, Squier turns to the question of the antiquity of the mounds. He brings forth the tree-ring evidence, and cites William Henry Harrison on the succession of trees in a second- or third-growth forest ecology. He introduces also an argument from geology of which much would be made by later writers: "The fact that none of the ancient monuments occur upon the latest-formed terraces of the river valleys of Ohio, is one of much importance in its bearings upon this question. If, as we are amply warranted in believing, these terraces mark the degrees of subsidence of the streams, one of the four which may be traced has been formed since those streams have followed their present courses. There is no good reason for supposing that the mound-builders would have avoided building upon that terrace, while they erected their works promiscuously upon all the others. And if they had built upon it, some slight traces of their works would yet be visible, however much influence we may assign to disturbing causes,—overflows, and shifting channels. . . . The time, since the streams have flowed in their present courses, may be divided into four periods, of different lengths,—of which the latest, supposed to have elapsed since the race of the mounds flourished, is much the longest."[122]

This admirable and classic study comes to a close on a note of uncertainty. Squier comments on the presence of exotic materials in the Ohio mounds— "native copper from Lake Superior, mica from the Alleghanies, shells from the Gulf, and obsidian (perhaps porphyry) from Mexico." These objects, denoting the existence of communication channels extending over a wide area of the continent, seem to him "seriously to conflict with the hypothesis of a migration, either northward or southward." And so, he concludes, "Further and more extended investigations and observations may, nevertheless, serve satisfactorily to settle not only this, but other equally interesting questions connected with the extinct race, whose name is lost to tradition itself, and whose very existence is left to the sole and silent attestation of the rude but often imposing monuments which throng the valleys of the West."[123]

6

Squier's Whigs finally won the election in 1848, the year his *Ancient Monuments of the Mississippi Valley* appeared. The Ohio newspaperman had become a national figure on the basis of his book—it is difficult for us to comprehend the impact that any sizable study of the Mound Builders had on Americans of the mid-nineteenth century—and the newly elected President Zachary Taylor saw a chance to further the cause of science while at the same time bestowing political patronage on a loyal supporter. He named Squier to be American charge d'affaires in Central America, thus allowing him to attempt to track the civilization of the Mound Builders to its source. Squier's career in Latin America was a long and notable one; he served in several diplomatic posts, found time to set up the Honduras Railroad Company, and carried on important archaeological investigations in Nicaragua and Peru, without, however, shedding new light on the Mound Builders.

Before leaving the United States, though, he returned to his native state of New York for a survey of the mounds of its western counties. His report, *Aboriginal Monuments of the State of New York,* written in 1849, appeared in the second volume of the *Smithsonian Contributions to Knowledge* series. In it Squier retracted some of his earlier statements, not merely on minor matters like the plating of silver, but on the nature and antiquity of some Mound Builders themselves. Although he continued to believe that the Ohio earthworks were products of a vanished race, he discovered to his surprise that those of western New York were much more recent:

"In full view of the facts before presented, I am driven to a conclusion little anticipated when I started upon my trip of exploration, that the earthworks of western New York were erected by the Iroquois or their western neighbors, and do not possess an antiquity going very far back of the discovery. Their general occurrence upon a line parallel to and not far distant from the lakes favors the hypothesis that they were built by frontier tribes, an hypothesis entirely conformable to aboriginal traditions. Here, according to these traditions, every foot of ground was contested between the Iroquois and Gah-kwahs, and other western tribes; and here, as a consequence, where most exposed to attack, were permanent defenses most necessary."[124] Thus he aligned himself, at least in part, with such "radicals" as Bishop Madison, Dr. McCulloh, and Henry Schoolcraft.

Another of Squier's projects before departing for Central America was to find a purchaser for his collection of Mound Builder artifacts. Here he did not do so well. He thought he had a deal with the New-York Historical Society, but at the last minute they refused to meet his price. The artifacts languished in dead storage in the Society's cellars until 1864, when they were purchased by William Blackmore of London. He intended to donate them to some worthy American museum, but was thwarted by the lack of a proper recipient. The logical place for the antiquities was the National Museum in Washington, D.C., an adjunct of the Smithsonian; but its Secretary, Joseph Henry, was just then engaged in a long and ultimately unsuccessful campaign to get his institution out of the museum business altogether. New York City's American Museum of Natural History did not yet exist; the state of Ohio had no facilities for displaying the material; and, after several attempts to place the relics in their native land, Blackmore let himself be persuaded by his brother to take them to England. There, in his home town, Salisbury, he founded the Blackmore Museum, which opened in September, 1867. (Later the mound relics were transferred to the British Museum.)

The Smithsonian could not extricate itself from the topic of the Mound Builders despite Secretary Henry's conspicuous lack of interest in the non-physical sciences. The third volume of the *Smithsonian Contributions to Knowledge* (1852) carried a paper by Charles Whittlesey, "Descriptions of Ancient Works in Ohio." Three years later, the seventh volume offered an essay by Increase A. Lapham on "Antiquities of Wisconsin." This was essentially a study of the effigy mounds of the Northern states; Lapham, in 1836, had been the first to detect the patterns of these mounds, although he was not the first to publish an account of them. He made his explorations under the auspices of the American Antiquarian Society, but through the agency of that group's librarian, Samuel F. Haven, Lapham's manuscript was turned over to the Smithsonian for publication.

In 1856, Haven's own views on the mounds appeared in the eighth of the *Smithsonian Contributions to Knowledge*. His lengthy article was entitled, "Archaeology of the United States, or Sketches Historical and Bibliographical, of the Progress of Information and Opinion Respecting Vestiges of Antiquity in the United States." As the title implies, it was not a report on original archaeological research, but an attempt at evaluating the work done on American prehistory up to that time. It was, one recent historian of the subject has said, "virtually the first attempt to write a history of American anthropology."[125]

Haven's approach is calm and judicious. He condemns those writers who have been "seduced into idle speculation founded on superficial resemblances" in trying to establish one or another foreign people as the authors of the mounds, and suggests that they should have been "seeking the answer in the mounds themselves." Considering the theories of Barton, Atwater, and Squier and Davis, Haven remarks that "none have led to a satisfactory solution."

His own notion of what a satisfactory solution would be lies close to the Madison-McCulloh-Schoolcraft outlook. He expresses the heretical view that the allegedly civilized and superior Mound Builders were not really so advanced at all; comparing the Ohio and Mississippi Valley structures with those of Mexico, Central America, and Peru, he observes, "There are no ruins of temples or other structures of stone, wrought by the hammer or the chisel, such as abound in Central America. There are no traces of roads and bridges to connect territorial divisions, or facilitate the commerce of an organized state, such as are found in Peru. There are no distinct evidences of arts and manufactures employing separate classes of population, or conducted as regular branches of industry. There are no proofs of the practice of reducing metals from their ores, and melting and carting them for use and ornament— none of a knowledge of chemistry or astronomy. . . . In a word, tokens of civil institutions, of mechanical employments, and the cultivation of science and literature however humbly such as appear among the remains of Mexico and Peruvian civilization, have no positive counterpart in the regions of which we are speaking. Whatever may have been the kind or degree of social advancement attained to by the ancient dwellers in the valleys of the Ohio and Mississippi, those domestic arts and habits of luxury which attend the division of labor and the accumulation of private wealth, had not been sufficiently developed to leave any symbols behind them."[126] Much later, in the 1877 *Report of the American Antiquarian Society,* Haven was even more explicit in his belief that it might be proved that the Mound Builders and the "red Indians" were of the same race.

7

Haven was perhaps too harsh on the mound folk, downgrading their abilities excessively to compensate for the exaggerations of most other observers. But his rational, circumspect assessment was a timely corrective; for another torrent of mythopoeic nonsense was then being unleashed upon the credulous American public. The children of the generation that had made Josiah Priest's absurd *American Antiquities and Discoveries in the West* the best seller of Andrew Jackson's era now rushed to confer the same success in the Millard Fillmore epoch upon William Pidgeon's farfetched *Traditions of De-coo-dah and Antiquarian Researches.*

The voluminous subtitle of this very queer book tells us a great deal about its nature and contents: *Comprising Extensive Explorations, Surveys, and Excavations of the Wonderful and Mysterious Earthen Remains of the Mound-Builders in America; the Traditions of the Last Prophet of the Elk Nation Relative to Their Origin and Use; and the Evidences of an Ancient Population More Numerous than the Present Aborigines.* Pidgeon, who claimed to be a trader with long experience among the Indians of the American West, registered his book for copyright in 1852, and the first edition appeared the following year; but it did not attain real notoriety until it was reissued in 1858 by the New York house of Horace Thayer. Pidgeon's fantasies, so appealing to the public, won no attention at all from professional archaeologists for twenty years; but then, in an insidious fashion, he began to turn up as a source cited in standard works on American archaeology, through the familiar process of the sanctification of myth by time.

Though Pidgeon had no idea whatever of how to organize themes to form a book, he was a vivid and compelling writer within the flamboyant tradition of his day, and that helped him win his wide audience. In his opening pages he strikes a good patriotic note, too, lamenting that Americans are too much concerned with antiquities of the Old World and ignore the wonders of their own land: "It yet remains for America to awake her story from sleep, to string the lyre and nerve the pen, to tell the tale of her antiquities, as seen in the relics of nations, coeval, perhaps, with the oldest works of man. This curious subject, although it is obscured beneath the gloom of ages, of which but little record remains, has nevertheless that record written in the dust, in the form of mighty mounds, aboriginal fortifications, and complicated tumuli, together with strange paintings, ancient skeletons, earthen effigies, and antique sculpture, that we imagine are worthy of rank among the most wonderful antiquities of the world. . . .

"Place the monuments, and secret repositories of the dead, together with the innumerable groups of complicated tumuli, and monstrous embankments, resembling fortifications, that abound in America, in any part of the Old World, and how would the virtuosi examine them, and the antiquarian fill volumes with their probable histories! . . . It would seem that no less ought to be expected at this day in America. While the traveller grows weary in Asia with tracing the time-worn trail of the centuries, or breaks the hard lava that encrusts the evidences of volcanic ruin, or sifts the dust in the desecrated catacombs of Egypt; or while the linguist reviews the history of primeval literature on the broken tablets recovered from long entombment in the vaults of time, why should less interest be manifested in the equally ancient relics of this broad country, which lie scattered in every state, and whose history is legibly written on the surface of her soil, from the Alleghany to the Pacific, in mighty mounds, strange effigies, and Herculean embankments?"[127]

The first builder of mounds, says Pidgeon, was Adam, who needed an altar upon which to offer sacrifices to the Lord. "It may scarcely be presumed," he says, "that mechanical knowledge, at so early an era in time, could have extended beyond the construction of the earthen mound." Noah, too, must have built mounds, and in the division of the earth among his three sons, Shem, Ham, and Japhet, the building of mounds was carried to every continent. Pidgeon rehearses the mound-building activities of Abraham and Lot, of the Israelites who erected "high places," and of Alexander the Great. He observes also that Alexander had extended his dominion to the New World: "Nor is this opinion founded in mere conjecture; on the contrary, it is sustained by an antiquarian record of literal import, discovered by a farmer of Monte Video, in Brazil, in 1827." This turns out to have been a flat stone inscribed in Greek with the name and date of Alexander's reign.

On the subject of pre-Columbian visits to the Americas, Pidgeon is the veriest of True Believers. A Roman coin supposedly found in Missouri and a Persian coin found on the banks of the Ohio establish the presence of Romans and Persians in the New World. The earthworks at Marietta, Ohio, seem to him "similar to the Roman camps described by Josephus . . . and various other earth-works, similar in construction, may be seen north to the lakes, and west to the Mississippi, west of which, we doubt whether the Romans ever held empire."[128] The circular enclosures he attributes to Danes and Saxons; he traces a continuous line of them from Sweden through England, Greenland, Pennsylvania, and lower Canada, to Wisconsin, "strong evidence of the migration of the Danes, Belgians, or Saxons, at some unknown era in time." He asks, "When we find on the shore of the Monongahela, or the highland of the Kickapoo, the identical Doom-ring [a circular earthwork] of Denmark, why should we hesitate to ascribe its origin to the ancient Dane?" And, "if the Dane, the Roman, and the Persian, may in the early times, have made their way to America, is it not rational to conclude that other nations may have done the same?"

He extends this "rational" process to show that large irregular earthworks are quite likely the product of emigrants from central Africa, that desiccated bodies found in Kentucky caves are mummies prepared according to ancient Egyptian techniques, and that Massachusetts' celebrated Dighton Rock displays "Phoenician letters, legibly engraved." The conch shells found in Western mounds become murex shells, from which Phoenicians once extracted a costly purple dye, and he follows Atwater in noting that the same shell "is known to have been highly esteemed by the Hindus." In six joyous pages, then, Pidgeon is "enabled to trace, amid the gloom of barbarian rule, the ancient existence of the Roman, the Grecian, the Persian, the Egyptian, the Phoenician, the Dane, and the Hindoo."[129]

Having established all this, Pidgeon proceeds to drop it almost completely. For most of his book he is concerned only with the fate of the Mound Builders and their replacement by the Indians, and contents himself with nothing more than vague implications that the Mound Builders were of European or Asian origin. "Less than three centuries ago," he writes, "North America was exclusively occupied by the red man of the woods. The very soil on which we tread and toil, three centuries ago sustained its millions of human beings without the aid of axe or plough. But whither have they gone? Forty-two tribes, familiarly known in the history of this country, within one century and a half, have become entirely extinct, and have scarcely left a trace of national existence behind them. Philanthropic statesmen may fold their arms, and tell us they are moving them west; but forty-two tribes bear mournful testimony to the fact, that we are moving them to eternity." If this sad fate is befalling the red man, he asks, how much more tragic is the doom that came over the red man's predecessor in our land? "It can not be any longer doubted that there has been a day when this continent swarmed with millions of inhabitants, when the arts and sciences flourished, when men lived, and labored, and reigned, and fought, and were in turn conquerors and conquered, subjects and kings, where now the deep silence of the forest has overcome all such evidences of life and civilization."[130] Pidgeon offers what he says is the authentic solution to the enigma of the Mound Builders' disappearance.

His interest in mounds, he relates, began in Frederic County, Virginia, in 1812. His "attention was arrested by the remains of an ancient stone-work that had previously been partially demolished by the removal of about four hundred wagon-loads of stone, used in the construction of a mill-dam in the vicinity."[131] He determined that this conical circular mound of stone "was an Indian cemetery, and for several years our reverence for the dead permitted it to remain without further desecration." Then an antiquarian friend informed him that the mound was clearly a "monument of national import" to its builders. His great-grandmother, the antiquarian said, had been held many years in captivity by the Indians, and had learned their traditions, among them one that held that such mounds were "dedicated to the great, containing only the relics of great kings, prophets, and chiefs of signal renown, that were gathered together periodically, and deposited in strata from time to time until the monument was full, when a new cemetery was commenced." This excited Pidgeon's youthful curiosity sufficiently to extinguish his reverence for the dead, and with some schoolmates he opened the mound and found it full of brittle, decaying bones. The discovery "engendered a desire for the acqusitions of Indian tradition that thirty-five years has failed to entirely satiate."

Pidgeon came to see, he declares, that the stone mound was Indian work, built in imitation of the more ancient earthen mounds. That led him to realize that "the successors of the mound-builders, either more or less remotely, were the North American Indians. Through them, should it be possible to recover any traditionary history, there might be a dim and uncertain, but still a welcome light thrown into the darkness of that oblivion which has hitherto enveloped" the Mound Builders.

But it was a while before he could undertake the recovery of this "traditionary history." After raiding every stone mound he could find in Virginia, Pidgeon departed for South America in 1826. In Venezuela he found truncated mounds resembling those of the southern United States, and visited a circular earthwork similar in outline though not in construction to that of Circleville, Ohio. These South American mounds, not otherwise recorded in archaeological literature, stirred Pidgeon to imagined views of "the habitations of a great people."[132]

In the spring of 1829, he set up shop as an Indian trader in Ohio's Miami Valley, and, having become much interested in tumuli and earthworks, visited all the adjacent sites. His base of operations was near Fort Ancient, the hilltop earthwork some thirty-five miles northeast of Cincinnati, and his "thirst for investigation was continually augmented by frequent conversations with antiquarians and curious travellers" who visited this "stupendous and wonderful" embankment. It seemed to Pidgeon that most of the researchers were in error in their opinions of the Ohio mounds, but he had as yet no theories of his own to put forth.

"In 1837, 1838, and 1839," he relates, "business pursuits led me to the immediate valley of the Upper Mississippi. There I soon observed that the mound-builders, in the construction of their works, had indulged in innumerable freaks of fancy, wholly unlike anything I had hitherto seen. . . . Perceiving that those mounds which were most remote from civilization retained their primitive form in greatest perfection, I resolved to make a tour of exploration in the unfrequented wilds of the west; and, in the spring of 1840, I repaired to the city of St. Louis, whence I embarked on the steamer Illinois for Galena, in the early part of April."[133]

At Galena, a bustling commercial community, he "might have been almost persuaded that I was in the midst of Jerusalem on a pentecostal day, for here were Jews out of almost every nation under heaven, together with natives of England, Ireland, France, Spain, and Germany—a truly motley mass of various creeds and tongues, yet all bound together by a common pecuniary interest." This "infant city," the last outpost of civilization in its parts, did not hold him long: "I secured a passage on board the steamer Otter, bound for the shot-tower at Helena, on the eastern shore of the Wisconsin river." The vessel touched at the "flourishing village" of Dubuque, fought its way upstream in the Mississippi against late spring floods, and entered the Wisconsin. At the village of Muscoda, Wisconsin, then occupied by "a few white families" and not much larger today, Pidgeon observed "relics of many an ancient mound, varying much in size and form; some resembling redoubts, or fortifications, others presenting the forms of gigantic men, beasts, birds, and reptiles, among which may be found the eagle, the otter, the serpent, the alligator, and others pertaining to the deer, elk, and buffalo species."[134] After remaining some days to examine these mounds, Pidgeon returned on the *Otter* to the "somewhat dilapidated" old village of Prairie du Chien, where the American Fur Company kept a trading post and the United States had a garrison "for the protection of the frontier settlements." He tarried awhile among the friendly French trappers and half-breed Indians of this outpost, and through them came to know the Indians of the vicinity. He learned their language, attended several of their feasts, and visited them frequently.

Pidgeon's Indian friends were displeased when he began to excavate in the mounds of Wisconsin. It developed that he was digging in "the graves of their departed friends, many of whom they had here, in imitation of their white neighbors, deposited in mounds. Some of them tendered their services to guide me to works equally interesting to me, and less sacred to them."[135] They brought him to a "flat embankment one hundred and thirty feet square, with an oval mound on the top, having an elevation of fourteen feet, the flat embankment being two feet and a half high. On sinking a spade in the small mound, I discovered that it was composed of ashes, small particles of charcoal, and sand. . . ." Pidgeon rolled up his sleeves and began to dig, while his

Indian companions sat by, grinning. Soon he came to the clay core of the mound. "But being much fatigued with my labor, I retired to the shade of a small tree which grew near by to rest myself; and while sitting there, wondering within myself what the anticipated relic would prove to be, an aged Winnebago squaw, whom curiosity had drawn to the spot, ascended the mound to view the excavation. She shook her blanket, and approached me; and, perceiving that I was fatigued, she presented to me a bladder filled with whiskey, and desired me to drink. I drank sparingly, and returned to my labor. She followed me to the pit, and looking into it, she thus addressed me—'Ah, how-she-mo-ko-mon, wah-wonk; cow-ean shu-rah; she-mo-ko-mon, sketch-ah-waw-wonk;' being interpreted, 'Ho, white man, you are a fool! There is no money there. White man, you are a very great fool!' and she went away, amid peals of laughter from the surrounding group."

12 De-Coo-Dah. Engraving from *Traditions of De-Coo-Dah,* by William Pidgeon, 1858.

The old squaw indeed had the last laugh, for the mound turned out to contain nothing of interest. But soon Pidgeon had more reliable guidance. While staying at Prairie la Cross, he learned that "an aged Indian acquainted with the history of the mounds, whose name was De-coo-dah, a man of undoubted veracity, revered and respected by those that knew him," had arrived to take part in a tribal festival. Shortly Pidgeon obtained an introduction to De-coo-dah, and through an interpreter explained to the formidable old man that he had come to survey and sketch the mounds, and wished to know their significance, so that coming generations might understand the history of the early occupants of the continent.

De-coo-dah expressed his anger at white men, who, he said, cared little for the mounds and destroyed them at whim or for their convenience. "Why does not the white man leave the record on the earth where it belongs?"

"Most of white men," replied Pidgeon, "care but little about things that are not directly connected with their real or imaginary pecuniary interest; but there are some white men that delight in promoting the welfare of others."

Pondering that, De-coo-dah looked Pidgeon full in the face for a minute, and, turning to the interpreter, exclaimed, "A good man—a good white man!" Pidgeon goes on, "Again fixing on me his eyes that now beamed with benevolence, he added, 'The red man's friend,' and extended his hand. I received it with a cordial grasp; he drew from his belt the big pipe of friendship, of antique structure, formed with a double tube for the admission of two stems, and asked for tobacco. I handed him a small plug, which he took, and after mixing it with bark, and rubbing them well together, filled the big pipe, introduced two stems, each about two feet long, sat down in front of me on a mat, and asked me to smoke with him. . . . We soon filled the wigwam with the fumes of friendship."[136]

Thus began Pidgeon's relationship with the man he calls his "adopted father." Through the winter of 1840–41, and again in 1841–42, they lived together in a cabin on an island near Prairie du Chien.

"De-coo-dah," says Pidgeon, "was of low stature, unusually broad across the shoulders and breast, his complexion somewhat darker than the Winnebago, with a large mouth and short chin; his limbs were well-proportioned, and he possessed undaunted courage. I furnished him with food and shelter from the inclemency of two severe winters, and he, in return, imparted to me many traditions not held or known by Indians of the present age. He remained several months with me before he spoke of traditions, using many stratagems to ascertain whether I was trustworthy or not. After satisfying himself on that point, he introduced the subject of traditions, by asking of me whether white men held tradition sacred. I told him that some white men possessed secrets which they did not tell to all."[137]

Among the secrets revealed by De-coo-dah, and which the trustworthy Pidgeon eventually published for the entertainment of thousands of palefaces, was the fact that "he claimed no lineal kindred with any nation now in existence, but was a descendant from the Elk nation, now extinct; that they were a mixed nation, claiming descent from those ancient Americans, the mound-builders; and that their traditions were sacredly kept by their prophets, from a family of whom he was descended."

Mound burial was one of those traditions. The making of effigy mounds was another. So, too, was the erection of mounds to mark great national events, such as the holding of the annual festival. De-coo-dah, who claimed to be in his eighty-ninth winter, said he had learned of these things from his great-grandfather, who had died seventy-eight years earlier at the age of one hundred fifteen. "My great-grandfather," De-coo-dah told Pidgeon, "had a great reverence for mounds; and said, that a new mound was erected at each national festival; that national festivals were frequently attended and held in union by several nations; and that at the place appointed for those union festivals, each nation erected a national monument significant of their number and dignity."

Pidgeon now sets forth, via De-coo-dah, a symbology of the mounds that for all its incoherence has about it the fascination of lunacy, like some monstrous bridge constructed of toothpicks. The revelation begins with an account of the so-called Amalgamation Mound, on the Wisconsin River about fifty miles above its junction with the Mississippi. This, according to Pidgeon, is a group of effigy reliefs and conical mounds stretching several hundred feet, presenting in outline the forms of two gigantic beasts, together with a well-delineated human figure. It was constructed, he asserts, "as a national hieroglyphic record, to commemorate an important event in the history of two ancient nations. These nations, once great and powerful, had become greatly reduced in numbers and resources by the adverse fortunes of war against a common enemy. Being no longer in a condition to maintain separately their national existence, they resolved to unite their forces, subject to one great head or Sovereign Ruler. And this earth-work was constructed as the great seal and hieroglyphic record of their union and amalgamation."[138]

De-coo-dah interprets the hieroglyphics. ("Horns appended to effigies represent warriors. One horn being longer than the other, shows one nation to have been the stronger of the two; and one horn having more prongs than the other, represents one nation as having more celebrated chiefs than the other, while some prongs, being longer than the others, represent some of the greater and more distinguished chiefs.") Truncated mounds were sacrificial altars; the figure pointing to the west symbolized the setting sun of the amalgamating nations; the human figure looking up at the noon sun stood for the greatness of the united powers. A stately oak firmly rooted in the bosom of the mound told Pidgeon that at least four centuries had gone by since its construction; but, he adds sourly, "The tree has since been removed and converted into shingles, and, in 1844, it formed a canopy over the drunken revels of Muscoda."

According to De-coo-dah, one earthwork is a "mound of extinction," marking the end of the nation symbolized by a buffalo effigy; for the Buffalo nation was uniting with the Elk nation when this mound was erected. The left forelimb of the buffalo is connected with the foot of the elk effigy. Nearby are "seven truncated mounds running east from the national mound." They are *"matrimonial memorials,* recording the international marriages of seven chiefs, which occurred during the erection of the work." And so on, for many more pages of detail about amalgamation monuments, in which two or more animal effigies are joined. Three small mounds extending from the third matrimonial memorial denote the birth of three children; the great length of the arms of the human figure represents immense territorial dominion; the even elevation of both arms signifies the equal status of the Buffalo and Elk nations in the merger. "Thus aided by tradition," comments Pidgeon, "we read in the hieroglyphical mounds of the earth, the dignity and destiny of nations unknown to written history," and he hopes that "a comparatively small portion of the funds expended in superficial surveys" of the mounds will go instead to "the acquisition of Indian traditions from the more secluded sons of the forest."[139]

Armed with the teachings of De-coo-dah, Pidgeon describes his interpretations of the four hundred earthworks he claims to have visited in the effigy-mound country, as well as the more familiar ones of Ohio. Fort Ancient is the first to be discussed. Pidgeon quickly disposes of the notion that this embankment could have been constructed "by the ancestors of the present race of Indians. The natural indolence of the Indian and his averseness to any kind of manual labor are well known. But these works bear testimony to a degree of enterprise and of patient industry, that would bring no discredit to any race or nation known to history."[140] Nor does he accept the common assumption that Fort Ancient's purpose was defensive. He disagrees with the diagram published by Squier and Davis, though praising the general excellence of their work, and challenges their interpretation of the "fort." He says that while a superficial examination supports the idea that the embankment was a military fortification, "when we reflect how few and simple were the implements of ancient warfare, we can not easily convince ourselves that so great labor could have been thus needlessly expended in the construction of a work which could not have materially contributed to the protection of its inmates."

From De-coo-dah he learns that the proper name of Fort Ancient is Moon City, and that its walls "were constructed by the successive labors of a long line of kings or rulers." Its purpose was religious: Pidgeon deduces from its name and crescent shape that it was a center for lunar worship. He comments on the twenty-five breaches or openings in the wall of the southern enclosure—certainly a superfluity of interruptions in an ostensibly defensive wall. "These are supposed by some to have been designed for gates or passways; by others, to have been the sites of block-houses, or places for lookout or of defence. But it appears evident to us . . . that these openings have all been made by the ravages of time, aided by the uprooting of trees which formerly grew upon the embankment, the wash of water, and the trail of men and beasts."[141] (The openings in Fort Ancient's wall have been a source of mystery to others trying to fathom the function of the enclosure. But the latest theory has come full circle—that the structure was a fort, and that the gaps in the wall are the sites of vanished wooden gates and blockhouses.)

The complex Newark enclosures, says Pidgeon, once comprised "a prophet's metropolis, or holy seminary of priests or prophets, with its holy circles, festival square, secluded walks, private avenues, and funeral-piles. The five residential circles were the permanent abodes of the senior fathers, who were appointed by the people to impart instruction to the junior prophets. These latter inhabited, in common, the pyramidal mounds within the octagon. To the octagon is appended a holy festival circle, known as such by its peculiar manner of construction, being formed with two avenues, the one from without, and the other communicating with the octagon. Upon the pyramidal altar, adjacent to the cluster of symbols of deities, was consumed the evening sacrifice offered at the appearance of each new-moon."[142] Near Chillicothe, De-coo-dah identified "the ruling prophet's resident circle," "the holy city," "the celestial city," and "the royal union city." When Pidgeon presented the aged De-coo-dah with a diagram he had previously made of the Circleville earthwork, "his eyes beamed with delight, and he exclamed, 'Sci-o-tee!' But when I informed him that a populous village now stood within the walls of the ancient enclosure, his frame trembled with emotion, and his visage grew dark with anger. I observed his excited state, and sought to change the subject. But my efforts were in vain, for memories of that ancient work seemed to engross all his thoughts. He soon, however, became more composed, and again repeated, as if to himself, 'Sci-o-tee!' . . . With an apparently unconscious movement of his hand toward the handle of his knife, he asked, 'Do the bones of my fathers rest in peace?' "[143]

Pidgeon reassured him, alas, in error, that the earthworks of Circleville were intact; and De-coo-dah, greatly relieved, provided an account of his visit to that ceremonial center seventy-six winters previously. Much is made of its system of matrimonial mounds.

In warmer weather, so Pidgeon relates, he and De-coo-dah visited many of the obscure effigy mounds of Wisconsin. At one, on the Kickapoo River thirty miles northeast of Prairie du Chien, Pidgeon beheld a "Sacrificial Pentagon," three to five feet high, twelve to sixteen feet thick at the base, and 1,200 feet in circumference. This drew from De-coo-dah a discourse on the symbolic values of the embankment's shape, as well as an account of human sacrifice among the Mound Builders. ("The victim, self-appointed, or determined by lot, as the case might be, repaired to the tent of the senior prophet, who, aided by his four junior associates, painted the face and adorned the body of the favored victim with a covering of the mistletoe, that being the holiest and most rare of evergreens.")[144]

At another time Pidgeon and De-coo-dah made a two-day canoe journey to a mound metropolis on the Bad-Axe River, where De-coo-dah "stopped suddenly at the base of a mound, and placing his right hand on his heart, and his left on his forehead, muttered, inaudibly, a short sentence, with his face westward." Following further gesticulations he cried out, "Alla Sha-lah, lu-lah; Alla Sha-lah, me-nah," which Pidgeon translates, "Great Spirit, save the king; Great Spirit, save the people." Next the old man "ascended to the summit, uttered a shrill war-whoop, and . . . began to sing and dance; at which he continued until, quite exhausted with exercise, he fell on his face and lay motionless."

At a third site De-coo-dah showed Pidgeon "memorials of migration. . . . Here we behold the six animal effigies, slightly differing in form, symbolizing the migration of the six tribes, and absence of tail to each effigy, records the circumstance that a portion of each tribe was dismembered and left behind. In their migration south, they tarried in these regions until after the death of their leader, as indicated in the human effigy." Buffalo and eagle effigies in the group tell the story of quarrels among the tribes, reconciliations, the succession of dynasties, marriages, and a good deal more. One group constitutes a record of twenty-two successive sovereigns and the extinction of their line. Another depicts the careers of ninety-six rulers belonging to six dynasties.

Out of all this there emerges the history of the Elk nation, builders of the

mounds. The combination of De-coo-dah's garrulousness and Pidgeon's in-
ability to tell any story in logical sequence makes the details a little difficult
to follow, however. It is particularly hard to identify Pidgeon's non-Indian
nation of Mound Builders, the Elks, with any of the various Phoenician, Egyptian, Persian, Greek, or Roman visitors he documented in the early part of the
book. What he does say is that De-coo-dah is virtually the last survivor of the
Elks, whose dispersion and downfall had occurred shortly before the landfall of
Columbus.

The valley of the Mississippi, according to De-coo-dah, "was, by his great-
grandfather's grandfather, traditionally spoken of to his grandfather as having
been the primitive residence of their nation, four hundred winters before the
birth of his father, which took place two hundred and thirteen winters gone by.
'So you perceive,' said De-coo-dah, 'it is more than six hundred winters since
this last dispersion. At the time of this general dispersion, the primitive Elk
nation, originally a branch or tribe of the ancient American, had become
mingled and amalgamated with the race of the red men from the south. A
portion of the original Elks, however, yet remained pure in blood, and returned
to the east, to unite with a remnant of the nation that occupied a territory
bordering on the rocky hills [the Allegheny mountains].' "[145]

There follows a jumbled account of civil strife "during the reign of the
great De-co-ta, who was a usurper, descended from the Black Tortoise nation,
which came from the south." Assassinations, fratricide, the destruction of
dynasties, the quarrels of "nations" hitherto unknown—all this had a powerful effect on Pidgeon's readers. It was as though he had unearthed a new *Iliad,*
and De-co-ta was a second Agamemnon. The tale, which is somewhat diminished in power by its incoherence, proceeds to tell of the division of the Elk
nation among three kings, Red-Deer, Black-Wolf, and Little-Otter, all grand-
sons of the murdered De-co-ta the Great. "The descendants of Little-Otter,"
De-coo-dah relates, "were probably the last in the great valley of the Mississippi
to relinquish the ancient form of hieroglyphical record. After his death, his
kingdom being divided between two chiefs only, its power and resources were
not greatly impaired; those two chiefs, the Black-Bear and the Big-Buffalo,
being highly honored and esteemed, lived at peace with each other for a long
time; and their people not being divided into small bands, continued to erect
memorial, matrimonial, and title-mounds, so long as they remained united.

"It was not until after this change in the form of government had taken
place, that festival mounds were erected by single bands. The bands being
generally small in comparison with the nations to which they had formerly
belonged, the erection of mounds became more difficult in consequence of the

increased amount of labor required to be performed by each individual. . . .

"Having lost sight of ancient order, those more modern union celebrations frequently engendered strife, and sometimes gave rise to murders that called for revenge. Thus the seeds of war were again sown." Further strife resulted in the construction of dozens of new mounds commemorating battles and dynastic changes. ("The Bald-Eagle was succeeded by lineal succession of Eagles through six generations, monumentally recorded on the highlands of the Kickapoo and Wisconsin. The sixth Eagle, however, was slain by the Big-Weasel, who succeeded him, and divided the command with the Red-Lion, his twin brother. . . .")

A *götterdämmerung* of the Mound Builders became inevitable; in a final conflict the quarreling chiefs destroyed one another and the survivors dispersed in small tribal bands. "After this final dispersion of the northern tribes, monumental commemorations ceased. The mound being the hieroglyphical sign through which the traditions were taught, and the knowledge of past events preserved, gradually losing its importance, came eventually to be looked upon with cold indifference. And thus the great fountain of tradition being dried up, it is by no means matter of wonder that its streams have ceased to flow."[146]

In his interpretation of these traditions Pidgeon finds "the evidences of a plurality of nations anterior to the occupation of North America by the modern Indian race. We suppose the Mississippi to have been the point at which those different nations came in contact with each other, from the fact that at that point a marked difference appears in the general form of their tumular monuments, and, moreover, the amalgamation or mixture of forms in the construction of those mounds or embankments exists to a greater extent along this river, than in any other region. . . . That those nations, differing in customs, came first in collision with each other at or near the junction of the Missouri with the Mississippi, is evident from the fact that as we go south from that point, the tumuli gradually partake of the pyramidal form, resembling those found in Mexico, South America, &c., and representing in miniature, the tumuli of Africa. On the contrary, as we advance north and east, the pyramidal form gradually sinks to the low conical, or flat mound, presenting many circles, squares, and triangular groups and embankments, resembling those found in the north of Europe."[147]

Pidgeon suggests that two great powers—one Danish, perhaps, and one Mexican?—waged war in North America until both were enfeebled and reduced in numbers. The Southern race of Mound Builders then "fell an easy prey to the wandering hordes (probably of Asiatic origin), who assailed them from the south"—the American Indians. The builders of truncated pyramids were absorbed and merged into the race of their red-skinned conquerors, Pidgeon says, and then the united powers turned against "the tribes of the north (probably of European descent.)" These, evidently, were De-coo-dah's Elks. New hostilities gave rise to new amalgamations, and then a dispersion of the tribes, a cessation of mound building, and the loss of the ancient traditions.

Through this kind of glib entangling of myths, Pidgeon was able to draw together virtually every story that had been told about the Mound Builders except the thesis that they were the Lost Tribes of Israel. He could imagine vast battles of ancient kingdoms; he could denigrate the Indians in the customary fashion; he could ascribe the mounds vaguely to Europeans and Mexicans. When necessary, he could blandly contradict his own statements: for, having said that the tradition of mound building had died out, he goes on to describe the death of De-coo-dah in 1842 and his interment in a burial mound west of Lake Superior. (Although Pidgeon had refrained from further mound excavations while dwelling with De-coo-dah, in deference to the old man's "aversion

13 An Ancient American battle-mound. Engraving from *Traditions of De-Coo-Dah,* by William Pidgeon, 1858.

. . . to the desecration of the monuments of his remote ancestors," he tells us that he lost no time sinking a shaft in the Amalgamation Mound and another in the Sacrificial Pentagon once the Elk prophet was dead.)

There is a good deal more to this fanciful work. One of the high points is De-coo-dah's description of the annual festival to celebrate the union of the ancient tribes. ("The oldest chief of the nations ascended the central mound, and sang a song of union. The four nations joined in the chorus, each in its own language. The clash of voices, and the absence of all harmony in this wild song, with its returning echoes, struck the ear in a confusion of harsh sounds, that seemed almost to make the trees of the forest shake."[148] Another is Pidgeon's theory, outlined in the closing pages, of the extinction of the Mound Builders through the sudden inundation of half the continent by a great flood. This remarkable concept involves the invention of a gigantic reservoir in the Blue Ridge Mountains, formed by the influx of the waters of the Delaware, Hudson, Schuylkill, James, Potomac, and Susquehannah rivers. Somehow, he

says, the mountains rimming this huge lake may have given way all at once; "nothing can be more reasonable than that the entire submersion of the lower country followed in quick succession, sweeping with the besom of destruction, man with all his works."[149] He adduces as proof of this the discovery of a whale skeleton far inland, evidently a stray from the Atlantic, who swam across the mountains on the breast of the vanished lake.

Traditions of De-coo-dah, then, is a crazy masterpiece of pseudoscience, the epitome of the grand era of humbug typified by Pidgeon's contemporary, P. T. Barnum. With delightful audacity Pidgeon orginally offered his manuscript to Joseph Henry for publication in the *Smithsonian Contributions to Knowledge;* the Smithsonian rejected it indignantly, whereupon Pidgeon turned to a commercial publisher and made a fortune with the book. For twenty years it was the object of fascination for laymen and bitter amusement for archaeologists; but then it achieved a brief but terrifying period of spurious respectability.

The first to lend credence to Pidgeon was Hubert Howe Bancroft, San Francisco's merchant-turned-historian, whose five-volume *Native Races of the Pacific States* appeared in 1875. Employing platoons of anonymous assistants, Bancroft digested whole libraries of sources to produce his voluminous works of history, and occasionally some odd things slipped through—as in his discussion of the effigy mounds of Wisconsin, "on which Lapham and Pidgeon are the prominent authorities."[150] A. J. Conant's *Footprints of Vanished Races* (1879) reproduced five of Pidgeon's diagrams of geometrical earthworks, three of his plans of effigy mounds, and a good deal of his "traditions." Ellen Russell Emerson's *Indian Myths* (1884) relied heavily on the tales told by De-coo-dah. The Marquis de Nadaillac's well-received *Prehistoric America* (1884) used seven of Pidgeon's diagrams by way of the Conant work.

In all this time apparently no one had actually gone to Wisconsin to check on the existence of Pidgeon's various hieroglyphic patterns of mounds. The job was undertaken in October, 1884, by T. H. Lewis of St. Paul, Minnesota, who reported on his findings in the January 1886 issue of *The American Journal of Archaeology.* Lewis, a surveyor, happened to be passing through a district on the Minnesota River where Pidgeon had located an "extensive group of tumuli and embankments . . . designed to commemorate the title and dignity of a great king or potentate." This group, the "Monumental Tortoise" mounds, included, according to Pidgeon, a central embankment in the form of a tortoise, 40 feet long, 27 feet wide, and 12 in height. "It is composed in part, of yellow clay, which was evidently procured at some distant place. The mounds of extinction (north and south of the central tortoise), are formed of pure, red earth, covered with alluvial soil, and are very perfect in form, each being twenty-seven feet in length, and six in greatest height. . . .[151] Nearby were "points of royal honor," "prophets' burial-mounds," "war-chiefs' burial-memorials," and other structures, all arranged in a markedly symmetrical pattern.

Lewis found a group of mounds, after a thorough search, at approximately the place Pidgeon had described. Since they were the only mounds in the vicinity, there could be no doubt that this was Pidgeon's "Monumental Tortoise" group. Lewis did indeed find the central "tortoise" effigy, but there, he wrote, the resemblance between what Pidgeon claimed to see and what existed ceased. "His heights and dimensions," said Lewis, "were undoubtedly mere estimates, and very poor ones at that. But how account for mounds of shapes so radically different from those that any other man ever heard of before or since our author's time? Or why so many more mounds represented than actually exist immediately around this central mound or tortoise?"

Lewis proceeded to visit and survey other mound groups mentioned by Pidgeon in southwestern Wisconsin and northeastern Iowa, as well as to interview many old settlers who remembered him. "I do not want to be understood as charging Mr. Pidgeon with a deliberate and intentional fabrication of arrangements and conformations of earthworks," Lewis declared. "But I have reason to know that it is not safe to quote his statements as authority." And, on a later page, he concluded in a more emphatic manner, "The result of all my researches in this respect is to convince me that the Elk nation and its last prophet De-coo-dah are modern myths, which have never had any objective existence; and that, consequently, the ancient history in the volume is of no more account than that of the Lost Tribes in the Book of Mormon."

8

The great debate on the Mound Builders raged on through the 1850's and 1860's. Throughout the world, the modern era in archaeology was beginning, and what had been the private province of antiquaries and scholars now excited extreme popular interest. The clank of picks and shovels was heard everywhere. In Egypt, such men as Auguste Mariette and Richard Lepsius were systematically assaulting the precincts of the Pharaohs. In Turkish-held Mesopotamia, a dashing young man named Austen Henry Layard had begun to dig in mounds along the Tigris in 1845, and shortly announced to a dazzled world that he had unearthed the Assyrian city of Nineveh. Layard's account of his work, published in 1848, was the literary success of the decade; everyone read it, everyone talked of Nineveh.

Charles Darwin's *Origin of Species,* propounding a Bible-subverting theory of evolution, was published in 1859. Two years earlier, the discovery of a strange, deformed-looking human skull at a place in Germany called Neanderthal had provided possible evidence of man's ancestral form. Archbishop Ussher's calculation that the world had been created in 4004 B.C. was destroyed. And still the archaeological revolution went on. In 1870, Heinrich Schliemann began the job of uncovering Homer's Troy, while other men looked thoughtfully toward Syria, Crete, and the Holy Land.

All at once, so it seemed, not merely the early historical era but prehistory itself lay bare. It was a confusing, exciting, bewildering time, when old concepts were swept away with each morning's newspapers, and the past suddenly seemed uncertain and transient. New syntheses were necessary. The public demanded popular and semipopular books that would impose some order on the chaos of new ideas of man's antiquity.

The notion that the world was many thousands or even millions of years old was stunning and disturbing. The related idea that man himself was of great antiquity, and had passed through several evolutionary stages on his way toward his present form, was even more disconcerting. For those who believed in vanished Mound Builders, though, the new chronology offered an apparent confirmation. Suddenly there was room in the past for forgotten empires of all sorts. Enthusiastic partisans of the Mound Builders thrust their heyday back to the dawn of time, and said that tens of thousands of years had elapsed since their downfall and the arrival of the American Indians. As early as 1799, Benjamin Smith Barton had suggested this heretical possibility; within sixty years it no longer seemed like heresy.

The archaeological findings coming from the Old World helped to bolster this enhancement of the Mound Builder myth. In 1848, G. R. Gliddon rushed out a book which, though entitled *Ancient Egypt,* dealt in good measure with Layard's just-published report on his Assyrian work. "From the ruins of Nineveh and Babylon," Gliddon wrote, "we have bones of at least two thousand five hundred years old; from the pyramids and the catacombs of Egypt both mummied and unmummied crania have been taken, of still higher antiquity, in perfect preservation; nevertheless, the skeletons deposited in our Indian mounds, from the Lakes to the Gulf, are crumbling into dust through age alone." Gliddon did not pause to consider that the difference between the desert climates of Egypt and Mesopotamia and the temperate climate of North America might have something to do with the relative states of preservation; and this argument from deterioration became an important peg, for a while, in the structure upholding the antiquity of the Mound Builders.

Another significant development was the discovery in America of the bones of the extinct ancestral elephants known as mammoths and mastodons. Thomas Jefferson had been the first to publish accounts of mastodons, giant ground sloths, and other relics of a vanished American fauna. By 1838, a professional dealer in fossils named Albert Koch had come upon a site in Missouri where the charred bones of a mastodon lay in association with broken spears, axes, and stone knives, very much as though the huge beast had been slaughtered and roasted for a prehistoric barbecue. This was the first time that anyone had shown human relics associated with mastodon remains, and the discovery might have been of pivotal value in establishing the fact of man's antiquity in the Americas, but for Koch's showmanlike traits; he was the Barnum of paleontology, and no one ever took him seriously.

Montroville Wilson Dickeson—he of the panorama of the mounds—in 1846 reported finding a human pelvis in association with the bones of mastodon, sloth, and other extinct animals near Natchez, Mississippi. This, too, seems to have been an authentic discovery, though Dickeson's reputation did not encourage many scientists to accept it. The question of man's relationship to the mastodon remained an open one for many years more; and, as occasionally happens, the eccentrics and cranks generally took the point of view that time has proved correct, while the cautious men of science were wrong. Man and mastodon *had* been contemporaries in North America, although this was not satisfactorily and indisputably demonstrated until the twentieth century.

Those who believed in Mound Builders a century ago also believed in the contemporaneousness of man and mastodon; the two romantic theories, one a myth and one a fact, were indissolubly conjoined. But in the imperfect state of archaeological knowledge of that era, it was possible to prove any sort of conclusion with the evidence at hand. If one assumed that the Mound Builders were hunters of mastodons, and that mastodons had become extinct many thousands of years ago, then it followed that the Mound Builders were of great antiquity. If one assumed that mastodons and giant ground sloths had died out around the time of Columbus (or still existed in the wild and woolly West somewhere), one could prove just as effectively that the Mound Builders were recent Indians. For those few who did not automatically link Mound Builders and mastodons, the situation looked quite different: it seemed to them that the mastodons were undoubtedly ancient, but that there was no necessary proof that they had survived into the era of the mounds. Until someone found a portrait of a live mastodon, or some comparable object, within one of the mounds, they said, the matter would have to remain unsettled.

The first major attempt to consolidate the archaeological and paleontological discoveries of the mid-nineteenth century into a coherent pattern of the past was made in *Prehistoric Times,* by Sir John Lubbock (later Lord Avebury). This work first appeared in 1865, and went on to reach a seventh edition in the twentieth century. Lubbock's chief interest was Old World prehistory, but he did not neglect that of the Americas. The exaggerated importance of the Mound Builders, even among such professionals as Lubbock, is demonstrated by his fourfold division of American prehistory: (1) original barbarism, (2) mounds, (3) "garden beds" [a decadent agricultural era], and (4) relapse into partial barbarism. In his discussion of the mounds, he relied chiefly on Squier and Davis, on Squier's later work on the New York mounds, on Haven's *Archaeology of the United States,* and on Lapham's *Antiquities of Wisconsin;* he also made passing references to Atwater and Schoolcraft. He did not attempt to attribute a high civilization to the Mound Builders or to define them as fundamentally distinct from the Indians; he saw them as one phase in the unbroken spectrum of American aboriginal life. Nor did he commit himself on the relationship of Mound Builders and mastodons. Though he believed that Koch's mastodons and Dickeson's Natchez find indicated considerable antiquity for man in the Americas, he did not correlate with the authors of the Ohio ramparts the early hunters, who, he thought, came here "little by little, year by year."

One of the most successful of the new popular works on American prehistory was John D. Baldwin's *Ancient America, in Notes on American Archaeology,* published by the firm of Harper & Brothers in 1872. This well-illustrated volume covered the Mound Builders, the various Mexican civilizations, the Incas, and the Pueblos; and, in characteristic emphasis, devoted some 200 of its 300 pages to the mounds. Baldwin's data on the mounds was drawn almost entirely from Squier and Davis; his conjectural sections represent an amalgam of much of the middle-of-the-road thinking of his time.

"Careful study of what is shown in the many reports on these ancient remains," wrote Baldwin, "seems plainly to authorize the conclusion that the Mound-Builders entered the country at the South, and began their settlements near the Gulf. Here they must have been very numerous, while their works at every point on the limit of their distribution, north, east, and west, indicate a much less numerous border population."[152] He feels that "the Mound-Builders had a certain degree of civilization which raised them far above the condition of savages," and doubts that they were related to the American Indians. "Some inquirers, not always without hesitation, suggest that the Indians inhabiting the United States two hundred years ago were degenerate descendants of the Mound-Builders," he says. "The history of the world shows that civilized communities may lose their enlightenment, and sink to a condition of barbarism; but the degraded descendants of a civilized people usually retain traditional recollections of their ancestors, or some traces of the lost civilization, perceptible in their customs and legendary lore. The barbarism of the wild Indians of North America had nothing of this kind. It was original barbarism. There was nothing to indicate that either the Indians inhabiting our part of the continent, or their ancestors near or remote, had ever been civilized, even to the extent of becoming capable of settled life and organized industry."[153] In repeating this familiar libel Baldwin rejects such legends as Heckewelder's tale of the Tallegewi: "The tradionary lore of the wild Indians had nothing to say of the Mound-Builders, who appear to have been as unknown and mysterious to these Indians as they are to us."

Baldwin believes that the Mound Builders were an ancient race, and cites customary proofs: the evidence of the river terraces, with no mounds on the most recently formed banks; the extreme condition of decay of the skeletons found in the mounds; the tree-rings; Harrison's point on the succession of forest growths. Since it seemed to him that it must have taken an extraordinarily long time to create the earthworks of the Mississippi Valley, and that the disappearance of the Mound Builders had occurred hundreds of years ago, their original arrival at the Gulf of Mexico must have come at an extremely early date.

Baldwin dismisses most of the wilder theories of the Mound Builders' origin. "Nothing can be more unwarranted or more absurd," he says, than the Lost Tribes of Israel theory, which he calls "a lunatic fancy." Samuel Mitchill's hypothesis of a migration of "Malays" from Polynesia via the Pacific strikes him as "much less improbable, though not satisfactory." That Phoenician voyagers may have reached the Americas appears quite reasonable to Baldwin, but if they were the founders of early American civilization, he points out, "it would be true also that they built in America as they never built any where else, that they established a language here radically unlike their own, and that they used a style of writing totally different from that which they carried into every other region occupied by their colonies."[154] Nor can he accept another hypothesis then beginning to win wide support: that the ancient Americans were refugees from the lost continent of Atlantis. This, he says, "is a fanciful theory which can not be proved," although he admits its "seductive plausibility" and seems to find in it much that is appealing.

His conclusion is that the Mound Builders "were unquestionably American aborigines, and not immigrants from another continent. That appears to me the most reasonable suggestion which assumes that the Mound-Builders came originally from Mexico and Central America. It explains many facts connected with their remains. In the Great Valley [of the Mississippi] their most populous settlements were at the south. Coming from Mexico and Central America, they would begin their settlements on the Gulf coast, and afterward advance gradually up the river to the Ohio Valley."[155]

The possibility of indirect influence, of secondhand imitation of Mexican traits by Northern aborigines, was evidently too subtle for 1872. Baldwin seizes upon the stone pyramids of Yucatán and the earthen pyramids of the United States and uses them to prove actual Mexican migration. "The high mounds also in the two regions are remarkably alike," he says. "In both cases they are pyramidal in shape, and have level summits of considerable extent, which were reached by means of stairways on the outside. The great mound at Chichén-Itzá is 75 feet high, and has on its summit a ruined stone edifice; that at Uxmal is 60 feet high, and has a similar ruin on its summit; that at Mayapan is 60 feet high; the edifice placed on its summit has disappeared. The great mound at Miamisburg, Ohio, is 68 feet high; and that at Grave Creek, West Virginia, is 75 feet high. Both had level summits, and stairways on the outside, but no trace of any structure remains on them. All these mounds were constructed for religious uses, and they are, in their way, as much alike as any five Gothic churches."[156]

From these and other arguments Baldwin decides that the Mound Builders' civilization stems from that of Mexico and Central America, and that, in turn, "did not come from the Old World; it was the work of some remarkably gifted branch of the race found on the southern part of the continent when it was discovered in 1492. Undoubtedly it was very old. Its original beginning may have been as old as Egypt, or even farther back in the past than the ages to which Atlantis must be referred. . . . Who can certainly tell its age? Whether earlier or later, it was original."[157]

Though Baldwin has cited three Mayan pyramids as prototypes for the mounds, he chooses to relate the Mound Builders to a different Mexican people—the Toltecs. Like all the theorists back to Benjamin Smith Barton who had fixed upon the mysterious Toltecs as the authors of the mounds, Baldwin works from the manuscripts and codices collected from the Aztecs at the time of the Spanish conquest of Mexico. "The Toltecs," he relates, "are said to have come into the country [Mexico] about a thousand years before the Christian era. Their supremacy appears to have ceased, and left the country broken up into small states, two or three centuries before the Aztecs appeared." He quotes Brasseur de Bourbourg, one of the protagonists of the Atlantis theory, on traditions establishing "the existence of an ancient empire known as Huehue-Tlapalan, from which the Toltecs or Nahuas came to Mexico, in consequence of a revolution or invasion, and from which they had a long and toilsome migration to the Aztec plateau." Brasseur de Bourbourg believed that Huehue-Tlapalan, which he placed in the Mississippi and Ohio valleys, was a stopping-off place for the Atlanteans after the cataclysm that drove them from their sundered continent. Baldwin ignores that point and simply asserts that Huehue-Tlapalan was the place where the Toltecs lived and built earthworks before they conquered Mexico.

But earlier Baldwin had said that the Mound Builders were emigrants *from* Mexico who landed on the Gulf Coast and spread northward up the Mississippi. So to make his Toltec theory hold together he has to postulate a double migration. First, in the really remote past, an ancient Mexican culture called the Colhuas sent colonists to the Mississippi Valley. After a long residence there, during which they built pyramids and ramparts of earth, these colonists returned to Mexico, "so much changed in speech and in other respects as to seem a distinct people,"[158] and, as the Toltecs, conquered and ruled their ancestral country. To explain the departure of the Toltecs from the Mississippi region he cites another Aztec tradition that the Toltecs were invaded by barbarous aboriginal tribes. "There was a terrible struggle, but, after about thirteen years, the Toltecs, no longer able to resist successfully, were obliged to abandon their country to escape complete subjugation. Two chiefs guided the march of the emigrating nation. At length they reached a region near the sea named 'Tlapalan-Conco,' where they remained several years. But they finally undertook another migration and reached Mexico, where they built a town called 'Tollanzinco,' and later the city of Tullan, which became the seat of their government."[159] Though Baldwin feels that the Toltecs abandoned Ohio in distant antiquity, he suggests that they maintained settlements along the Gulf and the lower Mississippi until relatively recent times: "The Natchez Indians found settled on the Lower Mississippi may have been a degenerate remnant of the Mound-Builders. They differed in language, customs, and condition from all other Indians in the country; and their own traditions connected them with Mexico."[160]

Baldwin's book is genteel and reasonable in tone, not particularly adventurous; it blazes no new paths, but merely attempts to give substance to earlier theories. A book that found much the same public as Baldwin's, but which was more aggressive in its thinking, was *Prehistoric Races of the United States of America,* by J. W. Foster, published in Chicago in 1873.

Foster was the president of the Chicago Academy of Sciences and the former head of the American Association for the Advancement of Science; though his specialty was geography, he had become enthralled by the Mound Builders when "for the first time I gazed upon the works of that mysterious people" at Newark, Ohio, and "my mind received a class of impressions which subsequent years have failed to efface." Though Foster writes rapturously of the "slumberous silence" that "filled the air . . . as I traced out the labyrinthine system of earthworks," his book is scarcely a romantic rhapsody after the manner of Pidgeon. His approach is doggedly modern; he is very much aware of writing in an era when startling revelations have overthrown old conceptions of the past.

He strikes that tone in the first sentence: "The combined investigations of geologists and ethnologists, prosecuted during the last quarter of a century, have thrown much light upon the origin of the human race, and developed facts which require us to essentially modify our pre-existing views as to the length of time during which it has occupied our planet." The task he sets himself is to grapple with the new discoveries and somehow yoke them to the established theories about the mounds.

Of man's antiquity in the New World he feels no doubt at all. He lists various instances of the discovery of human bones in association with those of the mastodon; he introduces such evidence as the famous Calaveras Skull, discovered 150 feet down in a California gold mine, which once was regarded as indisputable proof that man's advent in the Americas antedated even his appearance in Europe. (Alas, the Calaveras Skull was later shown to be no more authentic than Mark Twain's jumping frog from the same county!) Even overlooking subsequently discredited finds, Foster's catalog of evidence for man's antiquity in the Americas is impressive, though some fifty years more passed before the official scientific establishment came to share his views.

Nevertheless, Foster does not claim enormous age for the Mound Builders. Frederick Larkin, in his *Ancient Man in America* (1880), explained how the Mound Builders had transported such huge quantities of earth: by domesticating the mammoth and putting him to work. "We can imagine that tremendous teams have been driven to and fro in the vicinity of their great works," he wrote, and as evidence he offered a "copper relic" with an elephant engraved on it "in harness." But such extravagances were not for Foster. He offers a chart that bravely attempts to relate American prehistory to the newly discovered facts of European Stone Age life, and he ranks the American mastodons and mammoths as contemporaries of the beasts that roamed Europe during the glacial period: the cave bear, the woolly rhinoceros, and the European mammoth. He rates the American mastodon hunters on the same order of antiquity as the men who left flint blades in the caves of France; the Mound Builders are much more recent, he says, and he makes them the contemporaries of the Bronze Age societies of barbaric Europe just before the flourishing of Rome.

Yet within the context of the American civilizations Foster, for all his determined modernism, still clings to the myth of the Mound Builders as a separate race. He is bold enough to claim that mankind has existed "through thousands of generations"—a flat contradiction of scriptural belief—and, with a vigor refreshing for 1873, he ticks off briskly those who still tried to maintain that the world was precisely 5,877 years old that year. But, in discussing the Indian and the Mound Builder, Foster serves up this dizzying mixture of folklore and false anthropology:

"The Indian possesses a conformation of skull which clearly separates him from the pre-historic Mound Builder, and such a conformation must give rise to different mental traits. His brain, as compared with the European, according to George Combe, differs widely in the proportions of the different parts. The anterior lobe is small, the middle lobe is large, and the central convolutions on the anterior lobe and upper surface, are small. The brain-case is boxlike, with the corners rounded off; the occiput extends up vertically; the frontal ridge is prominent . . . His character, since first known to the white man has been signalized by treachery and cruelty. He repels all efforts to raise him from his degraded position: and whilst he has not the moral nature to adopt the virtues of civilization, his brutal instincts lead him to welcome its vices. He was never known voluntarily to engage in an enterprise requiring methodical labor; he dwells in temporary and movable habitations; he follows the game in their migrations; he imposes the drudgery of life upon his squaw; he takes no heed for the future. To suppose that such a race threw up the strong lines of circumvallation and the symmetrical mounds which crown so many of our river-terraces, is as preposterous, almost, as to suppose that they built the pyramids of Egypt."[161]

Here, cloaked in scientific trappings, are the sentiments of a nation then engaged in genocide. To proclaim the worthlessness of the American Indian was virtually an article of political faith in this era of Indian "removal;" and so Foster, like many predecessors, employs his learning to show that the Indians are worthless savages of an innately brutish nature. Though he does not mind attacking the prejudices of ignorant fundamentalists on the antiquity of man, he caters to another and much more terrible prejudice by parading arguments proving the Indians incapable of building the mounds. His chilling words, eerily reminiscent of certain German scientific researches of the 1930's, serve to remind us that the controversy over the origin of the mounds was not merely an abstract scholarly debate, but had its roots in the great nineteenth-century campaign of extermination waged against the American Indian.

Foster is haunted by the Neanderthal skull, with its low forehead and jutting brows. It inspires him to use Samuel Morton's methods against Morton's conclusions; for, under the influence of the Neanderthal discovery, Foster makes extensive cranial measurements that "have led me to infer that the Mound-builders' crania were characterized by a general conformation of parts, which clearly separated them from the existing races of man, and particularly from the Indians of North America."[162] His samples come from mounds near Chicago and Dubuque, and from Merom, Indiana. With much talk of lambdoidal sutures, superciliary ridges, glabellas, and occipital protuberances, he demonstrates that Mound Builders had thick, massive skulls, with low, flat foreheads and enormous ridges over the eyes—in fact, characteristics not too different from those of the Neanderthal skull.

As Foster identifies the governing characteristics of the Mound Builder "race," he drifts into an odd paradox. He has set out to show that a fundamental difference, both physical and mental, separates the diligent, well-organized, productive Mound Builders from the slothful, shiftless, drunken American Indians. But in the course of isolating the physical traits of the earlier race he finds himself reporting that "no one, I think, can view this fragment of a [mound] skull . . . without coming to the conclusion that its possessor was a ferocious brute," that "there is a deficiency of development, judged by the European standard," and that "this skull falls far below that of the average Teuton." Finally he admits, "All the [mound] specimens indicate a low intellectual organization, little removed from that of the idiot."[163]

What, then, of the "superior" Mound Builders?

The ingenious Dr. Foster is equal to the paradox. "The Mound-builders, assuming these skulls to be typical, were doubtless neither eminent for great virtues nor great vices," he declares, "but were a mild, inoffensive race, who would fall an easy prey to a crafty and cruel foe. Under the guidance of a superior mind, we can imagine that they would be content to toil, without weighing deliberately the nature or amount of the reward. Like the Chinese, they could probably imitate but not invent; and, secure from the irruption of enemies, they would, in time, develop a rude civilization."[164]

The glorious Mound Builders thus become the docile, dull-witted Mound Builders, placidly erecting their colossal ramparts to gratify ambitious prehistoric overseers whose own skulls have somehow failed to reach Dr. Foster's laboratory. It is, at any rate, a new approach, and has the virtue of depriving the American Indians of credit for the mounds without the need to postulate any very advanced ancient civilization in the United States. Thus Foster can avoid the whole question of colonization of Ohio by Mexicans, colonization of Mexico by Ohioans, and similar controversies.

In attempting to fix a date for the era of the Mound Builders he remarks, "The lapse of a few thousand years is all the time required to cover the most ancient of their structures," although he does feel that the ruins of Central America are more recent in origin than the mounds of the Mississippi Valley. Without committing himself to exact dates, he suggests that the mounds were abandoned at least six to eight centuries ago, and probably were first constructed some two thousand years earlier. He warns against uncritical acceptance of the evidence of tree rings, decayed skeletons, or Indian traditions in establishing the antiquity of the mounds. Tree rings do not afford "a chronometric scale by which to estimate the absolute lapse of time," he notes. "Inferences draw from the condition of skeletons form no reliable guide as to the lapse of time in which they have lain in the earth." As for Indian traditions, "little credence is to be attached" to them; "and yet so far as those traditions go, they are to the effect that the Mound-builders were a distinct race from themselves. . . . I would not make these traditions the basis of an argument for the high antiquity of these works; for among a people who have no written language, the lapse of a few generations would obliterate all knowledge even of the most signal events."[165]

9

The more there was published about the Mound Builders, the more passionate the debate grew, and the more energetically the archaeologists both professional and amateur searched for fresh evidence to prove their theories. Not all the excavation was scientific in intent, of course. In 1879 and 1880, the inhabitants of Charlestown, Missouri, learned that the handsome pottery found in their local mounds drew high prices from Eastern collectors. "A regular mining fever at once broke out," one archaeologist reported, "and spread so rapidly that in some instances as many as twenty-five or thirty men, women and children could be seen digging for pottery in one field at the same time. The specimens obtained were taken to Charlestown and sold to merchants, who in turn sold them to various museums, scientific institutions, and relic hunters. It is said that this trade brought to town several thousand dollars."[166]

In the course of this amateur activity, commercially inspired or otherwise, some evidence came to light that seemed to prove that mastodon, mammoth, and Mound Builder were contemporaries. In 1874, Jared Warner of Wyalusing, Wisconsin, sent to the Smithsonian a drawing of an effigy mound on his property that appeared to have the form of an elephant. In his accompanying letter he declared, "It has been known here for the last twenty-five years as the elephant mound. . . . The head is large, and the proportion of the whole so symmetrical that the mound well deserves the name. The mound was in a shallow valley between two sandy ridges, and was only about eight feet above high water."[167] The animal depicted was 133 feet in length, and had a proboscis 31 feet long. Sceptics pointed out that Mr. Warner's "elephant mound" had neither tusks nor tail, and that the proboscis, much too short to represent a true trunk, might well be the result of flood water adding earth to a bear-effigy mound. Others, though, took the mound as the intentional depiction of a mastodon.

14   Wisconsin elephant mound. Engraving from the *Second Annual Report of the Bureau of Ethnology*.

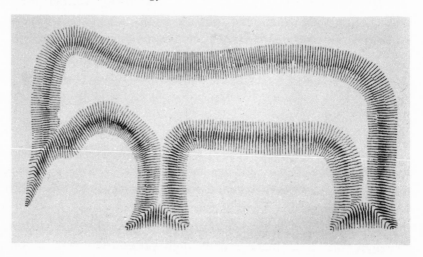

More bitterly contested discoveries of the same sort were made in and about Davenport, Iowa: two "elephant pipes" and three inscribed tablets of remarkable nature. The architect of these finds was the Reverend Jacob Gass, a Lutheran clergyman of Davenport, who, in 1874, came upon a group of mounds on the bank of the Mississippi about a mile south of the city. There were about a dozen of these mounds; he excavated two or three, finding in them such artifacts as copper axes, stone knives, spool-shaped copper implements, and pipes of a familiar Mound Builder type whose bowls were surmounted by animal effigies. These effigies of birds and animals were deftly carved; one had eyes of copper, another eyes of pearl. The Davenport relics were exhibited before the American Association for the Advancement of Science, meeting in Detroit in 1875, and attracted much attention.

The Reverend Mr. Gass did not become a figure of controversy until 1877. On January 10 of that year he returned to the Davenport mounds—known as the Cook group, from the name of the farmer on whose land they were—and opened a grave in Mound No. 3, a structure about three feet high and 60 feet in diameter. Gass was assisted by two students; five other citizens of Davenport were present as curious bystanders. On the surface of the grave, which was six feet wide and about ten feet long, were modern relics—glass beads and fragments of a brass ring—atop a layer of shells twelve or fifteen inches thick. Beneath this was a stratum of loose black soil or vegetable mold, eighteen or twenty inches thick, with fragments of human bones in it. At the bottom, five and a half feet below the surface of the mound, they came upon two inscribed tablets lying close together on a hard clay floor and encircled by a single row of smaller stones. The tablets themselves were covered with clay, and the inscriptions were not apparent until the clay was scraped off.

The larger tablet, twelve inches long and from eight to ten inches wide, was made of dark slate. It contained a pictorial scene on each side. One face showed a cremation scene: a fire burning on the summit of a mound, a number of bodies lying about it, with a group of supposed Mound Builders gathered in a ring around the mound. Above this picture was an arch formed by three crescent lines, representing the horizon, and in and above the crescent were hieroglyphics and letters. Roman and Arabic figures were included—the figure 8 was repeated three times, the letter O seven times, and F and N were also to be seen; other letters resembled Phoenician or Hebrew characters. The reverse face depicted a hunting scene. A large tree occupied the foreground, with animals and human beings arranged about it. The animals included bison, deer, hares, birds, goats, fish, and three that could be construed variously as moose, tapirs, or mastodons. Of the eight human figures, one was wearing a hat with a brim.

The smaller tablet, seven inches square with holes bored in two corners, became known as "the calendar stone." It contained twelve signs within three concentric circles. The signs were interpreted as the houses of the zodiac; the concentric circles were extraordinarily regular, one with a diameter of exactly two inches, the next three and a half, the next five inches.

A third inscribed tablet was unearthed on January 30, 1878, in Mound No. 11 of the Cook group. Once again the Reverend Mr. Gass was present, though the actual discoverer was Charles Harrison, the president of the Davenport Academy of Natural Sciences. In the mound was a pit containing a stone pile, two and a half feet by three feet, which the Davenport party considered an altar. Below the altar was a stone slab fourteen inches square, and beneath the slab was a stone vault, five inches deep and about thirteen inches by nine inches in length and breadth. Inside the vault lay a small quartz crystal, a shell, four arrow points, and a limestone tablet one and a half inches thick. Engraved on the tablet were a crescent to signify the moon, a circle supposedly representing the sun, and a human figure astride it, colored bright red and, of course, thought to represent a sun-god. A figure 8 and other characters were inscribed on the tablet, along with the outlines of a bird, an animal, and an ax, all quite crudely drawn.

The next Davenport discovery excited even more comment. In March, 1880, an elephant-effigy pipe turned up in a mound on the farm of P. Hass in Louisa County, Iowa. The excavator was another Lutheran minister, the Reverend Ad Blumer, of a neighboring city; he was assisted by the indefatigable Mr. Gass of Davenport. The mound was one of a group of ten; it was a flat cone, thirty feet in diameter, three feet in height. Near the surface was an eighteen-inch-thick layer of hard clay; below this was a foot-deep layer of burned red clay, hard as brick; under this was a bed of ashes, thirteen inches deep. In these ashes Mr. Gass found a small copper ax, and Mr. Blumer found the elephant pipe—or, at least, a pipe on which was mounted the effigy of a cumbersome-looking animal with a long snout. No tusks were visible; the eyes, ears, mouth, tail, legs, and feet were modeled in a lifelike, naturalistic way. At the "earnest solicitation" of Mr. Gass, the Reverend Mr. Blumer presented the elephant pipe to the Davenport Academy of Natural Sciences.

Very shortly the Academy came into possession of another such pipe, which had, in fact, been discovered prior to the other. As W. H. Pratt, then the president of the Academy, reported in *The American Naturalist* for April, 1882, "The first elephant pipe, which we obtained a little more than a year ago, was found some six years before by an illiterate German farmer named Peter Mare, while planting corn on a farm in the mound region, Louisa County, Iowa. He did not care whether it was elephant or kangaroo; to him it was a curious 'Indian stone,' and nothing more, and he kept it and smoked it. In 1878 he removed to Kansas, and when he left he gave the pipe to his brother-in-law, a farm laborer, who also smoked it. Mr. Gass happened to hear of it, as he is always inquiring about such things, hunted up the man and borrowed the pipe to take photographs and casts from it. He could not buy it. The man said his brother-in-law gave it to him and as it was a curious thing—he wanted to keep it. We were, however, unfortunate, or fortunate, enough to break it; that spoiled it for him and that was his chance to make some money out of it. He could have claimed any amount, and we would, as in duty bound, have raised it for him, but he was satisfied with three or four dollars."[168] The elephant shown on this pipe was similar to the other, but much more massive of body, with a pronounced trunk curled back almost to its forelegs.

The considered opinion of most scientists as of 1880 was that the mammoth and mastodon had vanished from the Americas thousands of years before. The occasional poorly documented discoveries of human artifacts in association with the bones of these extinct elephants had proved, at best, that the most primitive inhabitants of the New World had hunted them. But on the evidence of the Davenport pipes and the Davenport mastodon tablet, it now seemed clear that Mound Builders had been contemporaries of those beasts. By logical extension, the era of the Mound Builders must have been remote in time; and by further extension, the gap between the Mound Builders and the American Indians appeared huge. The great debate that had continued for most of the century had been resolved to the satisfaction of the majority. The existence of the Mound Builders as a distinct, ancient, and vanished race had been established, and the voices of those who ascribed the mounds to the ancestors of recent Indian tribesmen were drowned out.

Then a new voice was heard across the land: that of the United States Government, speaking through the instrumentality of the Smithsonian Institution. And the certainties of 1880 became the mythology of 1890.

▲▲▲ 5

THE DEFLATION OF THE MYTH

▲▲▲

John Wesley Powell, an authentic American phenomenon, first encountered the mounds as a boy in Ohio. He was born in 1834 in Mount Morris, New York, the son of an immigrant Wesleyan preacher of Welsh extraction. His birthplace was near Palmyra, New York, where Joseph Smith had found the golden plates of Mormon, and one of Powell's father's many difficulties was keeping his parishioners from succumbing to the new faith. New York State seemed unpromising soil for Wesleyans just then, and the elder Powell moved westward in 1838 by easy stages, first to Buffalo, then by steamship to Lake Erie, and by canal packet southwest to Chillicothe, Ohio, a community well populated by Welshmen.

The Powells settled in the nearby town of Jackson, purchasing a lot on Main Street and putting up a temporary log cabin that soon was replaced by a frame house. Jackson was a community of about 250 people, with six stores and three taverns. Among its citizens was George Crookham, a successful farmer, a self-taught man of science, and the most enthusiastic abolitionist in the county, who regularly helped escaping slaves north via the Underground Railroad. Crookham and the Powells had much in common: questing minds, convictions unsusceptible to mob intimidation, and love of learning. The new preacher was unpopular in Jackson because he believed that slavery was an abhorrence, and Crookham was unpopular for the same reason, so the two men drew together, and George Crookham became virtually a second father to young John Wesley Powell.

It was Crookham who gave the future director of the Smithsonian Institution's Bureau of American Ethnology his first look at the earthworks of Ohio. He was a kind of unofficial schoolmaster; on his property there was a rambling two-room log building, in which he kept his collections of plants, animals, and Indian relics, his apparatus for chemical experiments, and his library. In one of these rooms, used as a classroom, Crookham instructed, without fee, local boys who wished to improve themselves. He gave them the run of his museum, workshop, and library, and took them on field trips in the surrounding countryside.

Young Wes Powell was an avid pupil. Before he was ten, he had read Gibbon's *Decline and Fall of the Roman Empire,* Hume's *History of England,* and other learned works. On his walking tours with Crookham he had collected crawfish and minnows, pried fossils from the rocks, and examined unusual geological formations. They also visited the earthworks of Jackson and Ross counties. Powell dug in the mounds of Chillicothe, finding and treasuring flint points and other artifacts, while Crookham explained to him what was known about the Mound Builders *circa* 1844.

This youthful idyll was short lived. A gang of pro-slavery hoodlums burned down Crookham's museum and library, and the Powells began to think of moving on. In the summer of 1846, Powell sold his property in Jackson and bought 160 acres of land in South Grove, Wisconsin. Here Wes Powell come in contact with the shattered remnants of the Winnebago Indians who camped on his father's land, and he collected artifacts in the prehistoric earthworks at Delavan, a few miles away. He went on rambling excursions to study natural history, geology, and archaeology, and in other ways attempted to keep his inquisitive mind well stocked in his backwoods environment. The peaceful, friendly Indians fascinated him; as he watched the Winnebagos fishing and feasting, it seemed to him that these simple people had been maligned by the white men as severely as had the slaves whom George Crookham risked so much to help. It was the beginning of a powerful, passionate sympathy for Indian life.

In 1815 the Powells moved again, this time to northern Illinois. Wes, now seventeen, found a job as a schoolmaster at $14 a month, though his father hoped he would ultimately enter the ministry. He taught arithmetic, geology, and geography, and learned elementary geometry himself so he could teach it, lesson by lesson, to the pupils who followed a step or two behind him. His father became involved in the founding of a Wesleyan seminary and college at Wheaton, Illinois, and Powell went there to enroll in December, 1853. But he turned away bitterly when he discovered that there were no courses in the sciences or mathematics in the curriculum. He continued teaching school, now in Decatur, Illinois, where he excavated in mounds; in 1855 he registered at Illinois College, Jacksonville, but after a year he went off on a collecting trip across Wisconsin to study mollusks, and never returned. As the climax of that trip he traveled nearly the whole length of the Mississippi alone in a small rowboat.

In 1857, he was back at the Wesleyan college in Wheaton; the next year he studied a single term at Oberlin, where he learned a little Greek and Latin but failed to find the formal scientific training for which he was searching. Largely through a process of self-education, he attained a professional level in natural history and a deep knowledge of geology and archaeology.

From 1858 to 1860 he concentrated on the mounds of Ohio, Indiana, Illinois, and Missouri. At that time he shared the generally prevailing view that the mounds and other earthworks of the eastern half of the United States were vestiges of a people more ancient and more advanced in culture than the tribes of Indians that occupied the continent at the time of Columbus. "He began the preparation of a catalogue of mound-builders' arts," Powell said of himself many years later, "in the progress of which work many mounds were visited and a few excavated, and the catalogue grew from observations thus made in the field and from the examination of collections in various parts of the country. In the fall of 1859 certain mounds on the shore of Lake Peoria, in Illinois, were examined and skeletons were found in one of the largest, and with them works of art of various materials, especially of stone and pottery. At the bottom, with some articles of pottery, shells, stone implements, etc., an ornament was found made of copper skillfully cut in imitation of a spread eagle, with head turned to one side. Lying by the side of this were a few glass beads. These challenged attention, and the question was necessarily presented to him, Did these ancient people have the art of making glass? Subsequently the copper ornament was more carefully examined, and it appeared to be made of rolled sheet copper, or if the sheet was made by hammering this was so deftly accomplished that every vestige of the process had disappeared, leaving only flat surfaces on both sides, with a uniform thickness of metal. If these articles were the work of the mound-builders in pre-Columbian times, then the people must have possessed arts more advanced than those shown by the mound arts previously studied. Thus a suspicion arose as to the correctness of the prevailing opinion."[169]

Powell had no chance to confirm or deny this "suspicion" just then, because, as he relates, "national events interrupted the investigation, and carried the investigator into other fields of activity." At the outbreak of the Civil War he enlisted as a private in the Union Army, and rose through the ranks to become a major. While campaigning in Missouri, Tennessee, and Mississippi, Powell found time to discover and examine many groups of mounds, however. He reported later, "In these new fields, also, most of the works of art unearthed were of stone, bone, shell, and pottery, but in excavating a mound with stone graves, near Nashville, Tennessee, more glass beads were discovered and also an iron knife, very much rusted, which was afterwards lost. At the time of this find his former suspicion became a hypothesis that the mounds from which the glass, copper, and iron articles were taken were constructed subsequent to the advent of the white man on this continent, and that the contents gave evidence of barter between the civilized and savage races."[170]

During the slow, tense days before the battle of Shiloh in the spring of 1862, Powell opened Indian graves on the bluffs above the Tennessee River. In the battle, Powell was wounded in the left arm; it swelled and became infected, and an amputation followed. Despite this, Powell returned to duty after a brief convalescence, stipulating that his bride of six months would thenceforth be allowed to accompany him anywhere in the military zone.

At the end of the war Major Powell returned to academic life, taking a professorship at Illinois Wesleyan University at a salary of $1000 a year. His subject was geology, and shortly he was off on summer field trips to the Rocky Mountains with his classes. These expeditions led to his astonishing river journey in 1869 through the Grand Canyon of the Colorado; the one-armed major, accompanied by an odd band of mountain men and students, shot the rapids of the turbulent Colorado with true heroism and successfully carried out one of the most significant exploring trips in American history. On the strength of this achievement Powell became a nationally known figure and was made Director of the United States Geographical and Geological Survey of the Rocky Mountain Region, which in 1879 was merged with three other units to become the United States Geological Survey, eventually headed by Powell.

Throughout these years of geological studies, Major Powell retained his early interest in archaeology and ethnology. On his first expeditions to Colorado, in 1867 and 1868, he collected examples of Indian handicrafts—mainly garments, weapons, and pottery—for Illinois museums. At the suggestion of Joseph Henry of the Smithsonian, whose interest in Indian culture had awakened belatedly, Powell recorded the vocabularies of various Indian tribes as he traveled through the Colorado River area in 1869. Later he studied the Hopi Indians of Arizona, and in 1873 accepted an assignment to visit the Ute, Paiute, and Shoshone Indians. He realized that it was virtually the last chance to record the details of these vanishing cultures, and he was inflamed with vigorous conviction that such details *were* worth recording.

In 1876, at the great centennial exposition in Philadelphia, the Smithsonian staged an impressive display of Indian handicrafts. Powell took part in arranging this display. Later that year Secretary Henry authorized him to examine the 670 manuscripts on Indian linguistics in the Smithsonian collection; Powell winnowed through them and in 1877 produced a pioneering work of high importance, *Introduction to the Study of Indian Languages.* It established him as a professional ethnologist of the first rank; already an eminent geologist, he began to assume a position of leadership in this second field.

In a report to the Secretary of the Interior, filed in November, 1878, Powell voiced an eloquent plea for the creation of a government agency to support and carry on research on the North American Indians. "The work," he wrote, "is of great magnitude; more than four hundred languages belonging to about sixty different stocks having been found within the territory of the United States. Little of value can be accomplished in making investigations in other branches in the field without a thorough knowledge of the languages. Their sociology, mythology, arts, etc. are not properly known until the people themselves are understood, with their own conceptions, opinions, and motives. . . . The field of research is speedily narrowing because of the rapid change in the Indian population now in progress; all habits, customs, and opinions are fading away; even languages are disappearing; and in a very few years it will be impossible to study our North American Indians in their primitive condition, except from recorded history. For this reason ethnologic studies in America should be pushed with the utmost vigor."[171]

Powell had had predecessors in this enlightened view: Jefferson, Gallatin, and Schoolcraft, most notably. But none of them had succeeded in making ethnological research a government function. Powell had remarkable political skills; his status as a war hero and a Western explorer gave him enormous charismatic appeal; and he came along at the right time, when the nation, after decades of dedicated extermination of the Indians, was beginning to have a few twinges of conscience. Powell used this as an argument for his proposed government agency:

"The rapid spread of civilization since 1849 had placed the white man and the Indian in direct conflict throughout the whole area, and the 'Indian problem' is thus thrust upon us and it *must* be solved, wisely or unwisely. Many of the difficulties are inherent and cannot be avoided, but an equal number are unnecessary and are caused by the lack of our knowledge relating to the Indians themselves. Savagery is not inchoate civilization; it is a distinct status of society with its own institutions, customs, philosophy, and religion; and all these must necessarily be overthrown before new institutions, customs, philosophy, and religion can be introduced. The failure to recognize this fact has wrought inconceivable mischief in our management of the Indians. . . . The blunders we have made and the wrongs we have inflicted upon the Indians . . . have been cruel and inexcusable, except on the ground of our ignorance."

The government's response to this manifesto was uncharacteristically swift. On March 3, 1879, Congress passed a Sundry Civil Appropriation Bill that included funds for many things, among them:

"For completing and preparing for publication the contributions to North American ethnology, under the Smithsonian Institution, twenty thousand dollars: *Provided,* that all of the archives, records, and material relating to the Indians of North America, collected by the geographical and geological survey of the Rocky Mountains, shall be turned over to the Institution, that the work may be completed and prepared for publication under its direction. . . ."

Thereby Congress created the Smithsonian Institution's Bureau of Ethnology, later called the Bureau of American Ethnology. The same bill brought into being the United States Geological Survey, which Powell had hoped to head. But the directorship of the Geological Survey went to one of his rivals, Clarence King. Major Powell received a valuable consolation prize, though. At the recommendation of Spencer F. Baird, the new Secretary of the Smithsonian Institution, Powell was named the first Director of the Bureau of Ethnology. When ill health forced King to leave the Geological Survey in 1881, Powell inherited that bureau as well, and thereafter was an extremely busy man in the nation's capital.

2

On what was even then a markedly slim budget for such an ambitious enterprise, Powell led the Smithsonian into the active study of the American Indians. Congress had merely intended the $20,000 to cover the cost of completing and readying for publication the various ethnological researches of the geological survey expeditions, but Powell, construing his authority liberally, conjured up a department for continuing research. He hired a staff of a few persons and enrolled the nucleus of what would eventually be a wide-flung network of part-time field investigators. Powell saw the work of his bureau chiefly as anthropological rather than archaeological; he planned only to study the languages, arts, institutions, and mythologies of extant tribes, and originally there was no intention to use Bureau of Ethnology funds for excavations of mounds or ruins.

This orientation is evident from the First Annual Report of the Bureau of Ethnology, which Powell submitted in July, 1880, and which was published the following year. This massive volume in a gold-stamped binding of drab cloth was the first of forty-eight such annual reports that would appear before Depression economies forced their permanent discontinuance in 1932; the complete set is perhaps Powell's most impressive monument. But there was little in the first report about archaeology. A perfunctory introduction by Powell was followed by a group of "accompanying papers," most of them reports on work that had been under way before the bureau's formation. Powell himself contributed essays on Indian language and myth, on the Wyandot tribe, and on anthropology in general. Dr. Henry C. Yarrow, a doctor on the staff of the Surgeon-General of the United States, offered a paper on burial customs of the Indians. Among the other works in the 638-page volume were articles on Central American picture writing, cessions of land by Indian tribes to the United States, and sign language among North American Indians.

The only one of these papers that made any extended reference to the mounds was Dr. Yarrow's. He devoted eight pages to burial mounds, quoting Atwater, Bartram, and others, but made no theoretical conjectures. Powell, in one of his several essays, presented his own view of the mounds in a single terse paragraph: "With regard to the mounds so widely scattered between the two oceans, it may also be said that mound-building tribes were known in the early history of discovery of this continent, and that the vestiges of art discovered do not excell in any respect the arts of the Indian tribes known to history. There is, therefore, no reason for us to search for an extra-limital origin through lost tribes for the arts discovered in the mounds of North America."[172]

In that quiet, offhand way, Major Powell sounded the first battle cry of the coming revolution in American archaeology. On the same page he suggested that the concept of a single race of Mound Builders be discarded; "the wide extent and vast number of mounds discovered in the United States should lead us to suspect, at least, that the mound-builders of pre-historic times belonged to many and diverse stocks." An attempt to identify these separate stocks, he felt, would yield "but a meager harvest." Not even Powell then guessed how deeply the Bureau of Ethnology would soon be plowing that particular field.

An odd thing happened to Powell's bureau when it was time to renew its appropriation. A group of archaeologists, without letting Powell know, persuaded Congress to insert this passage in the appropriation bill of February, 1881:

"Add to the paragraph appropriating $25,000 for continuing ethnological researches among the North American Indians the following:

" *Five thousand dollars of which shall be expended in continuing archae-*

ological investigation relating to mound-builders and prehistoric mounds.' "

Powell was caught by surprise, and not entirely pleased. He had worked hard to get his appropriation boosted by $5,000, so that he could expand his ethnological work; now he learned that his entire increase had been irrevocably earmarked for an expansion of the bureau's responsibilities into a field that was beyond its present scope. He saw it as a dilution, for he did not have funds enough even to do the ethnology as he thought proper. But he obeyed Congress' behest, and set up a division within the bureau to investigate the mounds of the eastern half of the United States. He placed in charge of this division one of the archaeologists who had rammed the rider through Congress, a certain Wills de Haas. De Haas resigned almost at once, and late in 1881 Powell replaced him with Cyrus Thomas, who was destined to be the slayer of the Mound Builder myth. Thomas came from the southern tip of Illinois, the section known as "Little Egypt" after its principal city, the river port of Cairo. He had been first an entomologist and then a botanist in the service of the Geological and Geographical Survey of the Territories, one of the agencies now consolidated into Powell's other bureau, the United States Geological Survey. In some unspecified way Thomas had acquired the title of "professor," and his interests extended into many fields. When he came to the Bureau of Ethnology he was, he said, a "pronounced believer in the existence of a race of Mound Builders, distinct from the American Indians." Major Powell proposed to cure him of this aberration by putting him in charge of the bureau's mound explorations and letting him convince himself of his error. Powell provided Professor Thomas with one clerical assistant and three field assistants and told him to draw up a plan for a survey of the mounds.

There is no information on this change of bureau orientation in the Second Annual Report of the Bureau of Ethnology, which Powell submitted in September, 1882, This volume, somewhat smaller than its predecessor but still ponderous, says nothing about a program of excavations, for Powell's report on the bureau's activities was written in the 1880-81 fiscal year, before the expanded appropriation had gone into effect. The shift in the bureau's policies is evident, though, from the accompanying papers that make up the bulk of the volume. Among them are several ethnological essays, one on Iroquois myths, another on Zuni religious practices. But the book also includes papers on ancient artifacts from the Southwest, and on "The Art in Shell of the Ancient Americans," both of which would have been deemed beyond the range of the Bureau of Ethnology in its first two years. In addition, there is an essay on mounds.

The opening salvo in Major Powell's war against the myth of the Mound

Builders was fired by Henry W. Henshaw, a naturalist who had specialized in ornithology, and who had explored much of the American West. On behalf of the Bureau of Ethnology, Henshaw had made a field trip to the Indians of what was then Washington Territory, far beyond the mound zone. He had not excavated any mounds himself, nor did he claim any real firsthand knowledge of the subject. Henshaw seems an unlikely choice for the assignment, considering his apparent lack of qualifications. But, as he explains in the opening paragraphs of his paper, "Animal Carvings from Mounds of the Mississippi Valley," he approached the question of the mounds purely as an expert on natural history. Certain effigies of birds and animals had been recovered from the mounds, and from them certain conclusions had been drawn concerning the nature of the mounds and their builders. Henshaw now proposed to see if those conclusions were just. "It may be premised," he says, "that the writer undertook the examination of the carvings with no theories of his own to propose in place of those hitherto advanced. In fact, their critical examination may almost be said to have been the result of accident. Having made the birds of the United States his study for several years, the writer glanced over the bird carvings [from the mounds] in the most cursory manner, being curious to see what species were represented. The inaccurate identification of some of these by the authors of 'The Ancient Monuments of the Mississippi Valley' [Squier and Davis] led to the examination of the series as a whole, and subsequently to the discussion they had received at the hands of various authors. The carvings are, therefore, here considered rather from the stand-point of the naturalist than the archaeologist."[173]

What the burden of Henshaw's opinions would be was given away by Powell's preface to the paper. Where in the earlier report he had slipped his view on the mythical nature of the Mound Builders inconspicuously into print, now he blasts it forth. He denounces "the many false statements which corrupt the mass of literature" concerning the Indians, and cites "contradictions and absurdities." Discussing the varying concepts of migrations to and within the New World, Powell says, "With the unscrupulous zeal common to polemics, all observations were made through the medium adapted to a preconceived theory, while the garbling and perversion of the lower class of writers supplemented the phantasies of those better intentioned."[174]

The discovery of the mounds of the Mississippi basin, Powell goes on, opened "a new field . . . to enthusiastic theorists. Ignoring the fact that many of the historic Indians have practised the building of mounds, indeed that some are still building them, it was assumed that these works were the vestiges of a dense and extinct population whose advance in civilization was much superior to that of the known American Indians. From the size and forms of their mounds, their location, and the objects contained in them, writers have set forth the origin, migrations, numbers, institutions, art, and religions of their builders. This attempt was not illegitimate nor impracticable of execution if made after complete exploration and comparison in a scientific spirit, by experts possessing the requisite special training. It will be the duty of the Bureau of Ethnology to devote careful attention to this interesting field of archaeology. But those who have hitherto conducted the researches have betrayed a predetermination to find something inexplicable on the simple hypothesis of a continuous Indian population, and were swept by blind zeal into serious errors even when they were not imposed upon by frauds and forgeries."

Henshaw is no less aggressive in style; his piece is a brisk demolition job. He is careful to state at the outset that by his use of the term "Mound-Builders" he "is not to be considered as committing himself in any way to the theory that the Mound-Builders were of a different race from the North American Indian." Then he sets to work, and the first to be demolished is the revered Ephraim George Squier.

Tactfully Henshaw pays homage to "the skill and zeal" of Squier and Davis, and to "the ability and fidelity which mark the presentation of their results to the public." Then he falls on them for their attempt, on page 251 of their *Ancient Monuments,* to identify the animals shown on certain Ohio effigy pipes as "the lamantin, manitus, or sea-cow." Squier had written, "Seven sculptured representations of this animal have been taken from the mounds, of which three are nearly perfect. When first discovered, it was supposed they were monstrous creations of fancy; but subsequent investigation and comparison have shown that they are faithful representations of one of the most singular animal productions of the world."

Squier had quoted a lengthy zoological description of this animal, generally known as the manatee, and had declared, "These external features are faithfully and minutely exhibited in the sculptures from the mounds. The truncated head, small and scarcely distinguishable ears, thick, semi-circular snout, peculiar nostrils, tumid, furrowed upper lip, singular feet or fins, and remarkable moustaches, are all distinctly marked, and render the recognition of the animal complete. Only one of the sculptures exhibits a flat, truncated tail; the others are round. There is however a variety of the lamantin (*Manitus Senigalensis,* DESM.) which has a round tail. . . . It is smaller in size than the other variety."

The significance of these manatee effigies, according to Squier, lay in the fact

15

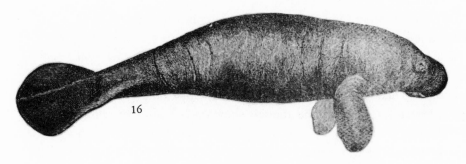

16

15   Manatee pipe, after Squier and Davis. Engraving from the *Second Annual Report of the Bureau of Ethnology*.

16   Manatee. Engraving from the *Second Annual Report of the Bureau of Ethnology*.

that "the manitus is found only in tropical waters," ascending no farther north than the rivers of Florida. The existence of manatee pipes in the Ohio mounds indicated, at the very least, some sort of trade route linking Ohio and the tropical shores of Florida, and even the possibility of a far-flung empire: "Either the same race, possessing throughout a like style of workmanship, and deriving their materials from a common source, existed contemporaneously over the whole range of intervening territory, and maintained a constant intercommunication; or else there was at some period a migration from the south, bringing with it characteristic remains of the land from which it emanated. The sculptures of the manitus are too exact to have been the production of those who were not well acquainted with the animal and its habits."[175] Thus Squier and Davis concluded from the presence of effigies of manatees and certain tropical birds that an extensive Mound Builder civilization, quite superior to any social organization of the fragmented Indian tribes, had once existed.

Here is an odd instance of thoughtful scientists reasoning from faulty premises twice over. We know today, from archaeological evidence, that Ohio *was* connected by trade routes with many distant parts of North America, and that something very much like Squier's hypothetical "Mound Builder" empire actually existed at one time, though it was not responsible for all the American mounds. But the so-called manatees and toucans on which Squier based this notion were not manatees and toucans at all. Henshaw proved that, even though he was incorrect in thinking that commerce linking Ohio and Florida in prehistoric times was a fantasy.

Henshaw's starting point is Squier's assertion that "some of these sculptures have a value, so far as ethnological research is concerned, much higher than they can claim as mere works of art. This value is derived from the fact that they faithfully represent animals and birds peculiar to other latitudes, thus establishing a migration, a very extensive intercommunication, or a contemporaneous existence of the same race over a vast extent of country."[176] Henshaw proceeds to show that the manatee pipes could not have been exotic items imported from Florida, for no such pipes had ever been found there; he demonstrates that the manatee did not range as far north as Ohio during Mound Builder days; and finally he shows that the zoological attributions of Squier and Davis are simply not to be trusted. What they had identified as an otter effigy, Henshaw shows to be the effigy of a squirrel; what they call a manatee, Henshaw demonstrates anatomically to be a North American otter. He ridicules Squier's explanation of the round tail on the effigies by pointing out that the round-tailed manatee, *M. senigalensis,* comes not from Florida but from Africa. "Elastic as has proved to be the thread upon which hangs the migration theory, it would seem to be hardly capable of bearing the strain required for it to reach from the Mississippi Valley to Africa," Henshaw says.[177]

In passing, Henshaw punctures the folly of another writer, E. T. Stevens, whose *Flint Chips* of 1870 was a guide to the Squier and Davis artifact collection in the Blackmore Museum. Stevens, discussing the manatee pipes, had said, "In one particular, however, the sculptors of the mound period committed an error. Although the lamantin is strictly herbivorous, feeding chiefly upon subaqueous plants and littoral herbs, yet upon one of the stone smoking pipes this animal is represented with a fish in its mouth." Noting that the pipe really shows a carnivorous otter and not a herbivorous manatee, Henshaw says, "Mr. Stevens apparently preferred to credit the mound sculptor with gross ignorance of the habits of the manatee, rather than to abate one jot or tittle of the claim possessed by the carving to be considered a representation of that animal."[178]

Henshaw goes on to show that the supposed tropical toucan illustrated in Squier and Davis is really a crow in one case, an eagle in another; several other tropical birds are similarly debunked. Then Henshaw attacks those who had drawn erroneous conclusions from the erroneous zoology of Squier and Davis. In particular he assails the respected, graybearded Sir Daniel Wilson, LL. D., F.R.S.E., author of *Prehistoric Man: Researches into the origin of civilization in the old and new world.* This work had first appeared in 1862, and had been revised and greatly expanded in 1865 and 1876. In an earlier book, *Prehistoric Annals of Scotland* (1851), Wilson had first introduced the term "prehistoric," which he defined as "the whole period disclosed to us by means of archaeological evidence, as distinguished from what is known through written records."

Wilson held that "the moundbuilders were greatly more in advance of the

17   Peregrine Falcon pipe from Tremper Mound. Courtesy Ohio Historical Society, Columbus, Ohio.

18 Raven pipe from Mound City. Courtesy Ohio Historical Society, Columbus, Ohio.

19 Toucan, after Squier and Davis. Engraving from the *Second Annual Report of the Bureau of Ethnology.*

Indian hunter than behind the civilized Mexican," a theory he based in part on the manatee and toucan pipes. He suspected that the Mound Builders had emigrated from Mexico or Central America, "bringing with them the arts of the tropics, and models derived from the animals familiar to their fathers in the parentland of the race." Citing such "accurate miniature representations" as those of the toucan, the manatee, and the jaguar, Wilson said, "The majority of these animals are not known in the United States; some of them are totally unknown within any part of the North American continent."

Henshaw repeats his attack on the manatee and toucan pipes, showing also that jaguars once roamed as far north as Louisiana, but that the so-called jaguar effigies probably depicted cougars, once native to the Mississippi Valley. Next he challenges Wilson's views on the presence of conch shells in the mounds. Wilson had exposed the error of John Delafield, author of *Inquiry into the Origin of the Antiquities of America* (1839), who had tried to prove a migration of the Mound Builders from India. Delafield had claimed that the conch was unknown in the New World, but abundant "on the coast of Hindostan," and that the shells had come in the baggage of the migrants. Wilson criticized this argument, observing that conchs were common in tropical America as far north as Yucatán. This, however, was three thousand miles from some localities where conch shells had been unearthed in mounds, and seemed to prove to Wilson that the Mound Builders had come from Mexico. Henshaw simply remarks that conchs have been found in the United States as far north as Beaufort, North Carolina, while a similar mollusk known to the Mound Builders and often confounded with the conch by archaeologists exists as far north as Cape Cod.

After dealing with a few more zoological errors, Henshaw devotes some pages to a criticism of the esthetic theories of Squier and Davis. Squier had written that the extreme realism of the Mound Builder carvings proves the superiority of Mound Builder culture over that of the Indians, who were given to grotesqueries in their art. Henshaw regards the idea that the Mound Builders were masters of realism as "simply preposterous," observing that "it is simply impossible to recognize specific features in the great majority" of the effigy pipes. Moreover, he casts doubt on the notion that one can determine the superiority or inferiority of a culture by measuring its reliance on artistic naturalism. Though he finds much Mound Builder art attractive, he regards it merely as "considerably above the general average of attainments in art of our Indian tribes, but not above the best efforts of individual tribes."

As a zoologist, Henshaw reserves his sharpest barbs for those who claimed to have found evidence of a relationship between Mound Builders and mastodons. Wisconsin's "elephant mound" seems to him no more than a nondescript bear effigy to which a fortuitous snout has become attached by flood action. Even though Henshaw is willing to admit—incorrectly, we now know—that the mastodon may have been alive within the past five hundred years, and so, "there are no inherent absurdities in the belief that the Mound-Builders were acquainted with the mastodon,"[179] he cannot admit the "elephant mound" to evidence. The absence of tusks, tail, and ears more than negates the presence of the short, stubby trunk; the slight resemblance, he says, is probably an accident of nature.

He is even less generous to the two elephant pipes of Davenport, Iowa. These he considers fakes, though he does not quite use that ugly word. "If the pipes are intentional imitations of any animal," he writes, "neither can be regarded as having been intended for any other than the mastodon. Yet . . . it is certainly surprising that if intended for mastodons no attempt was made to indicate the tusks, which with the trunk constitute the most marked external peculiarities of all the elephant kind. The tusks, too, as affording the most important product in primitive industries, ivory, would naturally be the one peculiarity of all others which the ancient artist would have relied upon to fix the identity of the animal."[180] Henshaw also makes much of the Davenport mastodons' lack of tails—a puzzling criticism, since the two effigies did show tails. He finds it "a curious coincidence that carvings found at a point so remote from the Elephant Mound, and presumably the work of other hands, should so closely copy the imperfections of that mound."

Relating the role of the Reverend Jacob Gass in bringing to light the two elephant pipes, Henshaw says, "The remarkable archaeologic instinct which has guided the finder of these pipes has led him to even more important discoveries. By the aid of his divining rod he has succeeded in unearthing some of the most remarkable inscribed tablets which have thus far rewarded the diligent search of the mound explorer. It is not necessary to speak in detail of these here, or of the various theories to which they have given rise . . . further than to call attention to the fact that by a curious coincidence one of the tablets contains, among a number of familiar animals, figures which suggest in a rude way the mastodon again, which animal indeed some archaeologists have confidently asserted them to be. The resemblance they bear to that animal is, however, by no means as close as exhibited by the pipe carvings. . . . Both figures differ from the pipes in having tails; both lack trunks, and also tusks.

"Archaeologists must certainly deem it unfortunate that outside of the Wisconsin mound the only evidence of the co-existence of the Mound-Builder and the mastodon should reach the scientific world through the agency of one individual. So derived, each succeeding carving of the mastodon, be it more or less accurate, instead of being accepted by archaeologists as cumulative evidence tending to establish the genuineness of the sculptured testimony showing that the Mound-Builder and mastodon were coeval, will be viewed with ever increasing suspicion."[181]

These charges were regarded in some quarters as perilously close to a libel against the good Mr. Gass; and, appearing in a huge volume bearing the imprint of the Government Printing Office, they represented a kind of scholarly overkill. The net effect of Henshaw's tirade was to stiffen public sentiment on behalf of the Davenport pipes, despite the cogency of the attack. In particular, Henshaw was troubled by the fact that, "if the Mound-Builders and the mastodon were contemporaneous, [why] have no traces of the ivory tusks ever been exhumed from the mounds?" The bones of muskrat and turtle, the horns of deer, the teeth of a host of animals had appeared, but of the mastodon "not a palpable trace remains. The tale of its existence is told by a single mound in Wisconsin, which the most ardent supporter of the mastodon theory must acknowledge to be far from a facsimile, and two carvings and an inscribed tablet, the three latter the finds of a single explorer." These were powerful points; but emotion begets emotion, and the heat of Henshaw's assault bred renewed fervor among the forces opposed to the views being put forth by the Bureau of Ethnology.

After some closing words on the esthetics of aboriginal art, Henshaw offers these conclusions, which could be regarded as a statement of Bureau of Ethnology policy as defined by Powell:

"That of the carvings from the mounds which can be identified there are no representations of birds or animals not indigenous to the Mississippi Valley.

"And consequently that the theories of origin for the Mound Builders suggested by the presence in the mounds of carvings of supposed foreign animals are without basis.

"Second. That a large majority of the carvings, instead of being, as assumed, exact likenesses from nature, possess in reality only the most general resemblances to the birds and animals of the region which they were doubtless intended to represent.

"Third. That there is no reason for believing that the masks and sculptures of human faces are more correct likenesses than are the animal carvings.

"Fourth. That the state of art-culture reached by the Mound Builders, as illustrated by their carvings, has been greatly overestimated."[182]

3

The Third Annual Report of the Bureau of Ethnology, covering the fiscal year 1881-82, was submitted by Powell in October, 1883, and was published in 1884. It still indicated a largely ethnological, rather than archaeological, orientation for the bureau, but for the first time Powell included a brief summary entitled, "Explorations in Mounds." Noting that in this fiscal year Congress had directed him to make such investigations, he cites the work of Wills de Haas in West Virginia and eastern Ohio, and of volunteer collectors in Tennessee, Arkansas, and Florida. Although Cyrus Thomas had replaced de Haas as head of the mound work during this fiscal year, Thomas is not mentioned; his contribution to the Third Annual Report was an essay on Mayan and Aztec manuscripts, which he had been engaged in studying at the time of his transfer to the mound project. There was no attempt in this report to continue the polemic tone of Henshaw's article. The only piece dealing with the mounds was a simple catalog, well illustrated, of artifacts found in mounds of North Carolina, Tennessee, and Arkansas. This reproduced a number of strikingly handsome works of ceramic art, showing that at least in the Southeast the Mound Builders had been unusually gifted potters. The purely descriptive commentary that accompanied these illustrations was the work of William Henry Holmes, himself a talented painter who had given up art for geology, then drifted into archaeology, and served Powell ably both in the Geological Survey and in the Bureau of Ethnology. (Holmes succeeded to the directorship of the latter upon Powell's death in 1902.)

The Fourth Annual Report, covering fiscal 1882-83, saw Powell's campaign against Mound Builder myths picking up momentum. Submitted in October, 1883—a day *before* the official submission of the previous year's report—it represented Powell's attempt to get up to date with his bureaucratic responsibilities, but printing delays kept it from appearing until 1886. The entry under "Mound Explorations" grew from half a page in the previous report to more than five pages here. Powell noted that "The Bureau of Ethnology was first organized on the basis of work developed by the Director while in charge of explorations and surveys in the valley of the Colorado River of the West. It therefore did not embrace any plan for archaeologic investigations in the eastern portion of the United States, and in particular did not contemplate researches relating to the mounds; but Congress having directed that such work should be added to the functions of the Bureau, a limited amount of work was accomplished in this field during the past year." Having delivered himself of this grumbled complaint against Congressional interference in his bureau, Powell is forced to admit, "The experience thus gained showed that a more thorough systematization of the work was necessary. Early in the year, therefore, a Division of Mound Explorations was organized, for a comprehensive examination of mounds and other ancient works in the United States east of the Rocky Mountains, and Prof. Cyrus Thomas, of Illinois, was appointed an assistant in the Bureau in charge of the division."[183] Powell lists three full-time assistants to Thomas, and five temporary helpers.

The work done during 1882–83 covered parts of Tennessee, Arkansas,

Illinois, Iowa, Georgia, Alabama, North Carolina, and Missouri. Some 4,100 artifacts were collected and placed in the National Museum. They included "three remarkable winged pipes of green chlorite slate of the finest workmanship, two large image pipes, gorgets, plummets, and boat-shaped ornaments," along with such humbler things as scrapers, hoes, diggers, axes, and hammers. And "among the articles obtained indicating contact with European civilization are some specimens of hammered iron from a North Carolina mound; some bracelets, brooches, crosses, and other objects of silver from a Wisconsin mound; fragments of copper plate bearing the impress of machinery on a metallic stamp from an Illinois mound, and a hog's tooth from an Arkansas mound."[184] All this served to reinforce Powell's original conviction that "a few, at least, of the important mounds of the valley of the Mississippi, had been constructed and used subsequent to the occupation of the continent by Europeans, and that some, at least, of the mound builders were therefore none other than known Indian tribes."

The fourth report continues the attack against the mythmakers. Though W. H. Holmes is present with another noncontroversial essay, the splendidly illustrated "Ancient Pottery of the Mississippi Valley," the vigorous note of the volume was struck by Garrick Mallery, one of Powell's most able contributors, in his "Pictographs of the North American Indians." This broad survey of Indian pictorial art and writing touched only incidentally, but incisively, on the Mound Builders and their purported inscribed tablets. Virtually all of the inscriptions found in mounds seemed fraudulent to Mallery; the instances of forgeries, he said, "have been equally divided between simple mischief and an attempt either to increase the marketable value of some real estate, supposed to contain more, or to sell the specimens."[185]

The plates from Kinderhook, Illinois, bearing "Chinese" characters designed by the village blacksmith after the lid of a Chinese tea chest, are cited. So is the discovery of David Wyrick, of Newark, Ohio, "who, to prove his theory that the Hebrews were the mound-builders, discovered in 1860 a tablet bearing on one side a truculent 'likeness' of Moses with his name in Hebrew, and on the other a Hebrew abridgement of the ten commandments. A Hebrew bible afterwards found in Mr. Wyrick's private room threw some light on the inscribed characters." To Mallery, any inscription emanating from the region about Newark was suspect, and he was not alone in that view. The April 11, 1884, issue of *Science* had remarked, "A correspondent from Newark, Ohio, warns us that any inscribed stones said to originate from that locality may be looked upon as spurious. Years ago certain parties in that place made a business of manufacturing and burying inscribed stones and other objects in the autumn, and exhuming them the following spring in the presence of innocent witnesses. Some of the parties to these frauds afterward confessed to them; and no such objects, except such as were spurious, have ever been known from that region."

The tablet from the Grave Creek Mound is mentioned, and Mallery has some fun with the would-be translators of the supposed alphabetical inscription; but he does not dismiss the tablet itself as necessarily fraudulent: "Any inscriptions purporting to be pre-Columbian showing apparent use of alphabetic characters, signs of the zodiac, or other evidences of a culture higher than that known among the North American Indians, must be received with caution, but the pictographs may be altogether genuine, and their erroneous interpretation be the sole ground of their being discredited."

For this reason, he makes no charges against the authenticity of the Davenport tablets, though he advises a conservative approach in interpreting the scenes they portray. However, the damage had already been done, so far as good relations between the Davenport Academy of Natural Sciences and the Bureau of Ethnology were concerned. Henry Henshaw's scathing words about the Davenport pipes, the tablets, and the ubiquitousness of Reverend Jacob Gass had stirred much wrath in Iowa, and early in 1885 came a fiery counterblast out of the West.

It took the form of a slender pamphlet entitled, *A Vindication of the Authenticity of the Elephant Pipes and Inscribed Tablets in the Museum of the Davenport Academy of Natural Sciences, from the Accusations of the Bureau of Ethnology of the Smithsonian Institution.* Its author was Charles E. Putnam, the incumbent president of the Davenport Academy of Natural Sciences, and it was printed by a Davenport firm, Glass & Hoover.

Here was outraged local scholarship striking back furiously at the Federal colossus! "In the sharp controversy now being waged among archaeologists, as to the origin of the Mound-builders," Putnam begins, "the Bureau of Ethnology connected with the Smithsonian Institution has taken a decided position as the champion of the theory that this mysterious race can be traced with comparative certainty to the ancestors of our American Indians." He quotes Powell's own words to this effect, supporting them with a quotation from the Marquis de Nadaillac's recent *Prehistoric America.* As representatives of the opposing viewpoint, Putnam gives J. W. Foster and his passage on the savagery and indolence of the American Indian, and cites Squier and Davis on the settled agricultural habits of the Mound Builders. But the Davenport Academy itself, Putnam says, "has postponed decision upon these important deductions, awaiting further discoveries." He describes the members of the Academy as "earnest seekers after truth."

For the "able and accomplished scholars" enlisted in the service of the

Bureau of Ethnology, Putnam has high praise; he speaks of their "consummate ability." But by his sixth page he reaches the nub of his complaint: "It is, however, to be regretted that, actuated by intemperate zeal to establish this theory [of the American Indian ancestry of the Mound Builders], its promoters have sometimes abandoned scientific methods, indulged in hasty generalizations, and even violated the amenities of literature." In this he refers to Henry W. Henshaw's paper in the Bureau of Ethnology's Second Annual Report, which took advantage of the "commanding position" occupied by the Smithsonian "in the world of science" to deliver "an attack of no ordinary severity . . . upon the Davenport Academy of Natural Sciences."

The Academy, Putnam insists, "has attained deserved eminence" in the field of archaeology. "Its inscribed tablets, elephant pipes, cloth-covered copper axes, and rare collection of ancient pottery have attracted the attention of archaeologists throughout the world of science. These remarkable relics, received with enthusiasm by antiquarians, are generally accepted as authentic additions to the 'unwritten history' of the past." He finds it reasonable "that discoveries so rare and unique should be subjected to severe scrutiny," but objects to Henshaw's innuendos of fraud.

Putnam relates the circumstances of the discoveries of the pipes and tablets: "The gentlemen engaged in the exploration are well known, and held in high

20   Davenport elephant pipe. Engraving from *A Vindication of the Authority of the Elephant Pipes and Inscribed Tablets,* by Charles E. Putnam, 1885.

esteem; their testimony as to all essential facts is clear and convincing, and the circumstances narrated seem to fully establish the genuineness of these relics. . . . From the social standing and high character of the principal discoverers, no question has been, or can be, successfully raised as to the authenticity of this discovery."

The testimony of several members of the Academy is adduced to prove the impossibility of fraudulent insertion of interpolated antiquities into the Davenport mounds. "The learned and lamented Dr. R. J. Farquharson, who was as guileless in character as he was eminent in science," so testifies, as does William H. Pratt, the Curator of the Academy, a man of "exact methods and untiring industry." The point that had drawn Henshaw's fire in particular was Jacob Gass' connection with all the elephant finds; Putnam explains this by quoting one of his fellow academicians to the effect that Gass "is a very tireless worker, and not easily discouraged. The mounds in this region are very numerous, but not one in ten contains anything of value. This causes most men to become easily discouraged, but not Mr. Gass. After opening, say, twenty or more mounds without result, he will commence the next with as much vigor as the first. His work is always thorough, and if there is anything to be found he finds it."

Putnam points out that if the authenticity of the Davenport discoveries were established, "then archaeologists will find in them strong corroborative evidence that man and the mastodon were contemporary on this continent, and that the Mound-builders were a race anterior to the ancestors of the present American Indians, and of higher type and more advanced civilization. As this conclusion would conflict with the theory announced by the Bureau of Ethnology, Mr. Henshaw was compelled to discredit these important discoveries. Before his 'destructive criticism' [the phrase is Powell's] the characters of men and the verities of science must alike be swept away to make room for a favorite theory. It was doubtless unfortunate for the Davenport Academy that its remarkable discoveries impeded the progress of this knight-errant of science; but if its elephant pipes and inscribed tablets were authentic and genuine, then his favorite theory would seem to be at fault."

Quoting some of Henshaw's "hints, innuendoes, imaginings, suspicions," Putnam strikes him at a vulnerable point. Henshaw had evidently based his discussion of the elephant pipes on "some coarse wood-cuts" published in "an Eastern magazine," and had "made this second-hand information the poor excuse for his unscientific screed." Thus he had written that the Davenport elephants had no tails, although photographs of the pipes in the possession of the Smithsonian would have shown him that the appendages did in fact exist. "This ludicrous blunder on the part of Mr. Henshaw clearly reveals the culpable carelessness of his scientific methods," Putnam declares. As for Henshaw's comment about the absence of ivory in the mounds, Putnam suggests that "at the era of the Mound-builders, the elephant and mastodon must have nearly reached the point of extinction on this continent, and hence would be infrequently seen and the article of 'ivory' uncommon." He does not rule out the possibility that future explorations in mounds still unopened will bring some ivory relics to light.

To demonstrate the coexistence of man and mastodon, Putnam brings forth a ninefold roster of evidence, beginning with Koch's discovery in 1838 of stone axes and arrowheads among charred mastodon bones in Missouri. Some of this evidence has been rejected by more recent archaeologists; a good deal has been granted authenticity; but none of it indicates any contemporaneousness of mastodons and Mound Builders, merely of mastodons and unknown primitive huntsmen of undeterminable culture.

In defense of the maligned Reverend Mr. Gass, Putnam objects to the "singular perversion of facts" by which Henshaw had made it appear that Gass was busily planting mastodon carvings all over Iowa. He mentions the many witnesses to each of Gass' discoveries, and asserts that "his character [is] above reproach. . . . Mr. Gass . . . is now preaching to a congregation at Postville, in northern Iowa, where he is, as he everywhere has been, highly esteemed by his people. He is a good classical scholar, well-grounded in Hebrew, but with a decided scientific bent of mind, which accounts for his perseverance and enthusiasm in these archaeological explorations." Putnam attacks Henshaw for having gone beyond his field of special competence, ornithology; for attempting to act as a dictator to archaeologists; and for approaching "the limits of legal libel, in misrepresenting the pipes by the use of false illustrations."

He strikes the David-and-Goliath theme by contrasting the privately endowed Davenport Academy, located "far from the centers of wealth and power," protected by its poverty from motives for the perpetration of fraud, with the wealthy, powerful Smithsonian, with great sums at its command. "Its paid collectors, going up and down the land in quest of valuable relics, may be strongly tempted to magnify their vocations by the practice of shameless deceptions," he suggests. "Its wealth may invite fraud. The modern manufacturer of ancient relics may turn his back upon our mendicant Academy and offer his wares to these scientific capitalists." After asserting that many specimens in the Smithsonian's own collection may be fakes, Putnam warns, "The shafts of criticism so ruthlessly hurled at other gleaners in the same field may turn out to be dangerous weapons, and, after the manner of the ancient boomerang, may, peradventure, return to smite the senders."

The attack now shifts to Powell, who is seen as a sinister puppet-master manipulating complaisant marionettes like Henshaw; Putnam repeatedly contrasts Powell's theories with those of Squier and Davis, to Powell's disadvantage. He finds it amusing that the classic work of Squier and Davis had been a Smithsonian publication, and that Powell's attempted re-evaluation of their findings shows that "that institution has not been engaged in the 'diffusion of knowledge' at all, but instead, during all these years, has been scattering error broadcast through the land. We are, therefore, called upon to retrace our steps, to unlearn the lesson we have so long conned, and to take our places at the feet of strange teachers. This is certainly discouraging to American scholarship, and the thoughtful student will wisely pause and make careful inquiry as to which, after all, is error—the earlier or the later deductions."

Greatly grieved, Putnam refers to several recently published papers that have taken for granted Henshaw's debunking of the Davenport finds: "The mischief is now done. The 'destructive' work, commanded by Major Powell, seems complete. The unsupported accusation is caught up with avidity, passed from writer to writer, from paper to paper, from book to book, gathering volume in its passage, until, at length, having attained portentous proportions, the fiction may pass into history as fact. The fiction is thus fairly launched on its journey round the world and down the years." And he concludes, "The purpose of this paper will have been accomplished, if we have succeeded in vindicating a generous and worthy man from foul aspersions; our young and growing Academy from the stigma of participation in a disgraceful deception; and our unique and valuable relics from all reasonable ground for suspicion."

Time has been unkind to the "unique and valuable relics" of the Davenport Academy. Whatever the elephant pipes may have tried to portray, elephants were certainly not found in Iowa at the time of the building of the mounds, nor for some thousands of years prior to that time. But Charles Putnam's spirited defense, even though it was a defense of error, sprang from a vital thesis. All too often, powerful scientific establishments had, through scorn or suppression, served to stifle independent thought. Putnam feared that Powell's new Bureau of Ethnology was using its great influence to impose an intellectual tyranny on American archaeology. Even though it happened that the Bureau of Ethnology was closer to the truth on the subject of the elephant pipes than was the Davenport Academy of Natural Sciences, Putnam's fears were not unjustified; in decades to come, and on other subjects, the archaeologists who spoke for the Smithsonian were indeed able to demand and receive absolute allegiance to their ideas, not always with beneficial effect. The outraged cry from Iowa was a valiant but futile attempt to halt the new juggernaut.

4

While the staff of the Bureau of Ethnology labored, sometimes none too tactfully, to deflate Mound Builder mythology, the disseminators of myth remained equally diligent. The supporters of the theory that the Mound Builders were survivors from lost Atlantis became particularly vocal just as Major Powell's men were swinging into high gear.

Atlantis has been vexing the minds of men since about 355 B.C., when Plato, then in his seventies and nearing the end of his career, composed a dialogue called *Timaeus*. The chief characters of the dialogue are Socrates and two friends, Timaeus and Critias. At one point in the discussion Critias relates the story of Atlantis, which he says has been handed down in his family since the time of his great-grandfather, Dropides.

Dropides, Critias says, had received the story from the great lawgiver Solon, who had heard it from Egyptian priests of the city of Sais, at the head of the Nile Delta, about 550 B.C. The priests had told Solon of Athens' grandeur nine thousand years previously, and of the glorious moment when a mighty enemy had come out of the Atlantic, entering the Mediterranean between the Pillars of Hercules (today the Strait of Gibraltar). These invaders came from an island larger than Asia and Africa put together, called Atlantis.

The Atlanteans attempted to subdue Greece and Egypt. "And then, Solon," said the priests, "your country shone forth. . . . Being compelled to stand alone, she defeated and triumphed over the invaders." Soon after this great victory, "there occurred violent earthquakes and floods, and in a single day and night of rain . . . the island of Atlantis disappeared, and was sunk beneath the sea."

In a second dialogue, *Critias,* Plato provided some further details about the lost continent. It had been, he declared, a place of great splendor and wealth, with soaring palaces and vast canals and majestic bridges. One temple, 600 feet long and 300 feet wide, was entirely covered by silver, and its roof was of gold. Within, the ceiling was fashioned from ivory inlaid with silver and gold. There were gardens, racecourses, parks, superb harbors thronged with ships, and wealth beyond measure. And all this had gone to the bottom of the sea in a single day and night.

Plato's Atlantis was fiction; his pupil Aristotle said of it, "He who invented it also destroyed it." But the fable was a compelling one, and it survived the downfall of Greek culture and the eclipse of Plato's own writings. When European seamen began venturing into the Atlantic in the fifteenth and sixteenth centuries, there were frequent reports that the remnants of the lost continent had been sighted; and when they reached South and Central America and found the highly developed civilizations of the Aztecs, Incas, and Mayas, it was easy to conclude that these were the descendants of refugees from that great land.

Though many writers speculated on the location and fate of Atlantis, the modern Atlantean cult received its impetus from the work of Charles-Étienne Brasseur (1814–1874), known as "Brasseur de Bourbourg." In 1864, this French scholar came upon a dusty manuscript in the library of the Historical Academy of Madrid: Bishop Diego de Landa's account of the culture of the Mayas of Yucatán, which he had done so much to destroy. Landa had made a record, inaccurate and confused, of the Mayan alphabet, and Brasseur de Bourbourg attempted to use it to decipher the three known surviving Mayan books. He produced a grotesque account of a volcanic catastrophe, presuming it to be a description of the disaster that had overtaken Atlantis. His translation begins, "The master is he of the upheaved earth, the master of the calabash, the earth upheaved of the tawny beast (at the place engulfed beneath the floods); it is he, the master of the upheaved earth, of the swollen earth, beyond measure, he the master . . . of the basin of water."[186] In another work, Brasseur de Bourbourg pointed out parallels between Plato's Atlantis and a legendary land described in the *Popol Vuh,* a chronicle from Central America that he had translated.

Brasseur de Bourbourg found a remarkable disciple in Ignatius T. T. Donnelly (1831–1901), a native of Philadelphia who emigrated in 1856 to Minnesota, where he practiced law and published a newspaper. Donnelly founded a city called Nininger, near St. Paul, but was bankrupted in the panic of 1857; the following year he was elected Lieutenant-Governor of Minnesota at the age of 28, and subsequently spent eight years as a Republican member of Congress for his state. While in Washington, Donnelly devoted himself energetically to self-education, apparently spending as much time in the Library of Congress as he did in the Capitol, and it was there that he began to gather materials for his study of Atlantis. Defeated for re-election in 1870, Donnelly began to organize his materials into book form, and in 1882 Harper & Brothers brought out his *Atlantis: The Antediluvian World.* This vigorous, entertaining book won immediate popularity, going through some fifty printings and several translations, and is still in print. It convinced many influential individuals of the authenticity of the Atlantis tale, among them William Ewart Gladstone, four times Minister of England, who was so moved by Donnelly's book that in 1882 he asked Parliament for funds to sponsor an expedition to search for the outlines of Atlantis in the ocean. (He did not get the money.)

Donnelly followed his first book with *Ragnarok: The Age of Fire and Gravel* (1883), in which he endeavored to prove that the onset of the Pleistocene glaciation was the result of the collision of the earth with a comet. Then he abandoned cosmological speculation to produce *The Great Cryptogram* (1885), which undertook to show that the works of William Shakespeare had been written by Sir Francis Bacon. This created a cult of its own. In 1890, Donnelly published a science-fiction novel, *Caesar's Column: A Story of the Twentieth Century;* he was elected about the same time to the Minnesota State Senate, and became one of the prime movers of the Populist Party, running twice for Vice-President of the United States on the Populist ticket. "His death in 1901," wrote his follower, Egerton Sykes, "left the world poorer for the loss of a great liberal mind, an impassioned champion of the eternal verities, and the founder of the modern science of Atlantology."[187]

The relation of Ignatius Donnelly to the story of the Mound Builders is apparent on the first page of *Atlantis: The Antediluvian World,* where he sets forth the basic theses of his work:

"1. That there once existed in the Atlantic Ocean, opposite the mouth of the Mediterranean Sea, a large island, which was the remnant of an Atlantic continent, and known to the ancient world as Atlantis.

"2. That the description of this island given by Plato is not, as has long been supposed, fable, but veritable history.

"3. That Atlantis was the region where man first rose from a state of barbarism to civilization.

"4. That it became, in the course of ages, a populous and mighty nation, from whose overflowings the shores of the Gulf of Mexico, the Mississippi River, the Amazon, the Pacific coast of South America, the Mediterranean, the west coast of Europe and Africa, the Baltic, the Black Sea, and the Caspian were populated by civilized nations."

There are nine more of these theses, asserting that the gods and goddesses of the Greeks, Phoenicians, Hindus, and Scandinavians were simply the kings, queens, and heroes of Atlantis; that Atlantis was the literal Garden of Eden; that Egypt was Atlantis' first mainland colony; that the Atlanteans were the first manufacturers of iron; that the Phoenician alphabet was derived from an Atlantean alphabet, and that the same alphabet was conveyed from Atlantis to the Mayas of Central America; and—

"12. That Atlantis perished in a terrible convulsion of nature, in which the whole island sunk into the ocean, with nearly all its inhabitants.

"13. That a few persons escaped in ships and on rafts, and carried to the nations east and west the tidings of the appalling catastrophe, which has survived to our own time in the Flood and Deluge legends of the different nations of the Old and New worlds."[188]

In the course of developing these ideas Donnelly weaves an amazing fabric out of every scrap of myth available to him, from the deluge legends of Mesopotamia to the chronicles of the native kingdoms of Central America. His underlying idea is an ultra-diffusionist one: that every development of civilization stems from the fertile land of Atlantis, whose colonists went out to all corners of the world. He cites, for example, the Toltec migration legends preserved, at third hand, by Spanish *conquistadores* who heard them from the Aztecs. According to these stories, "the Toltecs traced their migration back to a starting-point called 'Aztlan' or 'Atlan.' This could be no other than Atlantis. . . . The Aztecs also claimed to have come originally from Aztlan. Their very name, Aztecs, was derived from Aztlan. They were Atlanteans."[189] Donnelly observes that "The western shores of Atlantis were not far distant from the West Indies; a people possessed of ships could readily pass from island to island until they reached the continent. . . . The commercial activity of the Atlanteans would soon reveal to them the shores of the Gulf. Commerce implies the plantation of colonies; the trading-post is always the nucleus of a settlement; we have seen this illustrated in modern times in the case of the English East India Company and the Hudson Bay Company. We can therefore readily believe that commercial intercourse between Atlantis and Yucatán, Honduras, and Mexico, created colonies along the shores of the Gulf which gradually spread into the interior, and to the high table-lands of Mexico. And, accordingly, we find that all the traditions of Central America and Mexico point to some country in the East, and beyond the sea, as the source of their first civilized people; and this region, known among them as 'Aztlan,' lived in the memory of the people as a beautiful and happy land, where their ancestors had dwelt in peace for many generations."[190]

To support this theory Donnelly brings forth a long series of cultural parallels between Europe, the Near East, and the Americas, designed to trace the common origin of everything from Atlantis. The list is impressive, if wildly inaccurate. He asserts that one third of the Mayan language is pure Greek; that the flat-topped pyramids of Mexico are kin to the pointed ones of Egypt; that the Otomi language of Mexico is related to Chinese; that Chiapanec, a Central American tongue, resembles Hebrew; that Mayan "is not devoid of words from the Assyrian"; that styles of art are alike in the Old World and the New; that Etruscans and Mayas used the same type of corbeled arch; that there are strong similarities of myth and religion; that such cultural-traits as the use of spears, sails, metals, and agriculture are derived from a common source. Most of these statements, particularly the linguistic ones, are simply wrong; the others can be accounted for by explanations less elaborate than the hypothesis of a common (and lost) ancestral continent.

Mound building is one of the cultural traits Donnelly adduces. "The mounds of Europe and Asia were made in the same way and for the same purposes as those of America," he declares. "Herodotus describes the burial of a Scythian king; he says, 'After this they set to work to raise a vast mound above the grave, all of them vying with each other, and seeking to make it as tall as possible.' 'It must be confessed,' says Foster, 'that these Scythic burial rites have a strong resemblance to those of the Mound Builders.' Homer describes the erection of a great symmetrical mound over Achilles, also one over Hector. Alexander the Great raised a great mound over his friend Hephaestion, at a cost of more than a million dollars; and Semiramis raised a similar mound over her husband. . . . Foster believes that the grave-cists made of stone of the American mounds are exactly like the stone chests, or *kistvaen* for the dead, found in the British mounds. Tumuli have been found in Yorkshire enclosing wooden coffins, precisely as in the mounds of the Mississippi Valley. The articles associated with the dead are the same in both continents: arms, trinkets, food, clothes, and funeral urns. In both the Mississippi Valley and among the Chaldeans vases were constructed around the bones, the neck of the vase being too small to permit the extraction of the skull."[191]

Again, some of this is untrue, the rest generalized to the point where any trait could be said to be related to any other. But it forms a part of Donnelly's huge, rickety conceptual edifice. So, too, do the Davenport elephants:

"We find in America numerous representations of the elephant. We are forced to one of two conclusions: either the monuments date back to the time of the mammoth in North America, or these people held intercourse at some time in the past with races who possessed the elephant, and from whom they obtained pictures of that singular animal. Plato tells us that the Atlanteans possessed great numbers of elephants.

"There are in Wisconsin a number of mounds of earth representing different animals—men, birds, and quadrupeds. Among the latter is a mound representing an elephant, 'so perfect in its proportions, and complete in its representation of an elephant, that its builders must have been well acquainted with all the physical characteristics of the animal which they delineated.' [The quotation, which of course is inaccurate, is not attributed.]

"On a farm in Louisa County, Iowa, a pipe was plowed up which also represents an elephant. It was found in a section where the ancient mounds were very abundant and rich in relics. The pipe is of sandstone, of the ordinary Mound Builder's type, and has every appearance of age and usage. There can be no doubt of its genuineness."[192]

The Mound Builders, according to Donnelly, were offshoots of the Atlantean colonies in Mexico. "What would be more natural," he asks, "than that these adventurous navigators, passing around the shores of the Gulf, should, sooner or later, discover the mouth of the Mississippi River; and what more certain than that they would enter it, explore it, and plant colonies along its shores, wherever they found a fertile soil and salubrious climate?" He argues for a spread of the Mound Builders up the Mississippi and along its tributaries, halting at the Allegheny Mountains, but going westward as far as Oregon via the Missouri and Yellowstone rivers. He takes as typical of their works the Cahokia Mound at East St. Louis, Illinois, which is not typical at all, since it is a flat-topped temple mound of great size, unrelated stylistically or culturally to the conical burial mounds and earthen embankments of Ohio. Donnelly calmly insists that the Ohio mounds "were not cones but four-sided pyramids —their sides, like those of the Egyptian pyramids, corresponding with the cardinal points." That the Mound Builders "had attained a considerable degree of civilization" he shows by citing the geometrical accuracy of their enclosures, quoting Squier on this point. Donnelly adds, "They also possessed an accurate system of weights; bracelets of copper on the arms of a skeleton have been found to be of uniform size, measuring each two and nine-tenths inches, and each weighing *precisely four ounces.*"

The embankment at Fort Ancient, he claims, was large enough to "have held a garrison of sixty thousand men with their families and provisions." At a Newark mound he finds "a threefold symbol, like a bird's foot; the central mound is 155 feet long, and the other two each 110 feet in length. Is this curious design a reminiscence of Atlantis and the three-pronged trident of Poseidon?" He reports that "the Mound Builders made sun-dried brick mixed with rushes, as the Egyptians made sun-dried bricks mixed with straw." (The Mississippi Valley mounds were made of earth, not of brick.) He declares that "the Mound Builders also understood the art of casting metals, or they held intercourse with some race who did," and exhumes Hildreth's 1819 Marietta find of copper supposedly plated with silver, quoting Squier's revised opinion that "it is beyond doubt that the copper bosses were absolutely *plated,* not simply *overlaid,* with silver." A lengthy discussion of the advanced state of Mound Builder technology and art follows. Donnelly also offers Squier's manatee and toucan effigies as proof of contact between Ohio and the tropics.

Of the high antiquity of the Mound Builders he is convinced. The fact that the mounds had yielded many objects of copper and none of bronze indicates to him that the founders of the American colonies had left Atlantis before the discovery of the art of manufacturing bronze, though he concedes that an absence of tin in the Mississippi Valley may have hampered the development of an alloying technology there. He produces supposed skeletal evidence to prove that the Mound Builders were ancient, and quotes J. D. Baldwin on the absence of mounds on the most recent terraces of the river valleys. As for the withdrawal of the Mound Builders from the territory of the United States, Donnelly remarks, "the Mound Builders retreated southward toward Mexico, and probably arrived there some time between A.D. 29 and A.D. 231, under the name of Nahuas. They called the region they left in the Mississippi Valley 'Hue Hue Tlapalan'—*the old, old red land*—in allusion, probably, to the red-clay soil of part of the country."[193] He concludes, "The proofs, then, of the connection of the Mound Builders with Atlantis are:

"1. Their race identity with the nations of Central America who possessed Flood legends, and whose traditions all point to an eastern, oversea origin; while the many evidences of their race identity with the ancient Peruvians indicate that they were part of one great movement of the human race, extending from the Andes to Lake Superior, and, as I believe, from Atlantis to India.

"2. The similarity of their civilization, and their works of stone and bronze, with the civilization of the Bronze Age in Europe. [On his previous page Donnelly had admitted that no bronze artifacts had been discovered in the mounds.]

"3. The presence of great truncated mounds, kindred to the pyramids of Central America, Mexico, Egypt, and India.

"4. The representation of tropical animals, which point to an intercourse with the regions around the Gulf of Mexico, where the Atlanteans were colonized.

"5. The fact that the settlements of the Mound Builders were confined to the valley of the Mississippi, and were apparently densest at those points where a population advancing up that stream would first reach high, healthy, and fertile lands.

"6. The hostile nations which attacked them came from the north; and when the Mound Builders could no longer hold the country, or when Atlantis sunk in the sea, they retreated in the direction whence they came, and fell back upon their kindred races in Central America, as the Roman troops in Gaul and Britain drew southward upon the destruction of Rome.

"7. The Natchez Indians, who are supposed to have descended from the

Mound Builders, kept a perpetual fire burning before an altar, watched by old men who were a sort of priesthood, as in Europe.

"8. If the tablet said to have been found in a mound near Davenport, Iowa, is genuine, which appears probable, the Mound Builders must either have possessed an alphabet, or have held intercourse with some people who did. This singular relic exhibits what appears to be a sacrificial mound with a fire upon it; over it are the sun, moon, and stars, and above these a mass of hieroglyphics which bear some resemblance to the letters of European alphabets, and especially to that unknown alphabet which appears upon the inscribed bronze celt found near Rome. . . ."[194]

5

The Bureau of Ethnology did not bear singlehanded the burden of coping with this sort of misplaced ingenuity. Another powerful force for rationality at this time was Frederic Ward Putnam, Curator of the Peabody Museum of American Archaeology and Ethnology of Harvard University. Putnam— who was not related to Charles Putnam of Davenport, but who was connected to that family of New England Putnams to which Rufus Putnam of Marietta had belonged——was born in Salem, Massachusetts, in 1839. His first love was ornithology; but in 1856 he entered Harvard and came under the influence of the great naturalist Louis Agassiz, who aroused his interest in ichthyology. "His interests were always too living to become specialized in one secluded field," wrote the anthropologist A. L. Kroeber upon Putnam's death in 1915. "His studies were irregular, self-directed, and therefore the more fruitful." Kroeber speaks of Putnam's "special bent of mind toward direct, candid, and lucid observation of natural phenomena."[195]

Between 1864 and 1875, Putnam held a variety of curatorships in ichthyology at Boston and Salem. In 1873, his diligence and high professional standing brought him the post of permanent secretary of the American Association for the Advancement of Science, which he held for a quarter of a century. And two years later he was called to the curatorship of the decade-old Peabody Museum at Cambridge.

The Peabody owed its origin, in part, to the mounds. Othniel Charles Marsh, best known as a prodigious unearther of dinosaurs in the American West, had visited the Newark mounds in 1865 as part of a post-post-graduate tour after completing his paleontological studies in Germany. Marsh had induced his wealthy uncle, George Peabody, to endow a Peabody Museum of Natural

History at Yale, devoted primarily to zoology, geology, and mineralogy. But in the first flush of his short-lived enthusiasm for mounds, Marsh also persuaded Uncle George to set up, at Harvard, an ethnological museum. The selection of Frederic Putnam in 1875 to head the Harvard Peabody indicates how far he had wandered from his original zoological interests.

As an archaeologist and ethnologist, Putnam's role in the context of his day was that of a judicious liberal. While not subscribing to the prevailing myths of the American past, he was strongly convinced of the antiquity of man in the Americas—a position that was slightly unorthodox in the 1870's and 1880's, and downright heretical by the time of Putnam's death. Putnam was an ardent champion of the work of C. C. Abbott, who in 1873 had discovered an ancient Indian campsite in a gravel field near Trenton, New Jersey. Abbott claimed an extremely early date for the Trenton artifacts; in 1889, after prolonged study, he announced, "we are pretty sure of twenty or thirty thousand years now." Putnam backed him in this, even though a gradually hardening school of archaeological thought was coming to maintain that man had entered the Americas only two or three thousand years before, at the earliest. (The Trenton artifacts were later shown to be relatively recent.) In the steadily more vitriolic battle over the antiquity of New World man that developed in the early twentieth century, Putnam gently and consistently backed those who accepted the "long chronology."

On the subject of the Mound Builders he leaned slightly to the side of those who postulated a superior race. He began field work in Ohio in the summer of 1882; two years later, when the British Association for the Advancement of Science was meeting at Montreal, Putnam described the beauty of artifacts taken from the mounds, and said, "These relics seem to show a more complex social life, more abundant and varied artistic products, and a higher status altogether, than can be deemed consistent with the views of those who hold that these Mound-builders were merely the ancestors of our present Indians, and in the same state of culture."[196] Considering what we now know about the builders of the Ohio mounds, this statement is eminently sound: they *were* of "a higher status altogether" than the nomadic Indian huntsmen regarded in the nineteenth century as typical of the entire Indian people. Of course, anyone who said in 1884 that he thought the Mound Builders were superior to the contemporary Indians would seem to be affiliating himself with the extremist lost-race faction; but that was not Putnam's intent at all.

A more representative sampling of his theories on the mounds is to be found in the Twenty-second Annual Report of the Peabody Museum (1888). Here Putnam clearly states the idea, destined to win favor in later years, that instead of a single race of Mound Builders there was a succession of mound-building races in the Ohio Valley. He also expresses the belief, consistent with his views on man's antiquity in the Americas, that man and mammoth were contemporaries, but he does not make the mistake of his Davenport namesake in jumping to the fallacious conclusion that there was co-existence between mammoth and Mound Builder:

"In the great Ohio Valley we have found places of contact and mixture of two races, and have made out much of interest, telling of conflict and defeat, of the conquered and the conquerors. The long, narrow-headed people from the north, who can be traced from the Pacific to the Atlantic, extending down both coasts, and extending their branches towards the interior, meeting the short-headed and southern race, here and there. Our explorations have brought to light considerable evidence to show that after the rivers cut their way through the glacial gravels and formed their present channels, leaving great alluvial plains upon their borders, a race of men, with short, broad heads, reached the valley from the southwest. Here they cultivated the land, raised crops of corn and vegetables, and became skilled artisans in stone and their native metals, in shell and terra-cotta, making weapons and ornaments and utensils of various kinds. Here were their places of worship. Here were their towns, often surrounded by earth embankments, their fixed places for burning their dead, their altars of clay, where cremation offerings, ornaments, by thousands were thrown upon the fire. Upon the hills near by were their places of refuge or fortified towns. Preceding these were the people of the glacial gravels. The implements which had been lost by preglacial men have been found in the Miami Valley, as in the Delaware Valley. This would seem to give a minimum antiquity of man's existence in the Ohio Valley from eight to ten thousand years. From the time when man was the contemporary of the mastodon and the mammoth to the settlement of the region by our own race, successive peoples have inhabited this valley."[197]

A few years earlier Putnam had introduced a refreshing note of reason into the controversy over the metallurgical abilities of the Mound Builders. Ever since Dr. Samuel Hildreth had reported finding objects of copper and silver in the Marietta mounds, the legend of these abilities had grown continuously. Caleb Atwater, publishing Hildreth's account in his own paper of 1820, had added some notes on his findings at Circleville of traces of iron oxide. E. G. Squier, in 1849, had given credence to the idea that the Mound Builders could plate metal upon metal, and Ignatius Donnelly's book of 1882 had used the Hildreth-Atwater-Squier data to shore up his theory of an Atlantean origin for the Mound Builders. Certain other writers had distorted the story by failing to check on the original Hildreth and Atwater reports, so that the belief had become general that Hildreth had found a sword of iron or steel at Marietta, and that Atwater had found an iron blade and a plate of cast iron at Circleville.

Putnam dealt with these misconceptions in an article called "Iron from the Ohio Mounds," which appeared in the *Proceedings of the American Antiquarian Society* for April 25, 1883. He pointed out that the supposed fact of the discovery of iron artifacts in the mounds had given rise to four theories, some of which were mutually exclusive:

"*First,* as showing that the people who built the mounds had acquired the knowledge of manufacturing implements from iron, and hence were far in advance of the Indian tribes who afterwards occupied the country; or

"*Secondly,* that the ancient mound-builders had occasional intercourse with nations farther advanced in the arts than themselves.

"*Thirdly,* as proving beyond question the recent origin of the mounds: since the iron or steel weapons must have been obtained from the whites, and therefore the mounds were erected after contact of the Indians with the Europeans; or

"*Fourthly,* that, while the mounds themselves were very ancient, the iron was introduced in recent times in connection with intrusive burials."

Putnam was able to explode these theories by the simple method of quoting the relevant passage from Atwater. What Atwater had found at Circleville was no more than a piece of antler, in one end of which a hole had been bored; this he called "the handle of either a small sword or large knife," but distinctly stated, "no iron was found, but an oxyde remained of similar shape and size." This "oxyde," Putnam observes, "could be readily accounted for by one familiar with the traces of oxidized copper, iron-colored clay, and traces of oxide of iron, which are often met with in mound explorations." Atwater's other reference, to "a plate of iron, which had become an oxyde," goes on to speak of a *resemblance* to "a plate of cast iron." But nowhere did Atwater say that the plate was actually cast iron. If it had been iron at all, which was doubtful, it must have been meteoric iron found naturally and cold-hammered into shape.

The case of Hildreth's copper artifacts, "overlaid with a thick plate of silver," was more complex. Similar objects had been found in 1815 in Cincinnati, and reported in Drake's *Picture of Cincinnati,* published that year. Hildreth had suggested that these round copper plates might be "ornaments for a sword belt, or a buckler," but later archaeologists had simply termed them "spool-shaped objects" while awaiting some definite explanation of their function.

Putnam, as he examined the collections of the Peabody Museum, had become aware of the use of large earplugs in pre-Columbian Mexico and Peru; these studlike ornaments had been inserted in the distended earlobes of upper-class males. It struck him that the "spool-shaped objects" of the Ohio Valley might also be earplugs, thus demonstrating another cultural connection between the Mound Builders and the high civilizations of the Americas. But he hesitated to draw this parallel because he had never seen, among the human-effigy figures recovered from the mounds, any that depicted the studlike ear ornaments so commonly represented in the pottery figures of men from Mexico and Peru. On the contrary, human effigies from the mounds generally showed the ears as pierced by small holes for the suspension of earrings.

21   Copper ear plugs, Lauderdale County, Alabama. Courtesy Museum of the American Indian, Heye Foundation.

However, in the course of his 1882 mound excavations in Ohio, Putnam brought to light "a large number of these interesting copper ornaments, some of which are covered, or plated, with thin layers of silver, like those found by Dr. Hildreth, while at least one is overlaid in the same manner with a thin sheet of meteoric iron. During these explorations there were found a number of terra-cotta figurines of a character unlike anything heretofore known from the mounds, and one of these, representing in miniature a full length figure of a man, leaves little doubt that these 'spool-shaped objects' and 'bosses' are ear-ornaments. In this instance the ornament is distinctly shown as two large disks with the lobe of the ear between them. About thirty of these copper, and silver and iron-plated ear-ornaments were found on one altar in the Little Miami Valley, and in another mound of the same group three pairs were discovered with human skeletons, and in each case one was found on the right side and one on the left, near the skull."

The question of how adept the Mound Builders were at plating metals was settled by Putnam's careful study of the Hildreth specimens and these newly discovered ones: "The plating has been done simply by covering the outer surfaces of the objects with thin sheets of the overlaid metal, which were closely united to the copper simply by pounding and rubbing, and by turning the edges over and under the slightly concave edge of the copper foundation." However, Putnam says, "these ear-ornaments exhibit a degree of skill in working the native metals of copper, silver and iron, simply by hammering, which is conclusive evidence of the advance made by early American tribes in ornamental art."

Hildreth's "sword" from Marietta, much magnified by later commentators, is likewise viewed in perspective. Hildreth had reported merely "a plate of silver, which appears to have been the upper part of a sword scabbard." After remarking on the process whereby this report was twisted into a purported account of the finding of an iron sword, Putnam shows that the "scabbard" was probably an ornament for the hair, as shown on a pottery human effigy from Tennessee. He had found similar artifacts himself, some of copper, one of meteoric iron. Though he thus conceded the use of iron by the Mound Builders, he notes that what Hildreth took to be "iron rust" was more likely copper oxide.

"In this instance," says Putnam, "we see how easily [sic] it is to let our imagination run away with our facts. Not a shadow of a sword can be traced in this connection; the point of the supposed scabbard is a common copper bead; the supposed upper part of the scabbard is an ornament of a particular pattern, of which three others almost identical in shape are known from other mounds; and the 'bosses' or supposed ornaments of a sword belt are ear-rings. Yet for over sixty years archaeologists have had the mythical swords from the Marietta and Circleville mounds held over them as proofs that all the mounds were of recent date, and that these in particular were erected after contact of the Indians with the whites." Putnam might have added that the same swords were used with equal effect to prove the great antiquity of the mounds, the high technological attainments of their builders, and the possible Atlantean origins of the natives of the Ohio Valley.

6

Cyrus Thomas of the Bureau of Ethnology was now deep in the mound investigations that Congress had so unexpectedly thrust upon Major Powell's bureau. During the fiscal year 1883–84 the project expanded greatly. Thomas himself remained in Washington most of the time, like a general directing his troops from the rear lines; he plotted areas of attack, classified the artifacts that flooded toward the Smithsonian, and brooded over the task of covering all of the nation's thousands of mounds. Meanwhile, his three full-time field assistants and several part-time workers surveyed, sketched, dug, and collected. For purposes of field work Thomas divided the mound area into three zones: from Wisconsin to Ohio, from Ohio to Mississippi along the Mississippi Valley, and from eastern Tennessee and western North Carolina down the coast through Georgia and Alabama to Florida. Most of the Bureau of Ethnology's efforts were concentrated in the first of these zones.

Ideally, Thomas knew, the way to go about the enterprise was to prepare a comprehensive and accurate survey of all the mounds, with maps and illustrations, and to explore them by excavation only after these preliminaries were finished. But limitations of funds, lack of qualified personnel, and other handicaps made such a grand survey impossible. A full set of maps and charts of the mounds, Thomas discovered, would be so costly as to require the full appropriation of the Bureau of Ethnology for at least ten years. And while they were being prepared, the mounds would remain vulnerable to the raids of private collectors and the wanton destruction imposed on them by impatient farmers.

So he had to scrap the idea of charting first, investigating later. Too many mounds would be gone forever before the mapping was finished. An alternative plan was proposed: to select one particular zone of mounds and confine operations to it until all the ancient works in it were thoroughly examined, charted, excavated, and described in detail, and then to move on to another zone. But this, too, had drawbacks. It would leave Bureau of Ethnology personnel idle for much of the year, since they would not be able to work in the chosen zone in the winter, and probably their summer work would be handicapped by the planting and harvesting requirements of the farmers on whose lands most mounds were found. And the constant destruction of mounds by natural erosion, private excavation, and public ignorance would remove from study many of the most interesting monuments, no matter which zone was chosen first for intensive exploration.

So Thomas selected the middle course that left him open to a charge of spreading himself thin. He decided to carry on operations at a number of places at once, moving his men about to meet seasonal conditions, excavating sites as soon as they had been surveyed, without waiting for a broad pattern to emerge from the entire mound district, and leaving one site for another once its immediate value appeared exhausted.

The purpose of the work, said Thomas, was to answer the question posed by Major Powell: "Were the mound builders Indians?" If an affirmative answer were reached after careful study of the mounds and their contents, "then the investigation of the questions relating to their objects and uses would be merged in the study of the former habits, customs, art, beliefs, &c., of the Indians. There would then be no more blind groping by archaeologists for the thread to lead them out of the mysterious labyrinth; the chain which binds together the prehistoric and the historic ages of our country would then be known; a thousand and one wild theories and archaeological romances would be regulated to the shades of oblivion; and, the relations of all the lines of investigation to one another being known, these lines would lend common aid in solving many of the problems which have hitherto seemed destined to remain in complete obscurity. Should the result of the examination give a decidedly negative answer to the question, one broad field at least would be forever closed. . . ."[198]

The Fifth Annual Report of the Bureau of Ethnology, covering fiscal 1883–84, appeared in 1887. Major Powell was able to point in his report to a great deal of mound work. P. W. Norris had worked in the Kanawha Valley of West Virginia in late 1883; when cold weather forced a suspension there, he dug in Arkansas, but returned to West Virginia in May and June, 1884. James D. Middleton spent the summer and fall of 1883 exploring burial mounds in Wisconsin; in the winter he, too, went to Arkansas. L. H. Thing passed a few months of autumn and winter in exploring mounds of the southeastern counties of Missouri and the northeastern portion of Arkansas; John P. Rogan worked in Florida and Georgia, where he dug at the giant Etowah Mound near Cartersville. Dr. Edward Palmer's zone of operations was Alabama and southwestern Georgia, and John W. Emmert worked a short while in Tennessee and North Carolina.

From their research Thomas distilled the Bureau of Ethnology's first formal theoretical report on the mounds. It occupied more than a hundred pages of the Fifth Annual Report under the title, "Burial Mounds of the Northern Sections of the United States." Though only a preliminary version of Thomas' eventual huge work on the mounds, it stated all the essential conclusions of that work, and, despite its title, embraced not only the Northern mounds but those of North Carolina, Tennessee, and Georgia.

To no one's surprise, Thomas found nothing that tended to disprove Major Powell's earlier opinions about the builders of the mounds. Though he states again and again that his conclusions are preliminary and that it is premature to speculate, Thomas' own agreement with the Powell position is evident on every page. He opposes the "lost race" theory, and says, "whether the 'Indian theory' proves to be correct or not, I wish to obtain for it at least a fair consideration. I believe the latter theory to be the correct one, as the facts so far ascertained appear to point in that direction, but I am not wedded to it; on the contrary, I am willing to follow the facts wherever they lead."[199]

He concedes that the thought that a mighty nation once occupied the great valley of the Mississippi, with a chief ruler, a system of government, a religion, a mighty central city, is "fascinating and attractive." He sees the romance in the image of the disappearance of this nation "before the inroads of savage hordes, leaving behind it no evidences of its existence, its glory, power, and extent save these silent forest-covered remains." But he warns that this theory, when once it has taken possession of the mind, "warps and biases all its conclusions."

Lest he be thought too subservient a Powell acolyte, Thomas quotes the considered opinion of Frederic Putnam, who was independent of the Bureau of Ethnology: "That more than one of the several American stocks or nations or groups of tribes built mounds seems to me to be established. What their connections were is not yet by any means clear, and to say that they all must have been one and the same people seems to be making a statement directly contrary to the facts, which are yearly increasing as the spade and pick in careful hands brings them to light."[200] This supports the Powell-Thomas thesis that the theory of a single great race of Mound Builders ruling from Dakota to Florida, from New York to Louisiana, "is fast breaking down before the evidence that is produced." But Thomas is careful to quote Putnam's further statement, "That many Indian tribes built mounds and earthworks is beyond doubt, but that all the mounds and earthworks of North America were made by these same tribes or their immediate ancestors is not thereby proved."

Thomas' paper classifies the mounds by types into eight cultural districts:

1) The *Wisconsin district,* covering Wisconsin, northern Illinois, and northeastern Iowa, distinguished by effigy mounds.

2) The *Illinois* or *Upper Mississippi district,* marked by the simple conical tumuli found in eastern Iowa, northeastern Missouri, and northern and central Illinois.

3) The *Ohio district,* including Ohio, western West Virginia, and eastern Indiana, where earthen embankments and enclosures are found in conjunction with mounds.

4) The *New York district,* where he follows Squier in attributing the mounds to Indians of historic times.

5) The *Appalachian district,* of western North Carolina, eastern Tennessee, southwestern Virginia, and southeastern Kentucky, where the mounds are

similar to those of Ohio but where Thomas detected certain underlying cultural differences.

6) The *Middle Mississippi* or *Tennessee district,* including southeast Missouri, northern Arkansas, western Tennessee, and western Kentucky—a region of truncated pyramidal mounds.

7) The *Lower Mississippi* district, including the southern half of Arkansas, Louisiana, and Mississippi, similar to the last, but more densely populated, and showing a decided improvement in pottery technique.

8) The *Gulf district,* again a region of truncated pyramids, and not notably different from the last two.

Thomas also recognizes the existence of a Florida subdistrict; but he says that the data are insufficient for classification, a fact also evident in the absence of demarcations for his sixth, seventh, and eighth classes. Nevertheless, his eight groupings still remain current in archaeological thought, although vast alterations of terminology have occurred.

Following this attempt at classification, Thomas reports on the work his division has done thus far. He describes and charts mounds in Wisconsin, Iowa, Missouri, Ohio, Illinois, and several other states, backing up the archaeological findings with ethnological data gathered from explorers and researchers in the field. His purpose is to prove that a continuous spectrum of mound building can be found in some areas of the country from prehistoric times almost to the present. As an example, he produces an account of the mound burial of an Indian chief in Iowa in 1830, after the Black Hawk War; the dead chieftain went to his grave in a full military suit given him by President Jackson, and in his hands were placed trophies he had won from other Indian tribes and from the whites. Passing from state to state, Thomas gathers together accounts not only of his own men's work, but of the excavations of Putnam for the Peabody and of many private investigators, so that the report becomes a full account of American mound archaeology *circa* 1884. Hundreds of mounds are covered.

The value of Thomas' insistence that the mounds were not all built by the same culture at the same time becomes increasingly apparent as the evidence mounts. He allows himself a few hesitant conjectures; the effigy mounds, he says, "were built by the Indian tribes found inhabiting that section at the advent of the whites, or by their ancestors. . . . But the case is somewhat different in reference to the works of the Ohio district. Although the data here obtained point with satisfactory certainty to the conclusion that Indians were the authors of these works, it cannot be claimed that all or even the larger portion of them were built by Indians inhabiting the district when first visited by the whites, or by their ancestors."[201] In trying to identify the builders of these mounds, Thomas resorts to Heckewelder's old tale of the Tallegewi, tentatively suggesting that these were the people responsible for the famous Ohio and West Virginia mounds, and that, driven out of their homeland in some ancient war, they migrated to the Carolinas and became the modern Cherokees.

The ghost of yet another vanished race arises when Thomas turns to a consideration of the Etowah Mound of Georgia. In the course of John Rogan's work at Etowah in 1883–84, certain bizarre and striking artifacts of a previously unknown type had come to light. These were thin, evenly wrought sheets of copper, on which had been impressed, as if with stamping dies or machinery, intricate outlined figures of strange and fanciful appearance. Several of the plates showed profile views of full-length human figures with fiercely hooked noses and savage mouths; the figures were winged, wore complex

22 Copper plate engraving from Etowah Mound, Georgia. *From Report on the Mound Explorations of the Bureau of Ethnology, Twelfth Annual Report.*

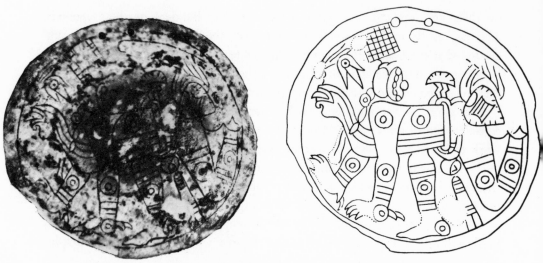

23   Shell disc with incised figure of mythical man-animal, Hale County,
Alabama. Courtesy of Museum of the American Indian, Heye Foundation.

headdresses, and were shown dangling severed human heads from their hands.
Some of the same motifs were found on pieces of engraved shell. All these
designs were vigorously executed and oddly powerful; to Major Powell, they
were reminiscent of the sophisticated yet barbaric art of the Aztecs and Mayas,
which also abounded in winged figures, men with beaked faces, and severed
heads. But Cyrus Thomas, studying the Etowah engravings more carefully,
found several features which were unknown to Mexican and Central American
art. For example, the wings on the two largest copper plates were represented
as rising from the back of the shoulders. "Although we can find numerous
figures of winged individuals in Mexican designs (they are unknown in Central
American)," wrote Thomas, "they always carry with them the idea that the
individual is partly or completely clothed in the skin of the bird. This is
partially carried out in our copper plate, as we see by the bird-bill over the
head, the eye being that of the bird and not of the man. But when we come to
the wings we at once see that the artist had in mind the *angel figure,* with
wings arising from the *back of the shoulders,* an idea wholly foreign to Mexican art. . . . That these plates are not the work of the Indians found inhabiting
the southern sections of the United States, or of their direct ancestors, I freely
concede. That they were not made by an aboriginal artisan of Central America
or Mexico of ante-Colombian times, I think is evident, if not from the designs
themselves, certainly from the indisputable evidence that the work was done

with hard metallic tools."[202] But Thomas was unable to guess at the identity of the creators of the Etowah plates; he could conclude only that "the Etowah mounds were not built by the Cherokees."

In a page and a half of summary, Thomas closes this 1884 report with eight points having to do with the builders of the mounds and their customs. "Different sections were occupied by different mound-building tribes," he asserts, "which, though belonging to much the same stage in the scale of civilization, differed in most instances in habits and customs. . . . There is nothing found in the mode of constructing these mounds, nor in the vestiges of art they contain, to indicate that their builders had reached a higher culture-status than that attained by some of the Indian tribes found occupying the country at the time of the first arrival of Europeans." He points out that the custom of erecting mounds over the dead had continued in some localities well into historic times, and that the character and condition of the mounds shows that "the mound-building age could not have continued in this part of the continent longer than a thousand years, and hence that its commencement probably does not antedate the fifth or sixth century." Tree-ring evidence to the contrary he dismisses; "the rings of trees are not a sure indication of age." And, finally: "All the mounds which have been examined and carefully studied are to be attributed to the indigenous tribes found inhabiting this region and their ancestors."[203]

7

Cyrus Thomas' next report on his mound work appeared outside the regular series of Bureau of Ethnology Annual Reports. Delays of several years had been encountered in getting these big volumes into print, and in August, 1886, Powell obtained Congressional permission to issue a series of supplementary bulletins. Five such paperbound bulletins appeared in 1887, and the fourth of these was Thomas' *Work in Mound Exploration of the Bureau of Ethnology.*

The twelve pages of text in this booklet comprise a sort of prospectus for Thomas' division. He outlines the purposes of the mound research, the methods of his survey, and the area covered. He tells how artifacts were collected in the field and shipped to the Bureau of Ethnology for cataloguing. "Hundreds of groups have been examined and, in most cases, surveyed, platted, and described," he says. "Over two thousand mounds have been explored, including almost every known type as to form, from the low, diminutive, circular burial tumulus of the North to the huge, truncated earthen pyramid of the South, the embankment, the effigy, the stone cairn, house site, &c. . . . The number of specimens obtained by the division since its organization is not less than thirty-eight thousand; fully one-half of these were discovered by the assistants during their explorations; the remainder were obtained by donations and purchase, though not more than $500 have been expended by the Bureau for this purpose."

He advises that a detailed report covering Bureau of Ethnology field work through the end of 1886 was in preparation, forming, "when printed, two quarto volumes of about five hundred pages each." It would describe all mounds studied; the artifacts taken from them would be analyzed and illustrated; and some general conclusions on the Mound Builders would be proposed. But Thomas could not resist announcing some of his findings in this bulletin:

"Some singular and rather unexpected discoveries . . . have been made, which it may not be amiss to mention. . . . From a mound in Wisconsin were obtained a few silver crosses, silver brooches, and silver bracelets, one of the last with the word 'Montreal' stamped on it in plain letters. These evidently pertained to an intrusive burial. In another Wisconsin mound, which stands in the midst of a group of effigies, was found, lying at the bottom on the original surface of the ground, near the center, a genuine, regularly-formed gunflint. In another, in Tennessee, some six feet high and which showed no signs of disturbance, an old fashioned, horn-handled case knife was discovered near the bottom. Far down in another of large size and also in comparatively modern Indian graves, at widely different points, have been found little sleigh-bells, probably what were formerly known as 'hawk bells,' made of copper, with pebble and shell bead rattles, and all of precisely the same pattern and finish. From a group in Northern Mississippi, in the locality formerly occupied by the Chickasaw, were obtained a silver plate, with the Spanish coat of arms stamped upon it, and the iron portions of a saddle. At the bottom of a North Carolina mound parts of an iron blade and an iron awl were discovered in the hands of the principal personage buried therein; with these were engraved shells and polished celts. . . . In addition to these, the assistants have obtained from mounds such things as brass kettles with iron bails, brass wire, wooden ladles, glass beads, &c. Some of these things clearly pertained to intrusive burials, but a large portion of them were evidently placed in the mounds at the time they were constructed and with the original interment, as shown by their positions when discovered."

All this was proof of the recent construction of many mounds, at a time of contact between Indian and white man. Thomas goes on to list thirteen general conclusions about the mounds—an amplified version of his eight-point summary in the Fifth Annual Report. Again he declares, "nothing trustworthy has been discovered to justify the theory that the mound builders belonged to a highly civilized race. . . . The links discovered directly connecting the Indians and mound builders are so numerous and well established that there should be no longer any hesitancy in accepting the theory that the two are one and the same people." He notes that archaeological work had confirmed the accounts of de Soto's chroniclers and other early explorers in the Southeast, who had written of mounds used by living tribes. And he chops at a few of the migration theories by saying, "The testimony of the mounds is very decidedly against the theory that the mound builders were Mayas or Mexicans, who, driven out of this region by the pressure of Indian hordes, migrated to the valley of Anahuac or plains of Yucatan. . . . It likewise gives a decided negative to the suggestion that the builders of the Ohio works were pushed south into the Gulf States and incorporated into the Muskokee group. A study of the pipes, aside from any other evidence, is sufficient to show that this theory is not tenable. Moreover, a study of the works of Ohio and their contents should convince the archaeologist that they were built by several different tribes and pertain to widely different eras." The simplistic, romantic picture of an integral empire of Mound Builders was coming apart under prolonged prodding; and what Thomas offered in its place was a complex view of many mound-building cultures, difficult to grasp, disturbing in its implications.

The publication of Thomas' promised major work on the mounds was certain to be an important event in American archaeology. It was awaited with eagerness in some professional quarters, and with tense, irritable impatience in others. But the immense job of collating, compiling, and illustrating dragged on and on. The Sixth Annual Report of the Bureau of Ethnology, published in 1888, contained an article by Thomas, but it was on the Mayan picture writing that he had been studying before being called to the mound project; Powell remarked that Thomas was still "engaged in preparing for publication the results of the operations of that division [of mound study]. The constant arrangement, comparison, and study of the material objects and facts ascertained required his close application." The story was the same in the Seventh Annual Report, which covered 1885–86, but did not appear until 1891. Thomas was still working on his manuscript, said Powell; and he reported the obsolete information that "During the summer of 1885 Prof. Thomas was in Wisconsin, engaged in investigating and studying the effigy mounds and other ancient works of that section."

The Eighth Annual Report appeared almost simultaneously in 1891, but it brought only small comfort for the impatient. Powell said that Thomas continued to labor on his manuscript, but had interrupted his writing to make field trips to Ohio and New York. The Major also announced that Thomas had completed a "preliminary list of the various monuments known, and of the localities where they are found, together with references to the works and periodicals in which they are mentioned. . . . It will be issued as a bulletin." The bulletin appeared later in 1891 as the twelfth in the Bureau of Ethnology's series: *The Catalogue of Prehistoric Works East of the Rocky Mountains.* It ran to 246 pages, with 17 plates and maps.

Prior to that, Thomas had sustained the interest of his followers with two more interim bulletins, both published in 1889. These contained material intended for his magnum opus, rearranged and compressed for the sake of unity. The first of these, Bureau of Ethnology Bulletin Eight, was entitled *The Problem of the Ohio Mounds.* This 50-page sketch for his larger work restates the now-familiar theories of the identity of Mound Builders and Indians, and dwells particularly on the encounters between sixteenth- and seventeenth-century explorers and the mound-building tribes of the lower Mississippi Valley. A good deal of material was reprinted from Thomas' paper in the Fifth Annual Report and from his 1887 bulletin. The evidence presented, says Thomas, "is so interlocked with other facts relating to the works of the 'veritable mound-builders' as to leave no hiatus into which the theory of a lost race or a 'Toltec occupation' can possibly be thrust. It forms an unbroken chain connecting the mound-builders and historical Indians which no sophistry or reasoning can break."[204]

Much of this bulletin is given over to a discussion of "The Cherokees as Mound-Builders." Thomas returns to his thesis that the Cherokees were Heckewelder's Tallegewi, forced to emigrate from Ohio to the Carolinas, and continuing to build mounds on a lesser scale in their new territory. He quotes Bartram and others on the "town houses" of the Cherokees, large communal buildings placed atop artificial mounds, in his attempt to show that the present mounds of Tennessee and the Carolinas are the remains of these sites, which had been constructed as late as the eighteenth century. Many arguments are brought forth to support this idea of Cherokee migration; but none of them are particularly convincing to the modern reader, since the earthworks of Ohio bear little resemblance to those of Tennessee and the Carolinas, and Thomas' effort to show a direct cultural link seems forced and labored. In his zeal to obliterate the lost-race theory, he was often too eager to embrace recent Indian tribes as the builders of the great enclosures and embankments.

The second 1889 bulletin was much more specialized. Under the title of *The Circular, Square, and Octagonal Earthworks of Ohio,* Thomas set out to examine the common belief that the Mound Builders had extraordinary geometrical talents. His discoveries did not quite match his expectations, and there is a certain heavy-handed charm in the way he reverses himself in mid-course.

The bulletin bristles with measurements and tables, lists of bearings and distances, all the arcane incantations of the surveyor's art. Skeptical of the accuracy of Squier and Davis' survey of the geometrical enclosures, Thomas sent surveyors of his own to go over the earthworks. He criticizes Squier and Davis for the lack of details, "the fact that their measurements are in most cases given in round numbers, and their omission to state whether these measurements were taken from the middle, the inside, or the outside of the walls." He speaks of "an inexcusable degree of carelessness, which is calculated to depreciate their work, and to a great extent destroys confidence in their measurements and figures." Thomas' own men, using a transit and a hundred-foot chain, came up with figures far more precise than those of Squier and Davis, corrected many of their errors, and applied more rigorous professional methods to the job. Some twenty-one pages along in this pamphlet, following many long lists of angles and innumerable folding diagrams, Thomas reports "somewhat unexpected results." The remeasurement of two large circular enclosures have shown, "first, that the figure is so nearly a true circle; and, second, that the radius is almost an exact multiple of the surveyor's chain. It is true that Messrs. Squier and Davis assert that this and some other inclosures are perfect circles, but their many errors in regard to dimensions, and our belief in the Indian origin of these works, led us to take this assertion cum grano salis. We were therefore surprised to find after a very careful survey the close approximation to a true circle in these cases."[205]

Surveys of other geometrical works likewise tended to confirm the faith of Squier and Davis in the ability of the ancient engineers, even though the actual figures they reported were frequently erroneous. "The first question which presents itself in view of these facts," says a somewhat embarrassed Cyrus Thomas, "is, How are we to reconcile them with the theory that the works were built by Indians?" His reply is that "we shall not attempt at this time a thorough discussion of this and other questions which arise in reference to these ancient works; nevertheless we may as well suggest some thoughts and note some facts which may aid in solving the problems."

Thomas insists that a careful study of the geometrical works "will satisfy any one, not biased by a preconceived theory, that their characteristics are essentially aboriginal." As an example of the consistency of the Ohio earth-works with aboriginal practice, he mentions the Iroquois custom of building polygonal forts; on the other hand, "there is nothing in their form or con-struction consistent with the idea that their conception is due to European influence." And his conclusion must have had a very lame look to his contempo-raries, although we know it to be correct: "That Indians can lay out true circles of moderate size will be admitted; that they are less able now to perform many things which necessity formerly compelled them to practice must also be admitted. No valid reason can be presented why Indians, taught by necessity and practice, could not lay off by the eye and by means at hand figures with which they were familiar more correctly than the white man without instru-ments."[206]

8

Sounding faintly distressed, Major Powell told the readers of the Ninth Annual Report of the Bureau of Ethnology that the fiscal year 1887–88 had passed without the completion of Cyrus Thomas' work on the mounds. In this report, published in 1892, Powell said that "the manuscript for the first volume . . . with the illustrations was presented for publication about a month before the close of the fiscal year. Work upon the manuscript, illustrations, and maps for the second volume was continued." On another page, though, Powell observed, "As the work of unfolding and systematizing the field notes, examining the collections and preparing the plats and illustrations proceeded, it was found that there were some omissions in the original ex-aminations which left the details of certain sections incomplete, and it became important to obtain as far as possible the missing information. The most serious hiatus was filled by an examination of the lake border of the United States from Detroit westward to the head of Lake Superior, for the purpose of ascer-taining whether the historic Indian localities along that line were marked by mounds or other ancient works."

The story was much the same in the Tenth Annual Report, which came out in 1893. Field work on the mounds had virtually ceased, except for "such investigations as were necessary to elucidate doubtful points," and Thomas toiled on. He was, Powell said, now occupied "in the preparation of the second and third volumes of his reports upon the mounds." To archaeologists of the day, Thomas' ever-burgeoning manuscript was taking on legendary characteristics of its own. But the Eleventh Annual Report, published in 1894, revealed that "Prof. CYRUS THOMAS was personally engaged during the entire year in preparing his report on the field work and collections of the preceding seven years. . . . His final report, which requires much comparison and reference as well as study of the works explored and objects obtained, was written as rapidly as was consistent with proper care and due regard for details. It will be incorporated in the Twelfth Annual Report of the Bureau." And later that same year the Twelfth Annual Report duly appeared, covering the fiscal year 1890–91, and devoted entirely to Thomas' monumental paper, "Report on the Mound Explorations of the Bureau of Ethnology."

Powell's original plan had been to publish it in two volumes (or perhaps three) in an occasional series called *Contributions to North American Ethnology,* which actually antedated the establishment of the Bureau of Ethnology itself. The first volume in this series had appeared in 1877, under the auspices of Powell's Geographical and Geological Survey of the Rocky Mountain Region, and was in effect a trial run for the later Annual Reports. Eight such *Contributions* were published through 1894; but then the series was abandoned, and Thomas' monograph was transferred to the Twelfth Annual Report, where it appeared as a single volume of 730 quarto pages.

The introduction to the paper, written by Powell, has an odd valedictory note. Powell reviews his involvement with the mounds from his youthful investigations through his Civil War moonlighting to the insistence of Congress that the Bureau of Ethnology investigate the earthworks. He traces the history of mound hypotheses from Thomas Jefferson and Benjamin Smith Barton through recent times, touching on the various "lost race" theories and his own conviction of their absurdities. He summarizes Thomas' conclusions, which parallel his own; and he announces with some relief that "general exploration of the mound region was discontinued and archaeologic field work was placed in the charge of Mr. William H. Holmes." (Holmes had begun work in the summer of 1890 in the vicinity of the District of Columbia, east of the mound zone, but by August of that year the obsession had caught him, too, for Powell tells us that "Mr. Holmes proceeded to the Mississippi valley for the purpose of reexamining some mound groups not previously explored with sufficient care." Holmes went on to study effigy mounds in Wisconsin, to dig up mound pottery in Arkansas, and to survey the Etowah group in Georgia; but so far as the Bureau of Ethnology was concerned, this was anticlimactic work, since Thomas had produced a definitive evaluation of the mound problem, and Major Powell was content to turn to other subjects.)

Thomas' "Report on the Mound Explorations" was the third of the three great syntheses of Mound Builder research written in the nineteenth century;

it dwarfs the earlier efforts of Atwater and of Squier and Davis both in physical bulk and in comprehensiveness of approach. And it was the last such synthesis that could ever be assembled, for, largely due to Thomas' work, the unitary concept of a "Mound Builder" culture was discarded, and future surveys would of necessity have to deal with local manifestations of the mound-building impulse.

The report was not intended for laymen, and little of it makes lively reading. The heart of it, covering nearly 500 pages, is simply a digest of field research, interspersed only occasionally with quotations from early explorers or with Thomas' interpretative conjectures. Methodically, grimly, ponderously, Thomas describes thousands of mounds: Pipestone County, Minnesota; Houston County, Minnesota; Dane County, Wisconsin; Crawford County, Wisconsin; and so on through the counties of Iowa, Illinois, Missouri, Arkansas, Louisiana, Mississippi, Tennessee, Alabama, Georgia, South Carolina, Florida, North Carolina, West Virginia, Ohio, Pennsylvania, New York, and Michigan.

A brief foreword states Thomas' conclusions, now arranged under eleven headings but amply familiar to anyone who had read his previous eight-point and thirteen-point formulations. His insistence on the continuity between Mound Builders and Indians is the strongest of these points, although he failed to recognize that there were gaps of hundreds or even thousands of years, in some cases, between the construction of certain mound groups and the arrival in those areas of the Indians of historic times. Thus his "apparently conclusive" proof "that the Cherokees were mound-builders and that to them are to be attributed most of the mounds of eastern Tennessee and western North Carolina" turned out not to be so conclusive, nor do today's archaeologists accept his argument that the Cherokees "were the author of most of the ancient works of the Kanawha valley in West Virginia" and "some of the principal works of Ohio." But these were errors on the side of conservatism, rising from Thomas' eagerness to disprove the fanciful tales then in circulation. No one today can quarrel with the last of his eleven theses: "Although much the larger portion of the ancient monuments of our country belong to prehistoric times, and some of them, possibly, to the distant past, yet the evidence of contact with European civilization is found in so many mounds . . . that it must be conceded that many of them were built subsequent to the discovery of the continent by Europeans."[207]

There follows a preface reviewing the mound activities of the Bureau of Ethnology, crediting Thomas' many co-workers and outlining the course of the project. A short section provides austere definitions of the types of mounds and earthworks examined. These are purely structural definitions; Thomas rightly discards such established terms as "Sacred Enclosures," "Sacrificial Mounds," etc., on the grounds that to use them is to presuppose a functional knowledge that should follow, not precede, an attempt at analysis.

Then Thomas begins his immense catalog of mound descriptions. The tone is dry and detailed. ("No. 22. Sixty feet in diameter and 5 feet high. First foot, soil; the rest black, mucky earth, with a slight admixture of sand. At the depth of 2 feet were seven skeletons, with heads in various directions, some stretched out with the faces up, others folded, also other bones. At the center, about 3 feet down, were a few rib bones, apparently the remains of a skeleton, over which lay a copper plate. . . .") The verbal descriptions are documented by stratification diagrams, surveyors' charts, and illustrations of recovered artifacts. Nearly all the mounds discussed by Thomas have since been destroyed, except only those spectacular ones preserved in public parks, and so modern archaeologists have had to rely on Thomas' published accounts for their entire knowledge of most of these sites. They have not always been able to find in Thomas the particular detail for which they are searching, and there is sometimes a petulant tone in their criticisms of his omissions or inclarities. But most writers accord him the respect due a pioneer; he was writing a book of finite length, and included everything remotely relevant, with no way of knowing that the irrelevancy of 1888 might become the sought-for clue of 1960.

The long series of excavation reports is generally objective, although Thomas sometimes pauses to underscore an artifact or a mound conformation that illustrates his basic conceptual structure. It is followed by an essay of some eighty pages on the types and distribution of mounds, showing with great force and skill the impossibility of assigning all the earthworks to a single "race." Lastly, under the heading, "General Observations," Thomas reviews the entire mound problem as it had unfolded since the eighteenth century, dealing in turn with each of the theories he has overthrown.

The indictment is a severe one. Thomas quotes from such writers as Baldwin, Foster, H. H. Bancroft, Squier, and Conant, picking out phrases like "An ancient race entirely distinct from the Indians," "a knowledge of art and methodical labor foreign to the red man," "the Mound-builder people and the Indians were distinct," "a nation with a central administration," and "one people, the subjects of one controlling government." He shows how myths perpetuated themselves from the lack of firsthand observation, tracing the heavy reliance of later authors on Atwater and Squier and Davis. Calmly, coolly, he deflates the lost-race myth with such lines as these:

"Yet, as will soon become apparent to any one who will study the different forms of these works with any care, the only similarity between the extremes of form and construction is the fact that they are built of earth. Between these extremes, if the earthworks of the world were classified, would fall much the larger portion of both hemispheres. The conical tumuli bear a far more striking resemblance to the mounds of Japan, Siberia, and northern Europe, and some of the burrows [sic] of the British isles than they do the effigy mounds of Wisconsin, the circles and squares of Ohio, or the pyramidal and truncated tumuli of the Southern States. It is probably not going too far to say that if the most skillful engineer of the present day were to undertake the task of building as many different forms of earthworks as his skill could devise, it would be difficult for him to exceed the variety now found."[208]

He challenges all past assumptions, showing that they do not stand up to scrutiny. Sometimes he is unfair and incorrect, as when he chides Squier and Davis for calling the Mound City tumuli "altar mounds," and denies that they were used for a religious purpose, when his real target should have been here as elsewhere the habit of making *a priori* functional guesses at all. (It happens that Squier and Davis were right about Mound City.) At other times he is penetrating in his analysis, as when he shows Albert Gallatin contradicting himself on the subject of Mound Builder agriculture, or where he disposes of those who, in maintaining that no Indians east of the Mississippi were capable of raising crops, overlook the evidence of early explorers. (Thomas quotes John Smith, Walter Raleigh, Père Marquette, and the Gentleman of Elvas, among others, to show that many Indian tribes were agriculturally self-sufficient and so could have sustained the great communal effort of building mounds.)

In the matter of the antiquity of the mounds, Thomas neatly pricks the argument from the river terraces, first hinted at by Atwater and made part of the canon by Squier and Davis. "The fact that none of the ancient monuments occur upon the latest formed terraces of the river valleys of Ohio, is one of much importance in its bearings upon this question," Squier had written. Thomas replies, "Few (for there are some) ancient works occur on the last formed river terrace in Ohio, for the very good reason that the builders had learned, probably by sad experience, that this lower terrace was subject to repeated overflows."[209]

A few lines on, Thomas displays his ability to argue on all sides of the question at once. For in the lower Mississippi region, where no such arrangement of terraces is found, the rivers are bordered by wide, low flood plains, called "bottoms," and as a rule the Southern mounds are built on the bottoms —just where they would be most vulnerable to flooding. Squier and Davis had not mentioned this, since their firsthand experience was confined to Ohio. Blithely disregarding his talk of "sad experience" just above, Thomas remarks, "A foolish idea has prevailed in the minds of many persons that the Indians and mound-builders were wiser in this respect than the people of the present day, and would never plant their villages where they were subject to overflow." He goes on to argue that along the lower Mississippi the mounds were deliberately placed on the bottoms to serve as points of refuge in time of flood, and that they are still used for that purpose in some rural areas. "One great hindrance to the mound explorations carried on in this region by the United States Bureau of Ethnology," he comments, "has been the unwillingness of the owners of mounds, on this account, to have them opened."

He handles the tree-ring evidence easily: "Recent investigations have served to destroy confidence in this hitherto supposed certain test of age, as it is found that even within the latitude of the northern half of the United States from one to three rings are formed each year." (Tree-ring dating has become an important tool of archaeologists; but Thomas was right to suspect the findings of the early dendrochronologists.) Another argument for the antiquity of the mounds and the racial distinctness of their builders is the magnitude of the earthworks, which to some had indicated the existence of superior technology and a cohesive, almost dictatorial, government. Thomas shows that Indians of quite recent times were able to organize governments and to carry out extensive works programs; and he asks where the tools of the supposed Mound Builders have gone, if superior technology were used in their building. "It is true that when we stand at the base of the great Cahokia mound and study its vast proportions, we can scarcely bring ourselves to believe it was built without some other means of collecting and conveying material than that possessed by the Indians. But what other means could a lost race have had? The Indians had wooden spades, baskets, skins of animals, wooden and clay vessels, and textile fabrics; they also had stone implements. Moreover, the fact should be borne in mind that this great mound is unique in respect to size, being more than treble in contents that of any other true mound in the United States. . . . As a general rule the labor necessary to build them could not have exceeded that which has often been performed by Indians. It is also more than likely that all the people of a tribe, both men and women, aided in the work, and that the large works were built by additions made during successive generations."[210]

What, then, of the inscribed hieroglyphic and alphabetic tablets found in certain mounds? Are these not proofs of a non-Indian origin? Thomas has some fun with the various translators of the Grave Creek Tablet, and then

turns once more to belabor the Davenport tablets and pipes. Far more dam-
agingly than Henshaw, Thomas examines the circumstances under which these
surprising artifacts were found, and uses his own experience as a field archaeologist to show that on the basis of the Iowans' own reported details the
tablets were almost certainly planted by pranksters. Generously, he expresses
his belief that Jacob Gass and the other members of the Davenport Academy
of Natural Sciences were innocent dupes, although this concession follows a
paragraph of such blistering mockery that it must have sent tempers soaring
in Iowa.

"Another objection to the theory that the mound-builders were Indians,"
Thomas goes on, "is based upon the oft-repeated statement of the Indians that
they know nothing of the origin of these works; that when they first entered
the territory they found them already built and abandoned." A good point,
but he has a good answer: "These same Indians have not the faintest tradition of some of the most important events in their own history dating back
less than two centuries. For example, De Soto's expedition, although it must
have been the most remarkable event in the past history of the southern
tribes, seems to have been forgotten by them when the French adventurers, one
hundred and thirty years later, appeared on the scene."[211] He proceeds to compare the accounts of mounds in Florida and Georgia—written by the Gentleman of Elvas, Garcilaso de la Vega, and Luis de Biedma—with the archaeological results of following de Soto's track, showing that Mound Builders
were still active there in the sixteenth century and that the mounds mentioned
by the chroniclers of de Soto can be identified. With some amusement, Thomas
comments that these eyewitness accounts by Europeans were forgotten within
a century, so that "these remains . . . begin to be discovered one by one, and
are looked upon by the new generation which has arisen, as strange and
mysterious mementos of a 'long lost' and 'unknown' race. . . . The imagination,
having once obtained the rein, runs back over the ages until it is lost in the
haze of the past. Is it strange that the 'untutored savage,' without writings or
records, should in a few—a very few—generations lose sight of the past when
our own civilized race forgets in the same time?"[212]

The next stage in the proof is to show similarities between artifacts and
customs of the Mound Builders and those recorded by observers of the recent
Indians. Thomas describes the architecture of the Mound Builders as seen in
the villages associated with the mounds, and compares it with that of Southern
tribes. "Prof. Swallow describes a room formed by poles, lathed with split cane,
plastered with clay both inside and out, forming a solid mass, which he found
in a mound in southeastern Missouri," Thomas reports, juxtaposing the state-

ment with such comments as that of the eighteenth-century French traveler La Harpe: "The Indians build their huts dome fashion out of clay and reeds." Thomas brackets the Gentleman of Elvas' account of an Indian town with clay-daubed palisade walls and Caleb Atwater's suggestion that the wall of an enclosure at Circleville once bore a similar palisade. He exhibits parallels in burial customs, in pottery, in tools, in agricultural techniques. Where Thomas confines himself to relating the Southern mounds to the seventeenth- and eighteenth-century Southern tribes, his arguments are generally unanswerable; where he attempts to make the same comparisons using evidence from the great Ohio mounds, he tends to distort the material, since exact parallels did not in fact exist.

At the end, briefly, Thomas considers the theory of a Mexican or Central American origin for the Mound Builders. He finds no evidence for a migration from the tropics to North America, and regards most of the supposed instances of cultural contact between Mexico and the mound region as exaggerated. But his discussion of this point, coming after more than seven hundred pages of evidence has been presented, shows signs of fatigue; his ideas are perfunctorily outlined and sketchily argued.

The work as a whole, however, is impressive. Despite Thomas' claim of objectivity, there is plenty of special pleading for his case; nevertheless, it represents a formidable gathering of data and a relatively rational assessment of it. It is difficult to disagree with Thomas' conclusion "that the mound-builders were divided into different tribes and peoples, which, though occupying much the same position in the culture scale, and hence resembling each other in many of their habits, customs, and modes of life, were as widely separated in regard to their ethnic relations and languages as the Indian tribes when first encountered by the white race."[213]

That statement needed refining—for actually the various mound-building groups did not occupy "much the same position in the culture scale." But it went to the essential truth of the situation, that archaeologists, as they sought to unravel the mystery of the mounds, had to be prepared to deal with diversity, not unity. Cyrus Thomas' great report marked the end of an era. No longer could one speak of "the Mound Builders" in quite the same way, with the old implications of a single empire. But Thomas had raised as many questions as he had answered. His work was not so much an epilogue as a prologue. It remained for archaeologists to examine the contents of the mounds more closely, to analyze the cultural traits of their builders, to discover relationships and differences—in short, to develop a coherent picture of the prehistoric American past.

▲▲▲ 6

THE HONORED DEAD:
ADENA AND HOPEWELL

▲▲▲

One of Cyrus Thomas' most useful contributions was a semantic clarification, long overdue, that helped to eliminate some of the confusion over the relation of Mound Builders to Indians. He asked, simply, "What is an Indian?" The standard nineteenth-century response was to point to the nomadic horsemen of the Western plains; but that was too simple. Also belonging under that vague heading, "Indian," were such peoples as the totem-pole builders of the Pacific Northwest, the pueblo dwellers of Arizona and New Mexico, the farmers who once had inhabited the Southeast, the forest huntsmen of the North, and many more. There were hundreds of totally unrelated Indian languages, thousands of tribal units. Indians were widely different in physical appearance; some groups were plump, others lean; some round-headed, others long-headed; some hawk-nosed, some flat-nosed. Though certain underlying commonly held traits provided a loose structure of meaning for the term "Indian," it was actually so vague that it defined very little other than the aboriginal inhabitants of the Americas in general. Since that was the case, Thomas asked, why set up high boundaries between the class of "Indians" and the class of "Mound Builders"? Why not accept the fact that the various mound-building tribes had simply been Indian tribes of a high culture and social organization?

Against the background of Thomas' common-sense semantics, other men groped toward a solution of the problem of the Mound Builders. Even before the publication of Thomas' final report, leading American archaeologists were seeking to reconcile the older theories with the new ideas propounded so vigorously by the Bureau of Ethnology. A typical approach is that of the Reverend Stephen D. Peet, whose book, *The Mound Builders: Their Works and Relics,* was published in 1892. Peet, an officer of the American Antiquarian Society and the editor of its journal, *The American Antiquarian,* saw himself as a neutral on a mined battlefield. His book testifies to that: he dedicated it to the officers of the Smithsonian Institution, but among the scholarly organizations in which he claims membership in a title-page list is the "Davenport Academy of Science."

"Some forty years ago," Peet begins, "it was held that the Mississippi valley must have been settled by a civilized people who had migrated from some historic country. Silver sword scabbards, iron knives, Hebrew inscriptions, triune vases, and other curious relics, were dwelt upon as proving this. The Mormon delusion grew out of an erroneous theory as to the 'lost tribes.'

"Latterly the opinion has gone to the other extreme. The Mound-builders were savages, and differed from the modern Indians only in that they used stone and pottery instead of iron and tin for their weapons and utensils. This opinion, however, is as far out of the way as the previous one."

Peet attempts to use Thomas' idea of a succession of cultures, while still retaining some vestige of the notion that the Mound Builders were conspicuously superior to any contemporary Indian tribes. His efforts are marred by his determination to steer clear of controversy, by his jumbled presentation, and by his often dubious scholarship ("Buddha, the great Egyptian divinity . . ."[214]). His central argument is "that there was a Mound-Builders' age in this country, and that it is as distinctive as was the neolithic age in Europe." He sees the Mound Builders as extremely early, culturally ancestral to the "cliff-dwellers" of the Southwest (whose romantic eyries were spawning a short-lived new archaeological myth-cult just about then) and the high civilizations of Mexico and Central America. "We imagine," Peet writes, "that the Mound-builders were the first people who occupied the territory after the close of the glacial period, that they followed hard on to the paleolithic people, that no other race intervened. This is, however, a matter of conjecture. Our reasons for holding this are as follows: 1. The appearance of the mastodon and mammoth. We contend that these animals and the Mound-builders were contemporaneous. . . ."[215] To Peet, the Davenport pipes and other similar relics are proof that man came early to the American continents, not that the mastodon and mammoth stayed late. He goes on to build an elaborate theoretical structure of mound-building cultures, whose flavor we can catch from a single passage: "While the representatives of all the districts are contained in the Ohio Valley, yet the different parts of that valley are to be considered, for the pyramid-builders never appeared on the eastern waters, the sun-worshipers never in the western part, the fort-builders erected their works in the middle part, and the serpent-worshipers merely passed through or crossed over the central part, and ultimately built their works in distant regions."[216]

This sort of work, simmering with half-digested ideas and proposing new

myths to replace old ones, was fortunately becoming extinct as the nineteenth
century drew to its close. Peet's book was no *Traditions of De-coo-dah*. He was
a reputable archaeologist, a member of the professional Establishment, but he
committed the nineteenth-century error of attempting to generate a synthesis
before the facts were in, and his text fell stillborn from the presses, a useless
mass of hypotheses and unfounded speculations. Such works swiftly gave way to
a different species of archaeological writing: the excavation report, deliberately
arid and bloodless, a solemn document with clearly marked sections labeled
"Discussion," "Speculation," or "General Observations." Although men had
been digging in the mounds since the 1780's, it was apparent as the century
ended that years of systematic work would be necessary before anyone could
dare to draw more than the most tentative conclusions about the era of the
mounds.

And the work began. William C. Mills of the Ohio State Museum published his report on Ohio's Adena Mound in 1902, on the Edwin Harness
Mound in 1907, on the Seip Mound in 1909. Clarence B. Moore of Philadelphia explored the mounds of Florida from 1892 to 1903, and spent the
years from 1905 to 1913 searching for mounds along the navigable rivers
of Arkansas, Louisiana, Mississippi, and Alabama, working from a specially
equipped flat-bottomed steamboat. Warren K. Moorehead of Ohio wrote on
Fort Ancient in 1890, and began his excavation of the important Hopewell
Group the following year. The Peabody Museum of Harvard sponsored a number of Ohio expeditions under F. W. Putnam. There were many more such
pioneers. Few of these men were primarily interested in substantiating some
preconceived theory; they were willing to wait until the late returns were in
before reaching conclusions. Their reports were published mainly in technical
journals. The general public went on thinking of a mysterious lost race that
deserved capital letters, the Mound Builders, but archaeologists increasingly
referred to "the so-called Mound Builders" or to "the supposed Mound
Builders." The concept of the Mound Builders had lost its viability, but, for the
moment, there was nothing to put in its place.

The situation was still in flux when Roland B. Dixon delivered the presidential address at the annual meeting of the American Anthropological Association in December, 1913. Dixon's talk, "Some Aspects of North American
Archaeology," was intended to sketch the current problems of archaeological
research. In connection with the Ohio Valley he remarked, "The history of
this region is a more than ordinarily complicated one, and . . . we must admit
here the presence of the remains of a number of different cultures." He called
the puzzle of the mounds "one of rather baffling complexity. A satisfactory
classification even of the various types present is by no means easy." The tone

of these comments is quite different from that of the nineteenth century; in place of the confident evaluations of Squier and Davis, Dixon offers hesitant, tentative statements well salted with confessions of doubt.

Through much of the first half of the twentieth century, American archaeologists wrestled with problems of culture sequence and time span. The question of taxonomy became paramount; there were fierce professional debates over the names and identities of the proposed chronological distinctions. Certain conventions won wide acceptance; others are still in dispute. Archaeological conferences to this day are punctuated by quietly passionate debates, and each decade sees the publication of some new system of terminology that wins adherents away from the older systems. There has been a magnificent flowering of technical terms to replace the old oversimplifications. A good example is the Midwest Classificatory System, first proposed in the 1930's. As Fay-Cooper Cole, one of its originators, describes it, "Each separate manifestation of a culture is known as a *component*. Components from which nearly identical materials are secured form a *focus;* several foci which resemble each other in a majority of their traits are classed together as an *aspect*. Aspects with a near majority of diagnostic triats in common are designated as a *phase,* while phases having several distinguishing traits in common constitute a *pattern*. In southern Illinois we recognize a Woodland and a Mississippi pattern each represented by different phases, aspects, and foci."[217] Other schools of archaeology reject these fine terminological distinctions, or provide their own names for the particular concepts involved. To a layman, these disputes are maddening—as they often are to archaeologists as well. But the professional regards them as necessary. Out of the clashing of theories, the thesis and antithesis of differing schools, comes the new synthesis that makes everything at least a little more comprehensible than it had been before. The bickering within the academic fraternity produces not only heat but light.

And so, since Cyrus Thomas' time, a structural sequence of cultural change in the mound zone has come into being. It is still tentative, still undergoing revision of minor details, and still subject even to major reconsideration. But it provides an intelligible guide to the course of prehistoric events in the United States, both within and without the region where mounds are found.

2

Of the several conceptual frameworks employed by modern archaeologists, perhaps the most easily grasped by laymen is that one that distinguishes between cultural *traditions* and chronological *periods.* This has been set forth most clearly in Gordon R. Willey's comprehensive *An Introduction to American Archaeology* (1966), the latest in the series of attempts at codifying and assembling the entire bulk of New World archaeological knowledge.

For Willey and those fellow archaeologists whose views he summarizes, a *culture* is a specific social group with a distinct way of life. Thus the Adena Culture of Ohio and surrounding states was typified by the construction of conical burial mounds, and its identifying traits include such other things as particular shapes of beads and pipes, the use of copper, and the habit of employing hard cradleboards to flatten the skulls of babies for decorative purposes.

The Adena Culture is considered a representative of the Early Woodland Tradition. A *tradition,* in this system, is a broadly defined way of life, practiced in more or less the same way by different cultures at different times. There was only one Adena Culture, but the Woodland Tradition can be traced in nearly all parts of the country as far west as the Great Plains. The hallmarks of the Woodland Tradition were the use of pottery, the beginnings of agriculture, and the development of permanent villages—all features of a cultural stage, not of a specific period in time. East of the Mississippi, many Indian groups began to reach the stage of development denoted by the term Woodland Tradition as early as 1000 B.C., but farther west another thousand years or more passed before the cluster of concepts comprising that tradition took hold.

A *period* is a fixed span of time during which a given tradition was dominant. In Ohio, where the Woodland Tradition was generally followed from about 1000 B.C. to A.D. 700, the term *Burial Mound Period* has been assigned to those centuries. This is an absolute measure of time; we can speak of events taking place during a certain period, but not during a certain tradition, since a tradition is not a unit of time but an abstract description of a way of life.

Willey recognizes a succession of four traditions in eastern North America: Big-Game Hunting, Archaic, Woodland, and Mississippian. These arrived in different sections at different times, so that it was quite possible for one area to be inhabited by tribes functioning in a Woodland Tradition pattern while backward tribes nearby still maintained the Archaic Tradition's way of life.

In the same geographical area Willey lists a sequence of four major periods, each pegged to a specific time span by the most reliable available chronological periods. These are the Paleo-Indian, Archaic, Burial Mound, and Temple Mound periods. (An annoying ambiguity has entered the system through no fault of Willey's, for it rested on terminology too firmly established to be replaced. There is both an Archaic Tradition and an Archaic Period. The former—a cluster of cultural traits—should not be confused with the latter—a designation covering the era from about 7000 to 1000 B.C. But such confusion is almost unavoidable, even among professionals.)

Approximate dates	Period	Tradition	Characteristics of Tradition
20,000(?)– 8,000 B.C. (Glacial Era)	Paleo-Indian Early Middle Late	Big-game Hunting Early Middle Late	Nomadic hunting cultures; stone weapons, knowledge of fire.
7,000– 1,000 B.C.	Archaic Early Middle Late	Archaic Early Middle Late	More or less permanent village life; with some seasonal travel; improved weapons, greater reliance on fishing and food-gathering.
1,000 B.C.– 700 A.D.	Burial Mound I Burial Mound II	Woodland Early Middle Late	Farming cultures with expanded population and more complex social structure; use of pottery; burial mounds.
700 A.D.– 1700 A.D.	Temple Mound I Temple Mound II	Mississippian Early Middle Late	Stockaded towns and agricultural life; fine pottery and art work; temple mound structures.

A *period* is a fixed span of time during which a given tradition was dominant; a *tradition* is a broadly defined way of life practiced in more or less the same way by different cultures at different times.

A *culture* is a specific social group with a distinct way of life. The Hopewell and Adena cultures existed during the Burial Mound Period and were representative of Woodland Tradition; many specific cultures—Tchefuncte, Poverty Point, Dalton, etc.—existed in the Mississippi Valley and southeastern United States during the Temple Mound Period and exhibited the characteristics of the Mississippian Tradition.

24   A Chronological Chart of the Prehistory of Eastern North America
(After Gordon R. Willey)

The four traditions are subdivided into Early, Middle, and Late phases. The four periods are likewise divided; Willey speaks of Early, Middle, and Late Archaic periods, Burial Mound I and II, Temple Mound I and II. Within this structure, each locality has its own cultural sequence; for example, in Louisiana, the Early Archaic Period is represented by the Dalton Culture, the Late Archaic by Poverty Point, Burial Mound I by Tchefuncte, Burial Mound II by Marksville and Troyville, Temple Mound I by Coles Creek, Temple Mound II by the Plaquemine and Natchez Cultures. This succession of cultures, as it moves upward through the chronological periods, displays the succession of traditions, from Archaic through Woodland to Mississippian. Ohio and Tennessee and Illinois present the same broad cultural sequence, but the local cultures themselves have other names and typifying traits.

In considering the development of American prehistory, it is important to remember that man reached the New World very late in his evolutionary career. Paleontologists have uncovered many human fossils of great age, quite different from modern man in physical form—such as *Pithecanthropus erectus,* the "ape-man" of Java; or *Homo neanderthalensis,* "Neanderthal man," the round-chinned, big-headed man of Ice Age Europe. From this fossil evidence they conclude that man emerged more than a million years ago, probably in Africa but perhaps in Southeast Asia, and that at least one human stock came through a series of evolutionary changes to assume more or less the present human form less than one hundred thousand years ago.

But there were no human beings at all in the Western Hemisphere during this evolutionary period. At least, no fossils of really primitive human forms have ever been discovered here. Pithecanthropus, Neanderthal man, and the other extinct human types never set foot in the New World. There were not even any manlike apes here, it seems; gorillas, chimpanzees, and other higher primates are strictly Old World natives. So far as the fossil record shows, the whole story of human evolution took place overseas, and when man got to the Western Hemisphere he was basically in his modern form.

As we have seen, general agreement was reached long ago that the route of early man to North America lay via the Bering Strait out of Asia. But the time at which this migration began long remained a matter for bitter scientific feuding. Those who adhered to the myth of the Mound Builders tended to ascribe an extremely high antiquity to the arrival of the first Americans; figures of ten, twenty, or even a hundred thousand years were lightly thrown about. The partisans of this view tended mainly to belong to the eccentric factions, although such a respected figure as F. W. Putnam of the Peabody lent his support to the so-called long chronology.

The fundamental reassessment of existing archaeological ideas begun by Major Powell and his Bureau of Ethnology led to the discrediting of the long chronology in the 1890's. The chief evidence in its favor came from the eastern seaboard, where C. C. Abbott and others had identified certain stone artifacts as being of Ice Age antiquity. In 1890, W. H. Holmes of the Bureau of Ethnology carefully examined the purported paleolithic sites and demonstrated that they were nothing more than workshops for the preliminary dressing of flint tools. The crude flint artifacts that had seemed to be so ancient were merely discarded factory blanks, and there was no reason to think that these were the work of other than recent Indians. For the next decade and a half, Holmes spoke out convincingly against the claims of overenthusiastic archaeologists who envisioned great antiquity for American man. The vigor and intensity of his attack brought about a sharp reaction away from the long chronology.

Early in the new century Holmes—by then director of the renamed Bureau of American Ethnology—acquired a protégé, Aleš Hrdlička, who became the fiercest of the opponents of the long chronology. Using the Smithsonian as his pulpit, Hrdlička denounced those who disagreed with him with such savagery that he succeeded in intimidating a generation of archaeologists. He was a formidable polemicist, and as he grew older, he rose above American physical anthropology like a colossus. He was hated and revered in almost equal measure; for, though he suppressed dissent and imposed an intellectual tyranny, he also exposed a host of frauds and demolished many misconceptions. With what one admirer, the late anthropologist Earnest A. Hooton, called "righteous scientific iconoclasm," Hrdlička shredded "dubious and spurious finds" and destroyed wild theories. Such an attitude was necessary and useful as a counterpoise to the previous approach of those who had speculated on the domestication of mammoths by the Mound Builders. Where Hrdlička went astray was in his lack of balance, his fanaticism, his dogmatic self-assurance. He was correct enough to say that there was no evidence that showed man's presence in the Americas hundreds of thousands of years ago. He properly rejected supposed Neanderthaloid and Pithecanthropoid skulls found in the Western Hemisphere. But he carried his theories to the opposite extreme, insisting that mankind in the Americas could be assigned an antiquity of, at best, three or four thousand years.

His first major work appeared in 1907 as the thirty-third Bulletin of the Bureau of American Ethnology. Entitled *Skeletal Remains Suggesting or Attributed to Early Man in North America,* it was a compact, uncompromising, and highly technical review of all the evidence that had been put forth thus far by the adherents to the long chronology. Among the material he dismissed was the pelvic bone found by Dickeson in 1846 near Natchez in association with the bones of the extinct mammoth and ground sloth. To admit that man had been a contemporary of those vanished beasts was, for Hrdlička, impossible; therefore he brushed the Natchez pelvis aside as a modern intrusion into the site. Hrdlička was correct anatomically in saying that the pelvis was modern in type; what he refused to concede was that even modern human bones found in the Americas might be ten or twenty thousand years old.

Of course, the remains of Mound Builders came in for his careful attention. In the 1870's, such archaeologists as J. W. Foster had commented on the jutting brows and low foreheads of certain skulls from the mounds, and had postulated the existence of a primitive "Mound Builder" race. Primitive races were anathema to Hrdlička. He devoted nearly half his slim book to an analysis of mound crania, showing that their alleged primitive characteristics were physical deformities or else were within the spectrum of contemporary Indian skeletal traits. Though he agreed that many skulls from the mounds did show low foreheads and other features usually termed ancient, Hrdlička commented, "no definite conclusion as to their antiquity can be based on this inferiority or peculiarity of type alone. The occasional and apparently nonpathological occurrence of such forms . . . offers one of the most interesting problems to American anthropologists, largely because everything points to the fact that these low cranial shapes are comparatively recent phenomena and not occurrences of geological antiquity." He called for further mound research, while adding that the mound bones he had examined "have in general much more affinity with those of the Indian than with those of any other people."[218]

In denying the antiquity of the Mound Builders, Hrdlička provided still more support for the Powell-Thomas thesis, which most leading archaeologists had come to favor in essence if not necessarily in detail. However, his dogged opposition to the whole concept of New World antiquity created an ugly atmosphere of tension among archaeologists, and greatly interfered with attempts to devise a chronological structure for American prehistory. It was difficult to see how all the events of New World development could have taken place within the three or four thousand years that Hrdlička would allow for them; but anyone who deviated from the Holmes-Hrdlička party line met with strict censure. The darker aspects of their attitude are unintentionally revealed in this 1925 comment by Holmes on certain Florida discoveries:

". . . the evidences of Pleistocene man recorded by Loomis at Melbourne, as well as by Sellards and others at Vero, are not only inadequate but *dangerous to the cause of science*."*

Science—of the Holmes-Hrdlička variety—was even more seriously imperiled in 1926 when J. D. Figgins of the Denver Museum of Natural History did some digging near the town of Folsom, New Mexico. Figgins excavated the skeleton of a bison that virtually everyone—even Hrdlička—agreed belonged to a species extinct for at least eight or ten thousand years. Lying alongside one of the bones was a stone weapon point. Here, surely, was new proof that man had been a contemporary of America's extinct giant fauna; but the experts fell on Figgins, calling the point "intrusive" and suggesting that it had been brought into proximity to the bison bones by the burrowing action of some rodent. So when Figgins came upon another association of man and bison in 1927, he halted work and invited a committee of experts to check the site themselves.

Three men came: Dr. Barnum Brown of the American Museum of Natural History, Dr. A. V. Kidder of Phillips Academy, and Dr. Frank H. H. Roberts, Jr., of the Smithsonian Institution. They looked at Figgins' extinct bison, and

* Emphasis added—R. S.

they observed the stone point neatly lodged between the bison's ribs. This was evidence that could not be argued away.

The Folsom point, as it was called, was a slender, delicately fashioned piece of stone about two inches long, with a narrow groove carved down each face. Its discovery was a dramatic turning point in American archaeology. Even Hrdlička was forced to admit that man's migration to the Americas must have begun "somewhere between possibly 10,000 or at most 15,000 years ago and the dawn of the protohistoric period in the Old World." Other Folsom points were found all over the country, from Alaska to Georgia. They proved beyond question that in the last Ice Age, when such great woolly beasts as the bison and the mammoth were common in North America, human beings lived among them and hunted them. Before long, archaeologist Frank Hibben found an even older type of point than the Folsom. In Sandia Cave, New Mexico, Hibben discovered larger, more crudely made points lying *beneath* a cache of Folsom points. On the basis of these and other pre-Folsom points, some archaeologists pushed the date of man's arrival in the New World back to thirty or even forty thousand years ago.

In the late 1940's the technique of dating through measurement of the radioactive decay of the isotope carbon-14 was developed, and it became possible at last to check some of these estimates. Bits of charcoal found at one Folsom site gave a carbon-14 dating of 10,780 ± 375 years. Among the pre-Folsom sites, one in California produced a carbon-14 dating of 30,000 years, and one in Texas a dating of more than 38,000 years. These dates are controversial and not all archaeologists accept their accuracy. However, it is certain that the ancestors of the Indians were in the Americas ten thousand years ago, and quite probable that they arrived fifteen or twenty thousand years before that. Archaeologists have uncovered a number of sites at which primitive Americans quite clearly had killed and butchered mammoths, mastodons, and other ancient mammals.

The skeletons of these early Americans remain elusive. Perhaps the first comers did not practice burial, merely leaving the bodies of their dead to weather away in the open. What may have been a burial site of this period was found in 1951 during the construction of a Virginia motel, but the burials were destroyed before they could be inspected by archaeologists.

Despite the lack of skeletal evidence, a good deal is known about these first Americans, based mainly on the weapon points. These people are most commonly classed as Paleo-Indians ("ancient Indians") and their culture is called the Big-Game Hunting Tradition. The time in which they flourished—down to about 8000 B.C.—is termed the Paleo-Indian Period.

The Paleo-Indians lived at a time when the climate of the United States was much colder than it is today. Glaciers covered much of the North. South of the ice sheets, the climate ranged from cold and snowy to cool and wet. Areas which are deserts today were chilly and rainy then. A distinctive fauna thrived in this climate: the mammoth, the great bison, the ground sloth, the saber-toothed tiger, the dire wolf. There were camels and horses and antelopes.

The Paleo-Indians depended on these Ice Age beasts for their food. They knew nothing of farming and had no villages; and, of course, they were incapable of building the huge mounds and earthworks with which they were sometimes credited by nineteenth-century theorists. They shaped sharp points from stone, and lashed them to pieces of wood to form spears and darts. Following the game animals from place to place, the Paleo-Indians killed the big beasts for food and clothing. At least some Paleo-Indian groups knew the use of fire. Judging by their points, which are found virtually everywhere in the United States, they were tireless nomads. The Big-Game Hunting Tradition did not differ greatly from one part of the country to another, though as thousands of years passed various styles of points came into fashion.

About 8000 B.C. the climate of North America began to undergo a great change, becoming warmer and drier. The glaciers vanished; the forested lands turned into deserts. The big-game animals started to die out. The mammoth, the camel, the horse, and the other large animals became extinct in North America. It was not a rapid extinction, but over the course of a thousand years or more man found himself forced to make great adjustments in his way of life. The Big-Game Hunting Tradition gave way to the Archaic Tradition.

The new way of life that developed seems to have arisen first in the woodlands of the East before 5000 B.C., possibly as early as 7000 or 8000 B.C., and spread slowly westward. In the East, the change in tradition coincides with a change in chronological period, from the Paleo-Indian to the Archaic Period. Some regions in Archaic Period times continued to practice the Big-Game Hunting Tradition long after others had moved into the Archaic Tradition.

We do not know whether these Archaic people are the lineal descendants of the Paleo-Indians, or if they represent a later wave of migration from Asia after climatic conditions had caused the extinction of the Paleo-Indians. Discovery of Paleo-Indian skeletal evidence would help to settle this point. The characteristics of the Archaic Tradition are improved weapons, greater reliance on fishing and plant-gathering, and the founding of more or less permanent villages. Archaic peoples learned how to stalk animals in the forests, how to strike them down with barbed or notched points. They made handsome chopping and scraping tools of polished stone, and discovered how certain seeds could be milled with grinding stones to make them edible. They built pit-houses in the ground and even some crude lean-tos, and kept close to these villages most of the year. They were not mound builders. Since Archaic Indians still did not cultivate their own food nor have any domestic animals, they had to travel with the seasons to some extent, moving in regular patterns to stay near their sources of fish and shellfish, meats, berries, and roots, but ultimately returning to the village that was their home base.

The Indians of Mexico and South America were far ahead of those occupying what is now the United States. While the relatively simple Archaic Tradition was dominant here, Indians to the south were mastering agriculture and pottery, and their cultures grew rapidly more complex. Farming was more efficient than food-gathering, and allowed the community leisure for development of social and spiritual concepts, as well as technical ideas. Villages grew larger, houses more elaborate, as the great city-building civilizations of Mexico and Peru entered their earliest stages. Some of the revolutionary new ideas from the south began filtering into the United States between 1000 B.C. and the time of Christ, and brought another cultural shift.

In the Southwest, the development of agriculture and pottery led toward the eventual flowering of the Pueblo culture. In the East and on the prairies, the Woodland Tradition developed. It was marked by a changeover to farming, the use of pottery, an expanding population, and a complex social and religious revolution. Though Archaic peoples had been content with simple burials, the Woodland Tradition folk devoted much effort to building tombs for their dead. This trait is noted in the chronological designation for the period that began in the East about 1000 B.C.: Burial Mound I. As the Archaic Tradition gave way to the Woodland Tradition, the Archaic Period came to its end and the Burial Mound Period began.

3

Archaeologists are now fairly sure who the first mound builders of North America were, but they have had some strange detours on their road to that knowledge. These pioneers of the earthworks are known as the Adena people, and their existence as a culture has been recognized since the beginning of this century.

The culture takes its name from that of the Chillicothe, Ohio estate of Thomas Worthington, who was Governor of Ohio from 1814 to 1818. In 1901, William C. Mills, curator of the Ohio State Archaeological and Histori-

25   The Adena pipe. Courtesy Ohio
Historical Society, Columbus,
Ohio.

cal Society, excavated the great mound on the grounds of Adena and found
within it log tombs, objects of mica, copper bracelets, and other distinctive
artifacts—including the famous Adena Pipe, a yellow and red clay effigy of a
stocky, perhaps dwarfed male figure. He was shown wearing ear-spools; the
deeply carved facial features seem to have a Mexican cast.

Mills regarded the artifacts found in the Adena Mound as sufficiently different from those discovered in most other Ohio mounds to warrant the designation of a distinct Adena Culture—this at a time when the concept of apply-
ing such local designations had barely come into general use. He extended the
term to cover certain other mounds that had been previously excavated, such
as the Grave Creek Mound in Moundsville, West Virginia, and the big Miamisburg Mound in Ohio. The traits he termed specifically Adena were conical
burial mounds, located singly or in groups; uncremated burials in log tombs;
the use of copper and mica; and the use of tubular tobacco pipes.

The place of Adena in the prehistoric pattern remained uncertain for a long
time. In 1930, Henry Clyde Shetrone, who had succeeded Mills as director
and chief archaeologist of the Ohio State Archaeological and Historical Society,
published a 496-page semipopular book, *The Mound-Builders,* in which he

devoted less than three pages to a discussion of the Adena Culture. "Far too little is known of the Adena type of mounds," wrote Shetrone, "and further exploration promises to enhance the importance of the culture."[219]

Two years later the first extensive study of the Adena Culture was published in the *Ohio State Archaeological and Historical Quarterly,* in which many of the basic reports on Ohio mounds had appeared. The paper was Emerson F. Greenman's lengthy "Excavation of the Coon Mound and an Analysis of the Adena Culture," in which Greenman identified 70 mounds as of the Adena type and isolated 59 cultural traits found in common in two or more of the mounds. Greenman's work was hampered by difficulties that have beset later investigators as well: many of the mounds had been ruinously excavated by artifact-hunting local citizens, and even those that had been opened by nineteenth-century archaeologists were in bad shape. The reports of these early archaeologists, Greenman found, were generally inadequate, and many of the mounds had been destroyed completely or in part by farming activities or industrial expansion.

Shortly after the publication of this report, the Federal Government began an extensive program of archaeology under the Works Progress Administration. A great many mounds were excavated, particularly in those Southern states where archaeological sites would be destroyed by flooding caused by the new Tennessee Valley Authority reservoirs; the WPA activity also concentrated heavily on sites closer to the Ohio mound region. One of the leaders of this enormous government-sponsored enterprise was William S. Webb, chairman of the department of anthropology of the University of Kentucky. In the course of the work, a number of new Adena mounds were examined for the first time, and some of the older ones were re-excavated. Webb, in collaboration with his University of Kentucky colleague Charles E. Snow, published in 1945 a comprehensive report on the new Adena findings: *The Adena People* (University of Kentucky Reports in Anthropology and Archaeology, Volume VI).

This attempt at a definitive work added 103 Adena sites to Greenman's 70, and expanded his list of 59 cultural traits to 218. By that time it was recognized that the Adena people occupied a significant place in Ohio Valley prehistory. Webb and Snow wrote:

"The point of origin of Adena man with his mound-building traits cannot yet be demonstrated, but it is certain that he was the *first builder of earthworks* in this region, and thus could not have derived these traits from any earlier occupant of the region. As a broad headed individual, with head deformation, one would suspect a southern origin, and his mound-building traits would point to the Middle American Area as a possible source."[220]

It was estimated that the Adena Culture had taken form about 1000 B.C., developing an elaborate cult of the dead and going to great effort to construct huge earthen tombs. About 400 B.C., archaeologists believed, a new group of settlers began to enter the territory of the Adena folk. These were the people of the Hopewell Culture, named for a site in Ross County, Ohio, where their typical traits were first uncovered. Skeletal evidence showed that the Hopewells had long, narrow skulls, while the Adenas generally had round, broad skulls. Thus the change in cultural pattern was the result of the arrival of a different stock, not merely of the passing of time.

The Hopewells—who in essence were the "Mound Builders" of whom nineteenth-century writers had made so much—adopted the basic pattern of Adena life, but expanded and transformed it. As Webb and Snow outlined it, the Adenas and the intruding Hopewells lived as uneasy neighbors for hundreds of years, with the Hopewells borrowing most of the Adena traits and carrying them to new heights. They built vast burial mounds and the celebrated earthwork embankments that covered hundreds of acres. By A.D. 500, the Hopewell Culture had reached its climax in a quasi empire with trade connections reaching across much of North America; then it began to fade, and shortly the older Adena Culture joined it in oblivion.

The report of Webb and Snow placed Adena in the sequence of cultural development in Ohio and made it the ancestral culture of the mound-building peoples. The details of the relationship of Adena to its successor, the dynamic Hopewell Culture, still awaited full clarification, however, and in the years that followed there was considerable research into the Adena problems. One of the leaders in this work was Raymond S. Baby of the Ohio State Museum, who excavated several important Adena mounds in Ohio. Baby's work largely amounted to salvage archaeology: he attempted to rescue what information he could from mounds that were about to be destroyed by commercial interests, and in some cases dug in mounds whose demolition was already under way. With much of the mound region of the United States undergoing vast industrial expansion in the years following World War II, virtually every mound not already protected by public ownership was jeopardized, and archaeologists were compelled to organize their work schedules according to the timetables of the bulldozer operators; mounds that were in no danger of immediate destruction were left unexplored while the archaeologists concentrated on salvaging the threatened ones.

One of the most important Adena excavations of the postwar years was a project in salvage archaeology. The Pittsburgh Plate Glass Company had purchased a tract of farmland at Natrium, West Virginia, for use as the site of a chemical factory. Prehistoric mounds are common there; the factory site was only a short distance from the Grave Creek Mound, the largest conical mound in the United States. An important mound was situated on the Pittsburgh Plate Glass property. Known as the Natrium Mound, it was almost 10 feet high and 55 feet in diameter, though there were signs that it had once been larger. A farmer who had cut away a small part of the mound for its soil, many years earlier, had reported finding Indian artifacts in it. Archaeologists suspected that it was an Adena mound, but there had never been any systematic exploration of it.

The Pittsburgh Plate Glass Company had already built a factory adjoining the mound. In 1948 it proposed to expand the factory, which would involve destruction of the mound. A company engineer notified the Smithsonian Institution of the plan, and told Dr. Frank H. H. Roberts, the co-ordinator of the Smithsonian's salvage-archaeology program, that the company was willing to co-operate in salvage work to the extent of suspending its construction work for three or four months while the mound was excavated. The company also agreed to provide four workmen and whatever mechanical equipment might be needed.

Dr. Roberts sent Ralph E. Solecki, a young archaeologist then with the Bureau of American Ethnology, to supervise the work. Solecki reached the mound on December 6, 1948, and excavation work began the next day. A telephone pole and the shrubbery atop the mound were removed; the bare surface was surveyed for artifacts; a Pittsburgh Plate Glass engineer prepared a contour map of the mound to guide the archaeologists. Then the digging began, first by hand, then with the aid of a bulldozer. Solecki had a trial trench dug, 125 feet in length, beginning 45 feet out from the mound and continuing over its crest for some 20 feet on the far side. The trench gave him an idea of the mound's inner profile. A second exploratory trench followed, and then the bulldozer was called into use. Employing recently developed salvage-archaeology techniques, the bulldozer operator was able to slice away the covering of the mound with amazing delicacy and speed; in less than six hours the mound was stripped to its core with no harm to essential structural features. Now the archaeologists went to work with shovels, trowels, and other conventional hand tools.

Within the mound were 51 features of interest—burials, fireplaces, groups of artifacts. Most of these were contained in an inner mound that had been erected over a stratum of yellow loamy earth. A simple horizontal log tomb had been built on a bark-covered clay floor; an extended skeleton lay within it. Elsewhere there were a number of cremation burials, associated with strings of copper beads, copper breastplates, and chipped stone blades and points. Solecki took hundreds of choppers, drills, beads, and hammerstones from Natrium Mound. The secondary mound, which had been heaped over the inner one, contained little of notice.

The artifacts recovered included 38 of the Adena traits on the 1945 Webb and Snow list; 11 new traits were identified and attributed to the Adena Culture. The mound yielded two anomalies, though: a birdstone and a boatstone. The birdstone—the stylized figure of a bird's beak, head, and shoulders, carved from gray sandstone—was of a sort common in Hopewell mounds, but it was surprising to discover one in an Adena mound. The boatstone, a keeled boat-shaped object believed to have been used as a weight for a spear thrower, was likewise a Hopewellian item. The presence of these two artifacts in the Natrium Mound was a good indication of Adena-Hopewell contact. But there were other perplexing aspects to this mound. It displayed most of the traits that Webb and Snow had said were typical of the late Adena Culture, and the two Hopewellian artifacts seemed to confirm this evaluation. Yet certain early Adena traits were observed also. Since Solecki felt that Natrium Mound represented a single cultural occupation over a relatively short span of time, it was difficult to account for artifacts displaying a range of more than a thousand years in style, except to say that "Natrium Mound may have been a culturally peripheral structure, both figuratively and literally. A cultural lag seems to have carried it well into early Hopewell times. This is reflected in the presence of such Hopewellian traits as the birdstone and the excavated boatstone, occurring apparently contemporaneously with objects of patently Adena type. On the other hand, artifactual remains of what has been called early Adena type . . . are also included in the list of traits from Natrium. Granting that these may have been survival traits, we are confronted here with the fact that we have a curious assemblage of mixed items, all presumably within one temporal horizon."[221]

About the time of Solecki's work on the Natrium Mound, the technique of carbon-14 dating was coming into general use, and the first reports on dates from the mounds were appearing. The results caused consternation, to say the least, among archaeologists. A group of Adena radiocarbon dates came out between A.D. 500 and A.D. 700. A group of Hopewell radiocarbon dates came out between 200 B.C. and the beginning of the Christian era.

These early reports seemed to invert the accepted order of things, making Hopewell ancestral to Adena, contrary to all that had been established thus far. It was a dizzying moment for American archaeologists. Some of them simply refused to accept the judgment of the newfangled technique, even though carbon-14 dating had been proven generally reliable within a small margin for error. As Ralph Solecki put it, "Even with the high order of accuracy attained by these chronological tests, an early Hopewell date preceding that of Adena is viewed with some skepticism by specialists in the light of what is known at present about Adena and Hopewell cultures."[222]

The faith of the skeptics was justified a few years later when further carbon-14 analyses were made. The results of this work were summarized in William S. Webb's second compilation of Adena research, *The Adena People No. 2* (1957), written in collaboration with Raymond S. Baby and including chapters by other Adena authorities. In this book Webb and Baby raised the number of known Adena mounds from 173 to 222, and added 23 new traits to their previous 218. In dealing with the question of the radiocarbon dates, they commented, "As yet the number of sites of Adena and Hopewell which have been subjected to radiocarbon dating is quite small, but enough dates have been obtained in the last three years to form a significant series. The first dates obtained for Adena unfortunately were from late Adena sites, and these, being more recent than Hopewell sites, suggested that Hopewell was older than Adena. Additional dates for Adena obtained recently have clarified the situation."[223]

Webb and Baby's tabulation of dates showed that the most recent Adena carbon-14 figures came from bark found at the Drake Mound, Kentucky, which registered an age of 1168 ± 150 years. The earliest Adena date, obtained from charcoal from the Toepfner Mound, Ohio, yielded an age of 2780 ± 410 years. This gave a range for Adena from about 800 B.C. to A.D. 900. Five samples taken from Hopewell mounds produced a range of from 600 B.C. to A.D. 1500. It was safe to return to the original theory that Adena had preceded Hopewell.

Some of these dates were still controversial, though. They seemed to show that the Adena Culture had lasted for seventeen hundred years and the Hopewell Culture for twenty-one hundred. The most recent dates were severely questioned, and further examination was called for. New tests left the early range basically unchanged, showing a beginning for Adena between 1000 and 800 B.C. and for Hopewell about 400 B.C. But the sample from the Drake Mound of Kentucky, previously calculated to show an age of 1168 ± 150 years, gave a new reading of 2200 ± 200, indicating that several other recent dates for Adena were questionable. Similarly, the most recent Hopewell dates were about A.D. 500, with the exception of one questionable date of A.D. 900. From the carbon-14 evidence, then, it appears now that these two mound-building cultures of the Ohio Valley flourished for about fifteen centuries, overlapping for most of the time, and both were in decay by the fifth century A.D.

The most recent study of the Adena Culture, published in 1963 by Pittsburgh's Carnegie Museum, takes into account these radiocarbon dates as well as important archaeological findings made after the publication of Webb and Baby's 1957 work. As a result, it calls into doubt many of the earlier conclusions about Adena, and offers new evaluations which, while not yet accepted by all archaeologists, are widely regarded as authoritative. The book is *Mounds for the Dead: an Analysis of the Adena Culture,* by Don W. Dragoo of the Carnegie Museum, and is based chiefly on Dragoo's excavation of the Cresap Mound in West Virginia.

Like Solecki's work at the Natrium Mound, this was a project in salvage archaeology. The Cresap Mound, about six miles up the Ohio River from the Natrium Mound, had long remained in the hands of the Cresap family, which guarded it from the raids of artifact-hunting vandals and eventually deeded it to the West Virginia State Highway Department, with the understanding that the mound was not to be disturbed in any fashion. In 1958 the State Highway Department relocated the road that ran past the mound, abandoning the right of way and selling the roadside land (including the mound) to the Hanna Coal Company. Hanna Coal announced the intended construction of an industrial plant on the mound site.

The unexpected shift in the status of the Cresap Mound did not go unnoticed by archaeologists, who persuaded Hanna Coal to permit a salvage excavation before the mound was destroyed. The Carnegie Museum was given the assignment of supervising the work; Hanna Coal supplied four full-time workers, a number of part-time men, and power machinery to carry away earth. The excavation of the mound began on June 2, 1958, and was completed on August 26.

The mound was 15 feet high and about 70 feet in diameter. In profile it had the classical Adena conical shape, although its height had been reduced by several feet through erosion. Atop it was a locust tree 22 inches in diameter at the base, whose removal was a difficult task and whose roots, spreading through the entire mound, plagued the archaeologists throughout their work.

Once the mound surface was cleared, a trial trench was cut that showed Dragoo where the base level of the mound lay; then he began digging at the outer margin of the mound, working inward from the southwest corner. Layers of earth about an inch thick were cut away by hoe and shoveled to the rim of the mound, where power equipment removed it. As the earth was gradually stripped away, an unexpectedly intricate inner structure was revealed. Dragoo found that the Cresap Mound had given him a stratified sequence covering a great span in the development of the Adena Culture. "I was at last presented with the previously missing key to Adena chronology," he reported. "Scraps of information that meant little before now took on new meaning."[224]

The mound had apparently been built on the site of an early house. Near the center of the mound was a large circular fire pit containing ashes and burned stones, surrounded by a circular clay floor about 40 feet in diameter and several inches thick. This rested directly on the loose gravel subsoil of the river terrace; an original layer of humus had been removed. Around the clay floor was a circular ditch about two feet wide, containing pieces of charcoal and burned earth; Dragoo speculated that the posts supporting the house had once been set in this ditch.

"The first use of the area for burial purposes occurred," he wrote, "when a shallow subfloor tomb was dug through the clay floor just west of the fire pit. Before this tomb was covered with earth a large crematory basin was dug into the clay floor just southwest of the tomb. Two extended adult burials were placed on the clay floor just south of the above features. A dark humus-laden earth was then placed over these features to a depth sufficient to cover them. Additional features containing human remains were gradually added and more earth over them until a small mound with a maximum height of 4.75 feet was formed. The earth of this small mound was a very dark, organic-laden, loamy soil."[225]

About midway in the growth of this mound, a second tomb was dug in the clay floor, and dark earth was heaped over it to form an "annex" to the first small mound. Another crematory basin was also dug. When the primary mound covered these adjoining features and had reached its full height, the center of activity moved to a point about 15 feet south of the fire pit, where an additional crematory basin was built, containing the remains of six individuals. Two other burials were placed beside it, and the region was covered by a small mound about three feet high. A similar mound, slightly more than five feet high, was subsequently erected over a tomb east of the fire pit. This mound grew in stages, and eight burials were enclosed in it.

Apparently this entire group of little mounds was covered by a wooden canopy, whose presence is indicated by small particles of charcoal on the surface of the mounds, and the absence of erosion gullies on them. This covering evidently was destroyed by fire. Next, a large crematory basin was constructed between two of the small mounds, and the entire site was covered with earth, forming a single mound of conical shape, 6.75 feet high at its peak. This was allowed to stand for some time; humus accumulated to a depth of several inches atop it, and erosion gullies developed.

Later, certain ceremonial artifacts were deposited on the mound in the course of further burials, and its height was increased to 8.2 feet. Then a depression was dug into the top of the mound and a cremation burial took place in it; 15 small copper beads and other objects accompanied this tribesman to his rest, and logs were placed above the burial. A cap of earth was added, bringing the summit of the mound to 13.25 feet, and then the mound was left undisturbed long enough for a 6-inch-thick layer of humus to collect.

"Eventually the mound again was used for the burial of the dead," wrote Dragoo. "This final act in the construction of the mound centered around a fire built at the top of the mound at the 13.25-foot elevation. On the surface of the mound around the fireplace had been placed burials 1, 2, 3, 5, 7, 8, 10, and 25. Over these burials and the fireplace a thick mantle of gravelly earth was placed until the mound was probably at least 17.0 feet in height. At the time of our excavation, erosion over the centuries had reduced the mound to 15.0 feet in height.

"With the addition of the above earth mantle, the building of the Cresap Mound by the Adena people drew to a close. The mound appears not to have been disturbed again until the Late Prehistoric (A.D. 1200–1600) when a man of that period was buried in a shallow pit dug into the top of the mound. Neither this intrusion nor two shallow probings of the mound during the past century caused any disturbance or damage to the mound's structure or contents. To us was presented the rare opportunity of excavating a basically undisturbed mound in which a clear chronological sequence of events could be traced."[226]

The artifacts taken from the mound included such prosaic things as scrapers, drills, blades, and projectile points, along with 370 copper beads, cups and awls made from bone, beads of shell, a polished boatstone, 4 pipes, and 22 tablets, one of them an unusual turtle effigy. The tablets, which lacked engraved inscriptions, were discovered at all levels of the mound, with the finest ones (including the turtle) at the top. Obviously these were late Adena tablets; they were related stylistically to ceremonial tablets found at other Adena mounds. The Cresap evidence showed an almost complete sequence of the evolution of Adena tablet styles, and served to link the top layer of the Cresap Mound to other mounds generally deemed late Adena. At no other mound had such a sequence been discovered; only Cresap displayed an accretion covering nearly the whole range of Adena life. From such evidence, Dragoo was able to reconstruct a view of Adena development quite at variance with that established by Webb, Snow, Baby, and others.

4

The picture of Adena life that has emerged from recent research shows a culture concentrated in the Ohio Valley within a radius of 150 miles from

Chillicothe, Ohio. There were two main centers of occupation, one along the Scioto River in southern Ohio and one on the Kanawha River near Charleston, West Virginia. Lesser centers were situated in eastern Indiana, northern Kentucky, western Ohio, and northwestern West Virginia. The most easterly of these minor centers was at Moundsville, West Virginia, surrounding the great Grave Creek Mound. A survey in 1909 showed 47 mounds in this area; most have been destroyed since then, although salvage archaeology at the Natrium Mound and the Cresap Mound was carried out in time.

From the heart of the Adena territory, it is possible to trace Adena influence north and east up the Ohio River to Pittsburgh, where a large Adena mound, since removed, was partially excavated by the Carnegie Museum in 1896. The spread of Adena continued into the Monongahela Valley, where Cyrus Thomas explored several small mounds later determined to be of the Adena type. The presence of Adena influence has been identified on the eastern shore of Chesapeake Bay, though no mounds were built there, and as far south as northern

26   Map of Adena sites.

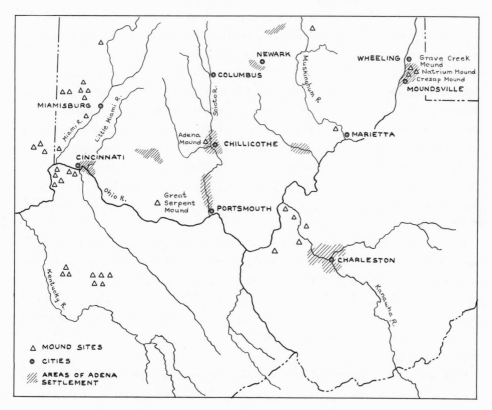

Alabama, where William S. Webb traced what seemed to be a late Adena group he called the Copena Culture. Adena traits also were reported in 1937 in New York State by William A. Ritchie of the New York State Museum; Ritchie identified the site as an example of the "Middlesex Complex," and suggested that it marked the arrival of a band of late-period refugees from the Adena heartland in Ohio. Only one group of Adena mounds is known in New York, on Long Sault Island in the St. Lawrence River. According to Ritchie, this is "the outpost most remote of any now known from the Adena heartland."[227]

The largest and most famous of the Adena sites is the Grave Creek Mound, entered by its owners in 1838 and later badly damaged by erosion; today it is a local tourist attraction and steps have been taken to halt its deterioration. Modern archaeological investigations were not conducted at Grave Creek until Delf Narona explored it in 1957. Don Dragoo considers the Grave Creek Mound a representative of late Adena life.

The nearby Natrium Mound, also regarded as late Adena by its excavator, Ralph Solecki, has been the subject of further discussion by Dragoo, who finds "a striking resemblance, both in the artifacts and the mound features, between the Natrium Mound and the middle and lower levels of the Cresap Mound."[228] Dragoo argues that the supposedly Hopewellian birdstone, one of the proofs of the lateness of the Natrium Mound, is not necessarily a Hopewell artifact at all, since birdstones were found in 1959 in New York and Ontario at sites that antedated by several centuries the oldest known Hopewell centers. As for the boatstone, also considered Hopewellian, one quite like it was discovered in the middle zone of the Cresap Mound, and so, Dragoo says, "the boatstone from the Natrium Mound appears less unusual in Adena and not necessarily a mark of Hopewellian influence." The revision of Adena trait sequences generated by Dragoo's meticulous unpeeling of the Cresap Mound allowed him to conclude that "none of the traits that mark late Adena was present in the Natrium Mound."[229]

The Cresap results have permitted a revision of the previously held views on Adena development; Dragoo has classified the several hundred known Adena traits into early, middle, and late styles, and his classification does not always agree with the distinctions drawn by Webb and his collaborators. Dragoo regards early and middle Adena as virtually continuous, and does not think it is yet possible to draw a fine line dividing them, while his late Adena styles are markedly different.

Early and middle Adena life, he says, were typified by the burial of the dead in conical mounds that occurred singly or in groups. Most bodies were simply stretched out on bark on the surface of the ground; a few selected individuals were placed in shallow pits lined with clay and covered with logs. Many bodies were cremated in oval or elliptical basins near the floor of the mound; burned and unburned artifacts were often placed with them.

In this period, Adena houses were circular, made of posts lashed together. The posts were arranged in a single row. Adena tools were of flint or bone; ornaments included copper beads, stone gorgets and pendants, and occasional headdresses made from deer or elk skulls with antlers. Sometimes the antlers were imitated in copper.

The transition to late Adena times was marked by the custom of burial in elaborate log tombs; the conical mounds now were usually constructed in groups, frequently with an earthwork in circular form nearby. These "sacred circles," found in many parts of the Adena territory, are different from the much larger enclosures attributed to the Hopewell people; none of them exceeds 500 feet in diameter. Dragoo thinks that the "sacred circles" were ritual centers, and that "the presence of elaborate log tomb burials of certain individuals in the mounds near 'sacred circles' is highly suggestive that these individuals were the leaders of the social and ceremonial activities of the group that used the earthwork."[230] Other diagnostic traits for late Adena are finely made stone tablets, tubular effigy pipes, the use of mica, and the presence of certain types of pottery, blades, and ornaments. At this time the style of house construction changed; Adena houses now were walled by double rings of posts, consisting of pairs of posts about a foot from each other and about 4½ feet from the adjoining pair. The circular dwellings ranged from 35 to 52 feet in diameter; larger buildings of similar construction apparently served as community centers.

Each village consisted of two to five houses, perhaps representing a family group. Clusters of these small villages were distributed over a wide area, and possibly such "greater villages" were the sustaining populations for the burial mound or earthwork centers. Most archaeologists believe that the Adena people were farmers; it had long been suspected that a culture devoted to such extensive works would need a steady and reliable food supply, rather than depending on hunting and gathering of wild vegetables, and this was confirmed in 1938 when fragments of pumpkin and squash were recovered from the fireplace of the Florence Mound, Pickaway County, Ohio. Radiocarbon dating of this material showed an age of 1425 ± 250 years. The rind of a gourdlike pumpkin was subsequently found at another late Adena site, the Cowan Mound in Clinton County, Ohio. These are the only two indications of Adena agriculture that have come to light so far. Corn, the basic component of most American

Indian agriculture, is totally absent. Dragoo feels that it would be an exaggeration to call the Adena people a true agricultural society; the absence of corn, and the presence of cultivated pumpkin and squash at only a couple of late Adena sites, leads Dragoo to adopt a relatively radical stance on this point.

"On the basis of our present knowledge," he writes, "it would appear that early Adena need not have been geared to an agricultural economy based on corn in order to have constructed mounds for the burial of the dead. The gradual build-up of a mound, for example the Cresap Mound, did not necessitate the expenditure of great amounts of labor at any one time. By the use of every source of food that was available from hunting, and gathering of wild plants, early Adena could easily have established the scattered pattern of settlement that marks the culture from the stable village life of later peoples with corn growing. . . . If agriculture, and specifically cultivation of corn, did become an important factor in Adena, I feel that it must have been very late."[231] Whether or not they were agriculturists, the Adena folk depended heavily on such wild plants as raspberry, chestnut, pawpaw, and walnut; they also collected snails and fresh-water mussels, and hunted deer, elk, black bears, raccoons, beavers, and many other animals.

The central fact of Adena life was the cult of the honored dead. This began simply, with the low mounds over burial pits found in the core of the Cresap Mound, and gradually became more extensive as Adena ceremonial practice expanded. At the outset the dead were treated in many ways: some buried extended in the flesh, others cremated, some left on exposed platforms until the flesh was gone and the bundled bones alone could be interred, and some dissected before burial, with just certain portions buried. One school of thought holds that only important leaders received a tomb burial extended in the flesh, while the common man was cremated; but Dragoo observes that "prized objects were often consigned to the crematory fires along with the bodies while some extended burials in tombs received no durable offerings." The significance of the various types of early Adena burials, then, is still in doubt; but there can be no doubt that the act of burial, with its implied belief in an afterlife, was vital to the Adena people even at the beginning of their development, and that fire was an important factor in their rites.

The grave goods interred in the burial mounds tell us a great deal about Adena craftsmanship. Most of the artifacts placed in the early Adena burial mounds were utilitarian: pottery, blades, drills, awls, scrapers. Evidently these were the property of the person with whom they were buried. Usually a single pipe was placed with each burial, though in one mound 32 pipes were arranged about a single individual. "Why?" Dragoo wonders. "Was this man the pipe-maker? Was this a way of paying tribute to a revered individual in which the men of the clan gave up their prized pipes? Was the pipe of special significance in their ceremonies? If so, why were pipes placed with some persons and not with others? Did only certain individuals have the rights to a pipe? These and many other questions goad the archeologist. . . ."[232]

The late Adena period, which saw so many sweeping changes in Adena customs, apparently produced a deepening and enriching of the burial cult that has yielded a rich harvest of superb Adena art. Now, it seems, burial was a privilege accorded fewer individuals; the honored dead lay in state in their sturdy log vaults while offerings of goods and food were placed beside them; their bodies were painted with pigments such as ochre or red graphite; sometimes a canopy was erected over the open tomb. When the flesh had begun to decay, the heaping of earth began. Frequently a second burial, with all the attendant ritual, took place on the site of an earlier one, so that some Adena mounds grew by accretion to tremendous sizes.

Within these late mounds have been found such objects as "trophy" skulls—clean, sometimes polished skulls placed on the thighs of an extended burial. Surely this must have had some ritualistic significance. Another evocative Adena object is the antler headdress, previously thought to be a Hopewell trait exclusively. These headdresses were usually made of the skullcap and antlers of an actual deer or elk, but some were fashioned from thin hammered copper sheets. Were they ceremonial crowns? The insignia of a chief or priest?

Other impressive grave goods include the effigy pipes, of which the finest is the human effigy from the original Adena Mound; copper bracelets made from heavy solid bars; small bowls decorated with a diamond pattern; handsome gorgets and other ornamental pendants; copper rings; abstract forms cut from thick sheets of mica; masks that included animal bones and teeth; and the striking flat stone tablets, usually covered with graceful, curving geometrical designs. The tablets in particular have fascinated archaeologists because of their great beauty. About a dozen engraved tablets and twice as many blank ones have been recovered, going back to the finding of the disputed Grave Creek Tablet in 1838. The patterns of most are abstract, with flowing lines and a curious quasi-symmetry of form; but a close inspection of the swirling loops and curvilinear outlines reveals that many of the "abstract" designs actually portray fierce birds with curving beaks and grasping claws. Webb and Baby have suggested that these birds are hawks, eagles, or vultures, and that their depiction on the tablets may be related to Adena burial customs:

"A study of the cremated remains of Adena has revealed that the skeletons had been denuded of flesh prior to burning. Before cremation of the bones by Adena people, the skeletons of those to be cremated had to be cleaned of the

27   The Berlin tablet. Courtesy Ohio Historical Society, Columbus, Ohio.

28   The Wilmington tablet. Courtesy Museum of the American Indian, Heye Foundation.

flesh. It is quite probable that they had some system of 'exposing' the bodies for a limited period of time to allow partial decomposition of the flesh before the shaman performed his duties of cleaning the bones and burning the remaining flesh in sacred fires. . . . If bodies to be cremated were thus exposed, whether on the earth, in trees, or on scaffolds, it would seem certain that they would have attracted the carrion crow or other vultures. Because of their flesh-eating habits these birds might have come to be highly respected by the people as agents of the spirit world who assisted them in the preparation of the skeletons for cremation. It would not be surprising, therefore, if the carrion crow or other vultures were deified, or, at least recognized as a potent influence in the Cult of the Dead."[233]

The function of the engraved tablets has come in for a good deal of discussion. Webb and Snow have speculated that they may have served as grinding stones for awls or knives used in ceremonial bloodletting: "If the participant in such a ceremony were a cult devotee, he would perhaps need some identification or record of his participation. What more natural way to accomplish this end than that the shaman, at the time, should draw or stamp upon the body of the individual the appropriate symbol of the cult?" The whetstone, in this interpretation, becomes the stamp used for imprinting the sacred design on the body of the initiated. Others have suggested that the tablets were used merely for stamping textiles, or that they had some cult significance wholly unknown to us.

The most conspicuous Adena ritual object—and one of the most famous of all American mounds—is the Great Serpent Mound in Adams County, Ohio. This is only conjecturally an Adena mound, for no human artifacts have ever been found in it; but excavation of a conical burial mound about 400 feet away has yielded characteristic Adena objects, including a copper breastplate, stone axes and points, and grooved pieces of sandstone.

The Serpent is one of four or five effigy mounds in Ohio, and is the largest known serpent effigy in the world. It consists of a low rounded embankment nearly a quarter of a mile long, depicting a gigantic serpent in the act of uncoiling. The serpent's head reaches a sheer rock precipice a hundred feet above the waters of Brush Creek; in seven great coils it writhes southward to its triple-coiled tail. Clasped in the open jaws of the serpent is an oval, thought by some to represent an egg, by others a frog. The serpent proper is 1,254 feet in length from tail to the tip of its upper jaw; the average width of the body is about 20 feet, its height four or five feet. The crescent wall forming the open jaws of the beast is 17 feet in width, and its ends are 75 feet apart.

Today this vast, sinuous monster is covered by a neatly manicured coat of grass, and it occupies the place of honor in a state park with adjoining picnic grounds. On a summer day hundreds of children swarm around the mound or climb the observation tower that affords a good view of its entire length. Yet this remarkable work —strangest and most awesome of all the mounds—came close to destruction in the last century, and was preserved only through the efforts of a few dedicated individuals.

The existence of the Great Serpent Mound has long been known. Atwater failed to mention it, but Squier and Davis included it in their survey, providing one of their customarily handsome maps. "No plan or description has hitherto been published," Squier wrote, "nor does the fact of its existence appear to have been known beyond the secluded vicinity in which it occurs."[234] He commented that "the serpent, separate or in combination with the circle, egg, or globe, has been a predominant symbol among many primitive nations. It prevailed in

29   The Great Serpent Mound. Aerial photograph, courtesy Museum of the American Indian, Heye Foundation.

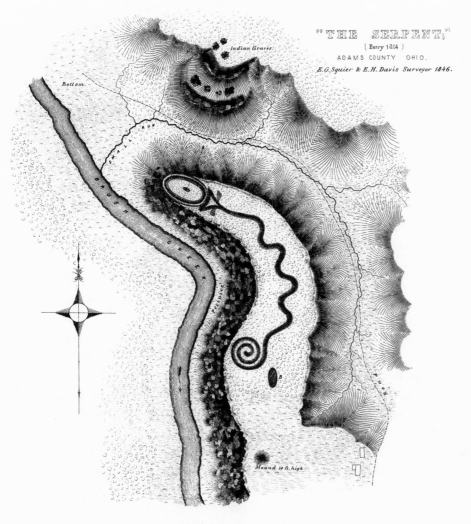

30   The Serpent. Diagram, Squier and Davis, 1848.

Egypt, Greece, and Assyria, and entered widely into the superstitions of the Celts, the Hindoos, and the Chinese. It even penetrated into America; and was conspicuous in the mythology of the ancient Mexicans, among whom its significance does not seem to have differed materially from that which it possessed in the old world. The fact that the ancient Celts, and perhaps other nations of the old continent, erected sacred structures in the form of the serpent, is one of high interest." This, of course, gave aid and comfort to those diffusionists who wished to prove a non-Indian origin for the mounds. Squier, noting the impossibility of tracing the connection of Ohio's Serpent to its Old World parallels, noted that such an investigation was "fraught with the greatest interest both in respect to the light which it reflects upon the primitive superstitions of remotely separated people, and especially upon the origin of the American race."

William Pidgeon, that self-appointed expert on primitive superstitions, claimed to have visited the Serpent in 1832 and again in 1849. His mentor De-coo-dah had showed him smaller serpent effigies in Iowa, Wisconsin, and Nebraska, telling him "that when the worshippers of reptiles were reduced by the fortunes of war, and compelled to recognise the sun, moon, and heavenly bodies as the only objects worthy of adoration, they secretly entombed their gods in the earth-work symbols which represented the heavenly bodies. . . ."[235] Hence the combination of serpent and oval (a sun or moon symbol, to De-coo-dah). The serpent effigies of the Northern states do exist, but are thought to have no cultural connection with the Ohio mound.

In the summer of 1883, F. W. Putnam of the Peabody Museum came to the Great Serpent. Describing his visit in an 1890 issue of *The Century,* Putnam wrote, "Leaving the wagon, we scrambled up the steep hillside, and pushing on through bush and brier were soon following the folds of the great serpent along the hilltop. The most singular sensation of awe and admiration over-whelmed me at this sudden realization of my long cherished admiration, for here before me was the mysterious work of an unknown people whose seem-ingly most sacred place we had invaded. Was this a symbol of the old serpent faith, here on the Western continent, which from the earliest time in the reli-gions of the East held so many peoples enthralled, and formed so important a factor in the development of succeeding religions? Reclining on one of the huge folds of this gigantic serpent, as the last rays of the sun, glancing from distant hilltops, cast their long shadows over the valley, I mused on the prob-abilities of the past; and there seemed to come to me a picture as of a distant time, and with it came a demand for an interpretation of this mystery. The unknown must become known."[236]

The mound then was the property of John J. Lovett, a farmer who was aware of its scientific importance and who had refrained from planting crops on the site. But Putnam was worried about the Great Serpent's future; already, there was talk of leveling the giant Cahokia Mound to get ballast for a railroad track, and who knew what might happen when farmer Lovett was gone?

In 1886, Putnam visited the Serpent again. The trip in those days was a strenuous one: he took a narrow-gauge railroad eastward from Cincinnati to the town of Peebles, a four-hour journey, had an early dinner in Peebles, and went on from there to the Serpent by hired carriage, taking another two hours and a half. Putnam found the mound partly obliterated by amateur excavators, the tramping of cattle and visitors, and the effects of rain. And Mr. Lovett said that he was about to sell his land, and that the mound would almost certainly be turned into a cornfield. Putnam managed to get a one-year option on the mound, and set out to raise the money for its purchase price.

He began his campaign with an impassioned letter to the Boston *Sunday Herald:* "To me it seems a greater loss than would be the destruction of our own monument on Bunker Hill, and yet what indignation would be aroused should some dynamite fiend topple that to the ground!" A group of Boston ladies organized a fund drive and raised $5,880, enough to buy the land and to care for the mound. In June, 1887, the title was conveyed to the Boston group. That summer Putnam spent eight weeks restoring the mound to the condition it had been in when Squier and Davis had made their chart forty years earlier. The restoration departed from their plan only in two small instances where Putnam believed the original survey had been in error; later archaeologists have had a few reservations about the authenticity of the reconstructed head and oval, but generally Putnam's restoration is thought to be a reasonable facsimile of the original. Putnam also built a fence with a turnstile, and installed a hitching post and horse trough for the convenience of visitors. In March of 1888, the Ohio legislature freed Serpent Mound Park from taxation, and in 1900 the Peabody Museum deeded it to the Ohio Archaeological and Historical Society to be maintained as a state park.

5.

For archaeologists there are three paramount questions not yet fully answered about the Adena Culture:

How did it originate?

What was its relationship to the Hopewell Culture?

Why did it decline?

It seems clear that the Adena people were intruders in the Ohio Valley, representing not merely a new cultural tradition but a new physical stock. The Archaic inhabitants of the region were mainly long-headed, with high-vaulted, narrow skulls and slender bodies. They lived in riverbank villages, feeding on shellfish, wild game, and seeds, and did not practice interment in burial mounds. Not only was the Adena Culture a sharp variant from this, but the skulls recovered in Adena mounds display a distinctive physical appearance.

The first description of an Adena skull was provided by Samuel Morton in his *Crania Americana* in 1839, though of course the Adena Culture had not yet then been identified. Speaking of a cranium found in a Chillicothe mound, Morton said, "This is, perhaps, the most admirably-formed head of the American race hitherto discovered. It possesses the national characteristics in perfection, as seen in the elevated vertex, flattened occiput, great interparietal diameter, ponderous bony structure, salient nose, large jaws and broad face. . . . Similar forms are common in the Peruvian tombs, and have the occiput, as in this instance, so flattened and vertical as to give the idea of artificial compression; yet this is only an exaggeration of the natural form, caused by the pressure of the cradleboard in common use among the American nations."[237]

Webb and Snow, one hundred and twenty years later, described the Adena type as having a large, round skull, a prominent forehead bordered below by sizable brow ridges, a jutting chin, and massive bones. The Adena folk were unusually tall and powerfully built; women over six feet tall and men approaching heights of seven feet have been discovered. It would seem that a band of strikingly different people of great presence and majesty had forced their way into the Ohio Valley from somewhere about 1000 B.C. However, Webb and Snow add the cautious note that their picture of the Adena physical type is based on less than a hundred skulls, nearly all of them from late Adena mounds, and nearly all found in the elaborately prepared log tombs. "The Adena people selected for the elaborate mound burial—the honored dead— cannot be regarded as representative samples of the Adena population," they point out. "It seems certain that many, if not most, of the ordinary people must have been cremated in the common form of burial preparation. Therefore we are dealing with a most unusual group."[238]

This leads to the picture of a small cadre of round-headed giants dominating and ruling an existing long-headed Ohio Valley population. However that may be, the question remains: where did the mound-building Adenas come from?

Webb and Snow, in 1945, suggested the Middle American area—specifically, Mexico. In this they adhered to a long tradition of claiming a Mexican genesis for the Mound Builders. They based their theory on the prevalence of round-headed people in prehistoric Mexico, on the shared custom of head-binding that led to deformed skulls, and on the mound-building traits of the Adena folk, which seemed derived from Mexican practices. This view has many adherents. Albert C. Spaulding's 1952 paper, "The Origin of the Adena Culture of the Ohio Valley," declared, "It would seem that the Adena culture appeared in the Ohio Valley as the result of a migration from lowland eastern Mexico" and that "the migrants would have been essentially tropical forest peoples whose culture possessed strong Circum-Caribbean affiliations."[239] He supplied a long list of cultural parallels: "the mortuary concept, with its tombs in earth mounds, multiple burials having a central inhumation with subsidiary in-humations or deposits of cremated remains . . . use of a considerable amount of grave goods including trophy skulls (one of which was painted), and sharp social differentiation shown in burial practices, with simple cremation for ordinary folk." About the same time, J. B. Griffin pointed out that the carved stone Adena tablets resemble certain Mexican tablets even in details of design.

In *The Adena People No. 2,* 1957, Webb and Baby reported "that nothing has developed since that time to change the basic conclusions" that the origin of Adena lay in Mexico. And Gordon R. Willey, in 1966, expressed the belief that the technique of corn agriculture had been exported from Mexico to the Ohio Valley in the Burial Mound I Period, shortly after 1000 B.C., although he admitted that no evidence of early corn cultivation there had yet been found. Presumably the mound-building concept had accompanied corn-raising north-ward. However, Willey says, "It should be made clear to the reader . . . that there is strong conflicting opinion on this question; and some authorities not only feel that agriculture was of no consequence in Burial Mound I times but that it played little part in the economy or the general development of Eastern Woodland cultures in the Burial Mound II Period." Though he re-marks that mound burial had developed early enough in Central and South America to have influenced eastern North America, "it may be that more than one point of origin is involved, or it may be that the idea was a completely independent development of the Eastern Woodlands."[240]

In an earlier period of archaeological speculation, it was frequently suggested that the mound-building idea had come out of Asia with the early Bering Strait emigrants. One of the first to state this was Caleb Atwater, who imagined a trail of mounds leading from the landing place of Noah's Ark across Asia into the Americas. (The opposite view was offered, in the early years of the twentieth century, by an Ohio Baptist minister who used the Great Serpent Mound as proof that the Garden of Eden had been located in Ohio, with the Serpent a visible reminder of Eve's deception of Adam.) The presence of mounds in Siberia tended to give some substance to the theory of an Asian origin for the mound-building custom. But this theory has been wholly discredited today.

Much of the northwestern part of North America was *terra incognita* in Atwater's time; since then it has become amply clear that a great gap in mound distribution exists in eastern Asia and northern Canada, separating the Siberian mounds from those of the United States. Furthermore, as Chester S. Chard pointed out in his 1961 paper, "Invention versus Diffusion: the Burial Mound Complex of the Eastern United States," there are no burial mounds at all in the part of Siberia closest to the Bering Strait. According to him, the first *kurgans,* as burial mounds are known in eastern Asia, appeared in the Old World between 2500 and 2000 B.C. in the Caucasus. The custom spread halfway across Asia to the vicinity of the Altai Mountains, but reached only into the southern Siberian steppe west of the Yenisei River. Even there— far from the Bering Strait—only miniature mounds were constructed until 1200 or even 1000 B.C. The greatest development of Siberian mound building came about 700 B.C., by which time the Adena Culture was already functioning. The Siberian mounds make use of stone in their construction, unlike those of Adena, and, Chard writes, "in form they are like an inverted saucer; extensive in ground plan but very low, only a few meters in height. The contrast with the tall, conical earth mounds of the Adena Culture is obvious. Not until about the first century B.C. in the final stage of the Tager Culture do you find hemi-spherical earth mounds that recall in any way those of eastern America, and none of these exceed 4½ meters in height."[241] Burial mounds were later used in Mongolia about A.D. 1 and in Japan about A.D. 250, too late to have in-fluenced the New World. In China, the Chou Dynasty, which came into being about 1000 B.C., constructed burial mounds, but these did not spread even to neighboring Japan, let alone to Ohio. Chard thinks that the Chou were western barbarians who may have carried *kurgan* burial into China from the Altai region.

Several ideas have been proposed by way of tracing the supposed Mexican intrusion into the Ohio Valley. One suggestion is that the puzzling Poverty Point site in northern Louisiana may have been a way station for migrants on their way from Mexico to Ohio. At Poverty Point, near the town of Floyd, in West Carroll Parish, a cluster of six mounds stands close to the banks of Bayou Mason. The largest mound is a flat-topped T-shaped structure 70 feet in height; the other mounds are from 4 to 21 feet high, and the entire group is laid out in a vague semicircle.

The Poverty Point mounds were first mentioned by Samuel H. Lockett in the Smithsonian Institution Annual Report for 1872, and received their earliest detailed examination about fifty years later when Clarence B. Moore spied them from his steamboat, *Gopher.* But little attention was paid to them until recent times, when aerial photographs of the group were taken for mapping purposes by the Mississippi River Commission of the U.S. Army Engineers. In 1953, these photographs were studied by James A. Ford, then on the staff of the American Museum of Natural History in New York. Ford was able to detect an unusual geometrical arrangement of the mounds that had eluded previous observers.

It seemed to him that the worn ridges that are today's Poverty Point mounds once constituted a set of six concentric octagons, the outermost one three fourths of a mile across; at some distant time in the past, a shift in the channel of the Arkansas River had washed away the eastern half of the octagons. In the report that Ford and C. H. Webb published in 1956 as one of the Anthropological Papers of the American Museum of Natural History, the speculation is offered that "if the concentric octagonal ridges were completed to the east in symmetrical fashion, the total length of ridge constructed would approximate 11.2 miles. Six feet high by eighty feet across the base is a conservative estimate of the average original dimensions of the ridge cross-section. A simple calculation gives the figure of about 530,000 cubic yards of earth," a mass "over thirty-five times the cubage" of the pyramid of Cheops in Egypt. The largest mound of this structure, Ford says, "is easily the most spectacular of the accomplishments of these people. It measures 700 by 800 feet at the base and rises to 70 feet above the surrounding plain . . . it can be estimated that the finished mound required something over three million man-hours of labor."

Yet Ford thinks the entire huge structure was constructed in a single concerted effort: "The few examples of chronological information that have been secured from excavations in various parts of the earthwork suggest that probably all of it was built and inhabited at about the same time. It is obvious that the figure was constructed according to an integrated plan that probably would not have prevailed if the town had grown by accretion over a long span of time." He estimates a population of several thousand, and calculates that it must have taken twenty million 50-pound basket-loads of soil to build the earthworks. From this he draws the conclusion "that this community must have been rather strictly organized. While a religious motivation may ultimately explain the large amount of earth construction, this effort was obviously well-controlled. The geometrical arrangement of the town . . . [is clearly the result] of central planning and direction. It is difficult to visualize how in a loosely organized society this quantity of essentially non-productive labor could have been expended."

Radiocarbon dates for Poverty Point fell between 1200 and 100 B.C. Ford and Webb, who thought that the site represented a southern colonial offshoot of the Adena or Hopewell mound-building cultures, preferred an 800–600 B.C. date for the flourishing of the community, which would place it several centuries after the emergence of Adena. But the artifacts found at Poverty Point are mostly of Archaic type; the site would be pure Late Archaic but for the presence of those astonishing earthworks. No Adena or Hopewell material has been found. And, though it seems impossible that such vast works could have been constructed without the support of an agricultural economy, no traces of farming have been detected at Poverty Point; its inhabitants did not even have pots to cook in, but prepared their food by heating balls of baked clay and throwing them into baskets or other containers of water that could not be placed over a fire.

Several possibilities exist: that Poverty Point was an indigenous Louisiana nonagricultural community which somehow took to building immense earthworks, or that there was influence from Ohio, or that the site represents a settlement of northward-bound migrants who eventually reached the Ohio Valley and established the Adena Culture. A more eccentric theory was propounded in 1930 by Henry Shetrone. Misinterpreting the baked clay balls used in cooking as "gambling cones" of a sort employed by certain Western Indian tribes, Shetrone suggested, possibly facetiously, that "considering the almost complete absence of potsherds and other ordinary domestic accumulations, perhaps the Poverty Point site is all that remains of an aboriginal Monte Carlo, curiously well named if prehistoric gambling led to the same financial state as in modern times."[242] More likely, Poverty Point was a sacred ceremonial city—but for whom? And when?

Another possible stopping-off place for Ohio-bound Mexicans has been pointed out in southern Louisiana on the shores of Lake Pontchartrain. Here was the home of the Tchefuncte Culture, first described by James A. Ford and George I. Quimby in 1945. They wrote at that time, "Tchefuncte and Adena are easily distinguishable by a majority of traits which they do not hold in common. . . . Indeed, it is surprising that there are any similarities between Tchefuncte and Adena, considering their spatial separation and environmental difference. We believe, however, that there is a fundamental similarity between the two cultures."[243] But which way the influences flowed—from north to south or south to north—remains unsettled.

A substantial school of archaeologists finds the Mexican hypothesis, including suggested Louisiana way stations, unacceptable. Webb and Baby, advocates of a Mexican origin, note that "it should be obvious that the ancestral Adena people could come from one of two, and perhaps both, directions, i.e., south and north," and a northern origin is now frequently postulated. Don Dragoo, whose excavation of the Cresap Mound armed him with such an extraordinary perspective on the whole range of Adena development, has pointed out that most of the "Mexican" traits found in Adena mounds come from *late* Adena mounds and are absent from those he has identified as early ones. "If we are to find the origin of Adena," he asks, "must we not look at the early stages of this culture? How can we use traits that are present in the late stage of a culture, but not present in the early stage, as indicators of origin? Are we to believe that the Adena people had all these ideas with them when they arrived from Middle America but that they did not use them for several hundred years? On the basis of the evidence as I see it, those who have looked towards Middle America for the origin of Adena culture have done so with almost a complete disregard for the facts of the chronological development of Adena culture in the Ohio Valley."[244]

He questions the resemblances Webb and his collaborators have seen between Adena practices and the burial and skull-deformation customs of early Mexico. He objects that the supposedly ancestral Mexican cultures had well-developed pottery techniques, using styles unlike any known for early Adena, and though he finds the Mexican theory "romantic and thought-provoking," he declares that "the time has come for serious consideration of other possible sources for the roots of Adena."

Dragoo finds signs of prototypical Adena in certain Late Archaic sites in the Northeast and in the lower Great Lakes area. In this he bases much of his thinking on the work of the New York archaeologist William A. Ritchie, who had found evidence of a formalized burial cult at the Muskalonge Lake and Red Lakes sites in New York. At these Archaic settlements, burial of bundled bones, cremations, and flexed bodies decorated with red ocher had been practiced in small sandy knolls. Although mound building itself was unknown among these people, Ritchie saw a "basic core of religiosity" in them, and "certain ideas possibly germinal to the development of the burial cult."

From New York, Dragoo traces the influence of this "basic core of religiosity" into Archaic cultures to the west, among them the Red Ocher Culture of Illinois and surrounding states, which practiced burial in low artificial mounds on natural prominences, and the Glacial Kame Culture of northwestern Ohio, northeastern Indiana, and southern Michigan, which buried its dead in kames, or natural knolls of gravel and sand deposited by glaciers in Pleistocene times. He sees a "coalescence of ideas and practices concerning the disposal of the dead that had developed in several widely scattered Archaic populations."[245] Thus he regards Adena more as a case of spontaneous local generation than of open invasion from a distant land. This, Dragoo recognizes, is a radical approach; he is forced to explain away the fact that Adena people had pottery, while the other burial-cult peoples of the East did not, by terming pottery an independent development among the Adenas, and he copes with the complication of the distinctive Adena physique by saying that "if, as Snow believes . . . the picture of Adena man is based upon the individuals of a selected group then our picture is not truly a representative cross-section of the Adena population." He believes that when more skulls have been recovered from early

Adena mounds, few of them will display the conspicuous chins and rounded crania of the "honored dead" of late Adena on which current physical assessments have been based.

6

The question of Adena's relation to Hopewell is equally unsettled at this time. Webb and Snow, in 1945, summarized the current theories by declaring that Adena was earlier than Hopewell and culturally ancestral to it; that the important burial and earthwork traits of Hopewell were derived from Adena prototypes; that Hopewell represented a stock of long-headed intruders into the territory then controlled by the round-headed Adena folk; that there was close contact and even intermarriage between Adena and Hopewell; and that all Adena sites had been abandoned before the final climactic flourishing of the great Hopewell Culture.

Dragoo, as might be expected, takes issue with much of this. He feels that "additional excavations and recent research by several workers, including Webb and associates, tend to cloud the picture as they then believed it to be." Since he rejects the thesis that Adena traits were directly derived from Mexico, he also rejects the theory that Hopewell traits were necessarily derived from Adena; Dragoo believes that the Hopewells were able to draw from the same pool of burial-cult beliefs common in the eastern United States of the Archiac Period that gave rise to Adena, and so that the evolution of the two cultures is largely parallel rather than sequential.

The origin of Hopewell, like that of Adena, is in doubt. The Hopewells had the agile bodies and long-headed skulls characteristic of the Archaic population of the eastern woodlands; those who see the Adenas as round-headed cultural innovators tend to see the Hopewells as a resurgent faction of the old long-headed stock. William Ritchie has pointed to the east end of Lake Ontario as a possible Hopewell starting point. There, about 1000 B.C., lived what he has called the Point Peninsula Culture, a non-mound-building group with certain similarities to Glacial Kame, Red Ocher, early Adena, and other burial-cult peoples. In 1952, James Griffin suggested that these Point Peninsula people may have found the culture of the Ohio Valley so attractive that they moved there en masse, blending with Adena to produce the Ohio Hopewell Culture. Other archaeologists see an Illinois origin for Hopewell; certainly the Illinois manifestations of Hopewell were related and probably ancestral to the astonishing flowering of Hopewell in Ohio. The Central Basin Culture of Illinois has been proposed as another Hopewell forerunner. Dragoo's conclusion is that "the similarities shared by Ohio Hopewell, Central Basin, Illinois Hopewell, and Point Peninsula were neither accidental, nor merely the result of trade, but the result of a common physical and cultural heritage."[246]

What was the impact on the Hopewell Culture as it consolidated its position in the Adena territory? And what was the impact of the newcomers upon the Adena folk?

The traditional idea, expressed by Webb and Snow, is that late Adena sites show "the beginnings of many of the customs which in Hopewell blossomed into important and highly specialized traits." They list such things as the practice of cremation, the use of copper and mica, the artistic carving of stone and bone, log tombs, earthworks, and so forth. Dragoo makes his familiar point about the discontinuity between early and late Adena; many of the traits which Hopewell allegedly borrowed from late Adena, he says, are absent in early Adena. He finds the changes between early and late Adena "as profound as the changes from Adena to Hopewell," and believes "that these changes were wrought from influences coming from outside of Adena rather than from within. It does not seem reasonable that the majority of the artificial and burial traits of late Adena should contrast so sharply with those of early Adena if there was a gradual development of these traits from early forms." His examination of Adena and Hopewell art, artifacts, and mounds leads him to the surprising and revolutionary conclusion that the sudden increase in the texture and density of life in late Adena times is largely the result of Hopewell influence on Adena—whereas most other archaeologists credit the Hopewell development to borrowing from the older and presumably more complex culture! Dragoo calls Hopewell "the catalyst" in the late transformation and expansion of the Adena way of life.

By late Adena times, the Adena Culture was distributed along all the tributaries of the Ohio River from southeastern Indiana to western Pennsylvania, with heavy concentrations in the Scioto Valley in south-central Ohio and along the Kanawha River in West Virginia. Ohio Hopewell's range at the same time was much more compact, centered chiefly in the Scioto Valley (where it overlapped Adena) and not going to the south or the east of that region. Dragoo sees this Hopewell concentration as a "wedge" driven into Adena territory from the northwest. According to Webb and Snow, this "mixing and blending of two different peoples brought about a hybrid vigor, genetically and culturally," that resulted in the magnificence of Ohio Hopewell.

After this collision, peaceful or otherwise, between the two cultures, Hopewell waxed and Adena steadily waned. The Adena people of the Scioto Valley apparently were incorporated in and submerged by the Hopewells. But along the borders of the territory taken by Hopewell, there evidently was continuing opposition to the newcomers. "The logical explanation of Hopewell's failure to cross the Ohio River into nearby Kentucky and West Virginia," says Dragoo, "would seem to be the presence of Adena peoples in sufficient numbers to hold back the tide. Such a situation implies the existence of both some physical and cultural resistance on the part of Adena peoples in these areas. The extensive spread and development of Hopewell Culture westward through Indiana and Illinois indicates that there were no major barriers in that direction."[247]

Perhaps as a result of Hopewell hostility, the late Adena folk pulled together in large centers. Their culture, which (if Dragoo is right) had been so greatly enriched by the impact of Hopewell, grew conservative. But an end was at hand: those Adenas who were not drawn into the Hopewell Culture began to leave the Ohio Valley, and a gradual exodus began several centuries before Christ.

Some Adena groups went south along the Tennessee River. Salvage archaeology work in northern Alabama in 1934, just prior to the construction of the Tennessee Valley Authority's Wheeler Dam, revealed a distinct burial-mound complex notable for its use of copper and the lustrous, brilliant ore of lead, galena. William S. Webb, who was in charge of this work, gave these people the name of the Copena Culture (*cop*per-gal*ena*). "The Copena People," Webb wrote, "fashioned beads of rolled sheet copper, bracelets, celts, rectangular breastplates, and, most diagnostic of all, copper reel-shaped gorgets. These are traits associated with late Adena and Hopewell. Further, they buried their dead in earth mounds and frequently laid the remains on and covered them with puddled clay. They occasionally covered graves with logs and bark. Cremation was practiced, and the deposit of cremated remains has been found occasionally."[248] Since the original 36 traits by which Webb defined the Copena Culture were similar to traits of Ohio Hopewell, Webb at first designated Copena as a southern branch of Hopewell, but by 1957 through further study of Copena artifacts, he had come to feel that "the cultural contribution of Adena may be evaluated correctly as greater than that of Ohio Hopewell to Copena." Dragoo has extended this interpretation to suggest that a Hopewell-influenced late Adena population moved into the Tennessee Valley and developed into a new culture, Copena, which was able "to perpetuate at least certain elements of Adena Culture in spite of strong cultural and physical influences from Hopewell and from peoples surrounding them in their new homeland in the Tennessee Valley."[249]

Other Adena bands went westward from the Ohio Valley. The Chesapeake Bay sites that display Adena influence were apparently settled during this time of cultural dispersal. The farthest outpost of Adena traits, on Long Sault Island in the St. Lawrence River, also represents a probable base for refugees. William Ritchie, who discovered and named this Middlesex Complex in New York State, saw at first only a random diffusion of Adena traits from Ohio to New York; but he restudied the Middlesex material in 1957 and 1958 in collaboration with Don Dragoo, and their two papers on "The Eastern Dispersal of Adena" reached the conclusion that the mound group in the St. Lawrence was the work "of actual splinter groups of Adena people and already resident groups, rather than random trait diffusions from an Ohio center."[250] They declared, "The wide scattering of Adena traits from the homeland in the Ohio Valley cannot, we think, be explained as the wandering of traders in search of new markets or raw materials. The finding of typical Adena objects made from Ohio Valley stone materials, and in the context of the Adena ceremonial burial pattern, at these farflung outposts, can best be explained by the actual presence of Adena people. Why would groups of Adena people want or find it necessary to leave the Ohio Valley, which had been their home for at least 600 years? The apparent answer to this question is that internal strife or outside force, or a combination of both these factors, drove them from the Ohio Valley. When we seek the cause of destruction in Adena, a movement of Hopewell people into the area appears to provide the logical clue."[251]

Far from home, far from the ancestral mounds and sacred circles, these Adena outcasts found it increasingly difficult to practice their traditional way of life. They had brought prized possessions with them from Ohio: gorgets, breastplates, beads, amulets. But the religion of the burial cult demanded that these be interred with the dead; and as the older people died, the supply of these treasures diminished. The traditions crumbled. Continuities were broken. A beaten, outcast folk no longer could summon the energy and discipline needed to construct mounds and earthworks. Probably by the first century A.D. the Adena way of life was extinct in its Ohio Valley birthplace, and the outlying groups could not survive much past that time. Those in New York and along the Atlantic coast gave up first; unable to maintain their old ways, forgetful of their great traditions, they let themselves be absorbed into local tribes. The Copena people hung on a few centuries longer, perhaps warmed by the radiance of the great Hopewell centers that had developed to their north. But by A.D. 400, probably, they had ceased to exist as a distinctive cultural group.

By then the bells were tolling for Hopewell, too. Before the Goths had burst into Rome, the mound-building era in the Ohio Valley had essentially come to its end.

7

The Hopewells were the Mound Builders of whom the nineteenth-century mythmakers dreamed. Although neither Phoenician nor Hindu nor Toltec, but merely long-headed American Indians out of the eastern woodlands, they filled many of the qualifications of that phantom race of superior beings to whom the Ohio mounds had so often been attributed.

They were the first empire builders of the United States. Whether there was ever such a thing as a Hopewell empire, a Hopewell nation, in the political sense, is open to doubt; but there is no question that Hopewell cultural influence was widespread and that wherever it reached it became overwhelmingly dominant. Some archaeologists have envisioned an actual Hopewell sovereignty, ruled from a central court in southern Ohio and extending its grasp westward across Indiana and Illinois into southeastern Iowa, northward to Wisconsin and Michigan, and southward down the Mississippi past St. Louis. A younger school of archaeologists has introduced the concept of a Hopewell "interaction sphere," lacking any centralized political control and held together by a common religion rather than by any real material bond. They compare it to the Islamic "interaction sphere," which under the original impetus of Mohammed and his Arabian followers spread rapidly to such diverse cultures as those of Turkey, Syria, Persia, and North Africa.

One representative of this school, Olaf H. Prufer of Cleveland, believes that "it is more appropriate to speak of a Hopewell cult than of a Hopewell culture." Prufer notes that the characteristic artifacts of the Hopewell complex are the same wherever they are found. Yet he says:

"In spite of this fact the Hopewell complex cannot be classed as a 'culture' in the anthropological sense of the word, that is, as a distinct society together with its attendant material and spiritual manifestations. On the contrary, the Hopewell complex was only one segment of the cultural totality in each area where it is encountered. A reconstruction of life in eastern North America from 500 B.C. to A.D. 900 reveals the existence of distinct cultural traditions in separate regions, each rooted in its own past. During the Hopewell phase each of these regional traditions was independently influenced by the new and dynamic religious complex. The new funeral customs did not, however, take the place of the local culture; they were simply grafted onto it."[252]

Whether a cult, or—as most archaeologists still believe—a tightly unified

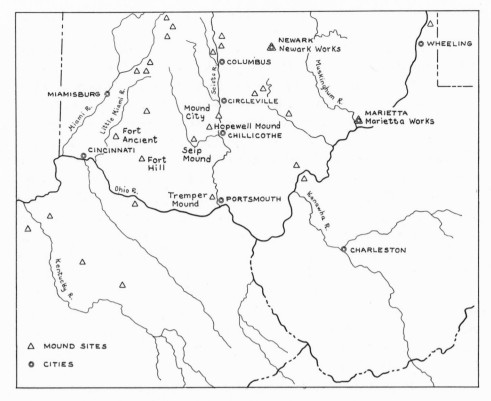

31   Map of Hopewell sites.

culture, Hopewell's geographical range was enormous, and its ability to send trade missions beyond its Midwestern heartland was even more impressive. Prufer himself testifies to this:

"One of the hallmarks of most Hopewellian traits is the emphasis on exotic raw materials which were either manufactured into a variety of objects or remained deliberately unmodified. These exotic materials—copper from the Upper Great Lakes region, mica from the Appalachians, fancy flints from various sources, obsidian from the Rockies or from the Southwest, large conch shells from the Gulf Coast, various sea shells from the Atlantic and Gulf Coasts, Grizzly Bear canine teeth from the Rockies, silver, meteoric iron, fossil shark teeth, to mention only a few—seem to have been crucial components in the material maintenance of the Hopewellian idea system. In order to obtain these materials a vast, and undoubtedly complex, exchange network had to be maintained through large areas of the United States. The exchange network itself seems to have provided the mechanical basis upon which this system spread, leading to a vast dynamic interaction sphere, the aim of which appears to have been exclusively the production of ceremonial objects primarily intended for deposition with the dead."[253]

The core of the Hopewell territory—the Scioto-Muskingum-Miami river system, tributary to the Ohio—was the place of the great construction projects that so thoroughly dazzled the minds and engaged the imaginations of white-skinned latecomers: the thousands of burial mounds, the colossal geometrical earthworks, the incredibly huge embankments and ramparts and avenues. The mound-building impulse weakened in direct proportion to the distance of Hopewellian settlements from southern Ohio; geometrical enclosures are almost entirely an Ohio specialty, and the burial mounds become smaller and less copiously filled with artifacts in the marginal Hopewellian areas. Although it appears that the Hopewells of the Illinois center were related by close ties of culture and genetics to those of Ohio, the argument for an "interaction sphere," for a Pax Hopewelliana embracing a loose religious confederation of many tribes, becomes strong when one considers how the outlying Hopewellians failed to display the startling energy of the Ohio mound builders. Had they been colonists from Ohio—or under the lash of some Ohio overseer—the cultists of Michigan, Wisconsin, Iowa, and other distant points might well have toiled more diligently to create imitations of the gigantic ceremonial centers of the Hopewell core.

By the name archaeologists have given it, the Hopewell Culture brings unexpected immortality to Captain M. C. Hopewell of Ross County, Ohio, whose farm near Chillicothe contained more than thirty mounds within a 110-acre rectangular enclosure. When it was decided to have an anthropological exhibit at the Chicago world's fair of 1893, Warren K. Moorehead excavated a number of Ohio mounds; the richest haul of artifacts came from Captain Hopewell's farm, and after the breakdown of the obsolete "Mound Builder" concept into separate cultures, the label "Hopewell" was placed on all sites sharing the traits found in artifacts from the original Hopewell Mound Group.

The identification of the separate mound-building entities did not come about without a good deal of confusion. As early as 1886, F. W. Putnam had recognized the independent existence of what he called the Fort Ancient Culture. Its manifestations were simpler and far less ornate than those found in lowland mounds, and so Putnam regarded the Fort Ancient people as predecessors of those who were still thought of simply as the Mound Builders. Between 1906 and 1917, W. C. Mills succeeded in dividing the latter into Adena and Hopewell phases. At the Robert Harness Mound, Mills reported in 1907, artifacts of the Fort Ancient type were found underlying Hopewell remains, and this confirmed the earlier belief that Fort Ancient was the ancestral culture. Since the Adena material tended to be less complex than the

Hopewell, it was assumed that Adena was less advanced and thus earlier than Hopewell.

It turned out later that Mills had been wrong about the Fort Ancient artifacts at the Robert Harness Mound. Despite his misinterpretation of the evidence, Fort Ancient was actually a much later culture than either Hopewell or Adena—and, in fact, had not been a mound-building culture. The Fort Ancient people had not constructed the hilltop rampart from which their name was derived; that was a Hopewell enterprise. Nevertheless, the name has stuck, so that laymen today must puzzle over the fact that the Fort Ancient people did not build Fort Ancient. And, gradually, the relationship of Adena to Hopewell became sufficiently clarified so that we can see Adena's earlier (but not necessarily ancestral) position.

Most of the mounds and earthworks that can be seen in Ohio today were made by the Hopewells. The most awesome, perhaps, is the great enclosure at Newark, which once covered four square miles. The long parallel earthen-walled avenues that so impressed Atwater and Squier have vanished, and only two important features of the Newark works remain. One, the Great Circle Earthworks, serves as a public fairground; it consists of an embankment about 1,200 feet in diameter, with earthen walls 8 to 14 feet high, enclosing 26 acres. At the center of the circle is the so-called "Eagle Mound," a bird effigy. Squier, writing of this enclosure when James Knox Polk was in the White House, said: "Here, covered with the gigantic trees of a primitive forest, the work presents a truly grand and impressive appearance; and, in entering the ancient avenue for the first time, the visitor does not fail to experience a sensation of awe, such as he might feel in passing the portals of an Egyptian temple, or in gazing upon the silent ruins of Petra of the desert."[254]

A long earthen avenue, now obliterated, formerly connected the Great Circle with a large square enclosure a quarter of a mile away, of which only a small section remains; from there a second avenue led westward a consider-able distance to the joined circle and octagon that comprised the finest part of the Newark works. Modern visitors must drive through the bustling town of Newark to get from one enclosure to the other; but the circle and octagon survive in Octagon State Memorial, the site of a municipal golf course. There has been surprisingly little mutilation in the course of converting the grand ceremonial center of a vanished people into a place of public amusement; the low flat-topped mounds within the octagon serve now to test the ingenuity of golfers, and the flags emerging from the holes do little to detract from the beauty and splendor of the scene. One walks through the golf course, with its flawless green carpet of grass, so stirred by the size and symmetry of

32 Newark golf course, with mounds. *Photograph by Barbara Silverberg.*

the ancient site that one scarcely has emotion left to object to the use to which it is put today.

Not many of the other geometrical enclosures, so abundantly figured in the pages of Squier and Davis, can be seen today; but of Hopewell burial mounds there is no shortage. Some of these are conical, elegant domes in the Adena manner; others are elongated and flattened on top, somewhat in the style of the Southern temple mounds of a much later era. Usually earthen enclosures surround the burial mounds, which were often constructed in large groups.

The Hopewell mounds are the most visible evidence of the complex cult of the dead that these people observed. Here the sacred rites and ceremonies were performed; here the tribal notables were laid to rest with what must have been remarkable pomp and circumstance. Some three fourths of the Hopewell dead were cremated; tomb burial in the flesh was seemingly the privilege only of a high caste.

The Hopewell funeral activities centered about mortuary houses built on specially prepared sites. First all trees and underbrush were cleared from the area where the mound was to rise; loose topsoil was removed, and the sub-surface usually was plastered with tough clay. Next, a layer of sand or fine gravel an inch or more in depth was strewn over the clay floor, and on this was erected a large wooden structure. The walls of these mortuary houses consisted of rows of single palisades. Some of the buildings were so big that they probably did not have roofs, but were stockades open to the sky; smaller, roofed apartments were often arranged around the inside of the main wall.

Burials of several kinds took place in the same mortuary house. Cremations were carried out in rectangular clay-lined crematory pits dug in the prepared floor; the bodies had first been stripped of flesh through exposure and decay or by cleaning. After the burning, ashes and bone fragments were gathered up and placed in log crypts on platforms near the crematory pits, or else were left in the pits themselves.

In an adjoining chamber, burials in the flesh were prepared. A rectangular tomb of log cribbing was built up on a low clay platform on the floor of the mortuary house; the dead one lay within, extended full length, surrounded by grave goods that had been ceremonially "killed," or broken, presumably to liberate their spirits so that they could accompany the deceased into the afterworld. These log tombs were similar to those of the Adena folk; the chief difference between Adena and Hopewell burials lies not in the preparation of the tombs but in the greater richness and quality of the Hopewell accompanying grave goods.

The individual graves within the mortuary house were customarily, though not always, covered with low mounds of earth. When the enclosure was filled with graves, it was intentionally set afire as part of the funeral rites. Then a single mound of earth was heaped over the whole site, sometimes while the embers of the burned mortuary house were still glowing. Probably the whole community took part in the building of the large tumulus. "Earth was carried in any convenient manner," wrote the Ohio archaeologist Henry C. Shetrone. "In detached clods, in carrying baskets, and doubtless even in buckskin aprons, each individual load being dumped upon the growing heap to add its little to the whole. The size, and often the form, of these individual loads are frequently readily discernible as exploration proceeds, owing to the fact that individual workers obtained their earth from various places, so that there appears a dumping of black soil here, a load of yellow clay there, and adjacent to either a basketful of another kind or color. In two instances the writer has found individual loads intact, where the weary or careless worker had dropped them on the common heap 'basket and all.' "[255]

A characteristic burial mound considered to belong to the early Hopewell period is the Tremper Mound on the Scioto River. Because of its distinctive form, it was considered at first to be an effigy mound, representing a tapir or even an elephant. Squier and Davis, the first to describe it, classed it with the effigy mounds. But excavation carried out in 1915 by William C. Mills and Henry Shetrone under the sponsorship of the Ohio State Museum showed it to be a burial mound that had been erected over a mortuary house. The main portion of the mound, an oval some 200 feet long and 100 feet wide, was the "body" of the supposed effigy; exploration showed that the "head," "tail," and "legs" were actually mounds covering annexes to the original building. Within, amid the charred remnants of wall posts and timbers, were clay crematory basins and troughlike receptacles for the ashes of the dead; a shrine room containing exquisite carved stone pipes and ornaments of bone, copper, mica, pearl, and other substances; and a compartment that had served as a kitchen or workroom.

Another important mound group now classed as early Hopewell is Mound City, near Chillicothe. Here twenty-four mounds lie within a 13-acre rectangular enclosure whose earthen walls may once have been topped by a wooden fence. Some of the mounds are hardly more than swellings on the earth; but the central mound is nearly 18 feet high.

Today Mound City seems idyllic and tranquil—a lovely cluster of grassy knolls lying just off a not-too-busy highway and just north of a surprisingly peaceful-looking state prison. But the mound group, now under Federal care, conceals a series of traumas that began with random excavations and ended

33   Mound City group. *Photograph by Barbara Silverberg.*

with virtual demolition. Squier and Davis visited the site in 1846, thrusting shafts down through the summits of the mounds and extracting more than 200 handsome effigy pipes; their detailed report on these excavations attracted several generations of furtive pot-hunting that left many of the mounds in poor repair. But real catastrophe came during World War I, when Mound City was selected to become Camp Sherman, a large military training center. Most of the mounds were leveled to make room for barracks, though last-minute intercession by the Ohio State Museum spared some. After the war Camp Sherman was pulled down, and Mills and Shetrone of the Ohio Archaeological and Historical Society conducted extensive excavations at Mound City in 1920–21. Even though the army had worked great destruction, the floors of many mounds containing the burial caches were still intact.

In one large mound Mills and Shetrone found twenty burials and a crematory basin; four cremated burials had been placed in a grave decked with thick sheets of mica. Today the so-called Mica Grave Mound has been cunningly fitted with a window so visitors can look into its depths and see this grave exactly as the archaeologists found it. Beyond it lies the Mound of the Pipes, where Squier and Davis recovered the artistic treasures that now occupy a remote corner of the British Museum. Farther on, one comes to the Death Mask Mound, the nucleus of the site. In this large mound Mills found burned fragments from a human skull, which Dr. Raymond Baby of the Ohio State Museum pieced together thirty years later. Baby showed that the fragments formed a mask designed to slip over a priest's face; holes drilled in the margin of the mask may have been used for ornamental attachment. The same mound yielded a collection of copper figures showing the human form, human hands, birds, turtles, and various animals. In the midst of one cremation lay a copper-covered wooden effigy of the death-cup mushroom, 13½ inches long—perhaps a priestly wand.

At the opposite side of the site, in a mound partly demolished by the building of Camp Sherman, Mills and Shetrone uncovered a large crematory basin and 6 cremation burials. Among the burial offerings were fragments of the tusks of mastodons or mammoths. It is easy to see the impact that these would have had if they had come to light in the nineteenth century; but by 1920 it was clear that there had been no face-to-face meeting of Hopewell man and mastodon, and that these tusk fragments had been discovered in fossil deposits by the Indians themselves, who revered them for reasons beyond our knowing.

After Mills and Shetrone finished their Mound City work in 1921, they restored the mounds to the condition they were thought to have been in a century before. The charts of Squier and Davis were valuable in this project.

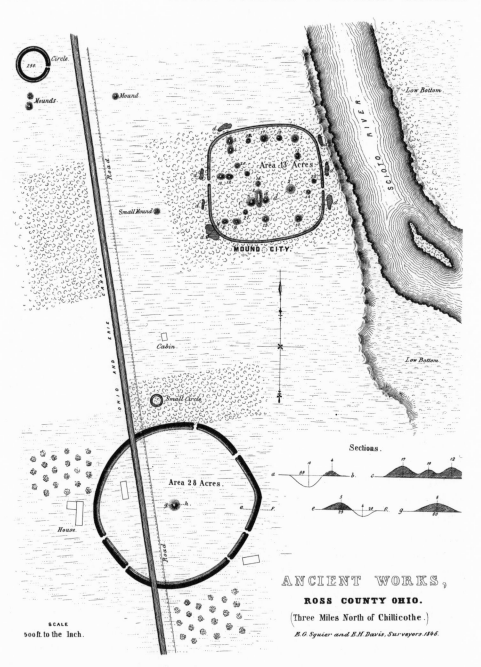

34   Diagram of the Mound City works. Squier and Davis, 1848.

The tract of fifty-five acres on which Mound City is located was given to the Ohio Archaeological and Historical Society by the War Department as a state park, and in 1923 it reverted to national ownership by presidential proclamation as Mound City Group National Monument. The present unspoiled appearance of the mounds is deceptive, then: they are, in fact, replicas of the originals, showing none of the scars of their recent past. Even the effects of an excavation in 1963, which yielded a great deal of important information, soon were concealed by grassy coverings.

The same is true of the great Seip Mound in Ross County, Ohio. This is the second largest of Hopewell tumuli, exceeded only by the central mound of the Hopewell Group proper. It is 30 feet high, 250 feet in length, and 150 feet wide. Today it stands in solitary majesty at the end of a long, narrow grassy field leading from the highway, and is hemmed in on both sides by private property; but formerly it was accompanied by several minor mounds, and stood within a square enclosure and two circular earthworks. Only remnants of these are left. Shetrone spent three summers at Seip, from 1926 through 1928, and took the mound completely apart. "The most striking feature of the examination," he wrote, "Was the finding of an interior sepulcher or vault, constructed of logs and timbers, in which reposed four adult skeletons, placed side by side and extended on their backs, while lying at their heads, transversely, were the skeletons of two infants. Whether or not this was a family tomb or a sepulcher devoted to the 'royalty' of the community, it is indisputable that the occupants were of the elect. The burials were accompanied by a rich array of artifacts, some of which were unique. There were thousands of pearls, from which circumstance newspaper reports at the time designated the interments as the 'great pearl burial.' Implements and ornaments of copper, mica, tortoise-shell, and silver were found in profusion. . . ."

One unusual burial feature was a skull adorned with an artificial nose of copper; copper rods about a foot long lay about the skull, and evidently had once been attached to the hair. A few years earlier Shetrone had found a double burial at the Hopewell Group that displayed the same bizarre artificial copper noses. Other Seip Mound finds included a ceremonial copper ax weighing 28 pounds, a set of copper breastplates, and a well-preserved burial shroud in whose woven fabric could still be seen abstract designs in tan, maroon, and black.

The excavation of the Seip Mound also resulted in the temporary mound burial of an archaeologist. Shetrone had directed the cutting of a 30-foot-high vertical slice at the side of the mound to facilitate making cross-section meas-

35   Hopewell skull with copper
nose from Seip Mound. Courtesy Ohio Historical Society,
Columbus, Ohio.

urements and photographs, and while this work was proceeding, the upper part of the cut section caved away and entombed him. He was unconscious when dug out, and suffered a number of broken bones; but shortly he was back at his post. At the conclusion of the work the Seip Mound was restored to its original dimensions. Nonetheless, the mound as seen today was assembled by archaeologists, not by prehistoric Indians, and this is a touchy point. Excavation means destruction. In order to find out what is in a mound, archaeologists must open it, and, if they are to do their work properly, level it to its base. But even if they use the same soil afterward to build a mound of the same size and shape, is it truly the same mound?

The Hopewell Group, mentioned by Atwater and Squier (but not under that name, for Captain Hopewell was not then its owner), was excavated in 1891–92 by Warren K. Moorehead on behalf of the World's Columbian Exposition Commission, and again from 1922 to 1925 by Henry Shetrone for the Ohio State Museum. Here the restoration problem was even more acute, for Shetrone, after excavating thirty-odd mounds, wrote, "Circumstances at the time precluded the restoration of the mounds examined, but it is hoped that this may be effected at a later date. . . . The earth composing most of the mounds remains practically where they originally stood." A complete restoration was never undertaken.

Squier and Davis excavated four of the mounds of this group, which they called the North Fork group because it was located on the north fork of Paint Creek. At the time, the land belonged to a certain W. C. Clark; when Atwater had visited the group a quarter of a century earlier, it had been owned by a Mr. Ashley and a Colonel Evans. So it is only an accident of time that the Hopewell Culture is not known to us as the Clark or Ashley or Evans Culture. Atwater thought that "the immense labour, and the numerous cemeteries filled with human bones, denote a vast population near this spot in ancient times,"[256] and Squier adds, "The amount of labor expended in the construction of this work, in view of the imperfect means at the command of the builders, is immense. The embankments measure together nearly *three miles* in length; and a careful computation shows that, including mounds, not less than three millions cubic feet of earth were used in their composition."[257]

From Mound No. 1 of the Hopewell Group, then reduced by ploughing to a height of only three feet, Squier and Davis took a remarkable collection of artifacts: "Several coiled serpents, carved in stone, and carefully enveloped in sheet mica and copper; pottery; carved fragments of ivory [bone]; a large number of fossil teeth; numerous fine sculptures in stone, etc." Another mound produced thin, finely made obsidian blades, scrolls cut from mica, woven fabric, bone needles, pearls, and much more.

36 Pottery head from Seip Mound, Hopewell culture. Courtesy Ohio State Historical Society, Columbus, Ohio.

Moorehead's examination of the same mounds showed that Squier and
Davis had scarcely exhausted the Hopewell Group; the artifacts he uncovered
are on display today at the Field Museum of Natural History, Chicago. Squier
and Davis had found a cache of 600 flint disks of some ceremonial nature,
remarking that they had barely disturbed the surface. Moorehead found 7,000
more. In another mound he exhumed more than 50 burials, with which
were found human jaws that had been cut and perforated as ornaments and
trophies, along with pipes, beads, and copper ornaments. But in the great central mound—*the* Hopewell Mound—Moorehead made his most important
finds. He drove five trenches across this tumulus, which was 500 feet long,
180 feet wide, and 33 feet high, and disclosed some 150 burials accompanied
by a rich assortment of copper offerings: circular, square, and diamond-shaped
figures, effigies of fish and birds, serpent heads, swastikas, and more, along with
67 copper axes (one weighing 38 pounds), and 23 copper breastplates. An
offering beside a crematory basin or "altar" included "mica ornaments, spool-
shaped ear ornaments, copper balls, many other copper objects, large beads,
bears' and panthers' teeth, carved bones, effigies carved out of stone, stone
tablets, slate ornaments, beautiful stone and terra-cotta rings, quartz crystals
worked into various forms, flint knives, and cloth." A striking headdress
with imitation deer antlers made of copper-covered wood came to light, and
artistically engraved human bones, effigies of birds and animals, and ornaments
made from the shells of ocean-going turtles.

37   Gooseneck effigy pipe from
     Hopewell Mound Group. Cour-
     tesy Ohio State Historical So-
     ciety, Columbus, Ohio.

38 Frog effigy pipe, Hopewell culture. Courtesy Museum of the American Indian, Heye Foundation.

39 Owl effigy pipe, Hopewell culture. Courtesy Museum of the American Indian, Heye Foundation.

40 Alligator effigy pipe from Esch Mound. Hopewell culture. Courtesy Ohio State Historical Society, Columbus, Ohio.

41   Bannerstone, Hopewell culture. Courtesy Museum of the
American Indian, Heye Foundation.

Thirty years later, Shetrone arrived to begin his four summers of work at the Hopewell Group. All existing mounds were exhaustively explored, and he ascertained that this amazing necropolis was not yet fully drained of treasure.

"In Mound 11," Shetrone wrote, "the Museum survey found a unique deposit. Alongside a crematory basin reposed the charred remains of a skeleton, accompanied by ornaments of mica and pearls. Adjacent to the burial was a large deposit of several hundred pounds of obsidian or volcanic glass. Encircling the burial and its accompanying phenomena was a border of boulders. The obsidian was in fragments, chunks, and chips, clearly the raw material used in fashioning obsidian knives and ceremonial spear- and arrowpoints. . . . The nearest source of obsidian supply was known to be the Rocky Mountains, and the question had been mooted whether these artifacts had been manufactured by the Hopewell artisans, or had been procured ready-made from Far Western tribes. Here, at last, was the answer. Many of the fragments of the raw material displayed bruised and battered edges, the result of its being carried pickaback halfway across the continent from the far-distant source of supply. It seems logical to suppose that the burial in this mound was that of the master flint-chipper of the community and that the material of his craft had been buried with him as a tribute to his important office."[258]

42 Obsidian ceremonial blade from
    Hopewell Mound Group. Courtesy
    Museum of the American Indian,
    Heye Foundation.

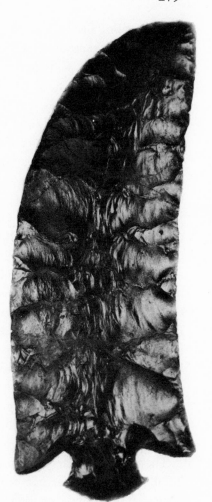

43 Copper fish, Hopewell culture. Cour-
    tesy Field Museum of Natural History.

44 Bird claw in Mica, Hopewell
    culture. Courtesy Field Museum
    of Natural History.

The catalog of Hopewell Group treasures seems almost infinite. The double burial in the central mound, distinguished by the presence of the artificial copper noses, was, said Shetrone, "an imposing example of barbaric splendor." A tall young man and a young woman lay side by side. "At the head, neck, hips, and knees of the female and completely encircling the skeleton were thousands of pearl beads and buttons of wood and stone covered with copper; extending the full length of the grave along one side was a row of copper ear ornaments; at the wrists of the female were copper bracelets; copper ear ornaments adorned the ears of both, and both wore necklaces of grizzly-bear canines and copper breastplates on the chest."[259]

Room after room in the Ohio State Museum in Columbus is filled with exhibit cases packed with Hopewell grave goods, and this is only a fraction of what has been found. The immense quantity and high quality of these objects reveal much about Hopewell life: the skill of the Hopewell artisans, the material wealth of the Ohio mound builders, the taste for exotic raw materials that brought far-flung trade routes into being, and above all the incredible fascination with death, the obsessive desire to send the departed into the next world accompanied with treasure. The Hopewells are the Egyptians of the United States, packing their earthen "pyramids" with a dazzling array. A single deposit from the Turner group in Hamilton County, Ohio, contained 12,000 unperforated pearls, 35,000 pearl beads, 20,000 shell beads, and nuggets of copper, meteoric iron, and silver, as well as small sheets of hammered gold, copper and iron beads, and more.

The relatively sparse and utilitarian grave deposits of the Adena folk look humble beside such largesse for the dead. There is a stunning vigor about Ohio Hopewell, a flamboyant fondness for excess, that manifests itself not only in the intricate geometrical enclosures and the massive mounds but in these gaudy displays of conspicuous consumption. To envelop a corpse from head to feet in pearls, to weigh it down in many pounds of copper, to surround it with masterpieces of sculpture and pottery, and then to bury everything under tons of earth—this betokens a kind of cultural energy that numbs and awes those who follow after.

From the Hopewell burial mounds, too, comes our only small clue to Hopewell political structure—but this is an extremely tenuous speculation. It has recently been found that many of the Ohio Hopewell skulls found in the richest burial deposits show bony growths known as exostoses along the inner ear canals. This is an extremely rare human trait, and it is genetically transmitted; so the supposition is that the Hopewell chieftains whose graves these are belonged to the same family—a hereditary aristocracy, in essence.

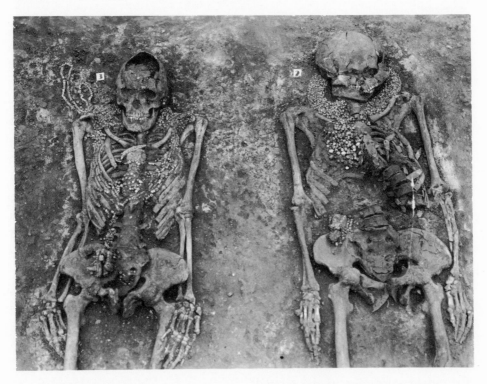

45   A Hopewell burial showing necklaces. Courtesy Illinois State Museum,
Springfield, Illinois.

8

On what fuel was this enormously vital, enormously profligate culture sustained? Surely a well-developed agriculture must have been necessary to keep these people going, since a group so concerned with making fine objects, conducting complex burial ceremonies, and erecting colossal mounds can hardly have had much time for hunting, fishing, and the always chancy gathering of wild nuts and fruits. Yet archaeologists have long been disturbed by the lack of any evidence that the Hopewells were agriculturalists—or that they even had permanent settled villages.

Cyrus Thomas called attention to this in the Twelfth Annual Report of the Bureau of Ethnology, and concluded that "the houses of the mound-builders were constructed of perishable materials." True enough; but even perishable huts leave traces that archaeologists can usually detect. Intensive field work covering more than a century revealed only about half a dozen Ohio Hopewell settlements, none of them in the immediate vicinity of any of the great ceremonial centers. In Illinois Hopewell, on the other hand, large villages are found associated with the mound groups and earthworks. Moreover, only at two Ohio Hopewell sites—Harness and Turner—were remains of corn found. This led to the seemingly untenable conclusion that the Hopewells were no-mads who lived by simple hunting and fishing, coming together at certain significant moments to create the great earthen structures and then wandering away again.

It was clearly absurd to think of the magnificent Hopewells as living in an Archaic-style food-gathering culture; but it was quite possible to consider the functional life of their great ceremonial centers as extremely short. Dragoo's work at the Cresap Mound had demonstrated that the Adena folk constructed their mounds over many generations, adding new burials and increasing the bulk of the mounds; thus the Adenas lived near their mounds and had a close relationship with them over periods that might extend across centuries. But, as Olaf Prufer of the Case Institute of Technology showed, this was not the situ-ation with the Hopewell mounds. With two special exceptions, they had each been built in a single stage. This was apparent not only from the structure of each mound but from radiocarbon dating. "The dates are so closely spaced for different features in the mound," Prufer wrote, "that it is far easier to conclude from them that they apply to a structure built at one go. In short, it does not seem as if the numerous burials contained in these large mounds represent successive interments of related individuals through time. What does this imply? It is difficult to believe that these dead people all belong to the same family or clan having died at the same time. Such a thing could be pos-sible in one or two cases, but we are dealing here with a repetitive pattern that can be traced from site to site, from mound to mound. It seems to me that this pattern may reflect a form of retainer burial along with the important individual for whom the mound was primarily intended."[260]

Prufer sees the stratified pattern of Adena mounds as showing a "vertical" burial custom, in which "individuals related through descent are interred through time. This pattern obviously does not hold true for Hopewell." If the Hopewells did indeed converge on a ceremonial center for a single mass epi-sode of multiple interments, there was no reason for the village sites to be close to the mound sites; there would not have been a continuing Adena-style intimacy between the villagers and their burial place. Prufer, who was con-vinced that the Hopewells were agriculturalists, began, in 1962, to look for Hopewell village sites away from the mounds—in the rich bottomlands along the rivers.

"I was struck by a possible parallel," he wrote, "between the Ohio Hopewell sites and the classical ceremonial sites of certain areas in Middle America, where the religious center remained vacant except on ritual occasions and the population lived in scattered hamlets surrounding the center. To apply such an assumption to the Ohio Hopewell complex meant granting the people agriculture; it meant, furthermore, that the bottomlands were the very zones in which to look for small farming communities."[261] He led survey teams through the valleys that turned up thirty-seven small village sites, the largest little more than 100 feet in diameter. Characteristic Hopewell utilitarian artifacts were strewn near the surface.

A farmer named Alva McGraw told Prufer of a site on his property along the Scioto River, two miles south of Chillicothe, which was soon to be destroyed by road construction. Prufer investigated. Unenthusiastically—for the surface indications were scanty—he had a trial trench dug—and found that he had stumbled upon the answer to one of the major Hopewell mysteries. Eight inches down lay a deposit of ancient village debris, a foot thick and 95 by 140 feet in area. It contained more than 10,000 pottery fragments, 2,000 mollusk shells, remains of wild plants, and both an ear and individual kernels of corn. Characteristic Hopewell artifacts were numerous.

The McGraw site told Prufer that the Hopewells had indeed been agriculturalists who had known the use of the most valuable of early American crops, corn. It revealed the other aspects of their diet: deer, rabbit, and turkey meat, hickory nuts and acorn, wild plums, turtles, fish, shellfish. "The inhabitants of the McGraw farmstead," Prufer reported, "evidently included craftsmen engaged in the production of grave goods for the Hopewell cult: cut and uncut mica was found in abundance. One bear tooth turned up in the midden. . . . There were also two ornaments made of slate that, like the bear-tooth ornament, were unfinished. Perhaps all these objects were discards; this would help to explain their presence in a refuse heap." Carbon-14 dating and other evidence suggested a date of A.D. 450 for the occupation of the McGraw site—late in Hopewell times.

The mixture of Hopewell and pre-Hopewell artifacts at this site seemed to support the "interaction sphere" theory of a Hopewell cult (not culture) superimposed on distinctive local cultures. Prufer does not believe that the McGraw site people who made the grave goods were the same as those who were buried in the great Hopewell mounds. He suspects that the Hopewell cult was brought to Ohio from Illinois by "a privileged minority who in some way had come to dominate some of Ohio's Adena people, among whom were the farmers of the McGraw site." Imposing their religion on the established tribes

of Ohio and surrounding states, these long-headed Hopewell intruders introduced new artistic styles as well as new burial customs, and turned the river-
bottom settlements into workshops to produce the wealth that went into the
mounds of their great chieftains. This theory has the advantage of separating
Hopewell cult centers from village life. But it is also possible to sustain the
older concept of a Hopewell Culture, and visualize hundreds of scattered
Hopewell villages where crops were grown and grave goods fashioned so that
at certain periods of convulsive ritualistic activity the vast mounds and enclosures could be constructed.

The origin of Hopewell life is a controversial matter. Ohio Hopewell radiocarbon dates show the culture taking form about 500 B.C., reaching its great
climax between 100 B.C. and A.D. 200, and disappearing between A.D. 550 and
750. This is roughly the same length of time as Adena endured, Hopewell
beginning and ending some five centuries later with a considerable overlap
between late Adena and classic Hopewell. As with Adena, there are those who
see a Mexican origin for the Hopewell traits, and those who regard them as
an outgrowth of purely local developments in the eastern United States during
the Archaic Period. (And, of course, many archaeologists believe that the
Hopewells borrowed their entire culture from the Adenas and magnified it
enormously, in a Romans-and-Greeks kind of relationship.)

Prufer thinks that "there is no doubt whatever that the classic Hopewell
ceramics and many of the flamboyant ceremonial objects found in the great
burial structures are not of local derivation. On the other hand, and quite
apart from specifically Adena-derived traits, a fair number of Ohio Hopewell
traits can be traced back to Adena antecedents and ultimately, perhaps, to a
generalized northern Early Woodland horizon. Of specifically local [Ohio]
ancestry I would consider to be the mound-building burial complex proper,
tomb structures involving the use of log-cribs, the use of mica, a preoccupa-
tion with copperwork. . . ." He feels that many of the other Ohio Hopewell
traits were derived from the earlier Illinois Hopewell settlements. "A major
exception to this might be the elaborate and huge geometric earthworks characteristic of Ohio which have no Illinoisan counterparts. It is possible that they
are elaborations of the earlier Adena earthen 'circles'; on the other hand they
may have been derived, in the course of the Hopewellian interaction, from the
South, bypassing the Illinois area."

A picture is emerging—via a composite of many archaeologists' thoughts—
of the long-headed Hopewells moving out of the Northeast into Illinois and
thence to Ohio, picking up useful traits as they went and creating in Ohio
a dynamic cultural center whose influence radiated outward over a wide area.

The Point Peninsula Culture of Ontario and central New York, identified by Ritchie, may mark the starting point of this movement, about 800 or 1000 B.C. Artifacts and burial mounds of what seem to be pre-Hopewell or proto-Hopewell styles have been found in New York State.

This does not rule out a simultaneous Mexican influence. The corn that is being found increasingly more often at Hopewell village sites seems to argue in favor of direct or indirect contact between Hopewell and Mexico, sending northward at least the techniques of corn agriculture and perhaps the inspiration for the gigantic Hopewell earthworks. In 1953, M. N. Porter listed nine cultural traits held in common by Hopewell and pre-classic Mexico; these included such things as head deformation, earplugs, burial mounds, log tombs, and the design motif of a feline figure. Prufer added six more traits to this list in 1964—vacant ceremonial centers, ceremonial use of mica, a serpent motif, et cetera. But at the same time he pointed out how shaky some of Porter's assumptions were: "The feline motif in Hopewell is a worse than dubious trait. The one instance reported from Turner, engraved on a human skull bone disk, has also been said to represent an owl." Though Prufer inclined to agree that there had been contact between Hopewell and Mexico, he noted "that none of the evidence is conclusive beyond the broadest generalities."

A much more positive adherent of the theory is Edward V. McMichael of the West Virginia Geological & Economic Survey. At the annual meeting of the American Anthropological Association in Philadelphia in 1961, he presented the hypothesis "that the climax of Ohio Valley Hopewell was stimulated by Mexican influences and that the mechanism for this influence was the Crystal River Complex of the Floridian Gulf Coast."[262]

The Crystal River Complex is found along Florida's Gulf Coast from Tampa Bay to the mouth of the Apalachicola River, and up that river and its tributary, the Chattahoochee, to a depth of 150 miles inland. The type site at Crystal River is located on the north side of the river, about four miles from the Gulf, in Citrus County, Florida. It includes two large temple mounds with ramps, a small residential mound, two burial mounds, and a plaza. Clarence B. Moore excavated the main burial mound and its surrounding platform in 1903 and 1906, discovering 411 burials and a rich collection of ceramic goods, shell ornaments, sheets of cut mica, polished celts, rock-crystal pendants, and copper plates, disks, and ear spools. Later the culture was shown to extend over a broad stretch of Florida. Many of its traits seem clearly akin to late Hopewell. Carbon-14 dates for various Crystal River Complex sites range from 537 B.C. (with a possible error of 150 years in either direction) to about A.D. 1.

There is no question about contact between Hopewell and Crystal River.

Flint knives of the Hopewell type have been found in Florida, and pottery from Florida has been found in Ohio; in addition, there is a whole constellation of common traits, such as ear spools, figurines, and panpipes. The suggestion has previously been made that Crystal River was a Hopewell-influenced settlement, but McMichael would reverse this, saying that the flow of ideas ran from south to north. As an example, he points to the truncated pyramidal mounds at Crystal River. Such mounds were unknown in Adena times and were not constructed by the early Ohio Hopewells; but they appear at such late Hopewell sites as Marietta, Newark, Ginther, and Cedar Banks. Flat-topped platform mounds are characteristic of the southern United States, but the obvious origin of the style was in Mexico. McMichael thinks that the Hopewells experimented with platform mounds after learning about them in Florida—and that their Floridian tutors, the Crystal River people, were in direct contact with the Mexican civilization centered about Veracruz.

He lists such Veracruz sites as Tajin, Tres Zapotes, and La Venta, all of which have been excavated since 1944. "At least portions of each of these sites," says McMichael, "relate to what is termed the Urban or Temple Formative, which predates the time of Christ. At these and other sites, most of the traits enumerated for the Crystal River Complex can be found and usually at the right time level." Among these are ear spools, pottery panpipes, pottery figurines, truncated pyramidal mounds, and flint-striking techniques.

The Mexican site most frequently discussed as a point of origin for the Ohio Valley mound-building concepts is La Venta, on an island covering two square miles, about a dozen miles inland from the Gulf of Mexico in a swamp near the Tonalá River. Archaeologists from Tulane University had found stone monuments there in 1925, including one of the colossal flat-nosed stone heads characteristic of Mexico's early and not yet well-known culture, the Olmec. Just before the Second World War, a National Geographic Society expedition visited La Venta and observed a huge earthen mound in the shape of a pyramid, 100 yards square at the base and about 100 feet high. North of this mound was a rectangular enclosure 75 yards long by 50 yards wide, bounded by long cylindrical columns of stone set side by side with no space between them. Other mounds lay nearby.

Excavation in the region of the mounds produced altars, carvings, statuettes, and larger stone statues, all in the Olmec style. La Venta was plainly an important Olmec center, and the National Geographic group worked at it for several further seasons. In 1955, the University of California added its support to the La Venta project, which was at that time under the direction of Philip Drucker and Robert F. Heizer. Their work was complicated by the discovery of oil at La Venta that year; what had been a secluded jungle outpost sprouted highways and oil derricks, and much of the site succumbed to bulldozers as airstrips and parking lots were laid down over the ancient plazas.

Before the government oil agency demolished the La Venta structures, though, the archaeologists gathered a great deal of information. They found that on the northern half of the island Olmec architects had erected an elaborate complex centering around the main pyramid. This clay mound, 240 by 420 feet at the base and more than 100 feet high, is all that survived obliteration by the bulldozers; it has not yet been entered by archaeologists. Flanking it were other constructions of a clearly ceremonial nature. Philip Drucker has suggested that the island of La Venta was a sacred shrine, inhabited by a group of priests and their servants, and visited regularly by Olmec worshippers from the surrounding countryside.

Many of La Venta's treasures were deliberately buried as soon as they were created. "Under tons of clay," wrote Drucker and Heizer, "went carefully worked figurines, their most precious gems, their gaudiest monuments. In one corner of La Venta's main Ceremonial Court, for instance, we uncovered a magnificent 15½-foot-square mask of the jaguar god. It was composed of 486 neatly cut squares of green serpentine, its mouth stained with brilliant orange sand; stylized plumes decorated the angular skull. . . . Yet seemingly no sooner was the mask finished than it was covered, first with a coating of olive-colored clay and then with some 500 additional tons of pink clay. Above ground at La Venta they left only pyramided mounds, sculptured monuments, platforms, and columns marking courts and submerged mosaics."[263] The archaeologists estimate that La Venta was constructed in four phases, beginning about 800 B.C., and remained in continuous use until about 400 B.C. Then La Venta was apparently destroyed; more than half its sculptured monuments showed signs of mutilation. It remained a holy place and a cult center for hundreds of years thereafter, but its temples and courts were deserted, visited only by worshippers who hurriedly buried their offerings and fled.

McMichael feels that traders or even colonists traveled in large canoes across the Gulf of Mexico from northern Veracruz to the northwest coast of Florida, and that the ideas that took root at Crystal River were passed along to the Hopewells before A.D. 1. The point remains uncertain, although the work of Ripley P. Bullen of the Florida State Museum in 1965 showed definite contact between Mexico and Crystal River about A.D. 440. Bullen discovered two previously overlooked stelae, or stone columns, of almost certain Mexican inspiration. Their carbon-14 dates are too late for them to have had any influence on the development of Ohio Hopewell; but if Mexicans were in Florida in A.D. 440, there is no reason why they could not have been there five or six hundred years earlier.

There are as yet no certain answers to the questions of Hopewell origins. Fifty years hence, the sequence of events may be obvious, and today's shrewdest theories may seem as quaint as the speculations of Caleb Atwater and Ephraim Squier. As it seems to us now, the Hopewells emerged from woodland obscurity, borrowed some ideas from the Adenas, some from distant Mexico, thought up some themselves, and fused a variety of cultural traits into a dazzling, wealthy society that flourished for centuries, indulged itself in splendid funereal habits unknown elsewhere in the prehistoric United States, imposed its elitist cult upon an area covering thousands of square miles, sent traders to the shores of far-off seas, created small masterpieces of ceramic art and sculpture and metal-work, amassed great treasure to thrust into earthen mounds, erected phenome-nal structures in geometrical patterns—and faded away, leaving behind the ramparts and tumuli that aroused such wonder in our great-grandfathers.

9

The end of Hopewell, like the end of any great culture, holds a special fasci-nation. By A.D. 550—perhaps even earlier—the Hopewells had ceased to build their ceremonial centers. In another two centuries they were gone, which is to say that their distinctive way of life had disappeared, their heartland was de-populated, and the people themselves had been absorbed into humbler tribes. We do not know what caused the crumbling of Hopewell. "Cultural fatigue," one authority, James B. Griffin, has suggested: "Ohio Hopewell marked a high peak in ceremonial and artistic forms based on a long tradition of cultural de-velopment in the area. In achieving this cultural peak they may have reached a level beyond which they found it impossible to go." But this implies a slow decay into a more modest culture, and evidence of the decline from the Hope-well peak has not been found; the end, when it came, was abrupt.

Griffin has since offered the possibility that climatic changes caused repeated crop failures and undermined the Hopewell economy. Others have postulated famines, plagues, civil war, and the invasion of Hopewell territory by savage tribes. One theory is just about as good as another, at this stage.

In the nineteenth century, men looked at the hilltop ramparts of Ohio and quickly saw the explanation of the disappearance of the Mound Builders. Surely they had been attacked by barbarians, had taken to the hills, and in their forts were gradually reduced by attrition and despair to the vanishing point. Hence

Josiah Priest, describing how "the remnant of a tribe or nation . . . making a last struggle against the invasion of an overwhelming foe . . . perished amid the yells of their enemies." Hence Jacob Bailey writing of "terror, havock, and desolation" and William Henry Harrison imagining the gallant last stand of the Mound Builders high above the Miami River of Ohio. Only the too-ingenious William Pidgeon disputed the common and obvious assumption that the hilltop ramparts were defensive forts; he thought they had too many openings in their walls to be effective barriers, and attributed religious purposes to such structures as Fort Ancient.

A number of modern archaeologists have taken the side of the eccentric Pidgeon against the more sober judgment of his contemporaries, seeing too many gateways in the "forts" for military installations and suggesting ceremonial functions for them instead. But for once, the simple conclusions of the early theorists seem to have been correct. The "forts" not only *look* like defensive structures, they *were* defensive structures, and probably marked the opening of the final phase of Hopewell life.

Fort Ancient is the most impressive of these structures that we can view today. It occupies a long, narrow headland plateau several hundred feet above the Little Miami River in Warren County, Ohio. The fort's earthen walls follow the edge of the plateau, which drops off steeply on the east and west and is bordered by deep ravines to the north and south. The only level approach is at the northeast, where the builders erected unusually high walls to hold off intruders. Today those walls are breached. State Route 350 spears right through the northern end of Fort Ancient.

The fort has three sections, known as the North Fort, the Middle Fort, and the South Fort, embracing about a hundred acres in all. The walls forming these sections have a total length of more than three and a half miles, and the distance from the north end of Fort Ancient to the south end is nearly 5,000 feet. Middle Fort is no more than a narrow isthmus linking the larger enclosures to its north and south; and the fancied resemblance of the three structures to North America, Central America, and South America produced the predictable sort of nineteenth-century speculations once it was pointed out.

The outer walls, which in some places are twenty feet high, in others only six or seven, are many feet thick. They are composed of earth and clay, taken from a ditch that runs parallel to their inner border, and here and there they are reinforced with flat stones, apparently to guard against erosion. The walls are broken by seventy openings or "gateways," some caused by the action of the elements, but most evidently intentional. Probably only five or six of these gaps actually represented gateways, the others once having been blocked by

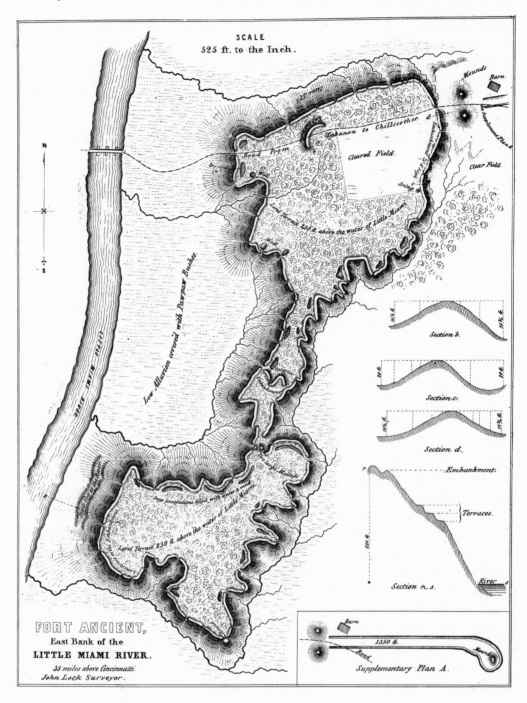

46   Diagram of Fort Ancient. Squier and Davis. 1848.

wooden defensive structures. Atwater had noted cinders "many feet in depth" near the wall of a similar fortification in a neighboring county, and later work has shown that this was no ceremonial pyre but the scene of a widespread and destructive conflagration.

Within Fort Ancient's North Fort are six small burial mounds. A low crescent gateway separates it from the Middle Fort, which has a second crescent gateway at its south end. This leads to the Great Gateway into the South Fort. To the west of this Great Gateway is a burial mound. Outside the fort proper are several other mounds and the largely obliterated remains of a walled avenue.

Fort Ancient came into the possession of the state of Ohio in 1891, and through subsequent purchases the size of Fort Ancient State Memorial has been expanded to 680 acres. Erosion damage has been repaired, and some mounds and sections of wall that excavators had harmed have been restored. Much of this work was done between 1933 and 1935 by the Civilian Conservation Corps; the result of their work is an inviting, perhaps overly well-manicured place with smooth, rolling lawns, gently curving walls, and the inevitable picnic tables on the grounds where Hopewell chieftains once swaggered in pomp and glory.

Somehow more authentic-looking, though far less attractive, is Fort Hill in Highland County, Ohio—unexcavated, unrestored, and covered with forest so heavy that the outlines of the fort are almost imperceptible. Fort Ancient, handsome as it is, has the air of being a museum exhibit; Fort Hill and some of the other surviving hilltop enclosures have lingering ghosts in their tumbled underbrush.

Olaf Prufer, who suspects that these structures had the defensive nature they appear to have had, remarks, "There is a certain incompatibility in the facts that on the one hand the Hopewellians did not make any identifiable efforts to protect their huge, numerous, and obviously wealthy ceremonial centers in the river valleys while on the other hand they erected large, apparently defensive hilltop enclosures in strategic positions on inaccessible hilltops from which they could hardly protect their ceremonial centers and associated villages."[264] The best resolution of this seeming paradox is that the hilltop enclosures represent the terminal phase of Hopewell: in Prufer's words, "The impression gained is that the people rather suddenly took to the hills, abandoning their centers in the wake of some danger."

Several small settlements have been discovered at the base of Fort Hill, suggesting that the Hopewells did not remain continuously immured in their forts, but took refuge in them only at times of severe crisis. What this crisis was, we

cannot suggest; but Prufer notes that about this same time the Indian population in more northerly areas began to protect its villages with stockades: "Unrest of some kind appears to have been afoot throughout eastern North
America."

This unrest may have triggered an irreversible collapse of Hopewell, because it cut off the supplies of imported raw materials that were so important
in the religious scheme. "Could the scheme itself be kept alive when the goods
were no longer available?" Prufer asks. "I suggest that the Hopewell cult could
survive only as long as its trade network remained intact and, further, that the
postulated current of unrest in eastern North America during the seventh and
eighth centuries A.D. was sufficient to disrupt that network. Whether or not
this caused the collapse of the Hopewell cult, there is no question that it did
collapse. By the beginning of the Late Woodland period, about A.D. 750,*
elaborate burial mounds containing rich funeral offerings were no longer
built."[265] The cult evaporated; its practictioners no longer were distinguishable
in North American Indian culture.

Succeeding developments in the Ohio Valley are cloudy. Possibly there was an
actual emigration from the region; certainly there was a sharp decline in population. Some time after the disappearance of Hopewell, the "Intrusive Mound
Culture" appeared—so called because it buried its dead in intrusive graves dug
into the tops and sides of old Hopewell mounds. These were simple hunting
folk of the forest; there had been a long regression from Hopewell grandeur,
and it is doubtful that any direct blood relationship existed. Much later—about
A.D. 1200, perhaps—the misnamed Fort Ancient Culture emerged. These people lived in and about Fort Ancient, but of course had had no part in its construction; other outposts of this culture were located through much of the
northern part of the former Hopewell territory. The Fort Ancient people lived
in small villages of a few dozen bark-covered huts, raised corn, beans, squash,
and sunflowers, and made decent if humble pottery. Occasionally they interred
one of their dead in a burial mound, but they were not really a mound-building
culture, and possibly they felt a certain awe as they moved among the great
structures, some already more than a thousand years old, that studded their area.

It has been suggested that the Fort Ancient people were lineal descendants
of the Ohio Hopewells. Perhaps. But attempts to trace the transition from
Hopewell through Fort Ancient to the historic Indian tribes have met with
little success thus far. Cyrus Thomas' idea that the Mound Builders of Ohio
were related to the Cherokees has had some respectable support in modern
times, notably from James B. Griffin; the Cherokees are members of the Iro-

---

* Some archaeologists prefer a date several centuries earlier.

quoian language family of the Northeast and upper Middle West, and Griffin and others have tried to demonstrate that the Iroquoians have their ancestry in Hopewell. Other archaeologists have connected the Hopewells with the Siouan stock, arguing that the Siouans, builders of the great Ohio Valley earthworks, were expelled from their homeland by the intruding Iroquoians and became the Indians of the Great Plains. This theory, quite popular in the 1930's, is rarely heard today. The currently favored view is that the Hopewells can be connected with the Algonkian group, which included many eastern tribes. As Prufer says, "The Algonkian interpretation appears to be the soundest at this time because it finds considerable archaeological support in the Hopewell Complex."[266] He notes that the hair style on certain extremely lifelike terra-cotta figurines from the Turner Mound group is typically Algonkian; that moccasins shown on a Turner figurine are in the Algonkian style; that Hopewell art has its parallels among the Algonkians; and that Algonkian priests in historic times wore antler headdresses similar to those from the Hopewell sites. He concludes, "This is quite an impressive list of apparently Algonkian-inspired traits. In the absence of anything more plausible, it seems best to identify the Hopewellians tentatively with an ancestral Algonkian group of peoples residing in Ohio." There seems good reason to think that the culture known to archaeologists as the Fort Ancient Culture is immediately ancestral to, or identical with, the historic Algonkian tribe known as the Shawnees.

But whatever the genetic trail leading from Hopewell to the Indians who occupied the Ohio Valley in the sixteenth through eighteenth centuries, the cultural tie was weak. When white men arrived in Ohio late in the eighteenth century, they found only simple farmers, and still simpler tribes that did not even know agriculture. With justifiable skepticism, the European intruders dismissed the possibility that these folk could have built the mounds and the enclosures. So they invented mythical Mound Builders of non-Indian blood, and wove fabulous tales about them, while outraged Hopewell spectres glowered in silent fury.

▲▲▲7

THE TEMPLE MOUND PEOPLE

▲▲▲

The mound-building impulse did not perish with the collapse of Ohio Hopewell. Hopewellian influence lingered in outlying regions; possibly there was an actual dispersal of the Ohio people themselves. William Ritchie has excavated what seem to be late Hopewellian mounds in New York State, raising the possibility that "small budded-off or shatter groups from the major centers down the Ohio Valley" had returned to New York, the possible first homeland of Hopewell. Hopewellian traces in such places as Kansas, Michigan, and Wisconsin may also have resulted from late dispersal.

In some of these fringe areas of what is known as the Burial Mound II Period, mounds shaped in animal effigies and other odd forms were constructed. The link connecting these effigy-mound people to Hopewell is exceedingly tenuous. Most of the Northern effigy mounds which so excited Pidgeon were built quite late, maybe even in the seventeenth or eighteenth century, a thousand years or more after the end of Ohio Hopewell. They represent at best a distorted echo of the basic mound concept. These impoverished cultures, heaping earth together in low hillocks of curious shape, have little in common with the splendor of classic Hopewell.

However, in the southeastern United States, some centuries after the end of Hopewell, the mound idea burst forth again in a quite different form. Once again great ceremonial centers were erected; once more an elaborate social system came into being; there were developments in art and in technology that rivaled and often exceeded Hopewell at its finest. But the cult of the dead was absent; the new mounds were not burial mounds, and the primary impetus of this new culture was not derived from the urge to see the dead into the next world accompanied by incredible treasures. In no real way were the Temple Mound cultures of the Southeast the lineal descendants of Hopewell; though some Hopewell ideas percolated into these new cultures, perhaps, it was more a case of parallel evolution than of direct transmission of basic concepts.

This new mound-building phase falls within the compass of a wholly new cultural tradition that replaced the Woodland Tradition in the eastern part of the United States. Archaeologists call this new way of life, which began to establish itself about A.D. 700 or perhaps a little later, the Mississippian Tradition. For all the opulence of the Woodland Tradition as expressed in its climactic culture, Ohio Hopewell, the new Mississippian represented a far more successful and advanced pattern.

The defining traits of the Woodland Tradition are the use of pottery, the employment of a mixed hunting and farming economy, and the observance of a cult of the dead, including eleborate rituals of burial and the establishment of ceremonial mortuary centers. The Mississippian Tradition, writes Gordon Willey in his 1966 survey of contemporary archaeological ideas, "stands in contrast to the Woodland tradition. There was some cultural continuity, but the differences are striking enough to justify regarding them as two separate traditions. . . . To begin with, the pattern of the major Mississippian site was unlike that of the Woodland sites. It was marked by rectangular, flat-topped platform mounds which served as bases for temples, chiefs' houses, and other important buildings. Frequently these platform mounds were arranged around rectangular open plazas. Although burial mounds did not disappear entirely in Mississippian cultures, they were dwarfed by the platform mounds and were relatively minor features at the major sites. Generally, in both earthwork construction and extent of settlement, Mississippian sites were larger than Woodland sites. Although large Adena and Hopewell mound and embankment groups have been found and the Poverty Point site in Louisiana is unusually large, it is nevertheless true that the largest of the Mississippian centers, such as Cahokia (Illinois) or Moundville (Alabama), are even larger than these. Then, too, the density of living refuse and house remains in their large Mississippian villages give evidence of more stable occupation than do the Woodland sites. These facts, together with the now frequent finds of charred maize, beans, and squash, and the Mississippian appearance of new and improved strains of maize, point to an intensification of agriculture and its increased economic importance."[267] Willey also mentions "ceramic innovations" that "effected a near-complete break with the past," such as improved modes of manufacturing and decorating pottery.

The Mississippian Tradition, it should be remembered, is a term used to describe a cluster of cultural traits. It does not refer to any one culture, nor does it denote a specific chronological era. The years during which this tradition flourished are thought to be from A.D., 700 to 1700, and this span of a thousand years is termed the Temple Mound Period, subdivided into Temple Mound I and II. (There are other systems of subdivision in use; one of them includes a

"Mississippi Period." Since there were dozens of Mississippian Tradition cultures during the Temple Mound Period, and one of the most important of these
was the Mississippi Culture, which flourished in Georgia, Alabama, and neighboring Southern states, archaeologists have the baffling option of being able to
speak of the Mississippi Culture of the Mississippian Tradition during the
Mississippi Period.)

The heartland of the Mississipian Tradition is the central Mississippi Valley
—northeastern Arkansas, southeastern Missouri, southern Illinois, and western
Tennessee. From here Mississippian ideas radiated up the rivers as far as the
Great Lakes region, and to the east and west. A second Mississippian heartland
in the lower Mississippi Valley developed more or less contemporaneously,
spreading through Alabama, Georgia, and the rest of the Gulf Coast states.
Beyond much doubt the basic Mississippian ideas stemmed from Mexico, for
they follow Mexican thought in many ways. The fundamental Mississippian
concept was that of the flat-topped, steep-sided temple mound, an earthen
pyramid 80 to 100 feet high, covering acres of ground, and bearing a wooden
temple at its summit. This development in the United States followed shortly
in time the initiation of a great pyramid-building movement in Mexico, the
most splendid results of which we can still see at such Mayan centers as
Chichén Itzá and Uxmal. Though the Mexican influence on Hopewell and
Adena is still a matter for conjecture, there is little doubt that Mexican thought
underlies the Mississippian Tradition. But there is no evidence for a mass migration of Mexicans into the United States; the contact was probably indirect,
in the form of visits by Mexican traders to the Gulf Coast of the United States.
Transmission of ideas up the Mississippi could easily have taken place. Since
no sites in northeastern Mexico or western Texas show Mississippian traits, it is
unlikely that there was any significant overland contact between Mexico and
the Mississippian centers.

The high culture of the American Southeast coalesced out of a mosaic of
relatively isolated Archaic and Woodland groups. Unfortunately for laymen,
these have been extensively studied, so that any discussion of pre-Mississippian
life in the area quickly dissolves in a welter of phases, aspects, complexes, and
other technicalities, each applicable only to one local sequence. On the lower
Tennessee River, for example, the story begins about 5000 B.C. with the Eva
Phase of the Middle Archaic Period—hunting and fishing folk who made large
chipped-stone points and attached them to darts that were hurled with weighted
atlatls, or throwing sticks. They lead through the Three Mile Phase into the
Big Sandy Phase, which persisted into the Burial Mound I Period (1000–300
B.C.). Meanwhile, Alabama prehistory shows cultures named Dalton and

Lauderdale; Florida offers the Suwanee, Mount Taylor, and Orange; Georgia provides Dalton and Stallings Island; Louisiana yields Dalton, Jones Creek, and Amite River. Pursuing the development of these Archaic cultures is an exhausting task for the specialist and a bewildering one for the layman.

During the period known as Burial Mound I, when the big news in American life was being made in the Ohio Valley by Adena and then by Hopewell, the future centers of the Mississippian Tradition were occupied by much simpler folk observing most of the features of the Woodland way of life. Here we have such Woodland Tradition cultures of the Southeast as Watts Bar and Candy Creek in Tennessee, Deptford in Georgia, and Tchefuncte in Louisiana, preceded by the transitional Late Archaic Poverty Point Culture. The early Woodland Tradition cultures of the Southeast made fairly good pottery and perhaps built small burial mounds of sand or earth. One Woodland site in Georgia shows rock effigies in the shape of birds with outstretched wings; these hilltop rock mounds are associated with small dome-shaped heaps of rock which may have been burial mounds.

At this time, also, certain cultural outposts right on the Gulf of Mexico were apparently exposed to direct contact with Mexico. The Crystal River Culture, already mentioned, is the most significant of these. Whether concepts passed up the Mississippi from Crystal River to Hopewell or came down to Florida from Ohio is still unclear, but in any event a variety of Hopewellian ideas began to circulate in the intervening territory. In the Burial Mound II Period, the climax of Ohio Hopewell, cultural life in the Southeast became much richer, as is shown in the remarkably beautiful pottery produced at this time. Burial practices also grew more complex, undoubtedly a result of a diffusion of Hopewell ideas.

But the Hopewell influence in the Southeast seems relatively remote in Florida and southwest Georgia, where vigorous local cultures developed in Burial Mound II—among them the ones termed Santa Rosa-Swift Creek and Weeden Island. These people had mortuary cults, and buried their dead under conical mounds of sand, accompanying them with mass offerings of superb and distinctive pottery and other artifacts. However, these customs seem to have reached them at second hand, and to show only a vague debt to the mighty Hopewell system to the north. The Weeden Island Culture appears to mark one of the transitional points from the Woodland Tradition to the Mississippian, and from the Burial Mound II Period into Temple Mound I. These people, who occupied a 400-mile stretch of the Florida Gulf Coast southward from Mobile Bay, were round-headed folk who practiced skull deformation and lived in small villages on the coast and for some fifty miles inland along rivers.

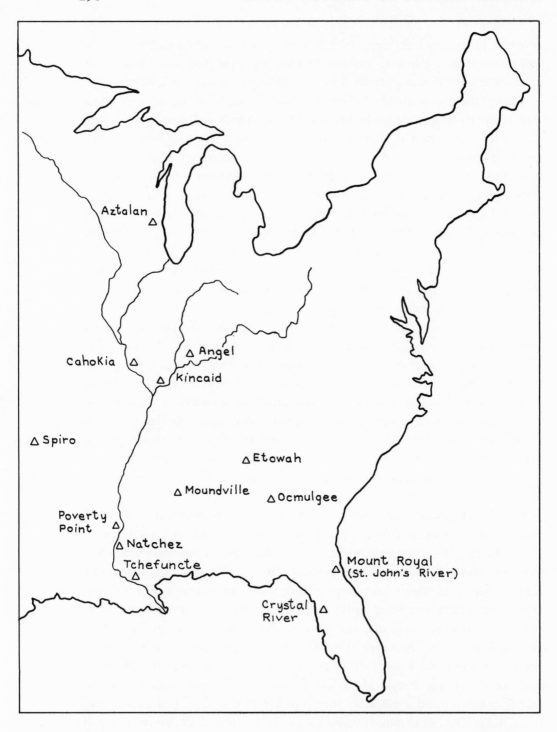

47   Map of Temple Mound sites.

They practiced some farming, but the ease with which ample supplies of shell-fish could be obtained tended to discourage the development of extensive agriculture. At some Weeden Island Culture sites, large, rectangular platform mounds with ramp approaches were constructed—harbingers, it would seem, of the new order of things that soon would spread over thousands of square miles.

The Southern cultures farther to the west show more marked signs of contact with the Ohio Valley during Burial Mound times. We have already noted the puzzling proto-Hopewellian traits at Poverty Point, the late Archaic Period site in northern Louisiana. The succeeding Burial Mound I Period produced Louisiana's Tchefuncte Culture, with dome-shaped burial mounds as high as 15 feet and sometimes more than 100 feet in diameter. Burial Mound II in Louisiana brings the Marksville Culture, which spread over much of the lower Mississippi Valley. The Marksville people, who may have flourished while Ohio Hopewell was in its greatest expansion and who seem to have had extensive contact with the classic Hopewell centers, buried the dead in large conical mounds of earth, some of which were 150 feet in diameter at the base and 25 feet high. One Marksville site shows the remnants of a semicircular earthen embankment 10 feet high, which had served as an enclosure for the mounds and a plaza; this is a strikingly Hopewellian feature. Marksville mounds were built in layers; bodies were placed on top of one layer of earth and covered with another. The burials were flexed or extended. Log tombs were sometimes employed.

The Marksville Culture was succeeded in Louisiana in Burial Mound II, sometime after A.D. 300, by the Troyville Culture, which was quite similar in many ways. Troyville sites are more numerous, and generally larger, than Marksville ones, although the burial mounds tend to be smaller. The influence of Troyville has been detected in Texas, Arkansas, Mississippi, Alabama, and Florida. Troyville artifacts include ear spools made of copper from the Great Lakes region, platform pipes, perforated bear teeth, and other objects familiar from northern Hopewellian sites. Toward the end of the Troyville Culture, though, pyramidal temple mounds appear. To James A. Ford, one of the leading authorities on Louisiana archaeology, Troyville represents the local transition from a burial-mound-building Woodland Tradition culture to a platform-mound-building Mississippian Tradition culture. Others feel, though, that the platform mounds associated with late Troyville sites actually belong to a successor culture, Coles Creek.

In any event, Marksville, Troyville, and Coles Creek compose a cultural continuum, and Coles Creek definitely marks the arrival of the Mississippian

Tradition in Louisiana and adjacent Mississippi, just as Weeden Island marks it on the Florida Gulf Coast. Coles Creek is typified by excellent pottery with smooth polished surfaces; generally red and white, or red, white, and black in color, Coles Creek ware shows strength of imagination combined with simplicity of form, and some vessels of new patterns appear, such as flat-bottom beakers and shallow bowls with wide flanged rims. The changes in pottery technique in Louisiana at Coles Creek parallel those in Florida at Weeden Island. Coles Creek peoples constructed villages in the true Mississippian style, containing ceremonial centers consisting of groups of flat-topped pyramidal mounds with temples at their summits. The mounds, which were 40 to 80 feet high, and as big as 200 feet square at the base, had ramps leading to their tops, and were arranged about a large central plaza.

The same cultural evolution has been observed at many other sites, covering an enormous geographical range. In Illinois, a Woodland Tradition settlement was supplanted by a Mississippian village that created the immense Cahokia Mound. In eastern Tennessee there appeared an early Mississippian phase known as Hiwassee Island, marked by stockaded towns containing platform mounds and numerous dwellings; ramps or stairs led up the sides of the mounds to the rectangular buildings on top, which had fireplaces, small platforms ("altars"), and seats. The new tradition reached into central Georgia, where the Swift Creek Culture of Burial Mound II was followed by the Macon Plateau Culture of Temple Mound I; on the Georgia coast the Deptford Culture of Burial Mound I developed into the Hopewell-influenced Wilmington Culture, and then into the Savannah Culture of Temple Mound I. Similar successions can be traced in other Southern states. The northernmost reach of the Mississippian Tradition was southern Wisconsin, where the great Aztalan Mounds of Jefferson County were built. Aztalan consists of an earthwork enclosing two pyramidal platform mounds; the whole site, which once was defended by a palisade of clay-covered logs, covers some 10,000 square yards. Aztalan probably represents a colonial offshoot of Mississippian Indians who came up the river from Cahokia in Illinois.

The Mississippian Tradition's westernmost expansion carried it into Texas, Arkansas, and Oklahoma, where the Caddo Culture took form. This culture is named for the Caddoan-speaking Indians who were in possession of parts of Texas and Louisiana when the first white explorers arrived. Caddoan villages were usually flanked at either end by platform mounds bearing temples or other important buildings; burials were in cemeteries, not in mounds, although in a few instances bodies were buried within the temple mounds. Caddoan pottery was unusually handsome, even for Mississippian peoples, who were nearly all masters of the ceramic arts. A long sequence of cultural development has been worked out for the Caddo region, leading through Burial Mound times into the Temple Mound Period. One early Caddo site in eastern Texas, the Davis Site of the Gibson Phase, has been proposed by the archaeologist A. D. Krieger as the earliest appearance of the Mississippian Tradition in the United States. Krieger asserts that Mississippian ideas entered the United States overland from Mexico, and points to the "Gilmore Corridor," a route of streams and prairie running from northern Mexico through Texas to northern Louisiana. In historic times Indians had used this corridor as a road-way between Texas and Mexico; since it is inhospitable to agriculture, Krieger does not suggest any slow entry of Mississippian traits into Texas via the corridor, but thinks that Mexican farming ideas and related concepts may have passed fairly swiftly northward along it, until they reached the fertile agricultural lands of the Caddo region on the western rim of the lower Mississippi Valley. Other archaeologists agree that there probably was some diffusion of Mexican traits along the Gilmore Corridor; but they point to the similarity of Gibson Phase pottery to Coles Creek ware, whose antecedents lie well back in the Burial Mound Period, and argue that any spread of concepts was westward out of Louisiana into Texas, not vice versa. Any Mexico-to-Texas contact, they say, came only after the Mississippian Tradition settlements in Texas had been established as a result of influence from Coles Creek.

The vectors of radiation of the Mississippian cultural revolution are still unclear. Were the new ideas carried out of Mexico through Texas, as Krieger says, and thence into the Gulf Coast states and up the Mississippi? Or did they arrive first in Mexican canoes landing on the shores of Louisiana, Mississippi, Alabama, or Florida? One school of thought holds that the Mississippian traits made their way immediately to the central Mississippi Valley, an area already sensitized to progress by the recently departed Hopewells. Then, after the new tradition had begun vigorous growth in the region between St. Louis and Memphis, cultural missionaries carried the temple-mound traits as far north as Aztalan in Wisconsin, and to the south and east into Georgia and Florida. More likely there were several simultaneous thrusts, all getting under way about A.D. 700, with Mississippian concepts spreading out of centers on the lower Mississippi in Louisiana and farther to the north in the Missouri-Illinois-Arkansas-Tennessee quadrangle. Certain it is that by A.D. 900 most Indian tribes living along the Mississippi and its major tributaries knew something about the gospel of the platform-mound religion; and within another three centuries, a chain of major ceremonial centers stretched across the continent from Oklahoma to Alabama.

2

The early commentators on the Mound Builders—even those who believed that all the mounds were the work of a single race—realized that there was something different about the giant flat-topped mounds that were seen here and there in the Northern states and so much more commonly in the South. Squier, who reported that he was "in possession of very little authentic information respecting the monuments of the Southern United States," noted that their distinctive form, "as well as their usually great dimensions, have induced many to regard them as the work not only of a different era, but of a different people. Mounds of several stages, closely resembling the Mexican *Teocalli* in form and size; broad terraces of various heights; elevated passages and long avenues, are mentioned among the varieties of ancient structures which abound from Florida to Texas."[268] One of the first good accounts of these mounds was that of William Bartram, who set down detailed descriptions of such now-vanished structures as the Rembert Mound, in Georgia, with its "spiral path or track leading from the ground up to the top" and its "niches or sentry boxes" that "seem to have been meant for resting places or lookouts."

Late in 1773, Bartram came upon the Ocmulgee mounds, east of the present city of Macon, Georgia, and gave them glancing mention in his book. These mounds had been known nearly forty years; one of the companions of Oglethorpe, the founder of the Georgia Colony, had written of "three Mounts raised by the Indians over three of their Great Kings who were killed in the Wars." Other travelers visited the mounds, learned that the contemporary Indians of the region had no traditions of their origin, and were told that ghostly singing could sometimes be heard at them in the early morning hours. Though Cyrus Thomas and other archaeologists of the late nineteenth century devoted much attention to the mounds of Georgia, the Ocmulgee group somehow went untouched; as late as 1930, not much more was known about it than that the large pyramidal mound was a temple mound of a Mississippian Tradition culture, and that a second mound had been used for burials.

In December, 1933, the Smithsonian Institution's Bureau of American Ethnology began excavations at Ocmulgee, using labor supplied by the Civil Works Administration. Other New Deal agencies were intimately involved in the work; the Works Progress Administration underwrote most of the cost of the project, and the Civilian Conservation Corps contributed an additional force of laborers. The program lasted eight years and saw the removal of tons of earth and the recovery of hundreds of thousands of artifacts. A. R. Kelly, the first director of the Ocmulgee work, published the essential paper on the project, "A Preliminary Report on Archeological Explorations at Macon, Georgia," in a 1938 Bulletin of the Bureau of American Ethnology; subsequently the National Park Service issued a booklet dealing with post-1937 excavations there.

Kelly uncovered a story with many chapters. About 3000 B.C. the site was occupied by an Archaic people who left as evidence of their presence huge mounds of mussel, clam, and oyster shells, mixed with the bones of deer, bear, rabbit, turkey, and other wild creatures. About 2000 or 1500 B.C., these food-gathering folk learned how to make a coarse undecorated pottery, and took their first steps toward Woodland Tradition life. There are gaps in the stratification, indicating that the site was abandoned from time to time, or that it served only as an occasional campground for wandering tribes who followed their food sources along the Georgia rivers. But about 1000 B.C. a semipermanent farming settlement developed. Pumpkins, beans, sunflowers, and tobacco were the probable crops.

There seems to have been some contact between Ocmulgee and the Adena folk in early Burial Mound times. No burial mounds were constructed, but certain motifs stamped on pottery have Adena affinities, and the unusual hilltop bird effigies made of rock, previously mentioned and found not far from Ocmulgee, seem to relate to Adena bird symbolism. In Burial Mound II, Ocmulgee produced pottery of the Swift Creek type, named for a culture found at a site only a few miles down the river. This is more delicate ware than earlier pottery from the site, indicating both greater craftsmanship and a more sedentary way of life. There was a large increase in population at Ocmulgee in this time—about A.D. 300 to 700—and indications of Hopewell influence have been traced.

The first temple mounds at Ocmulgee date from about A.D. 900. Kelly, writing in 1937, believed that he was working in "a cultural continuum with new trait complexes coming toward the end of a long period of internal development," and that "it is quite possible that the mound building on the Macon Plateau comes in as a culmination of civilizational processes taking place in the area."[269] But the current theory is that the Macon Plateau Culture that flourished at Ocmulgee during Temple Mound I was intrusive, the result of an extensive migration of Mississippian folk who started near St. Louis and took several generations to reach central Georgia.

These people cultivated corn as well as the minor crops, and the bounty of corn enabled them to build a large village and to establish a major ceremonial complex. On the high ground above the river they constructed rectangular

wooden temples, and a circular chamber with a clay-covered wooden framework, among their thatched houses. Archaeologists believe that these were the
tribal community centers, the summer and winter temples where councils were
held and rituals performed. One of the winter temples remains in part: a low
clay wall outlining a circular area 42 feet in diameter. A clay bench about six
inches high, divided into 47 seats, runs along the base of the wall; a clay platform in the shape of an eagle effigy runs from the wall on the west side of the
building to a sunken central fire pit. This eagle effigy bears design features that
link it to a religious cult that flourished in late Temple Mound times in many
parts of the Southeast. The winter temple also contains shallow basins, one for
each seat, which may have been vomitoriums for a "black-drink ceremony."
This is conjecture; but the Creek Indians of the area in historic times practiced
a ritual purgation by taking the "black drink," an herb tea made of the leaves of
a shrub called *Ilex cassine,* which induced vomiting. They would fast four days,
until their bodies were completely cleansed. Since there are many continuities
between the Creeks and the Temple Mound people, this is a reasonable explanation for the presence of the basins in the temple.

At the west end of the village arose a burial mound, which was one of the
first to be explored by the 1933 expedition. A. R. Kelly wrote that the mound,
"a large conical truncate, had been partially destroyed by steam-shovel excavations in cutting the right of way of the Central of Georgia Railway. The remaining half of the mound stood as a shell, crescentic in shape where the
shovels had taken proportionately greater materials from the central portion of
the mound." The exposed north face of the cut revealed several superimposed
clay platforms, and when Kelly's workers had made a careful vertical cross-
section, it was apparent that the mound consisted of five distinct flat-topped
cones of clay, each succeeding mound having been built upon a predecessor,
with striking contrasts in the colors of the clays and sands used in the construction. The innermost of the mounds had six log-tomb burials underneath its base.
The decomposed flesh had been partly stripped from the bones before burial; the
bodies had been liberally decked with masses of shell beads and other ornaments. A clay stairway, consisting of 14 steps six feet wide, had been erected
from ground level to the summit of the mound. Later, a second mound had
been superimposed on this one; it had had a building atop it, for Kelly found
the outlines of poles in the second mound's clay summit. A third, fourth, and
fifth flat-topped mound had been placed over this core, each time with a wooden
building at the top. In the sod over the summit of the last mound were intrusive Indian burials of the late seventeenth century, incorporating such European artifacts as pipes and glass beads.

The temple mound at Ocmulgee evolved in the same composite manner. Originally the temples had been at ground level; but they were rebuilt on their sites, and each time an old building was leveled a small platform was built as the foundation for the new one. One platform gradually increased in height until it became the great mound dominating the group, nearly 50 feet high and some 300 feet broad at the base. Lesser temple mounds rose about it. When one of these was excavated, it proved to cover the site of a cultivated field, which perhaps had been land sacred to one of the gods, supplying corn for use in the rituals. If we are right in linking Creek customs to those of the Temple Mound folk, the most important ceremony of the year was the summer corn festival, the *puskita* or "busk." As it was practiced among the Creeks, the busk had indisputably Mexican features: all the fires of the village were extinguished, precisely as in the Aztec New Fire ceremony, and only after prolonged rituals of purification were new fires lit and old sins forgiven. Boys entering manhood received new names; men and women danced far into the night, circling round the central temple mound while sacred rites were performed in the wooden building high above on its flat summit.

After two or three centuries, the Temple Mound people abandoned Ocmulgee. The migrating urge that had carried them halfway across the continent may have come upon them again about A.D. 1200; or they may have been exterminated by the original population of the area; or possibly some unimaginable pollution occurred in the village, compelling its people to go elsewhere. The site was unoccupied during the entire Temple Mound II Period, covering the thirteenth through seventeenth centuries. Early in the eighteenth century Creek Indians, probably descendants of the Temple Mound folk, returned to the area to form what is called the Ocmulgee Old Fields Culture. This was a large and thriving Indian community at the western edge of the old Temple Mound site; the presence of knives, swords, bullets, flints, pistols, muskets, iron axes, brass and copper bells, and the like indicates prolonged contact with European traders, but these Creeks of the historic period maintained their ancient festivals and at least some of their mound-top ceremonies for several generations more. When William Bartram visited Ocmulgee in 1773, however, no Indians lived anywhere near the site.

Though Ocmulgee was deserted during the cultural climax of the Temple Mound II years, a site only three miles down the river was one of the centers of the vigorous expansion of Mississippian Tradition life at that time. This was Lamar, where two mounds and a village site remain. Lamar was a palisade-enclosed settlement on an island surrounded by river and swamp; within the palisade was a plaza separating the two mounds, which were built of successive

levels of earth capped with a smooth layer of clay. Spiral ramps led to the
ceremonial buildings, which were made of poles, thatching, and clay plaster.
The dead were buried in grave pits within the village, not in mounds. The
economy was a well-developed farming tradition, centering on corn, beans, and
squash, though hunting was important. Lamar pottery was unusual and skillful,
and the presence of typical Lamar ware at sites in Florida, Alabama, the
Carolinas, and Tennessee indicates the wide range of this culture. No doubt
some of this Lamar ware reached outlying areas by trade; but villages of the
Lamar type extended over a large region, and the prevailing customs of the
Lamar folk remained important there even after mound building had largely
ceased. The Creeks, who were closely related culturally and genetically to the
Temple Mound people, made pottery in the Lamar fashion in historic times.
So, too, did the Cherokees, an Iroquoian people who arrived late in the Southeast and allowed themselves to be influenced by the earlier culture. The various
towns of the Lamar site were still strong and active when de Soto marched
through the Southeast in 1540–42.

The most spectacular of the Lamar villages was Etowah, near Carterville
in northern Georgia. There are three outstanding mounds on this site along
the north bank of the Etowah River; the largest of these, a roughly rectangular
flat-topped pyramid more than 60 feet high and covering an area of over
three acres, contains 4,300,000 cubic feet of earth and is second in volume
only to the Cahokia Mound among American earthworks. A graded ramp runs
up the east side of this structure.

De Soto may have visited Etowah. Cyrus Thomas thought so, identifying
it with the Indian town of Guaxule mentioned by Garcilaso de la Vega.
Garcilaso spoke of an unusually large mound at Guaxule, which "had round
about it a roadway on which six men might march abreast." Thomas commented, "This language is peculiar, and, so far as I am aware, can apply to
no other mound in Georgia than the large one near Cartersville."[270] This is a
problematical point; but whether or not Etowah was Garcilaso's Guaxule, there
is no real reason why the Spaniards could not have stopped there, since it was
a large and active settlement that lay along de Soto's general route.

However, it also lay along William Bartram's general route in 1773, and he
said nothing about it. The first definite description of the Etowah group was
the work of the Reverend Elias Cornelius, whose account appeared in *Silliman's
Journal* in 1819:

"I have but one more article of curiosity to mention under this division. It
is one of those artificial mounds which occur so frequently in the western
country. I have seen many of them and read of more, but never of one of such

dimension as that which I am now to describe. . . . I visited it in company with eight Indian chiefs. The first object which excited attention was an excavation, about 20 feet wide and in some parts 10 feet deep. Its course is nearly that of a semicircle, the extremities extending toward the river, which forms a small elbow. I had not time to examine it minutely. An Indian said it extended each way to the river, and had several unexcavated parts, which served for passages to the area which it incloses. To my surprise I found no enbankment on either side of it. But I did not long doubt to what place the earth had been removed; for I had scarcely proceeded 200 yards when, through the thick forest trees, a stupenduous pile met the eye, whose dimensions were in full proportion to the intrenchment. I had at the time no means of taking an accurate admeasurement. To supply my deficiencey I cut a long vine, which was preserved until I had an opportunity of ascertaining its exact length. In this manner I found the distance from the margin of the summit to the base to be 111 feet. And, judging from the degree of its declivity, the perpendicular height can not be less than 75 feet. The circumference of the base, including the feet of three parapets, measured 1,114 feet. One of these parapets extends from the base to the summit, and can be ascended, though with difficulty, on horseback. The other two, after rising 30 or 40 feet, terminate in a kind of triangular platform. Its top is level and, at the time I visited it, was so completely covered with weeds, bushes, and trees of most luxuriant growth that I could not examine it as well as I wished. Its diameter, I judged, must be 150 feet. On its sides and summit are many large trees. . . . One beech tree near the top measured 10 feet 9 inches in circumference. . . . At a short distance to the southeast is another mound, in ascending which I took 30 steps. Its top is encircled by a breastwork 3 feet high, intersected through the middle with another elevation of a similar kind. A little farther is another mound, which I had not time to examine.

"On these great works of art the Indians gazed with as much curiosity as any white man. I inquired of the oldest chief if the natives had any tradition respecting them, to which he answered in the negative. I then requested each to say what he supposed was their origin. Neither could tell, though all agreed in saying, 'they were never put up by our people.' It seems probable they were erected by another race who once inhabited the country. That such a race existed is now generally admitted. Who they were and what were the causes of their degeneracy or of their extermination no circumstances have yet explained. . . ."[271]

Squier and Davis discussed the Etowah mounds, misplacing them, however, into Alabama. They reproduced a plan of the group drawn by the erratic naturalist Constantine Rafinesque and not overly reliable, and found it necessary to deny that these or other Southern mounds had been erected by de Soto's men, as was claimed locally. "Had Hernando de Soto erected one tenth of the works which have been ascribed to him, in the States bordering the Gulf, in Tennessee, and even in Kentucky," Squier wrote, "he must have found ample demands on his time and exertions. It is most likely, however, that the intervals between his tedious and toilsome marches were occupied more profitably . . . than in the erection of vast earth structures of this description; which, when finished, could not possibly have served him any useful purpose."[272]

Several archaeologists visited Etowah between 1871 and 1873; by then, the mound summits and the surrounding plazas had been cleared of forest growth and were under cultivation. The Bureau of Ethnology began its explorations there in 1883; Cyrus Thomas sent his assistant, John Rogan, to excavate some of the smaller mounds, and Thomas himself worked at the site for a while. It was Rogan who brought to light the first of the famous copper plaques at Etowah showing winged human figures wearing bizarre headdresses and eagle masks. Though these compelling designs had an undeniably Mexican look, displaying that taste for the vividly grotesque so marked among the Aztecs and Mayas, Thomas shrewdly pointed out that none of the Etowah motifs were literal Mexican designs; though they might have an Aztec flavor, they were indigenous creative products. Later archaeologists would develop this valuable suggestion of Thomas' into a major concept, the Southern Cult, a religious movement thought to have swept through the entire Temple Mound civilization about A.D. 1500.

W. H. Holmes, who came to Etowah for the Bureau of Ethnology in 1890, after Thomas had withdrawn from field work to write his massive report, discovered more engraved designs in the unmistakable Etowah style. The mounds went undisturbed until the winter of 1925, when Warren K. Moorehead investigated them for Phillips Academy, Andover, Massachusetts. Moorehead was then a veteran of more than thirty years of mound work—it was he who had excavated the original Hopewell Mound in 1891–92—and his work at Etowah was the climax of a notable career. He spent parts of three winters there, excavating the village site and the third largest mound, a structure 22 feet high and 180 feet in diameter at its base. He took this mound apart completely, replacing the earth afterward. In his report, *Etowah Papers* (1932), Moorehead told of finding ceremonial swords and knives bearing a resemblance to the ritual blades of Mexico; pottery vessels in color, one of which showed a double symbol representing the sun and the four winds; circular gorgets of shell, with engraved designs of woodpeckers, human figures in antlered head-

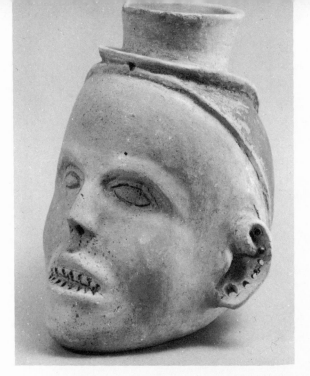

48 Effigy jar from Fortune Mound, Alabama. Courtesy Peabody Museum, Harvard University.

49 Effigy vessel from Pecan Point, Arkansas. Courtesy Museum of the American Indian. Heye Foundation.

50 Kneeling man effigy from Temple Mound. Tennessee.
Courtesy University of Tennessee.

dresses, and severed heads; and other artifacts bearing equally strange and oddly awe-inspiring motifs. Moorehead believed that Etowah was the dominant village, "the hub," of a widespread culture whose hallmark was this mysterious style of art. Unlike Thomas, he saw an overt and not merely indirect Mexican influence, and suggested that a band of Indians from eastern Yucatán had spread through the West Indies into Florida and, after a long occupation there, had moved northward into the southern United States and thence to the Mississippi Valley, constructing huge earthen mounds as they went.

Artifacts in the Etowah style came to light at a number of other major Temple Mound sites. Perhaps the most intense expression of the style—purer even than that of the type site at Etowah—was found at the huge ceremonial center of Moundville, in northern Alabama. This gigantic complex on the south bank of the Black Warrior River was first examined by Clarence B. Moore in 1905 and 1906, and has had some attention from Alabama archaeologists more recently, but many of its secrets are still intact.

Moundville consists of nineteen square and oval flat-topped mounds, from 3 to 23 feet in height, arranged in a rough circle about two others, 22 and 57 feet high. The shorter of these covers the greatest area of the group, 195 by 351 feet. On the north side of the taller central mound is an artificial platform about 1⅔ acres in size. Most of the mounds have one or more graded ramps leading to their summits. The entire group is located on a level plain well above the flood level of the river.

Moore, in two seasons of work, excavated 560 burials. Some 455 of these came from a cemetery at the base of certain mounds; the rest were found in the mounds themselves. No objects of European origin were unearthed. The artifacts associated with the burials included pottery decorated in a characteristic Temple Mound II manner, with deeply incised patterns, some abstract, some of birds or animals. Typical Moundville designs, engraved on pottery, disks of shell and stone, and pipes, make much of such motifs as the swastika, the human hand, skull, eye, and arm, the eagle, the ivory-billed woodpecker, the heron, and the horned toad. Snakes are shown occasionally with wings, calling to mind the famed Feathered Serpent of Mexico. There are grotesque, improbable juxtapositions: one double-headed figure on a water bottle from a grave has the head and the neck of a heron, the fanlike tail of the woodpecker, and a long, serpentine tongue. The reduplication of the figure, with identical forms inverted relative to one another and joined along the baseline, is reminiscent of the design of kings, queens, and jacks in modern decks of playing cards. These intricate symbolic designs from Moundville evoke a mood of brooding fantasy. Here are profiled skulls with great toothy jaws; here are staring eyes in strange isolation, some of them weeping; here are hands adrift in limbo, marked with clear fingernails and even the creases of the joints; here are crosses within sunburst circles, eyes sprouting in the palms of human hands, fingers pointing to nowhere, formidably beaked birds, men with terrifying animal masks, bones, and a host of geometrical forms which, while representing nothing concrete, somehow arouse a vague feeling of uneasiness. The flavor, as at Etowah, is Mexican; but the design motifs, morbid, weird, and haunting, are nearly all unique to the United States of Temple Mound II.

This style of art was not confined to Alabama and Georgia. It has been found as far west as the Spiro Mound in eastern Oklahoma, where one of the greatest tragedies of American archaeology occurred. There are at Spiro eight mounds of varying sizes and a village site; the largest mound in the group had been used both as a temple mound and as a burial site, and contained a rich collection of Mississippian Tradition artifacts. A farmer, plowing at the base of the mound, accidentally exposed part of this hoard and, with the market for "Indian relics" always good, he and his friends began to mine the mound for private profit. In 1933, a commercial company was formed for the exploitation of Spiro. The proprietors cut away the overburden of earth with horse-drawn scrapers, and when this proved too slow, simply gutted the great mound by blowing it apart with dynamite. This split open the central tomb, giving them access to the treasures it contained, and these were hauled out in wheelbarrows and sold on the spot to dealers, collectors, and aggrieved museum representatives. The account books of this novel and deplorable venture show entries such as "Shell beads—1200 lbs." and "Pearl beads—2 gallons." Naturally, the site was all but destroyed for scientific purposes, and its exploiters put the finishing touches on their job when their two-year lease expired and could not be renewed: they expressed their disgruntlement at their eviction by touching off a huge charge of powder that demolished most of what remained.

The shattered mound and its partly intact neighbors were taken over by a WPA archaeological project in 1935, and the following year the University of Oklahoma began a program of excavation. This work, carried on from 1936 to 1941 under the direction of Forrest E. Clements, was surprisingly successful in salvaging artifacts and data from the vandalized mound group. Meanwhile, a dedicated pair of amateur archaeologists, Mr. and Mrs. Henry W. Hamilton of Marshall, Missouri, devoted some sixteen years to tracing the dispersed Spiro objects that had been sold commercially, gathering enough information to permit a reassembling of the Spiro society. Spiro has its own set of motifs, but they are clearly akin to those found at Etowah and Moundville, representing the variations one might expect considering the great distance between the Oklahoma ceremonial center and those of Alabama and Georgia.

51 Effigy figure from Spiro Mound, Oklahoma. Courtesy Museum of the American Indian, Heye Foundation.

52 Wooden antler mask from Spiro Mound, Oklahoma. Courtesy Museum
of the American Indian, Heye Foundation.

3

This related assortment of symbols, design elements, and artifacts carries
with it a fascination as irresistible as that exerted by the eerie Hopewell styles.
Cyrus Thomas identified it late in the last century as something typical of the
Southern mounds; Warren Moorehead, in 1932, groped toward a view of a
religious movement linking a number of ceremonial centers and characterized
by this strange style of art; in an important symposium published in 1940,
The Maya and Their Neighbors, Philip Phillips of the Peabody Museum,
Harvard, remarked on the traits and tentatively linked them to a hypothetical
Mexican-influenced cult. A number of other archaeologists, from the nineteenth
century on, saw in these objects the traces of the ubiquitous and shadowy Toltecs. If the Toltecs had brought feathered serpents, skulls, and human sacrifice
into the classic Mayan centers at Uxmal and Chichén Itzá in Yucatán, the
argument went, they might well have exported some of their bizarre and bloodthirsty ideas to the lower Mississippi Valley.

By 1941, these hazy notions of a Southeastern religious movement influenced by or even dominated from Mexico had crystallized into the theory of the Southern Cult—also known to archaeologists as the Southern Death Cult, the Buzzard Cult, and the Southeastern Ceremonial Complex. The Southern Cult concept was the work of A. J. Waring, Jr., and Preston Holder, who prepared a paper on it early in 1941. As it happened, the first reference in print to the Southern Cult appeared in an article by two other archaeologists, James A. Ford and Gordon R. Willey, published in *The American Anthropologist* for July–September, 1941. Ford and Willey had consulted the unpublished manuscript of Waring and Holder, and—giving due credit—they discussed in their essay, "An Interpretation of the Prehistory of the Eastern United States," the existence of a Southern religious movement "which shows little relationship to anything which has previously transpired."

The original paper of Waring and Holder finally appeared in the same periodical in 1945, entitled "A Prehistoric Ceremonial Complex in the Southeastern United States." They analyzed the so-called cult traits, listing fifty-one in all. Among the traits isolated were these:

Axes with head and handle made of a single piece of stone.

Stone batons or clubs.

53 Shell gorget from Spiro Mound, Oklahoma. Courtesy of Museum of the American Indian, Heye Foundation.

Shell pendants with background cut out to form crosses.

Copper pendants with circles or weeping-eye symbols.

Shell gorgets showing fighting cocks, woodpeckers, rattlesnakes, or spiders.

Pottery jars or bottles painted, modeled, or engraved with circles, crosses, hands, skulls, rattlesnakes, flying horned serpents, and feathered serpents.

Rectangular or circular stone paint palettes, often with scalloped rims, bearing such cult symbols as skulls or horned and winged rattlesnakes.

Large stone figures with Negroid features.

Copper plates showing warriors in eagle costumes, sometimes carrying a human trophy head in one hand and a baton in the other.

Specific cult motifs included the weeping eye, the hand with eye or cross in the palm, the human-skull motif, barred ovals, bones, bi-lobed arrows, and others, all long familiar from Etowah and Moundville. Waring and Holder took note of the variant forms from Spiro, and observed that cult practices seemed to differ widely at the centers then known; at Etowah all the cult material had come from stone-vaulted graves in a single platform mound, while at Spiro it came from a series of log-roofed chambers in a small conical mound near a platform mound; at Moundville the designs were freely used on the engraved grave ware in village-site burials, as well as in mound burials throughout the group. They pictured a chain of cult ceremonial centers across the whole lower half of the nation from Oklahoma to Georgia.

The idea of the Southern Cult stirs the imagination in a way that mounds alone, however massive, cannot do. It brings the Temple Mound people to vivid life the way the sight of the Newark octagon, for example, gives life to the Hopewells. We are free to conjure up impressive processions to the tops of the great mounds, strange rites within the temples at their summits, the blaze of a sacred fire atop the great earthern heaps, perhaps ritual human sacrifice, the wearing of amulets decorated with the icons of unknown gods. There is a touch of fantasy about the Southern Cult material that excites wonder and arouses a sense of widening vistas. The mounds become the platforms for lost cathedrals; the village folk are something more than diligent farmers to us, as we contemplate the regalia and paraphernalia of their religion. Their poetry, their history, the names of their kings, are forever lost to us; but here are wands, scepters, holy plaques, ritual vessels, all speaking of elaborate ceremonies shrouded by time, and all decorated with the nightmarish figures that these folk held sacred.

So fertilizing is the Southern Cult to the imagination that it has provoked the usual complement of mutually exclusive theoretical constructs. The early view of the cult, and one that still appeals to many, is that it represents a

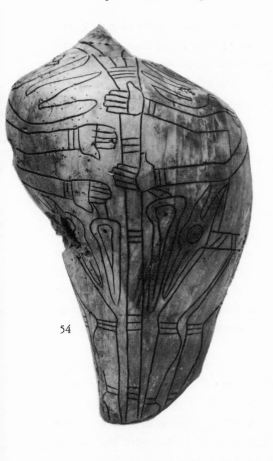
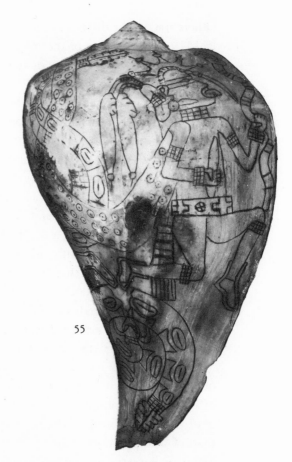

54   Incised conch shell from Spiro Mound, Oklahoma. Courtesy Museum of the American Indian, Heye Foundation.

55   Incised conch shell from Temple Mound, Oklahoma. Courtesy Museum of the American Indian, Heye Foundation.

Messianic movement that sprang up early in the sixteenth century as a reaction to the arrival of the Spaniards in the New World. Thus a 1946 paper on Spiro by Kenneth Gordon Orr asks if the cult were "stimulated by a culture crisis . . . developing from a knowledge and fear of aggression from European invaders." Some who follow this theory believe that the cult came into being sometime after 1540 in response to de Soto's bloody and disastrous march across the Southeast. His route embraced virtually the whole of the cult-center area, and his policy of calculated murder along the way undoubtedly sent a traumatic wave rippling through the numerous farming settlements along his orbit.

Others trace the cult to an earlier culture shock: the fall of Mexico to Cortés in 1519. The toppling of the might Aztec empire very likely reverberated into the tranquil farming country of the Temple Mound folk—particularly if there was frequent contact between Mexico and the United States at that time. The doom of the Aztecs might well have inspired the creation and swift growth of an apocalyptic cult among those to the north who correctly assumed that their turn would be next.

The innate drama of this theory has been marred somewhat by the hard truths of carbon-14 dating. It begins to look as though the cult—if it really was a cult—had come into being as early as the fourteenth century, and perhaps even earlier. The Craig Mound, one of the Spiro group, has yielded a cluster of radiocarbon dates from A.D. 818 to 1084, according to a study published in 1964. Shells engraved with cult designs have been found in this mound. The tentative conclusion is that the complex which produced the engraved shells of the Craig Mound flourished between A.D. 800 and 1100, and died out by 1250. This tends to indicate that the cult may have originated at Spiro, spreading northward and eastward to reach such centers as Moundville and Etowah in the fifteenth or sixteenth centuries.

Implicit in this idea is the thought that the cult is the fictitious construct of over-ingenious archaeologists, and that there never was any mass movement of despair in response to the Spanish incursions. A. J. Waring, Jr., has suggested that the Temple Mound religion was an expression of vitality rather than of terror, and that the symbols we find so frightening were merely emblems of harvest and renewal, used in some rite foreshadowing the busk or summer corn festival of the Creeks.

Since carbon-14 dates are still subject to revision, it may be that the Spiro evidence is misleading, and the picture of the cult as a sixteenth-century phenomenon can be rehabilitated. The question of the origin of the cult motifs is similarly in doubt. The feathered serpents and other grotesqueries point to Mexican influence, but proof of direct contact with or stimulus from Mexico is still lacking, and Cyrus Thomas' observation that the Etowah motifs are essentially non-Mexican remains accurate. It has been argued that the Southern Cult traits were wholly Southeastern expressions of native mythological traditions.

William S. Webb and Raymond S. Baby, in *The Adena People No. 2*, tried in 1957 to show an Adena or Hopewell ancestry for the cult. Waring and Holder had pointed out in their original paper that "there existed an earlier level of ceremonialism, namely that typified by a group of burial customs seen throughout the Southeast, of which the 'Hopewell Culture' may well be the culmination. . . . Work is as yet too incomplete to make any definite statements, but when the definitive synthesis of archaeological evidence of late Southeastern ceremonialism is finally written, we feel that cognizance of the earlier level will have to be taken in the interpretation of many of the later aspects." And in an article published that same year, 1945, Alex D. Krieger had remarked, "We have shown that many of the techniques, artistic concepts, and ritualistic associations which underlie the Southern Cult material were already well developed in Hopewellian times. . . . It is my present belief that the late cult owes considerably more to Hopewell than it does to any specific late influence from Middle America." To this Webb and Baby added the proposition "that the Southern Cult may have developed indigenously out of Adena-Hopewell or under the influence of that total cultural complex."[273]

Somewhat slyly Webb and Baby comment on the debate, more than a decade old, as to how the cult ideas reached the United States: "One remembers how much consideration has been given to the means of diffusion and the comparison of the different possible routes of migration, from Mexico via the Southwest, or directly along the Texas coast, or by way of the West Indies and Florida, or on the water route along the gulf coast. The suggestion has also been made that special early expeditions in historic times suddenly brought slaves into southeastern United States who introduced the cult. Some proponents of the Southern Cult, becoming discouraged with attempts to explain its rise, have recently expressed doubt of its very existence. In considering the possible relationship of Adena-Hopewell to the Southern Cult, it becomes apparent that it is unnecessary to worry about the possible routes of diffusion."[274]

Webb and Baby list the fifty-one cult traits as defined by Waring and Holder, and supply a remarkably convincing list of Adena-Hopewell parallels. They find the antler headdresses of Etowah rooted in masks and headdresses of Hopewell; they relate the cult's rattlesnakes to Adena's Great Serpent Mound; they see artistic kinships in a variety of animal effigies and engraved designs. Their case is a substantial one, but it seems derailed by chronology. Webb and Baby rely on carbon-14 figures no longer accepted, which show Adena persisting as a still vigorous mound-building culture as late as A.D. 700. That carries it up to the beginning of Temple Mound I, and supplies at least the possibility that the Southern Cult's ancestry is in the Ohio Valley. But now it appears that Adena had ceased to matter as a cultural force at least five hundred years before the emergence of Mississippian Tradition cultures. As for Hopewell, it seems to have lost vitality by A.D. 550, which leaves a gap of several centuries to the first Temple Mound developments. Several centuries is a long time for traits to remain dormant, even among primitive peoples. Furthermore, there is no evidence yet (except from remote Spiro in the West) of cult manifestations in Temple Mound I. The cult seems to have been a spontaneous outburst in Temple Mound II, after A.D. 1200 and probably *well* after. It strains probability to think of the cult traits slumbering nearly a thousand years after the collapse of Hopewell and bursting into sudden vitality in Temple Mound II.

4

Many important Mississippian sites lie outside the Southeast, and testify to the ability of the temple-mound concept to make its way into outlying territories. The greatest mound structure of all, Cahokia, is among these distant outposts.

Cahokia Mound is the central tumulus of what may once have been a group of several hundred mounds within a seven-mile radius in Madison County, Illinois. Today about eighty of the mounds survive, though some have been destroyed in recent years by superhighway construction; the heart of the group is preserved in Cahokia Mounds State Park, a pleasant green enclave of 225 acres lying just east of the formidably industrialized city of East St. Louis, Illinois.

The main mound is the giant of American earthworks, so huge that it seems only a natural hill until one notices its flat-topped outline. It is a truncated pyramid about 1,080 feet long and 710 feet wide, raising to a maximum height of some 100 feet and covering approximately 16 acres. Its volume has been calculated at 21,690,000 cubic feet. It rises in several terraces, now very much obscured by erosion and the growth of vegetation. From the summit, one has a view not only of the factory buildings of the adjoining city, but of the dome-shaped mounds that cluster about it, and which would be impressive sights in themselves if they were not dwarfed by the giant temple mound.

The prehistory of Cahokia goes back well beyond the Temple Mound Period, but the details are only now beginning to come into focus as a result of very recent work by the Illinois State Museum. Evidently Woodland Tradition settlements gave way to a transitional Mississippian village in Temple Mound I, which blossomed into the immense political and religious center of Temple Mound II. It is assumed that Cahokia was colonized by Mississippian folk coming up the river from the South, but this idea, like much else currently believed about Cahokia, may have to be discarded when the report on current excavations there has been published and evaluated. Pottery found at Cahokia,

56 Cahokia Mound, Illinois. Courtesy Illinois State Museum, Springfield, Illinois.

dating from the period A.D. 900–1050, has been correlated with pottery types from the Southeast of that time; but it has been harder to find parallels for the Cahokia material from the twelfth and thirteenth centuries. Objects showing Southern Cult motifs are relatively unimportant.

One interesting new suggestion is that Cahokia may have served as a sort of solar observatory. Salvage archaeology in 1960 and 1961 in advance of highway construction on the borders of the park unearthed a great many four-foot-deep postholes, about two feet in diameter. Warren L. Wittry of the Cranbrook Institute of Science in Detroit plotted the positions of these postholes and found that they comprised portions of four precise circles, ranging from 240 to 480 feet in diameter. He discovered twenty of a supposed forty-eight postholes in the perimeter of the second largest circle; carbon-14 dating for this figure was about A.D. 1045. A colleague found a twenty-first hole in 1963, near the center of the circle but displaced more than five feet to the east.

Wittry speculated that lines of sight taken from this off-center posthole might show some of the perimeter posts in significant solstice or equinox positions. Adjusting his calculations for solar positions of a thousand years ago, he worked out the angle for the sunrise at the summer solstice, and found that one of the perimeter posts was in direct line with it. Later computations showed that the other circles offered line-of-sight demarcations of the summer and winter solstices. While there is the strong possibility that all this is merely coincidental, it seems at present as though the Cahokia agriculturalists, to whom a knowledge of the change of seasons must have been important, may indeed have forecast the optimum planting times by squinting along these sighting points.

The colossal center at Cahokia was abandoned in the sixteenth or early seventeenth century. French explorers later in that century passed close to it without encountering any sign of occupation. From 1809 to 1813, the village was inhabited by a colony of French Trappist monks, from whom the great mound took its early name, Monks' Mound. Malaria drove the monks away; but about 1815 the mounds were visited by H. H. Brackenridge, whose description of them was published by the American Philosophical Society and excited great interest. Squier and Davis devoted half a page to Cahokia; subsequently there was considerable amateur digging there, such as that described by William McAdams in his *Ancient Races of the Mississippi Valley* (1877). He told of "excavating near the base of the great temple mound of Cahokia, whose towering height of over 100 feet gave a grateful shade for our labors," and of finding "in a crumbling tomb of earth and stone a great number of burial vases, over one hundred of which were perfect. It was a most singular collection, as if the mound-builder, with patient and skillful hand, united with artistic taste in shaping the vessels, had endeavored to make a representation of the natural history of the country in ceramics." A scientific investigation of Cahokia had to wait until 1922, when the University of Illinois sponsored excavations directed by Warren K. Moorehead and Jay L. B. Taylor. After thirty years of further neglect, Cahokia is again coming under close inspection, and the nature of its link to the Mississippian Tradition centers to the south may soon be more fully understood.

A few hundred miles east of Cahokia is the Temple Mound II center known as Angel, outside Evansville, Indiana. Angel lies close to the Ohio River at the point where Indiana, Illinois, and Kentucky converge. It consists of an enclosure and six well-spaced mounds, preserved today in a park adjoining a rapidly expanding residential community. At the center of the group is an oblong, flat-topped mound 30 feet high, with an apronlike ramp at its south

57 Temple Mound burials,
Wycliffe, Kentucky.
*Photograph by Barbara
Silverberg.*

end. A large platform mound nearby is topped by a conical mound 20 feet in height; there are four smaller conical mounds. A low crescent wall extends for about half a mile about the group. Angel has been subjected to long and careful investigation, directed for twenty-seven years by Glenn A. Black of the Indiana Historical Society. Black, who died in 1964, worked at Angel nearly every summer, first with a large WPA crew and then with the aid of students taking a summer course in field archaeology at Indiana University. A vast quantity of material was recovered; summer work at Angel has continued since Black's death, and the expected publication of his definitive work on the Angel Group will add much to our knowledge of the northern outposts of the Temple Mound cultures.

Cahokia and Angel form a rough triangle with Kincaid, in southern Illinois, at the third vertex. Kincaid is a major Temple Mound II site on the Ohio River opposite Paducah, Kentucky; it is located near the confluence of the Ohio with the Mississippi, Cumberland, Tennessee, and Wabash Rivers, and thus held a commanding position on the routes leading from the Southeast. The Kincaid mounds first came to the notice of archaeology in 1934, when Colonel Fain King of Wycliffe, Kentucky, suggested to Fay-Cooper Cole of the University of Chicago that he examine them. (Wycliffe is also a mound center; a burial-mound complex there, deftly excavated so that the burials remain *in situ,* is open to visitors today as a commercial venture run on behalf of a local hospital.) Cole toured Kincaid and found "an extensive aboriginal settlement and a number of large mounds—part of them truncated pyramids. A portion of the site had recently been plowed, and at various points an unusual amount of potsherds and other village debris appeared. This surface material apparently belonged to the Middle phase of the Mississippi cultural pattern."[275]

Cole had previously taken part in a University of Chicago survey of Cahokia and other Illinois mounds. At his suggestion, bolstered by the favorable report of his colleague Thorne Deuel, the University purchased the site and excavated there through 1942, with several weeks of final work in 1944. The work revealed a sequence of cultural development indicating the transformation of Kincaid from a series of small hamlets into a great ceremonial center. Platform mounds were built, and structures of considerable size and importance, some protected by palisades, rose at their summits. The magnitude of these mounds and their accompanying plaza show a highly organized social and political structure. One, a truncated mound 30 feet high, covers about two acres; excavating it was made difficult because the Kincaid family, former owners of the land, had, in 1876, built a substantial dwelling on top of it. Another, 20 feet high, 485 feet long, and 195 feet wide at the base, was partly excavated and proved to have an intricate nine-level structure. Few traces of Southern Cult material were found, leading Cole to conclude tentatively "that the 'cult' did not enter the area until after Kincaid was abandoned or that it did not reach this area."[276] Carbon-14 dating had not yet come into wide use when Cole's report on Kincaid was completed in 1950, but a reliable tree-ring count, using modern techniques, produced some accurate dates. The rings of one charred house post found in the village site, when matched to a master chart, showed that the tree from which the post had been made had been alive from 1483 to 1588; allowing for the loss of a few outer rings, Cole estimated that the tree was cut between 1598 and 1613. Other specimens of wood from the village registered various sixteenth-century dates, but no later ones; and, since no European trade materials of any kind were found even in the most recent strata at Kincaid, it appears that the site was abandoned before the arrival of the white man.

The Mississippian Tradition seeped into many parts of the country, following river routes that carried it to Tennessee and Arkansas, to Missouri, to Kentucky. In Arkansas and Tennessee, particularly, high artistic levels were reached; one of the splendors of the period was the human-effigy pottery of the Temple Mound II days, portraying in clay the faces of strange-looking individuals with decorated cheeks and mouths, and slitted eyes that may betoken dreaming or, more likely, death. That remarkable flair for the bizarre so characteristic of the builders of the temple mounds was never more forcefully demonstrated than in these effigy pots and in the realistic, powerful stone sculptures of certain Mississippian sites along the Tennessee and Cumberland rivers.

5

The end came. We do not know how or why. It is simplest to say that the Temple Mound cultures were shattered by the arrival of the white man, with his contagious new diseases and his fondness for collecting slaves who could be worked to death; and no doubt de Soto and his successors had much to do with the disruption of a way of life that had grown complex and magnificent over some eight centuries. Certainly there were still many thriving centers of Temple Mound life when de Soto came; just as certainly, these centers were virtually abandoned by the late seventeenth century. We can well imagine a combination of syphilis, measles, and despair snuffing out the villagers of the Southeast.

But though the Mississippians withered at the white man's touch, they seem

58 Effigy vessel from the Tennessee Valley. *Author's collection, photograph by Barbara Silverberg.*

already to have been in decline at many of their greatest settlements, and the arrival of the Spaniards was only the final blow. The archaeological evidence appears to indicate a steady blight descending on the Southeast in the sixteenth and seventeenth centuries, and not necessarily one that can be explained by the depradations of the whites. We have no prehistoric census figures; but the Frenchmen who occupied Mississippi at the beginning of the eighteenth century learned from the Indians themselves that even in regions where the white man's malign effects had not been felt, populations had been declining a long time. Thus a certain De la Vente, living among the Natchez Indians in 1704, wrote:

"Touching these savages, there is a thing that I can not omit to remark to you, it is that it appears visibly that God wishes that they yield their place to new peoples. One may learn from the most aged that they were formerly incomparably more numerous than they [now are].

"The Natchez . . . assure us that they came here to the number of more than 5,000. The other nations say that many centuries ago they were, some 3,000, others 2,000, others a thousand, and all that is reduced now to a very moderate number. What is certain is that our people in the six years in which they have been descending the river know certainly that the number has diminished a third, so true is it that it seems God wishes to make them give place to others."[277]

De la Vente thought that the reason for this decline was the intensity of war and scalp-collecting among the Indians. But disease and Spartan discipline seem to have been more important; one French observer writing in 1700 speaks of "a flux of which the savages almost always die," and another of the same period declares, "The women of the Mississippi are fecund, although the country is not extremely well peopled with savages. The severe way in which they rear their children makes a large part of them die; and diseases like fever and smallpox, for which they know no other remedy than to bathe however cold it be, takes off a great number of them. The girls, although given as they are to their pleasures, have means of guarding against pregnancy."[278]

Whatever the causes, the natives of the United States had been drained of the energy that inspired the building of mounds. Just as Adena and Hopewell had vanished to leave simpler non-mound-building farmers in their place, so did the Temple Mound folk of the Southeast subside into a less ambitious way of life. Huge mounds no longer were built. The old ways lingered on, reduced and diluted; about the old mounds of the doubtless revered ancestors the familiar festivals and rituals still continued, but in a mechanical, ever less meaningful way, until their inner nature was forgotten and their practitioners could no longer remember that it was their own great-great-grandfathers who had built the mounds.

When the white men came to the Southeast, they found a loose confederation of tribes in Georgia and Alabama, amounting to some thirty thousand Indians in fifty good-sized towns. The dominant Indians of this confederation called themselves the Muskhogee, but English traders, meeting a branch of the Muskhogee who lived along the Ocheese Creek, called them Creek Indians, and as Creeks they have since been known. Other tribes in the same general part of the country spoke related Muskhogean tongues, although they were not necessarily genetically related to the Creeks. These were the Chickasaw and the Choctaw Indians. Like the Creeks, they lived about the old temple mounds, and sometimes built low mounds of their own on which to place temples and dwellings of chiefs. To the north of these Muskhogean-speaking peoples lived the Cherokees, whose language was Iroquoian, indicating a migration from the land to the west and north; except for language, though, the Cherokees were similar to their Muskhogean neighbors, having assimilated their farming techniques and even their reverence for the mounds.

As Bartram and other eighteenth-century observers discovered, these latter-day dwellers in the Temple Mound region had only faint and foggy notions of their own history, and though it seems likely that the Creeks were direct descendants of the Temple Mound people, there is no solid confirmation of that hypothesis in Indian tradition. In the nineteenth century, a pioneering ethnologist collected a Chickasaw myth about the mounds which indicates just how little these people understood of them. The myth is a migration legend telling of the lengthy eastward passage of a Chickasaw tribe across the continent from the place "far off toward the west" where "many people came out of the ground." Wherever they stopped, said the Chickasaw informant, "they remained there for four years; they marched with an advance guard moving about in front. When they saw the ocean and found that they could not go farther they stopped there. They rested by a large river. Then they learned that some people were living on the other side. They wanted to know what sort of people were living there and went near, when a fog covered them so that they were moving about in it and so stopped not able to see anything. They discovered that the strangers had something which smelt very good and they wanted it, and they considered how they could get it. While they were considering over it they made a long mound and another round mound. They said that this action would give them help. When they were ready they caused a wind to blow on the people covered with fog living there, and the fog was cleared away. Then they killed and took many captive and exterminated that town."[279] Another

Chickasaw mound myth, communicated to Henry Schoolcraft about 1850 by a white trader, said that the mounds were "navels of the earth." The Mississippi, they thought, "was the center of the earth, and those mounds were as the navel of a man in the center of his body."

One group of Southeastern Indians who evidently remained much more conscious of its Temple Mound heritage was the Natchez, a Muskhogean tribe living in some seven small villages along St. Catherines Creek, east of the present city of Natchez, Mississippi. We know a great deal about these people, largely due to the writings of the French who lived with them from 1698 to 1732, studied them in detail, and eventually, after an Indian rebellion, exterminated them.

The first recorded contact between the Natchez and Europeans apparently took place in 1682, since de Soto's chroniclers do not mention them, even though the Spaniards passed right through Natchez country. The French expedition of La Salle encountered them on March 26, 1682; La Salle called them "the Natché," and thus "Natchez" in its Americanized pronunciation does not give an accurate rendition of their own pronunciation of their name. La Salle had hoped to plant a colony near the mouth of the Mississippi, but the scheme miscarried, and not for another sixteen years did the Natchez have to submit to permanent French intrusion.

At the center of the Natchez villages was Emerald Mound, an extensive 35-foot-high mound covering seven acres. Each village had its own temple mound and a mound for the chief's dwelling, and these were described in some detail by the French.* What is most fascinating about this only authentic survival of a Temple Mound state into historic times is what we know of its social structure; if we are correct in believing that the Natchez system is a true representative of Mississippian culture, then it is our only slice of Temple Mound anthropology, as distinct from archaeology.

The Natchez government was an absolute monarchy. At its head was a ruler called the Great Sun, who was considered divine and had total power over his subjects. "When he [the Great Sun] gives the leavings of his dinner to his brothers or any of his relatives," wrote one of the French observers, "he pushes the dishes to them with his feet. . . . The submissiveness of the savages to their chief, who commands them with the most despotic power, is extreme . . . if he demands the life of any one of them he [the victim] comes himself to present his head."

The Great Sun's foot never touched the bare earth. Clad in a regal crown of swan feathers, he was carried everywhere on a litter, and when he had to

* See page 23 of this book.

walk, mats were spread before him. He and a few priests were the only ones permitted to enter the temple atop the mound, where an eternal fire burned and the bones of previous Great Suns were kept. When a Great Sun died, his entire household—wife and slaves—was killed to accompany him in the after-life.

The immediate relatives of the Great Sun were members of a privileged class called "Suns." All of the important functionaries of the tribe were chosen from the ranks of the Suns, who were regarded with the greatest deference by the lower orders. Beneath the Suns in importance was a class called the "Nobles." Beneath them were the "Honored Men," and below them was a large body of despised and downtrodden commoners known by the uncomplimentary name of "Stinkards." The class divisions were sharply drawn and there was no social mobility; once a Stinkard, always a Stinkard.

The unusual feature of this class system is the way it revolved from genera-tion to generation. All Suns, including the Great Sun himself, were required to choose their mates from the Stinkard class. Thus every Sun was the offspring of a Sun and a Stinkard. The children of female Suns married to Stinkards were Suns themselves, but the children of male Suns were demoted to the Noble class. The son of the Great Sun, therefore, could never succeed his father, for he would be only a Noble. The Great Sun's successor was usually the son of one of his sisters, who, since Sun rank descended through the female line, had to belong to the highest caste.

The children of Nobles also had to marry Stinkards. The offspring of female Nobles were Nobles also; the children of male Nobles were demoted another class and became Honored Men. It worked the same way among them: the children of male Honored Men became Stinkards. Since there were always a great many more Stinkards than members of the three upper classes, most Stinkards married other Stinkards, and their children, of course, were Stinkards too. But a good many Stinkards were selected as mates for Suns, Nobles, and Honored Men, and so their children rose in the class structure.

The ones whose lot was least enviable were the Stinkard men who married Sun women. Although their children were Suns, these men had no power themselves, and were regarded simply as stud animals. They could not eat with their Sun wives, had to stand in their presence like servants, and might at any time be executed on a whim and replaced by another Stinkard.

As with many Indian tribes, the men ruled, but the power of descent was matrilineal. Female Suns elected the new Great Sun; females alone could trans-mit their rank to their children. It was an intricate and clever system which guaranteed a constant transfusion of new blood into each of the four classes.

Whether this unusual arrangement was common to all Temple Mound peoples must forever remain unknown; but it seems safe to say that some sort of class system was found among them all, and probably an absolute monarchy as well. It could be that the Natchez, the last survivors, evolved this extremely specialized social structure independently, as a manifestation of a decadent culture's last surge of creativity.

The Natchez rebelled against the French in 1729. In a prolonged and bloody campaign, they were nearly wiped out; the survivors were scattered among other Southeastern tribes, who looked upon them as gifted with mystic powers.

A good deal is known of Creek culture, too, and it appears likely that the Creeks were simply Temple Mound folk who had forgotten their ancestry, though they remembered the ancient customs to some extent. A typical Creek town was arranged around an open plaza, with the chief's house at one end and a ceremonial building at the other. These important structures were usually elevated on low mounds. The streets were often straight and well laid out. Each house had its own garden plot where vegetables were raised, but the main fields, divided into family plots, were outside the town.

The center of the plaza contained two important features: the Hot House, or winter temple, and the open court where the game of *chungke* was played. The Hot House was a round building 50 feet in diameter, plastered with mud. A fire burned constantly inside, but there was no smoke hole, and the atmosphere could hardly have been pleasant. Women never entered the Hot House. In it, each warrior of the tribe had his own bench, and there he would go to smoke his pipe or rest or talk with his friends—a kind of men's club. An adjoining open cabin served the same purpose in summer.

Chungke, or "chunkey," was the popular game of the Southeast, and seems to have been of great antiquity, going back to Adena-Hopewell times. It was played by two men who used 8-foot poles tapered to flat points at their ends. One man would bowl a stone disk, 5 inches across and 1½ inches thick, down the field, and both players, running abreast, would hurl their poles javelin-fashion toward the stone. The player whose stick landed closer to the point where the stone stopped rolling scored a point; if his pole actually touched the stone, he tallied two points.

The Creeks were divided into two groups, the "Whites" and the "Reds," each including some twenty-five clans. They also were divided into Upper Towns and Lower Towns, the Upper also being known as the Peace Towns, the Lower as the War Towns. The White Clans were Peace Clans; the Red, War Clans. In theory, all the peacetime responsibilities of Creek life were assigned to the White Clans of the Upper Towns. The Miko, or principal chief of the confederacy, was always chosen from a White Clan. White Towns were sanctuaries for fleeing murderers. The clansmen of the Upper Towns were charged with carrying out such civil ceremonies as the *puskita,* the eight-day summer harvest festival. On the other hand, all the ceremonies of war were the affair of the Lower Towns; members of the Red Clans were supposed to organize war parties, lead raiding expeditions, and take care of the religious rituals having to do with war, which in the Southeast was something combining aspects of play and religion rather than a matter of conquest or extermination.

The division between Upper Towns and Lower Towns soon became blurred geographically, and many of the Lower Towns were actually north of the Upper Towns as some tribes changed residences. And in most villages both Red and White Clans could be found, though the chief always came from a White Clan.

These customs were already undergoing a breakdown when the white men put an end to Creek life for good late in the eighteenth century. The Creek territory was simply too tempting; a process of nibbling at Creek land accelerated until it was blessed by Congressional decree in 1830. Under the act confiscating all Indian land east of the Mississippi, the Creeks and their neighbors, the Choctaws, Cherokees, Chickasaws, and Seminoles, comprising the Five Civilized Tribes, were removed at government expense and given land in Oklahoma. Though the tribes have survived there and have attained considerable prosperity, due in part to oil wealth, few vestiges of the ancient ways remain.

Outside the Temple Mound heartland, Indians who had no real part in the mound-building enterprise seemingly acquired the habit in a kind of temporal lag during the seventeenth century. Among them were the Cherokees, whom Cyrus Thomas erroneously credited with the construction of the Ohio mounds. He was correct in thinking that the Cherokees had entered the Southeast relatively recently, but their passage through Ohio had occurred long after the Hopewells had reared their mighty structures. The Cherokees' own traditions confirm this picture of them as latecomers. One of Thomas' colleagues, James Mooney, assembled a classic collection of Cherokee myths published in the Nineteenth Annual Report of the Bureau of American Ethnology (1897–98), and among them was this account of "The Old Sacred Things":

"Some say that the mounds were built by another people. Others say they were built by the ancestors of the old Ani-Kituhwagi [the ancient Cherokees] for townhouse foundations, so that the townhouses would be safe when freshets came. The townhouse was always built on the level bottom lands by the river in order that the people might have smooth ground for their dances and ballplays and might be able to go down to water during the dance.

"When they were ready to build the mound they began by laying a circle of stones on the surface of the ground. Next they made a fire in the center of the circle and put near it the body of some prominent chief or priest who had lately died—some say seven chief men from the different clans—together with an Ulunsuti stone, an uktena scale or horn, a feather from the right wing of an eagle or great tlanuwa, which lived in those days, and beads of seven colors, red, white, black, blue, purple, yellow, and gray-blue. The priest then conjured all those with disease, so that, if ever an enemy invaded the country, even though he should burn and destroy the town and the townhouse, he would never live to return home.

"The mound was then built up with earth, which the women brought in baskets, and as they piled it above the stones, the bodies of their great men, and the sacred things, they left an open place at the fire in the center and let down a hollow cedar trunk, with the bark on, which fitted around the fire and protected it from the earth. This cedar log was cut long enough to reach nearly to the surface inside the townhouse when everything was done. The earth was piled up around it, and the whole mound was finished off smoothly, and then the townhouse was built upon it. One man, called the fire keeper, stayed always in the townhouse to feed and tend the fire. . . .

"All the old things are gone now and the Indians are different."[280]

When European explorers entered Tennessee and the Carolinas in the seventeenth century, they found the Cherokees in command of a vast region along the Tennessee Valley. They were in constant war with their neighbors, particularly the Creek Indians to the south and the Chickasaw to the west. By most reports, the Cherokees had not been in the area long, but had come as invaders from some other part of the country, probably from the north. Though many of the Cherokees were forcibly moved to Oklahoma in 1830, a number of them refused to go, and their descendants have reservations in North Carolina to this day. Cyrus Thomas, investigating Cherokee country in the 1880's, found numerous mound sites along the rivers, and concluded from this that the Cherokees had been mound builders while living in Ohio, and that upon their arrival in the Southeast they had erected some mounds themselves and had taken possession of the existing mounds of displaced tribes.

A truer appraisal of the Tennessee Valley mounds emerged half a century later when the construction of the TVA dam system brought the need for a salvage-archaeology program in the region. As work began on Norris Dam, the first of the TVA projects, in October of 1933, it became apparent that the new lakes to be created would wipe out much of the area's prehistory. William S. Webb, then chairman of the University of Kentucky's department of anthropology and later celebrated as an expert on the Adena Culture, was chosen to direct the Norris Basin salvage-archaeology work, using labor supplied and paid by government relief agencies.

Webb began his survey on January 8, 1934. The site of the future Norris Lake was rich in unexplored mounds. These seemed mainly to be burial mounds; so Cyrus Thomas had identified similar structures in other parts of Tennessee. But Webb was aware that many of these mounds were simply the sites of Indian town houses, or communal ceremonial buildings, which had collapsed and had become covered with accumulations of earth. These town houses were generally the biggest and most conspicuous features of any village; but the mounds that covered them could not be considered mounds in the sense used by Thomas and other students of the Mound Builders. As Webb said in discussing one of these Norris Basin pseudo-mounds:

"Although the mound contained 49 identifiable burials, it was not a 'burial mound' in the ordinary sense; that is, it was not erected for the purpose of burial, or built up, as true burial mounds often are, by successive additions of earth used to cover the burials which from time to time were deposited on top of the previous burials. This mound, which at the center was some 8 feet higher than the old village surface, seems to have been a true town-house site. The mound of earth was actually formed by the collapse of structures raised on wooden posts. Each structure had several feet of earth on its roof. As the wooden structure decayed and fell in ruins its earthen roof raised the level of the mound. On this the new structure was built. It appeared that at least three successive buildings had been erected here."[281]

One of these large mounds was roughly circular in shape, 90 feet in diameter and 10 feet in height. A vertical face cut in the mound told Webb that it was made up of layers of yellow and red clay, with a foot-thick layer of black humus at the bottom. Below the humus was the yellow clay subsoil of the general area. Using 40 men supplied by the government, Webb staked the mound in 10-foot sections and had each section cut horizontally to the floor line. Soon it became apparent that the mound covered a large building which had burned and collapsed—the town house Webb had been looking for. Charred logs, still tied together by split cane and thatched with grass, lay beneath the clay. Two fireplaces in the form of shallow pits were uncovered at the north end of the mound; they were about three feet in diameter and contained charcoal and stones. Several larger fireplaces were found at the southern end of the mound. At floor level was a fireplace, or perhaps an altar, consisting of a nearly square clay platform 6 feet 10 inches long and 6 feet 8 inches in width, raised six inches above the floor. Near it, against the southeast wall of the building, was a thronelike seat made of fire-hardened clay, perhaps used by a chieftain or high priest.

Webb did not think the burning of the town house had been accidental: "It does not seem necessary to assume any special motive for such destruction beyond the desire to erect a new town house on the site of the old one. . . . It seems certain that these structures were made of logs, each with the larger end set in the earth and the smaller end bent inward to form a portion of the roof. . . . From this method of construction it is believed that the weight of the covering of earth on the roof and the pressure of the earth piled against the walls caused the walls of the structures to lean and the roof to sag badly as time passed, thus necessitating numerous attempts at minor repairs. . . . Even with such repairs, the time eventually came when the building, because of decay, became unsuited for further use and a new structure was necessary. It is natural to suppose that in most cases the old town house was on the most desirable site for such a building and probably on ground consecrated for that purpose. In order to have a new structure, the old one must either be removed or a new site chosen and prepared. . . . The burning of such a structure was an easy and effective way to clear the site for the new building." As successive town houses were built on the same site, a good-sized mound accumulated.

At a site near Caryville, Tennessee, Webb gained an indirect clue to the age of the mounds. This was Irvin Village Site, marked by a low earth mound 100 by 150 feet in size. This mound contained two large rectangular town houses that had been burned in ancient times. At a depth of 18 inches, workmen shoveled out a worn copper coin, struck in 1787 by New Jersey, prior to the introduction of national coinage. Webb pointed out that the coin must have been carried into the town house "by some men, red or white matters not, *before* the town house with its earth-covered roof collapsed to bury it 18 inches or more below the top of the mound. The important possibility certainly presents itself that this town house was open and the floor was accessible to someone in 1787 or thereafter. The suggestion seems to point to a comparatively late occupancy of this site by its builders." At a nearby village site, burials after the fashion of the eighteenth-century Creeks and Chickasaws were found.

But why had Cyrus Thomas failed to see that the Tennessee mounds were town-house sites? Webb, who found that Thomas' report on this region, "while sufficiently complete for his purpose, leaves much to be desired by way of detailed information," explained it as a failure of technique: "A careful study of the reports of these excavations as presented by Thomas seems definitely to show that the excavators did find collapsed and burned town houses in these mounds, although they did not recognize their finds as such, and seemingly had little idea of the real significance of their observations. Although they found burials in a number of these mounds, the interpretation seems to be in error, for the excavators appear to have regarded the burials, where they were found, as the chief features. The opinion is here ventured that the burials were probably intrusive into a mound formed by the collapse of one or more structures which had been built on the site."[282] Thomas' mistake arose from his method of cutting trenches through the centers of mounds, thereby overlooking the post molds and other evidences of walls along the outer borders.

Who built the Norris Basin town houses?

The Cherokees were known to have used such structures. A dramatic encounter between white man and Indian took place in one on March 23, 1729, when an English officer, Sir Alexander Cuming, entered the Cherokee town house at the village of Keowee and compelled three hundred assembled Indians to swear allegiance to King George II. Ludovick Grant, a Scottish trader, wrote an eyewitness account of this episode, declaring, "Sir Alexander carried with him into the Town House, his gun, Cutlass, and a pair of pistols; and one of the Traders telling him that the Indians never came there armed, and did not like that any should. He answered with a wild look, that his intention was if any of the Indians had refused the King's health to have taken a brand out of the fire that burns in the middle of the room and have set fire to the house. That he would have guarded the door himself and put to death every one that endeavored to make their escape that they might have all been consumed to ashes."

Webb concluded from this that the town house at Keowee must certainly have had only one door and no windows; otherwise Sir Alexander could not have hoped to hold three hundred Indians at bay singlehanded. That matched the archaeological evidence of the Norris Basin town houses, and confirmed the description of Bartram, who visited a Cherokee town in North Carolina in 1776: "There is but one large door, which serves at the same time to admit light from without and the smoke to escape when a fire is kindled."

But Bartram also described the town house as a circular building made of logs lashed together at top and covered with a thin coating of earth. All the town houses Webb had excavated had been rectangular. Moreover, the other contemporary accounts of Cherokee town houses spoke only of circular buildings. This was the chief obstacle to accepting a Cherokee origin for the Norris Basin town houses. Webb made a chart of 62 traits typical of the Norris Basin

Indians—burial customs, pottery styles, tool and ornament types—and matched the list against known Cherokee traits as reported by four other archaeologists. He found that one of his sites had 66 per cent of its traits in common with the Cherokee list, and the other nearly as many. "Nevertheless," he cautiously concluded, "it would appear the part of wisdom to regard the possible connections with the historic Cherokee, while not positively denied, still not definitely established."

Webb suggested that the rectangular town houses might be pre-Cherokee buildings, and that the Cherokees, upon their arrival, had adopted many of the culture traits of this earlier group, merely altering the design of the town house to fit their own ideas. Many of the Cherokee town houses, said Webb, were built on top of mounds left by these unknown predecessors—perhaps Creek Indians or some other Muskhogean group, who were themselves but the diluted remnants of an earlier and grander Temple Mound culture.

The picture that emerges is one of a progressive attenuation of the mound-building impulse through the sixteenth and seventeenth centuries, until nothing remained but forgetful Creeks and imitative Cherokees. In the far north, the effigy-mound people built their low pictorial tumuli as late as the eighteenth century; in Ohio, mound activity had ended centuries before. There is good evidence that mound burials continued in a sporadic way on the Great Plains well into the nineteenth century; but these interments of great chiefs were simple gestures of honor, perhaps spontaneously conceived, with none of the ceremonial trappings that accompanied mound burial among Adenas and Hopewells.

In essence, then, mound building came to an end in the United States in the seventeenth century, and what followed was a kind of convulsive reflex action. For a thousand years the Adenas had heaped up earth; for five centuries more after their passing, the Hopewells had reared their elaborate enclosures and embankments; and then, while Europe passed through the crises of the Crusades and the Black Death and the tumultuous Renaissance, the builders of temple mounds had constructed their titanic platforms. After that, a swift and puzzling decline, and a slow fading out of the old mound-building urge.

Grass and shrubbery sprouted on the slumbering mounds. Saplings grew to mighty trees. Those in whose veins ran the blood of Hopewells or Temple Mound folk slipped into sleepy ruralism or into something not far from savagery. Then came the white men, who stared, and wondered, and speculated, and spoke of vanished races. The mythmakers did their work, and the sober-minded archaeologists undid that work, and the bulldozers came to shear away much of what had inspired the myth. And yet some mounds remain, celebrated in their vicinities as tourist attractions, although virtually unknown to Americans beyond the mound zone itself. It is difficult to comprehend now the intensity of the interest those mounds provoked a century and more ago, or to grasp the deeper motives that led so many to believe that they were the work of superior beings hidden in the mists of time. But the interest was real, and the controversy over the myth was passionate, and the resolution, as resolutions tend to be, was a prosaic one of the phases and complexes and cultural sequences. Archaeologists today smile at the fancies of yesteryear.

Yet there is magic in the mounds even now. Forget the labors of Cyrus Thomas and the other debunkers; cast from your mind the diligent toil of William Webb and Don Dragoo and Olaf Prufer and James Ford and Warren Moorehead and Henry Shetrone and William Mills and all those others who have shown us why we must not think of the builders of the mounds as the Mound Builders. Stand, as I did, in the midst of the Newark octagon on a summer afternoon, and walk along Fort Ancient's wall, and scramble to the top of Cahokia, and look down from the observation tower upon Great Serpent Mound. All is green and silent; and, looking about at these mysterious grassy monuments, one succumbs easily to fantasy, and feels the presence of the ghosts of departed greatness, and then, in warm understanding, one reaches out across the decades to the makers of the Mound Builder myth.

59 Outer wall of the South Fort, Fort Ancient. *Photograph by Barbara Silverberg.*

SOURCES OF QUOTED MATERIAL

▲▲▲

1. Herodotus, Book IV, Chap. 71
2. Thomas, 1894, xli
3. Gentleman of Elvas, 135
4. *Ibid.,* 147
5. Garcilaso, 13
6. *Ibid.,* 170
7. *Ibid.,* 171
8. *Ibid.,* 299
9. *Ibid.,* 303
10. Gentleman of Elvas, 175
11. Garcilaso, 314
12. *Ibid.,* 320
13. Gentleman of Elvas, 175
14. Thomas 1887a, 39
15. Thomas 1894, 652
16. *Ibid.,* 653
17. *Ibid.*
18. *Ibid.*
19. Quoted in Winsor, I, 398
20. Squier and Davis, 75
21. Thomas 1894, 22
22. Bartram, 25
23. *Ibid.,* 34
24. *Ibid.,* 64
25. *Ibid.,* 66
26. *Ibid.,* 88
27. *Ibid.,* 192
28. *Ibid.,* 246
29. *Ibid.,* 232
30. *Ibid.,* 328
31. *Ibid.,* 206
32. *Ibid.,* 331
33. Quoted in Hindle, 324
34. Jefferson, 97–100
35. Baily, *Journal.*
36. Haven, 31
37. Brerewood, 96–7
38. Quoted in MacGowan, 15
39. Atwater, 196–7
40. Thomas 1889a, 43–5
41. Thomas 1894, 600
42. Haven, 32
43. Atwater, 111–12
44. *Ibid.,* 123–24
45. *Ibid.,* 129
46. *Ibid.,* 140
47. *Ibid.,* 144
48. Squier and Davis, 72
49. Atwater, 167
50. *Ibid.,* 162
51. *Ibid.,* 168–72
52. Squier and Davis, 208
53. Squier, 187
54. Atwater, 178
55. *Ibid.,* 188
56. *Ibid.,* 199
57. *Ibid.,* 202
58. *Ibid.,* 205
59. *Ibid.,* 209
60. *Ibid.,* 213
61. *Ibid.,* 239
62. *Ibid.,* 219
63. *Ibid.,* 221
64. *Ibid.,* 248
65. *Ibid.,* 331
66. *Ibid.,* 343
67. Shetrone, 1930, 18
68. Squier and Davis, 306
69. Thomas 1894, 612
70. Dahl, 184
71. Haven, 41
72. Dahl, 87
73. Turner, 35
74. Bancroft 1890, 60
75. *Ibid.,* 69
76. Hallowell 1960, 82

77. Atwater, 186
78. Foster, 190
79. *Ibid.*
80. Mallery, 250
81. Thomas 1894, 635
82. Trans. Am. Ethn. Soc. I, 371–2
83. In Baldwin, 42
84. Trans. Am. Ethn. Soc. II, 217
85. Atwater, 209
86. Morton, introduction
87. *Ibid.,* 260
88. *Ibid.,* 81
89. *Ibid.,* 82
90. Squier and Davis, 290
91. Trans. Am. Ethn. Soc. II, 134
92. Squier and Davis, xxxiii
93. *Ibid.,* 7
94. *Ibid.,* 8
95. *Ibid.,* 9
96. *Ibid.,* 14
97. *Ibid.,* 16
98. *Ibid.,* 41
99. *Ibid.,* 42
100. *Ibid.,* 44
101. *Ibid.*
102. *Ibid.,* 47
103. *Ibid.,* 61
104. *Ibid.,* 118
105. *Ibid.,* 119
106. *Ibid.,* 121
107. *Ibid.,* 135
108. *Ibid.,* 139
109. *Ibid.,* 143
110. *Ibid.,* 144
111. *Ibid.,* 161
112. *Ibid.,* 145
113. *Ibid.,* 146
114. *Ibid.,* 161
115. *Ibid.,* 162
116. *Ibid.,* 188
117. *Ibid.,* 196
118. *Ibid.,* 242
119. *Ibid.,* 272
120. *Ibid.,* 288
121. *Ibid.,* 301
122. *Ibid.,* 305
123. *Ibid.,* 301
124. Squier, 83
125. Hallowell 1960, 5

126. Haven, 154
127. Pidgeon, 11–12
128. *Ibid.,* 17
129. *Ibid.,* 20
130. *Ibid.,* 5
131. *Ibid.,* 22
132. *Ibid.,* 39
133. *Ibid.,* 41
134. *Ibid.,* 44
135. *Ibid.,* 7
136. *Ibid.,* 8
137. *Ibid.,* 57
138. *Ibid.,* 61
139. *Ibid.,* 71
140. *Ibid.,* 259
141. *Ibid.,* 260
142. *Ibid.,* 257
143. *Ibid.,* 98
144. *Ibid.,* 91
145. *Ibid.,* 162
146. *Ibid.,* 169
147. *Ibid.,* 177–8
148. *Ibid.,* 134
149. *Ibid.,* 319
150. Bancroft 1875 IV, 749
151. Pidgeon, 73
152. Baldwin, 31
153. *Ibid.,* 58
154. *Ibid.,* 173
155. *Ibid.,* 70
156. *Ibid.,* 72
157. *Ibid.,* 184
158. *Ibid.,* 217
159. *Ibid.,* 203
160. *Ibid.,* 55
161. Foster, 300
162. *Ibid.,* 275
163. *Ibid.,* 298
164. *Ibid.,* 299
165. *Ibid.,* 375
166. Thomas 1894, 183
167. Peet, 42
168. Henshaw, 156
169. Thomas 1894, xxxix
170. *Ibid.,* xl
171. Darrah, 225
172. Bureau of Ethnology First Annual Report, 74
173. Henshaw, 124

174. *Ibid.,* xxxi
175. Squier and Davis, 254
176. *Ibid.,* 242
177. Henshaw, 131
178. *Ibid.,* 129
179. *Ibid.,* 153
180. *Ibid.,* 155
181. *Ibid.,* 157
182. *Ibid.,* 166
183. Mallery, xxx
184. *Ibid.,* xxxii
185. *Ibid.,* 247
186. De Camp, 36
187. Donnelly, xi
188. *Ibid.,* 1
189. *Ibid.,* 89
190. *Ibid.,* 225
191. *Ibid.,* 112
192. *Ibid.,* 133
193. *Ibid.,* 230
194. *Ibid.*
195. American Anthropologist 1915, 715
196. Science, Sept. 26, 1884
197. 22nd Annual Report of Peabody 1888, 53
198. Thomas 1887a, 4
199. *Ibid.,* 80
200. *Ibid.,* 81
201. *Ibid.,* 58
202. *Ibid.,* 105
203. *Ibid.,* 108–9
204. Thomas 1889a, 29
205. Thomas 1889b, 21
206. *Ibid.,* 33
207. Thomas 1894, 18
208. *Ibid.,* 602
209. *Ibid.,* 626
210. *Ibid.,* 631
211. *Ibid.,* 643
212. *Ibid.,* 656
213. *Ibid.,* 528
214. Peet, 59
215. *Ibid.,* 36
216. *Ibid.,* 123
217. Cole, 3
218. Hrdlička, 97
219. Shetrone 1930, 169
220. Webb and Snow 1945, 317
221. Solecki, 379
222. *Ibid.,* 380
223. Webb and Baby, 109
224. Dragoo, 16
225. *Ibid.,* 18
226. *Ibid.,* 20–21
227. Ritchie, 201
228. Dragoo, 144
229. *Ibid.,* 168
230. *Ibid.,* 214
231. *Ibid.,* 225
232. *Ibid.,* 211
233. Webb and Baby, 101
234. Squier and Davis, 96
235. Pidgeon, 244
236. Century Magazine, Apr., 1890, 871
237. Morton, 47
238. Webb and Snow 1959, 38
239. Spaulding, 266
240. Willey, 268
241. Chard, 23
242. Shetrone 1930, 379
243. Ford and Quimby, 92–3
244. Dragoo, 231
245. *Ibid.,* 243
246. *Ibid.,* 267
247. *Ibid.,* 280
248. Webb and Baby, 74
249. Dragoo, 282
250. Ritchie, 200
251. Ritchie and Dragoo 1959, 63
252. Prufer 1964b, 93
253. Prufer 1965, 132
254. Squier and Davis, 68
255. Shetrone 1930, 194
256. Atwater, 183
257. Squier and Davis, 29
258. Shetrone 1930, 207
259. *Ibid.,* 211
260. Prufer 1964a, 72
261. Prufer 1964b, 94
262. McMichael, 125
263. Drucker and Heizer, 370
264. Prufer 1964a, 69
265. Prufer 1964b, 102
266. Prufer 1964a, 82
267. Willey, 292
268. Squier and Davis, 104

269. Kelly, 15
270. Thomas 1894, 689
271. *Ibid.,* 293
272. Squier and Davis, 112
273. Webb and Baby, 102
274. *Ibid.,* 104
275. Cole, v

276. *Ibid.,* 231
277. Swanton 1911, 39
278. *Ibid.*
279. Swanton 1928, 57
280. Mooney, 395
281. Webb, 163
282. *Ibid.,* 217

BIBLIOGRAPHY

▲▲▲

ATWATER, CALEB
    1820   Description of the Antiquities Discovered in the State of Ohio and Other Western States. *American Antiquarian Society, Archaeologia Americana, Transactions and Collections, Vol. 1.*

BABY, RAYMOND S.
    1954   Hopewell Cremation Practices. *Ohio Historical Society, Papers in Archaeology, No. 1.*

BAKELESS, JOHN
    1950   *The Eyes of Discovery.* Dover Publications, New York.

BAKER, FRANK C., and others
    1941   Contributions to the Archaeology of the Illinois River Valley. *American Philosophical Society, Transactions, Vol. 32, Pt. 1.*

BALDWIN, J. D.
    1872   *Ancient America in Notes on American Archaeology.* Harper & Brothers, New York.

BANCROFT, HUBERT HOWE
    1875   *The Native Races of the Pacific States of North America.* Vol. 4, *Antiquities.* Vol. 5, *Primitive History.* D. Appleton and Company, New York.
    1890   *History of Utah.* The History Company, San Francisco.

BARTRAM, WILLIAM
    1958   *The Travels of William Bartram.* Edited by Francis Harper. Yale University Press, New Haven.

BILLINGTON, RAY ALLEN
    1949   *Westward Expansion: A History of the American Frontier.* The Macmillan Company, New York.

BOLAND, CHARLES MICHAEL
    1961   *They All Discovered America.* Doubleday & Co., Garden City, New York.

BRANDON, WILLIAM
    1961   *The American Heritage Book of Indians.* American Heritage Publishing Co., New York.

BREBNER, JOHN BARTLET
    1933   *The Explorers of North America, 1492–1806.* Adam & Charles Black, London.

BRENNAN, LOUIS A.
    1959   *No Stone Unturned: An Almanac of American Prehistory.* Random House, New York.

BREREWOOD, EDWARD
1614 *Enquiries Touching the Diversity of Languages.* John Bill, London.
BROOKS, VAN WYCK
1944 *The World of Washington Irving.* E. P. Dutton, New York.
BROWN, EDWARD HOAGLAND
1949 Harvard and the Ohio Mounds. *New England Quarterly,* Volume 22, No. 2.
BULLEN, RIPLEY P.
1966 Stelae at the Crystal River Site, Florida. *American Antiquity,* Vol. 31, No. 6.
CALDWELL, JOSEPH R.
1953 The Rembert Mounds. In *Smithsonian Institution Bureau of American Ethnology, Bulletin* 154. Washington, D.C.
1958 Trend and Tradition in the Prehistory of the Eastern United States. *Illinois State Museum, Scientific Papers,* Vol. 10, and *American Anthropological Association Memoirs,* No. 88.
1964 Interaction Spheres in Prehistory. In Hopewellian Studies, *Illinois State Museum, Scientific Papers,* Vol. 12, Springfield.
CALDWELL, JOSEPH R. and ROBERT L. HALL, editors
1964 Hopewellian Studies. *Illinois State Museum, Scientific Papers,* Vol. 12. Springfield, Illinois.
CHARD, CHESTER S.
1959 New World Origins: A Reappraisal. *Antiquity,* Vol. 33, No. 129.
1961 Invention versus Diffusion: The Burial Mound Complex of the Eastern United States. *Southwestern Journal of Anthropology,* Vol. 17, No. 1.
COLE, FAY-COOPER and others
1951 *Kincaid: A Prehistoric Illinois Metropolis.* University of Chicago Press, Chicago.
COLE, FAY-COOPER and THORNE DEUEL
1937 *Rediscovering Illinois.* University of Chicago Press, Chicago.
DAHL, CURTIS
1961 Mound Builders, Mormons, and William Cullen Bryant. *New England Quarterly,* Vol. 34, No. 2.
DARRAH, WILLIAM CULP
1951 *Powell of the Colorado.* Princeton University Press, Princeton.
DE CAMP, L. SPRAGUE
1954 *Lost Continents: The Atlantis Theme in History, Science, and Literature.* The Gnome Press, New York.
DE VOTO, BERNARD
1952 *The Course of Empire.* Houghton Mifflin, Boston.
DONNELLY, IGNATIUS
1949 *Atlantis: The Antediluvian World.* Revised by Egerton Sykes. Gramercy Publishing Co., New York.
DRAGOO, DON W.
1963 Mounds for the Dead. *Carnegie Museum, Annals,* Vol. 37. Pittsburgh.
DRIVER, HAROLD E. and WILLIAM C. MASSEY
1957 Comparative Studies of North American Indians. *American Philosophical Society, Transactions,* Vol. 47, Pt. 2.

DRUCKER, PHILIP and ROBERT F. HEIZER
  1956 Gifts for the Jaguar God. *National Geographic Magazine,* Vol. 110, No, 3.
DRUCKER, PHILIP, ROBERT F. HEIZER and ROBERT J. SQUIER
  1959 Excavations at La Venta, Tabasco, 1955. *Smithsonian Institution Bureau of American Ethnology, Bulletin* 170, Washington, D.C.
DUFFIELD, LATHEL FLAY
  1964 Engraved Shells from the Craig Mound at Spiro, LeFlore County, Oklahoma. *Oklahoma Anthropological Society, Memoir* No. 1. Oklahoma City.
FAIRBANKS, C. H.
  1956 Archaeology of the Funeral Mound, Ocmulgee National Monument, Georgia. *National Park Service, Archaeological Research Series,* No. 3. Washington, D.C.
FIGGINS, J. D.
  1927 The Antiquity of Man in America. *Natural History,* Vol. 27, No. 3.
FORD, JAMES A.
  1952 Mound Builders of the Mississippi. *Scientific American,* Vol. 186, No. 3.
FORD, JAMES A. and GEORGE I. QUIMBY
  1945 The Tchefuncte Culture. *Society for American Archaeology, Memoirs,* No. 2.
FORD, JAMES A. and CHARLES H. WEBB
  1956 Poverty Point: A Late Archaic Site in Louisiana. *American Museum of Natural History, Anthropological Papers,* Vol. 46, No. 1.
FORD, JAMES A. and GORDON R. WILLEY
  1941 An Interpretation of the Prehistory of the Eastern United States. *American Anthropologist,* Vol. 43, No. 3.
FOSTER, J. W.
  1874 *Prehistoric Races of the United States of America.* Third edition. S. C. Griggs and Co., Chicago.
FOWKE, GERARD
  1910 Antiquities of Central and Southeastern Missouri. *Smithsonian Institution, Bureau of American Ethnology, Bulletin* 37. Washington, D.C.
  1922 Archaeological Investigations. *Smithsonian Institution, Bureau of American Ethnology, Bulletin* 76. Washington, D.C.
GARCILASO DE LA VEGA
  1951 *The Florida of the Inca.* Translated by John Grier Varner and Jeannette Johnson Varner. University of Texas Press, Austin.
GENTLEMAN OF ELVAS
  1907 The Narrative of the Expedition of Hernando de Soto. In *Spanish Explorers in the Southern United States 1528–1543,* edited by F. W. Hodge and Theodore H. Lewis. Charles Scribner's Sons, New York.
GOSLIN, ROBERT
  1957 Food of the Adena People. In *The Adena People,* No. 2, W. S. Webb and Raymond S. Baby. Ohio Historical Society, Columbus.
GREENMAN, EMERSON F.
  1932 Excavation of the Coon Mound and an Analysis of the Adena Culture. *Ohio State Archaeological and Historical Quarterly,* Vol. 41, No. 3.
  1964 *Guide to Serpent Mound.* Ohio Historical Society, Columbus.

GRIFFIN, JAMES B.

    1943   *The Fort Ancient Aspect.* University of Michigan Press, Ann Arbor.

    1952   Editor. *Archaeology of the Eastern United States.* University of Chicago Press, Chicago.

    1958   The Chronological Position of the Hopewellian Culture in the Eastern United States. *Museum of Anthropology, Anthropological Papers,* No. 12, University of Michigan, Ann Arbor.

    1960   Climatic Change: A Contributory Cause of the Growth and Decline of Northern Hopewellian Culture. *The Wisconsin Archaeologist,* Vol. 41, No. 2.

HALLOWELL, A. IRVING

    1959   Backwash of the Frontier: The Impact of the Indian on American Culture. *Smithsonian Institution Annual Report,* 1958. Washington, D.C.

    1960   The Beginnings of Anthropology in America. In *Selected Papers from the American Anthropologist,* 1888–1920, edited by Frederica de Laguna. Row, Peterson & Co., Evanston, Illinois.

HAVEN, SAMUEL F.

    1856   Archaeology of the United States. In *Smithsonian Contributions to Knowledge,* No. 8. Washington, D.C.

HAY, C. L. and others

    1940   *The Maya and Their Neighbors.* Appleton-Century, New York.

HENSHAW, HENRY W.

    1883   Animal Carvings from the Mounds of the Mississippi Valley. In *Smithsonian Institution Bureau of American Ethnology, Second Annual Report,* 1880–81. Washington, D.C.

HEWITT, J. N. B.

    1939   Notes on the Creek Indians. Edited by John R. Swanton. In *Smithsonian Institution Bureau of American Ethnology, Bulletin* 123. Washington, D.C.

HINDLE, BROOKE

    1956   *The Pursuit of Science in Revolutionary America.* University of North Carolina Press, Chapel Hill.

HOLMES, W. H.

    1883   Art in Shell of the Ancient Americans. In *Smithsonian Institution Bureau of Ethnology, Second Annual Report,* 1880–81. Washington, D.C.

    1886   The Ancient Pottery of the Mississippi Valley. In *Smithsonian Institution Bureau of Ethnology, Fourth Annual Report,* 1882–83. Washington, D.C.

HRDLIČKA, ALES

    1907   Skeletal Remains Suggesting or Attributed to Early Man. *Smithsonian Institution Bureau of American Ethnology, Bulletin* 33. Washington, D. C.

JEFFERSON, THOMAS

    1955   *Notes on the State of Virginia.* Edited by William Peden. University of North Carolina Press, Chapel Hill.

JONES, HOWARD MUMFORD

    1964   *O Strange New World.* The Viking Press, New York.

JUDD, NEIL M.

1967   *The Bureau of American Ethnology: A Partial History.* University of Oklahoma, Norman, Oklahoma.

KELLY, A. R.

1938   A Preliminary Report on Archeological Explorations at Macon, Ga. In *Smithsonian Institution Bureau of American Ethnology, Bulletin* 119. Washington, D.C.

KRIEGER, ALEX D.

1945   An Inquiry into Supposed Mexican Influence on a Prehistoric Cult in the Southern United States. *American Anthropologist,* Vol. 47, No. 4.

1949   Importance of the "Gilmore Corridor" in Culture Contacts between Middle America and the Eastern United States. *Texas Archaeological and Paleontological Society, Bulletin* 19. Abilene.

LEWIS, T. H.

1886   The "Monumental Tortoise" Mounds of "De-coo-dah." *American Journal of Archaeology,* January, 1886.

LEWIS, T. M. N. and MADELINE KNEBERG

1946   *Hiwassee Island.* University of Tennessee Press, Knoxville.

LORANT, STEFAN

1946   *The New World.* Duell, Sloan & Pearce, New York.

MACGOWAN, KENNETH and JOSEPH A. HESTER, JR.

1962   *Early Man in the New World.* Revised edition. Doubleday & Co., Garden City, New York.

MCMICHAEL, EDWARD V.

1964   Veracruz, the Crystal River Complex, and the Hopewellian Climax. In Hopewellian Studies, *Illinois State Museum, Scientific Papers,* Vol. 12. Springfield.

MALLERY, GARRICK

1866   Pictographs of the North American Indians. In *Smithsonian Institution Bureau of Ethnology, Fourth Annual Report,* 1882–83. Washington, D.C.

MARTIN, PAUL, and others

1947   *Indians Before Columbus.* University of Chicago Press, Chicago.

MATHEWS, CORNELIUS

1839   *Behemoth: A Legend of the Mound-Builders.* Weeks, Jordan & Co., Boston.

MILLER, CARL F.

1950   Early Cultural Horizons in the Southeastern United States. *American Antiquity,* Vol. 15, No. 4.

MILLS, WILLIAM C.

1902   Excavation of the Adena Mound. *Ohio State Archaeological and Historical Quarterly,* Vol. 10, pp. 452–79.

1907   Exploration of the Edwin Harness Mound. *Ohio State Archaeological and Historical Quarterly,* Vol. 16, pp. 113–193.

1909   Exploration of the Seip Mound. *Ohio State Archaeological and Historical Quarterly,* Vol. 18, No. 3.

1916   Exploration of the Tremper Mound. *Ohio State Archaeological and Historical Quarterly,* Vol. 25, pp. 263–398.

1922   Exploration of the Mound City Group. *Ohio State Archaeological and Historical Quarterly,* Vol. 31, pp. 423–584.

MOONEY, JAMES
1900   Myths of the Cherokee. In *Smithsonian Institution Bureau of American Ethnology, Nineteenth Annual Report,* 1897–98. Washington, D.C.

MOORE, CLARENCE B.
1903   Certain Aboriginal Mounds of the Florida Central West Coast. *Philadelphia Academy of Natural Sciences, Journal,* Vol. 12.

1905   Certain Aboriginal Remains of the Black Warrior River. *Philadelphia Academy of Natural Sciences, Journal,* Vol. 13, Pt. 2.

1907   Moundville Revisited. *Philadelphia Academy of Natural Sciences, Journal,* Vol. 13, Pt. 3 .

1915   Aboriginal Sites on the Tennessee River. *Philadelphia Academy of Natural Sciences, Journal,* Vol. 16, Pt. 2.

MOOREHEAD, WARREN K.
1890   *Fort Ancient: The Great Prehistoric Earthwork of Warren County, Ohio.* Robert Clarke & Co., Cincinnati.

1892   *Primitive Man in Ohio.* G. P. Putnam's Sons, New York.

1922   The Hopewell Mound Group of Ohio. *Field Museum of Natural History, Publications 221, Anthropological Series,* Vol. 6, No. 5. Chicago Natural History Museum, Chicago.

1928   The Cahokia Mounds. *University of Illinois, Bulletin,* Vol. 26, No. 4. Urbana.

1932   *Etowah Papers.* Yale University Press, New Haven.

MORGAN, RICHARD G.
1965   *Fort Ancient.* Ohio Historical Society, Columbus.

MORGAN, RICHARD G. and EDWARD S. THOMAS
1950   *Fort Hill.* Ohio State Archaeological and Historical Society, Columbus.

MORTON, SAMUEL G.
1839   *Crania Americana.* J. Dobson, Philadelphia.

MYER, WILLIAM EDWARD
1928   Two Prehistoric Villages in Middle Tennessee. In *Smithsonian Institution Bureau of American Ethnology, Forty-first Annual Report,* 1919–24.

MYRON, ROBERT
1964   *Shadow of the Hawk: Saga of the Mound Builders.* G. P. Putnam's Sons, New York.

NARONA, DELF
1957   Moundville's Mammoth Mound. *West Virginia Archaeologist,* No. 9.

ORR, KENNETH GORDON
1946   The Archaeological Situation at Spiro, Oklahoma. *American Antiquity,* Vol. 11, No. 4.

PEET, STEPHEN D.
1892   *The Mound Builders: Their Works and Relics.* Office of the American Antiquarian, Chicago.

PENNELL, FRANCIS W.
  1942   Benjamin Smith Barton as Naturalist. *American Philosophical Society, Proceedings,* Vol. 86, No. 1.

PENROSE, BOIES
  1952   *Travel and Discovery in the Renaissance.* Harvard University Press, Cambridge.

PHILLIPS, PHILIP, J. A. FORD, and J. B. GRIFFIN
  1951   Archaeological Survey in the Lower Mississippi Alluvial Valley, 1940–47. *Peabody Museum Papers,* Vol. 25, Harvard University, Cambridge.

PIDGEON, WILLIAM
  1858   *Traditions of De-coo-dah.* Horace Thayer, New York.

POPE, G. D., JR.
  1956   Ocmulgee National Monument, Georgia. *National Park Service Historical Handbook Series,* No. 24. Washington, D.C.

POWELL, JOHN W.
  1881   On Limitations to the Use of Some Anthropologic Data. In *Smithsonian Institution Bureau of Ethnology, First Annual Report,* 1879–80.

PRUFER, OLAF H.
  1964a The Hopewell Complex of Ohio. In Hopewellian Studies, *Illinois State Museum, Scientific Papers,* Vol. 12. Springfield.
  1964b The Hopewell Cult. *Scientific American,* Vol. 211, No. 6
  1965   The McGraw Site: A Study in Hopewellian Dynamics. *Scientific Publications of the Cleveland Museum of Natural History, New Series,* Vol. 4, No. 1.

PUTNAM, CHARLES E.
  1885   *A Vindication of the Authority of the Elephant Pipes and Inscribed Tablets.* Glass & Hoover, Davenport, Iowa.

PUTNAM, F. W.
  1883   Iron from the Ohio Mounds. *American Antiquarian Society, Proceedings,* Vol. 2, New Series, Pt. 3.

QUIMBY, GEORGE IRVING
  1960   *Indian Life in the Upper Great Lakes.* University of Chicago Press, Chicago.

RITCHIE, WILLIAM A.
  1944   The Pre-Iroquoian Occupation of New York State. *Rochester Museum of Arts and Sciences, Memoirs,* No. 1.
  1965   *The Archaeology of New York State.* Natural History Press, Garden City, New York.

RITCHIE, WILLIAM A. and DON W. DRAGOO
  1959   The Eastern Dispersal of Adena. *American Antiquity,* Vol. 25, No. 1.
  1960   The Eastern Dispersal of Adena. *New York State Museum and Science Service, Bulletin* No. 379. Albany, N.Y.

SHETRONE, HENRY C.
  1926   Exploration of the Hopewell Group of Prehistoric Earthworks. *Ohio State Archaeological and Historical Quarterly,* Vol. 35, No. 1.
  1930   *The Mound Builders.* D. Appleton, New York.

SHETRONE, HENRY C. and EMERSON F. GREENMAN

   1931   Explorations of the Seip Group of Prehistoric Earthworks. *Ohio State Archae-ological and Historical Quarterly,* Vol. 40, No. 3.

SILVERBERG, ROBERT

   1963   *Home of the Red Man.* New York Graphic Society, Greenwich, Conn.

   1964   *Man Before Adam.* Macrae Smith, Philadelphia.

   1965a *The Old Ones: Indians of the American Southwest.* New York Graphic Society, Greenwich, Conn.

   1965b *Scientists and Scoundrels: A Book of Hoaxes.* Thomas Y. Crowell, New York.

   1967   *The Morning of Mankind.* New York Graphic Society, Greenwich, Conn.

SOLECKI, RALPH

   1953   Exploration of an Adena Mound at Natrium, West Virginia. In *Smithsonian Institution Bureau of American Ethnology, Bulletin* 151. Washington, D.C.

SPAULDING, ALBERT C.

   1952   The Origin of the Adena Culture of the Ohio Valley. *Southwestern Journal of Anthropology,* Vol. 8, pp. 260–68.

SPINDEN, H. J.

   1930   The Population of Ancient America. In *Smithsonian Institution Annual Report,* 1929. Washington, D.C.

SQUIER, E. G.

   1850   Aboriginal Monuments of the State of New York. *Smithsonian Contributions to Knowledge,* No. 2.

SQUIER, E. G. and E. H. DAVIS

   1848   Ancient Monuments of the Mississippi Valley. *Smithsonian Contributions to Knowledge,* No. 1.

STARR, S. F.

   1960   *The Archaeology of Hamilton County, Ohio.* Cincinnati Museum of Natural History, Cincinnati.

STEGNER, WALLACE

   1953   *Beyond the Hundredth Meridian.* Houghton Mifflin, Boston.

SWANTON, JOHN, R.

   1911   Indian Tribes of the Lower Mississippi Valley. *Smithsonian Institution Bureau of American Ethnology, Bulletin* 43. Washington, D.C.

   1928a The Interpretation of Aboriginal Mounds by means of Creek Indian Customs. In *Smithsonian Institution Annual Report,* 1927. Washington, D.C.

   1928b Social Organization and Social Usages of the Indians of the Creek Confederacy. In *Smithsonian Institution Bureau of American Ethnology, Forty-second Annual Report,* 1924–25.

THOMAS, CYRUS

   1887a Burial Mounds of the Northern Sections of the United States. *Smithsonian Institution Bureau of Ethnology, Fifth Annual Report,* 1883–84. Washington, D.C.

   1887b Work in Mound Exploration of the Bureau of Ethnology. *Smithsonian Institution Bureau of Ethnology, Bulletin* 4. Washington, D.C.

   1889a The Problem of the Ohio Mounds. *Smithsonian Institution Bureau of Ethnology, Bulletin* 8. Washington, D.C.

1889b The Circular, Square, and Octagonal Earthworks of Ohio. *Smithsonian Institution Bureau of Ethnology, Bulletin* 10. Washington, D.C.

1891 Catalogue of Prehistoric Works East of the Rocky Mountains. *Smithsonian Institution Bureau of Ethnology, Bulletin* 12. Washington, D.C.

1894 Report on the Mound Explorations of the Bureau of Ethnology. *Smithsonian Institution Bureau of Ethnology, Twelfth Annual Report,* 1890–91. Washington, D.C.

TURNER, WALLACE

1966 *The Mormon Establishment.* Houghton Mifflin, Boston.

UNDERHILL, RUTH M.

1953 *Red Man's America.* University of Chicago Press, Chicago.

WARING, A. J., JR. and PRESTON HOLDER

1945 A Prehistoric Ceremonial Complex in the Southeastern United States. *American Anthropologist,* Vol. 47, No. 1.

WAUCHOPE, ROBERT

1966 Archaeological Survey of Northern Georgia. *Society for American Archaeology, Memoirs,* No. 21.

WEBB, WILLAM S.

1938 An Archaeological Survey of the Norris Basin in Eastern Tennessee. *Smithsonian Institution Bureau of American Ethnology, Bulletin* 118. Washington, D.C.

WEBB, WILLIAM S. and RAYMOND S. BABY

1957 *The Adena People, No. 2.* Ohio Historical Society, Columbus.

WEBB, WILLIAM S., RAYMOND S. BABY, and JAMES B. GRIFFIN

1957 *Prehistoric Indians of the Ohio Valley.* Ohio Historical Society, Columbus.

WEBB, WILLIAM S. and CHARLES E. SNOW

1945 The Adena People. *University of Kentucky Reports in Anthropology and Archaeology;* Vol. 6. Lexington.

1959 *The Dover Mound.* University of Kentucky Press, Lexington.

WILLEY, GORDON R.

1949 Archaeology of the Florida Gulf Coast. *Smithsonian Miscellaneous Collections,* Vol. 113. Washington, D.C.

1966 *An Introduction to American Archaeology.* Vol. 1. Prentice-Hall, Englewood Cliffs, New Jersey.

WILLEY, GORDON and PHILIP PHILLIPS

1958 *Method and Theory in American Archaeology.* University of Chicago Press, Chicago.

WILLOUGHBY, CHARLES C.

1922 The Turner Group of Earthworks. *Peabody Museum of American Archaeology, Harvard University, Papers,* Vol. 8, No. 3.

WINSOR, JUSTIN

1889 *Narrative and Critical History of America.* Vol. 1, *Aboriginal America.* Houghton Mifflin, Boston.

WISSLER, CLARK

1942 The American Indian and the American Philosophical Society. *American Philosophical Society, Proceedings,* Vol. 86, No. 1.

INDEX

▲▲▲